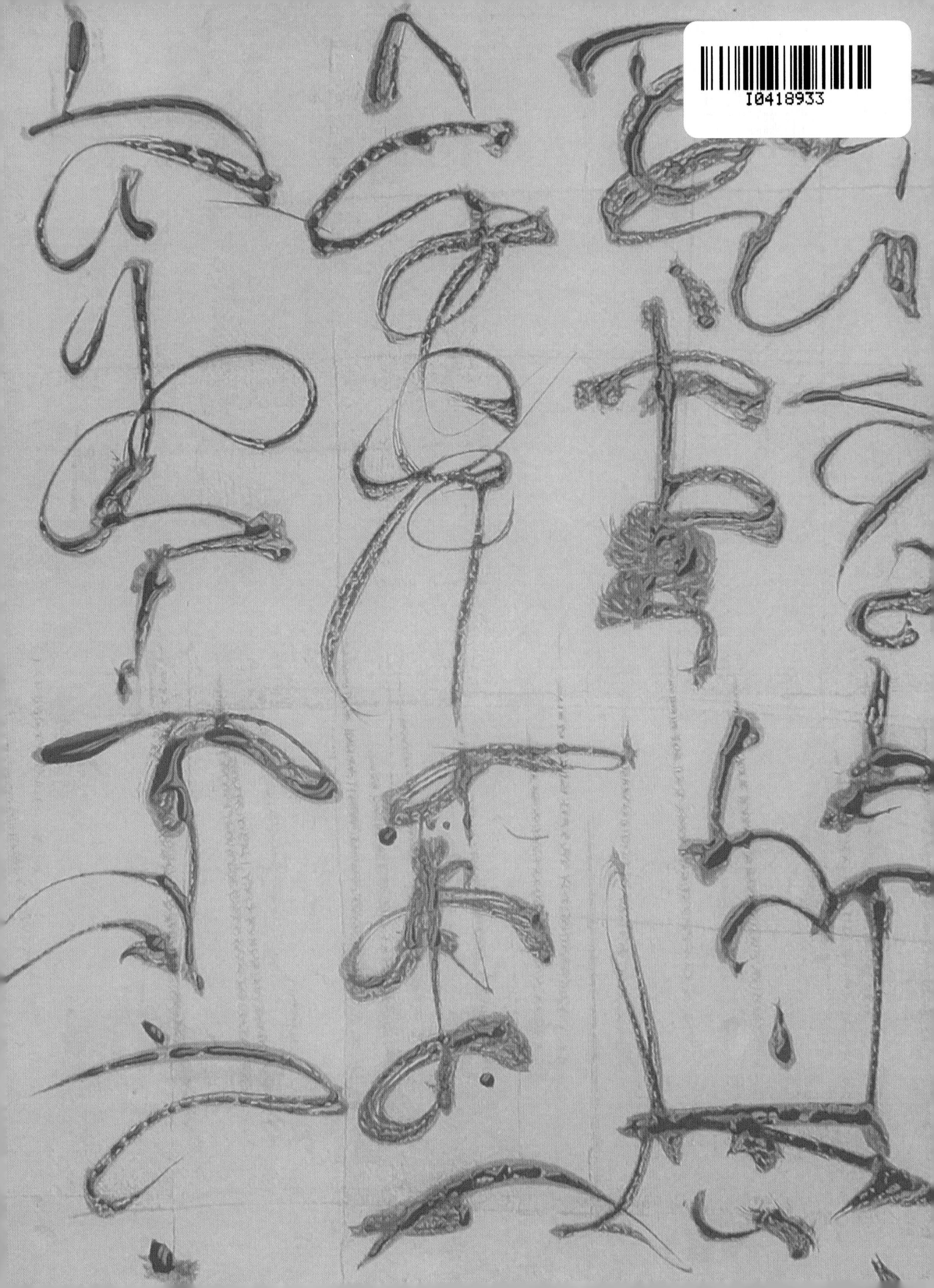

Gel Plate Printing for Mixed-Media Art

Taking Your Visual Storytelling to a New Level

Robyn McClendon

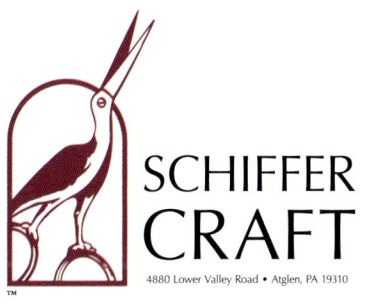

SCHIFFER
CRAFT

4880 Lower Valley Road • Atglen, PA 19310

Other Schiffer Craft Books on Related Subjects:

Prints Galore: The Art and Craft of Printmaking, with 41 Projects to Get You Started, Angie Franke, ISBN 978-0-7643-5628-5

The Painted Word: Mixed Media Lettering Techniques, Caitlin Dundon, ISBN 978-0-7643-5647-6

Print It! 15 Fun Printing Projects for Kids, Amy Appleyard, ISBN 978-0-7643-6067-1

Cover and interior design by Ashley Millhouse
Photography by Shen Daughtry, Zion Jones
Type set in IvyPresto Display/FreightSansCmpPro

ISBN: 978-0-7643-6694-9
Printed in China
6 5 4 3

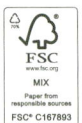

Published by Schiffer Craft
An imprint of Schiffer Publishing, Ltd.
4880 Lower Valley Road
Atglen, PA 19310
Phone: (610) 593-1777; Fax: (610) 593-2002
Email: Info@schifferbooks.com
Web: www.schifferbooks.com

For our complete selection of fine books on this and related subjects, please visit our website at www.schifferbooks.com. You may also write for a free catalog.

Schiffer Publishing's titles are available at special discounts for bulk purchases for sales promotions or premiums. Special editions, including personalized covers, corporate imprints, and excerpts, can be created in large quantities for special needs. For more information, contact the publisher.

We are always looking for people to write books on new and related subjects. If you have an idea for a book, please contact us at proposals@schifferbooks.com.

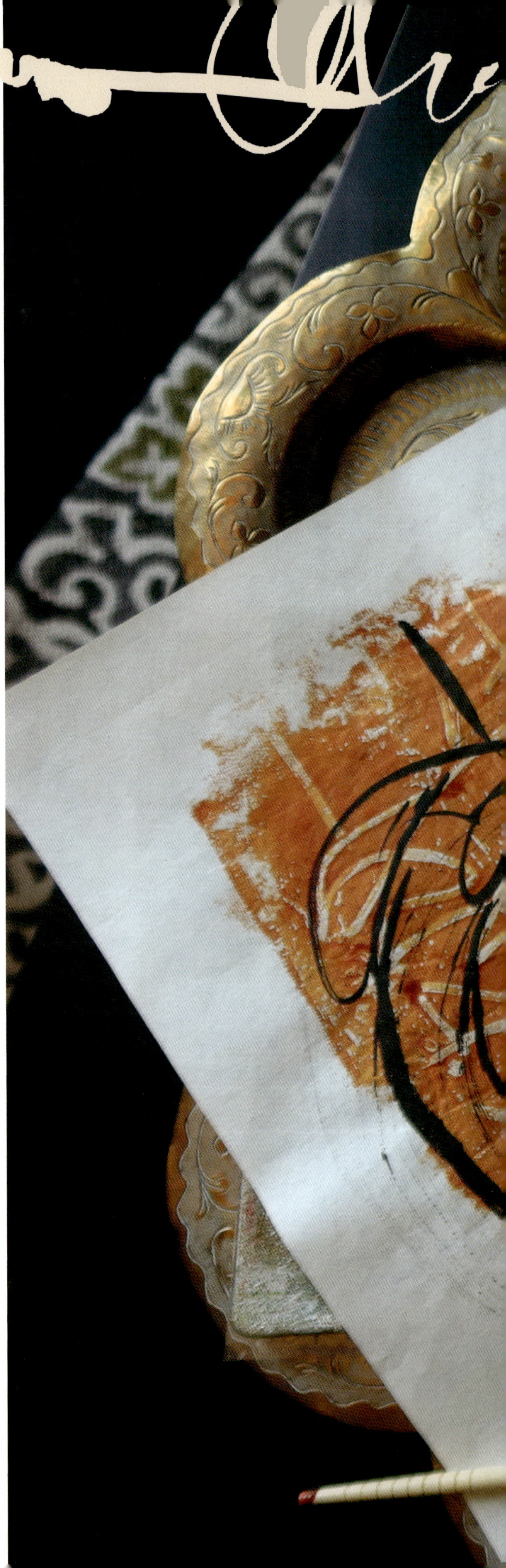

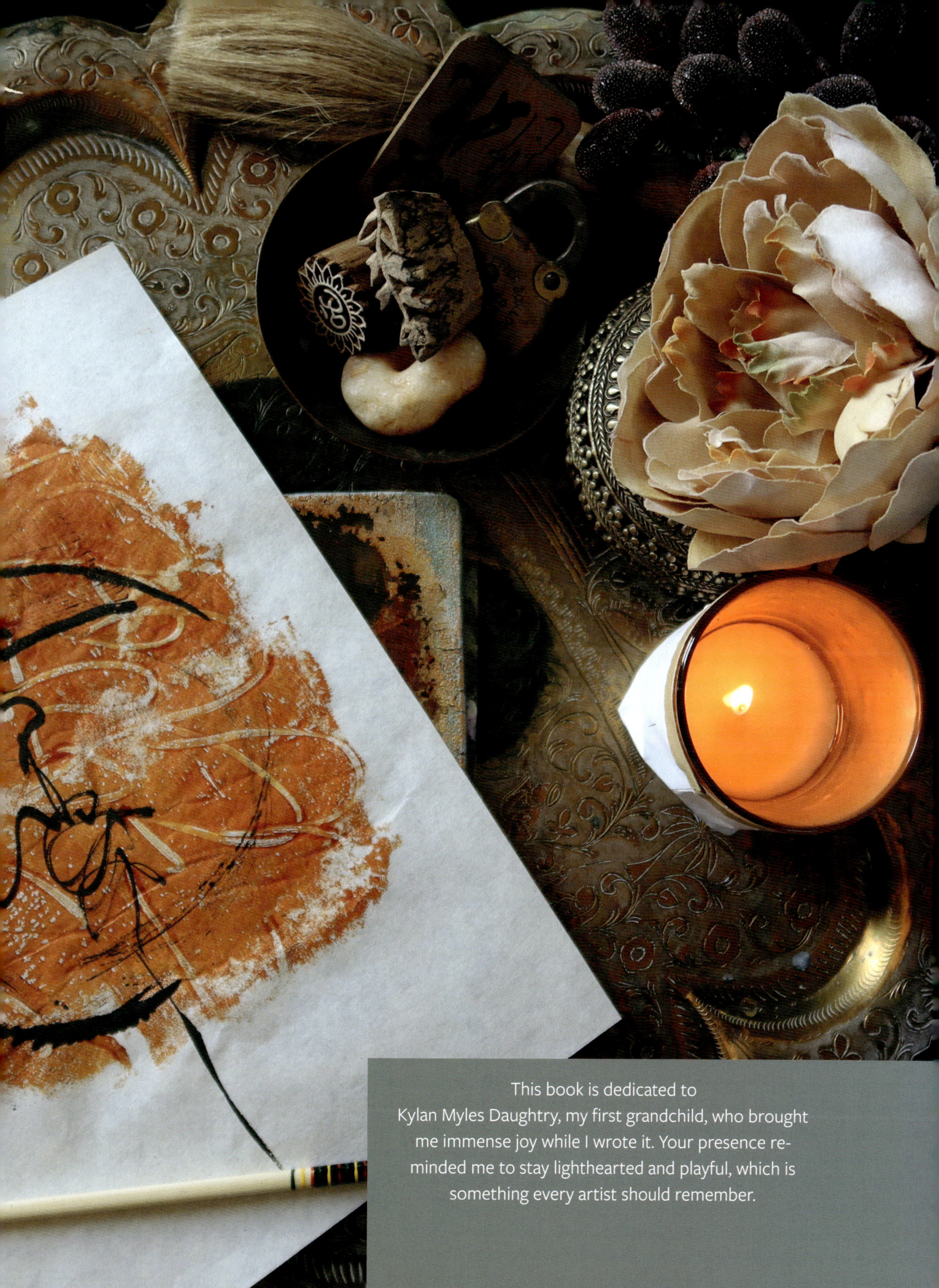

This book is dedicated to
Kylan Myles Daughtry, my first grandchild, who brought
me immense joy while I wrote it. Your presence reminded me to stay lighthearted and playful, which is
something every artist should remember.

Contents

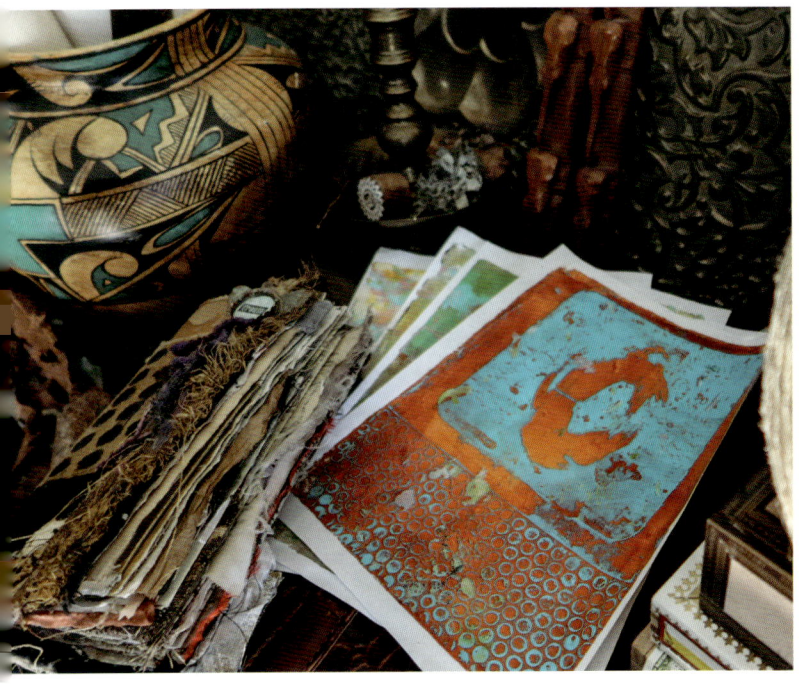

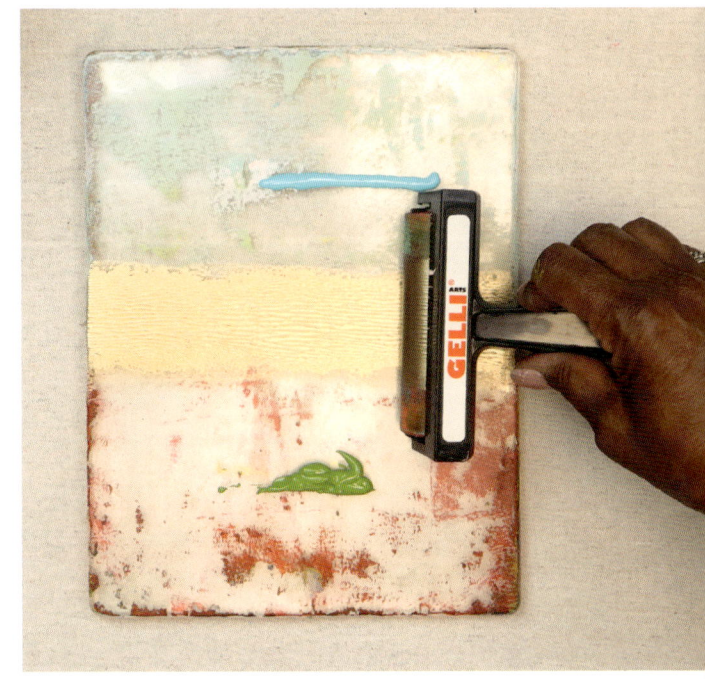

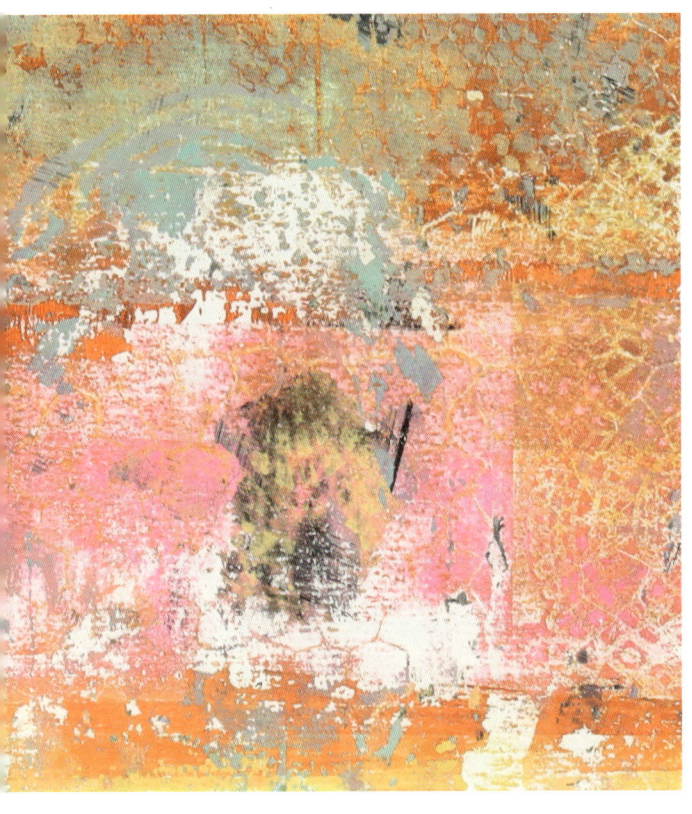

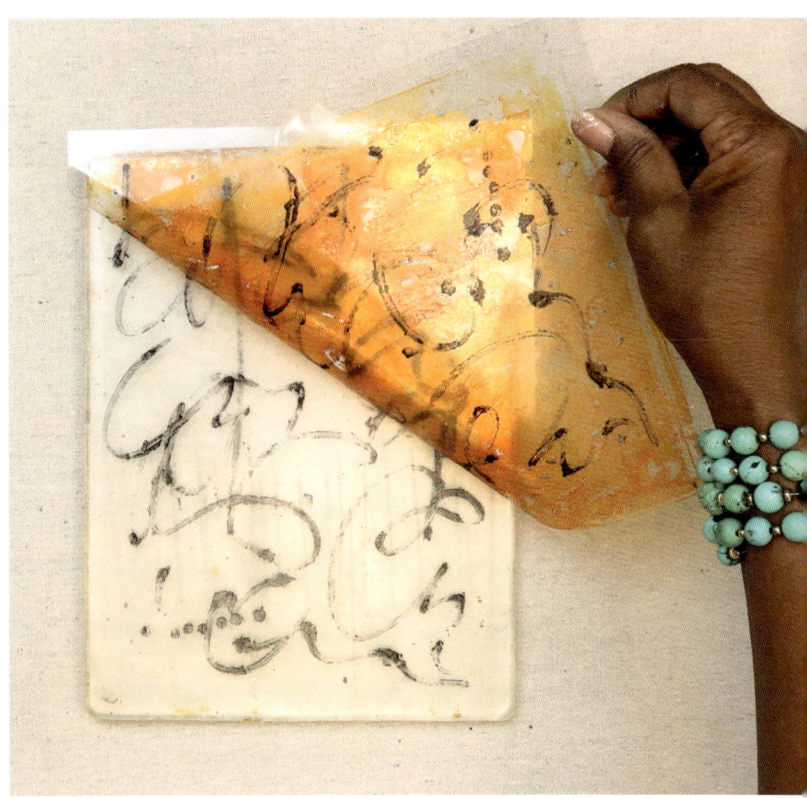

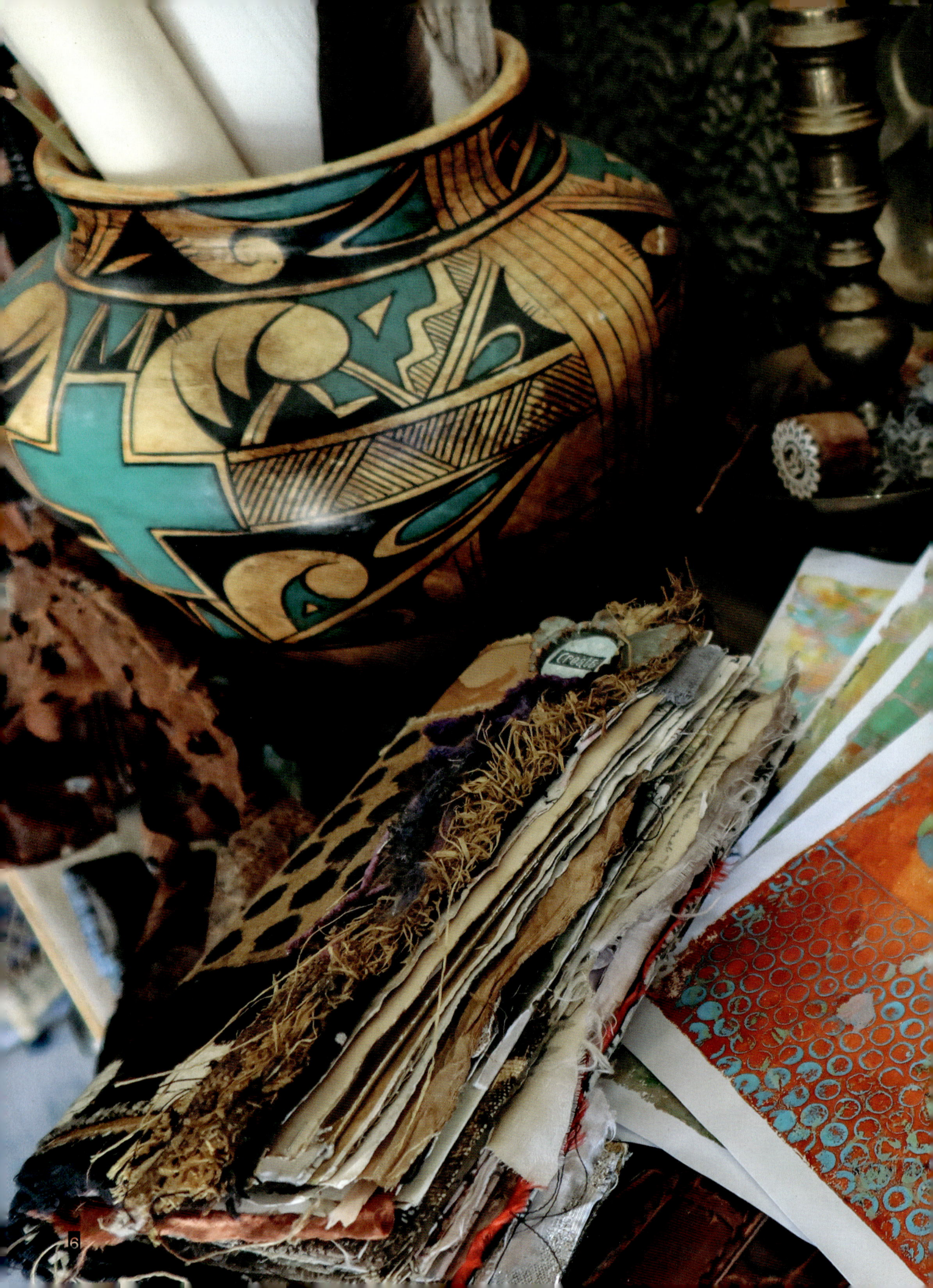

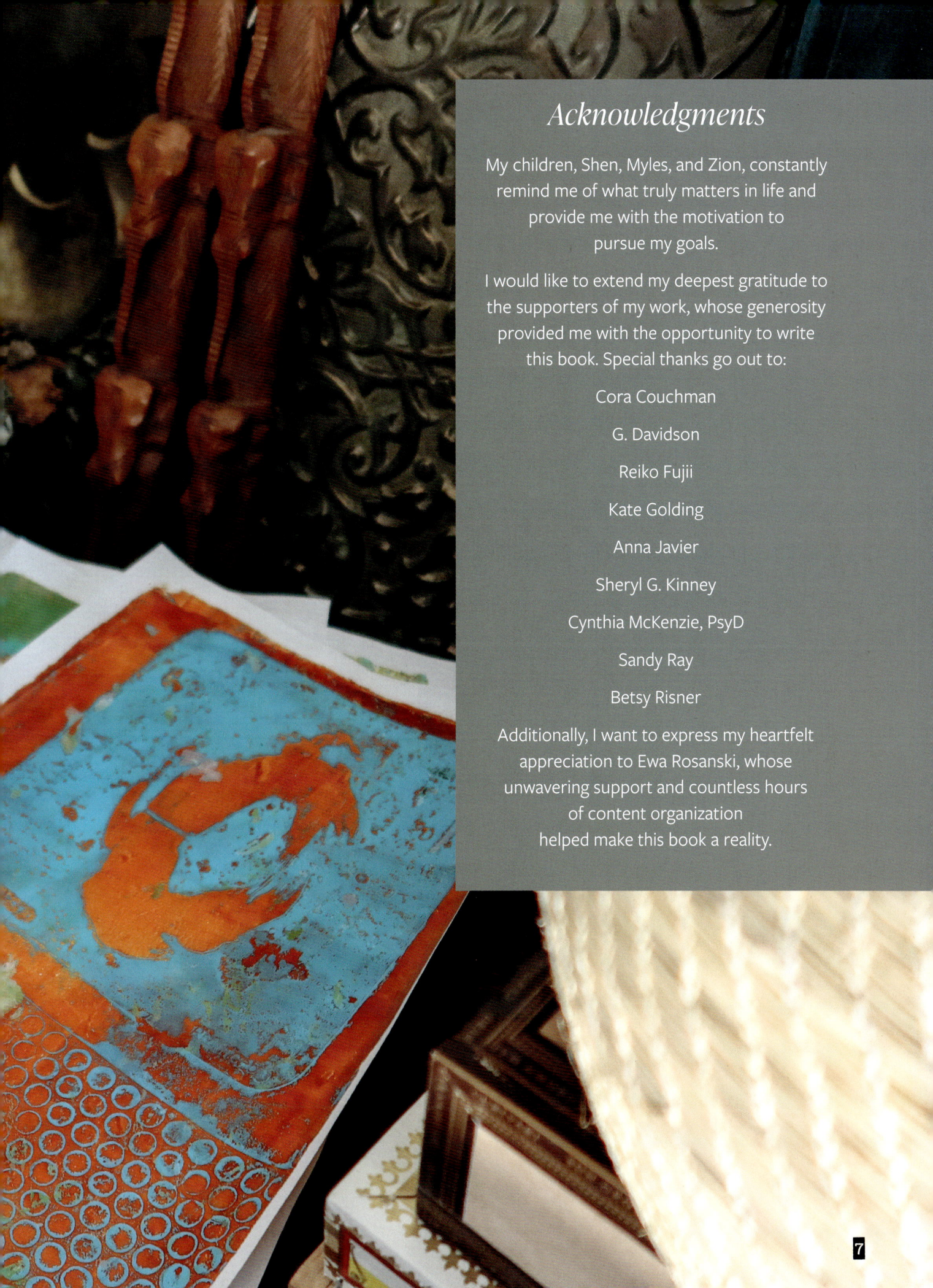

Acknowledgments

My children, Shen, Myles, and Zion, constantly remind me of what truly matters in life and provide me with the motivation to pursue my goals.

I would like to extend my deepest gratitude to the supporters of my work, whose generosity provided me with the opportunity to write this book. Special thanks go out to:

Cora Couchman

G. Davidson

Reiko Fujii

Kate Golding

Anna Javier

Sheryl G. Kinney

Cynthia McKenzie, PsyD

Sandy Ray

Betsy Risner

Additionally, I want to express my heartfelt appreciation to Ewa Rosanski, whose unwavering support and countless hours of content organization helped make this book a reality.

Welcome!

Welcome to our adventure in gel plate printing. This book has been a dream of mine for many years, and it is my biggest wish for you to fall in love with the art of gel plate printing.

The gel plate is often thought of as "just" a printing tool; however, it is actually an amazing mixed media tool as well.

In this book I'm presenting it to you through my ArtMythos philosophy. ArtMythos incorporates a wide array of subjects, but at the heart of its approach is telling our stories visually. Furthermore, this book teaches solid printmaking techniques while also supporting the artist's inspirational process. The beauty of making successful prints relies very much on learning to balance the controlling and guiding of the artwork while allowing elements of surprise.

Combining mixed media, my ArtMythos philosophy, and techniques inspired by traditional printmaking will support you in being present and connected to what you wish to create, and in knowing how to guide the mixture of paint on the plate for a desired effect.

You'll practice trusting a process and releasing the need for control in order to experience the joy of a creation that is a blending of the artist's vision and the unknown. The gel plate allows for these seemingly contrasting elements, control and letting go, to be experienced at the same time. This is powerful, and for many, therapeutic and healing.

You will soon see that the gel plate, compared to other creation tools, doesn't require a lot of supplies. Especially if you are a beginner and feel overwhelmed with the large amount of space and supplies needed for certain forms of art creation, the gel plate will be your best friend. All you need is the gel plate, acrylic paints, a brayer, and paper; any paper will do (copier, tracing, old envelopes, etc.). No canvas necessary. Most importantly, what this means is that you can get into the process and start having fun right away instead of feeling like you're working with precious materials, which might cause tension as you try to enter your creative flow.

Which brings us to another important part of my teaching philosophy in ArtMythos: fun, experimenting, and playfulness are just as important as the other elements in art. It has been my experience that artists struggle with having created a habit of entering their creative space with a very serious mind. My approach is one of practice and exploration, and gel plate printing is one of the best tools to support sessions that are built around an atmosphere of practice. Last but not least, through this approach you will discover and practice new ideas and your own personal preferences that you can later apply to other forms of art with confidence.

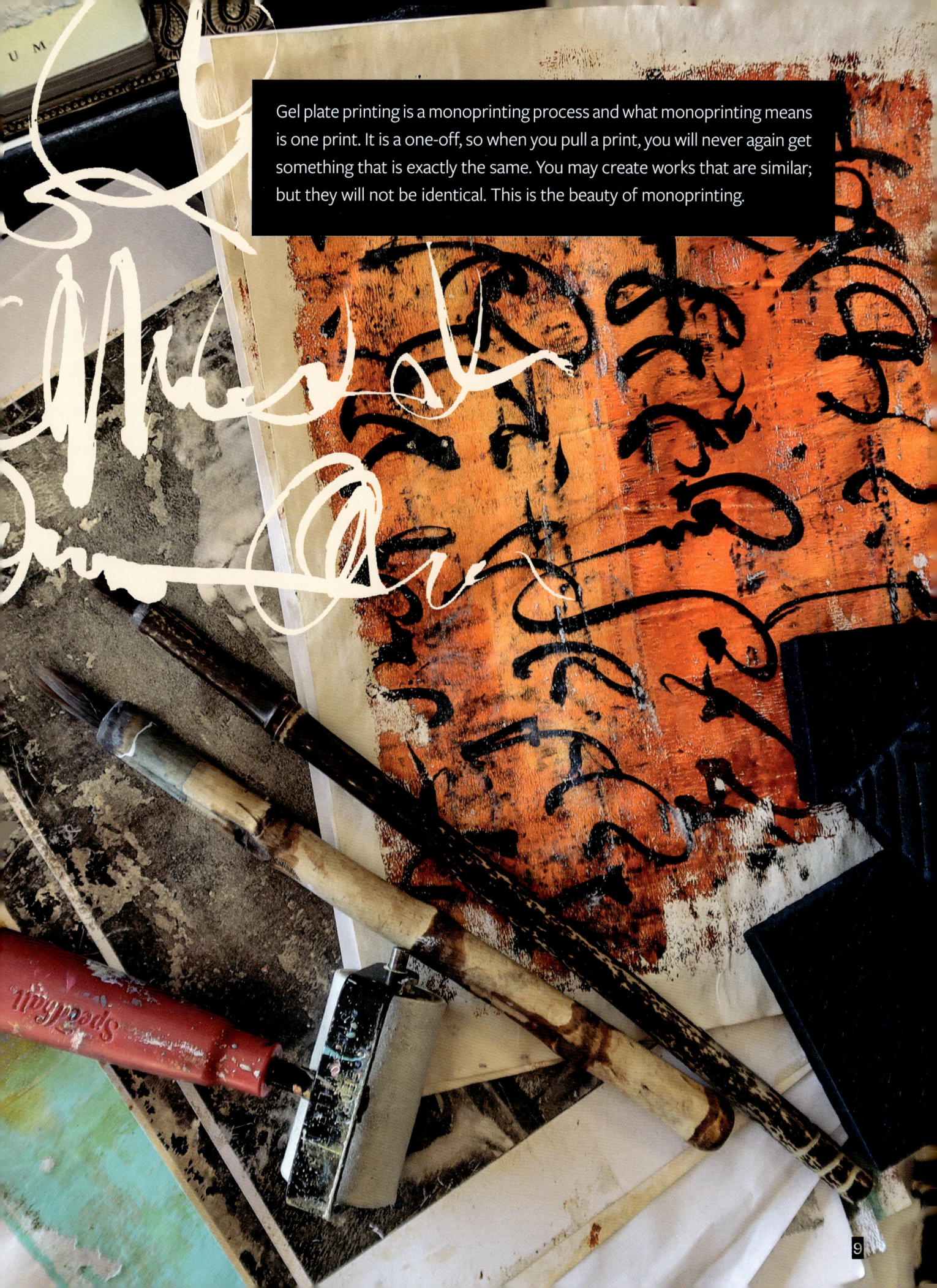

Gel plate printing is a monoprinting process and what monoprinting means is one print. It is a one-off, so when you pull a print, you will never again get something that is exactly the same. You may create works that are similar; but they will not be identical. This is the beauty of monoprinting.

My Journey to the Gel Plate

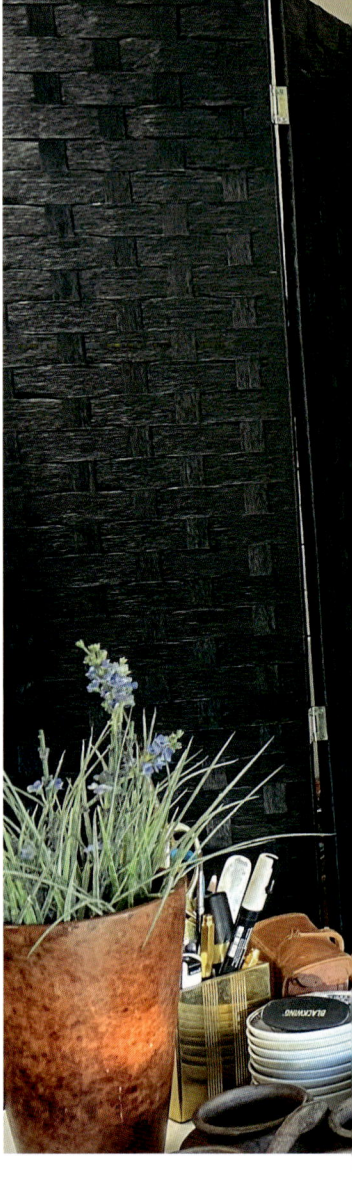

Because my gel plate work reflects a very personal mix of my experiences, I'd like to share a few things about myself before we get started. My long and rich experience in the arts and in teaching culminates in my gel plate techniques, and I'm excited to share with you what I have learned.

As a small child I was always creating things and knew early on that my life would be filled with creative endeavors. After earning degrees in graphic design / photography and in anthropology/archaeology focused on the art of Benin, I worked in arts management while generating a body of artwork and exhibiting nationally and internationally, including in the Smithsonian Museums, the Corcoran Art Gallery, and the Museum of Modern Art. My work is in the National Museum for Women in the Arts and in the permanent book collection of MOMA as well as in other notable collections.

Papermaking and bookbinding were dying art forms in the '80s, and so I apprenticed with artists to learn them. I subsequently taught in universities and museum systems as an adjunct professor, and as an itinerant K–12 art teacher throughout the state of Maryland, reviving art programs in schools whose budget had eliminated art from their programs.

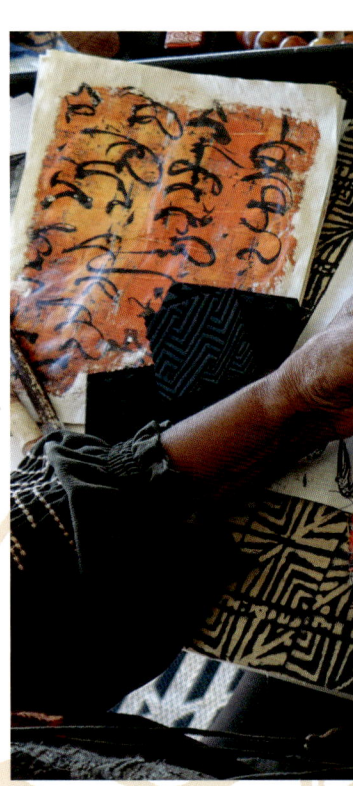

My design experience has won notable commissions, including creating a distinctive crystal sculpture award for Dr. Dorothy Irene Height, the founder and president of the National Council of Negro Women. Additionally, I have designed stationery products for *Essence* magazine and for UNICEF, and fabric designs featured by Target and IKEA.

As an artist, healer, Reiki master, and artaeomythologist, telling stories and helping others to heal is at the core of who I am and what I feel called to do. It embraces all that I am inspired to share with the world.

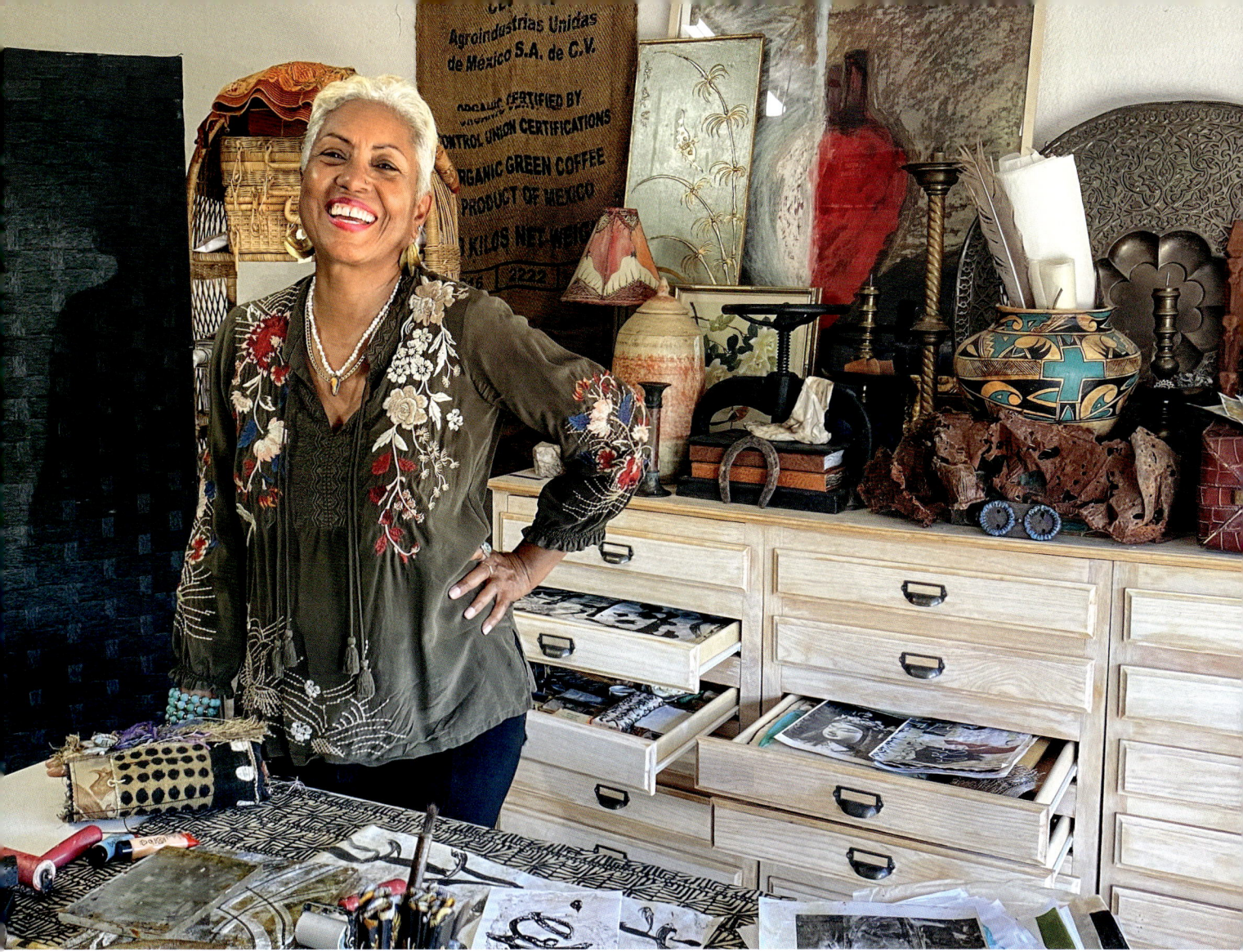

Using the ArtMythos Inspirations

As you learn the techniques, you'll notice "ArtMythos Inspirations." These sections give you ways to help you effectively tell your stories visually.

ArtMythos is a series of processes and technique and is the guiding philosophy for my approach to art as a working artist and instructor. This philosophy highlights storytelling as common thread and the importance of establishing visual vocabularies sufficient to create variety and depth of expression. Visual dialogues will result from many of the ArtMythos practices, which creates nonverbal exchanges between you the creator and your viewer.

1

Getting to Know Your Gel Plate

The gelatin plate, or gel plate, is a multipurpose mixed-media tool that is incredibly user-friendly. The gel plate techniques I have developed, many based on the art of monoprinting, enable you to empower your work by creating strong visual dialogues.

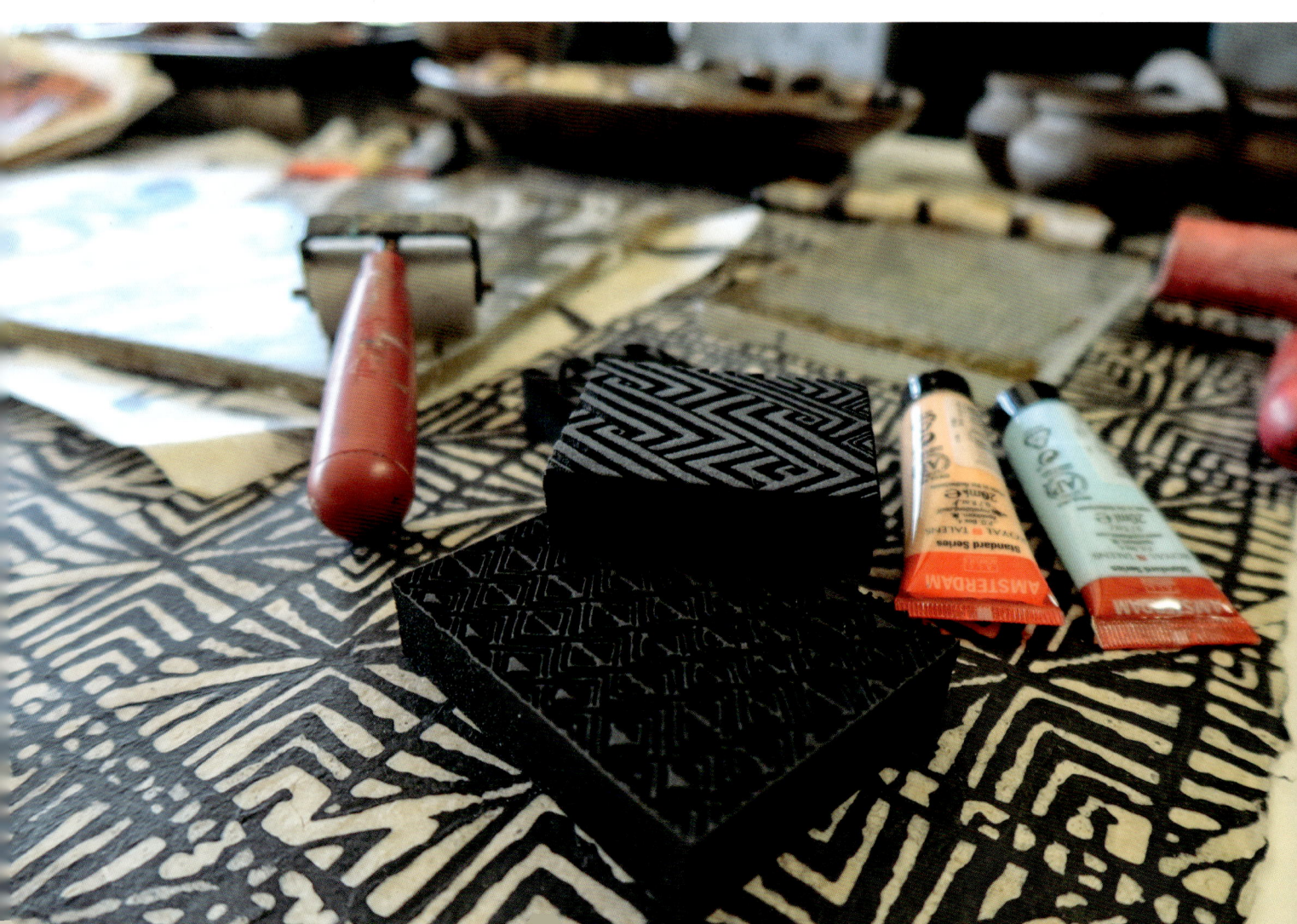

With the techniques in this book, which are presented in a specific order for most effective learning, a person who has never used the gel plate before will be able to create art within just a few short sessions, art to feel really good about! The pieces you will be creating will not feel underdeveloped. With these techniques on the plate, you will see an added richness through layers that will elevate your work, something that very few other art tools allow you to accomplish in such a short time.

When I first became aware of the gel plate, the Gelli® Plate specifically, I had just moved out of a 4,000-square-foot home with a separate studio in New Mexico to Chicago. I had sold a lot of my equipment for the move. Before I actually found studio space in Chicago, I lived in a six-flat and for ten months, my space was limited.

However, I did have a hallway. It was 5 feet wide by 20 feet long.

So one morning, I was thinking about where I could paint. I looked at that hallway and thought, "I probably could do something in there." I had space for a little table and some of my paints, but definitely not for an easel or much else.

I'd been on YouTube looking for inspiration and I came across the gel plate from Gelli Arts®. It looked fascinating to me, although a little like kid's play (this was ten years ago), but I was thinking, "I can see the potential of this monoprinting plate." I saw that all I needed was the plate, brayers, and papers, and a space for the papers to dry. I definitely had the space for the papers to dry due to that hallway! Most importantly, I saw the potential for making the kind of art I wanted to make, even in my limited space.

During my first few sessions on the gel plate was when I started working my "Old Wall" and "Patchwork" techniques. I also made my own stencils. The more I worked, the more potential I saw of layering upon layering, just like in traditional printmaking and monoprinting, but at a fraction of the cost of equipment and skill needed to use traditional printing tools. I was sold.

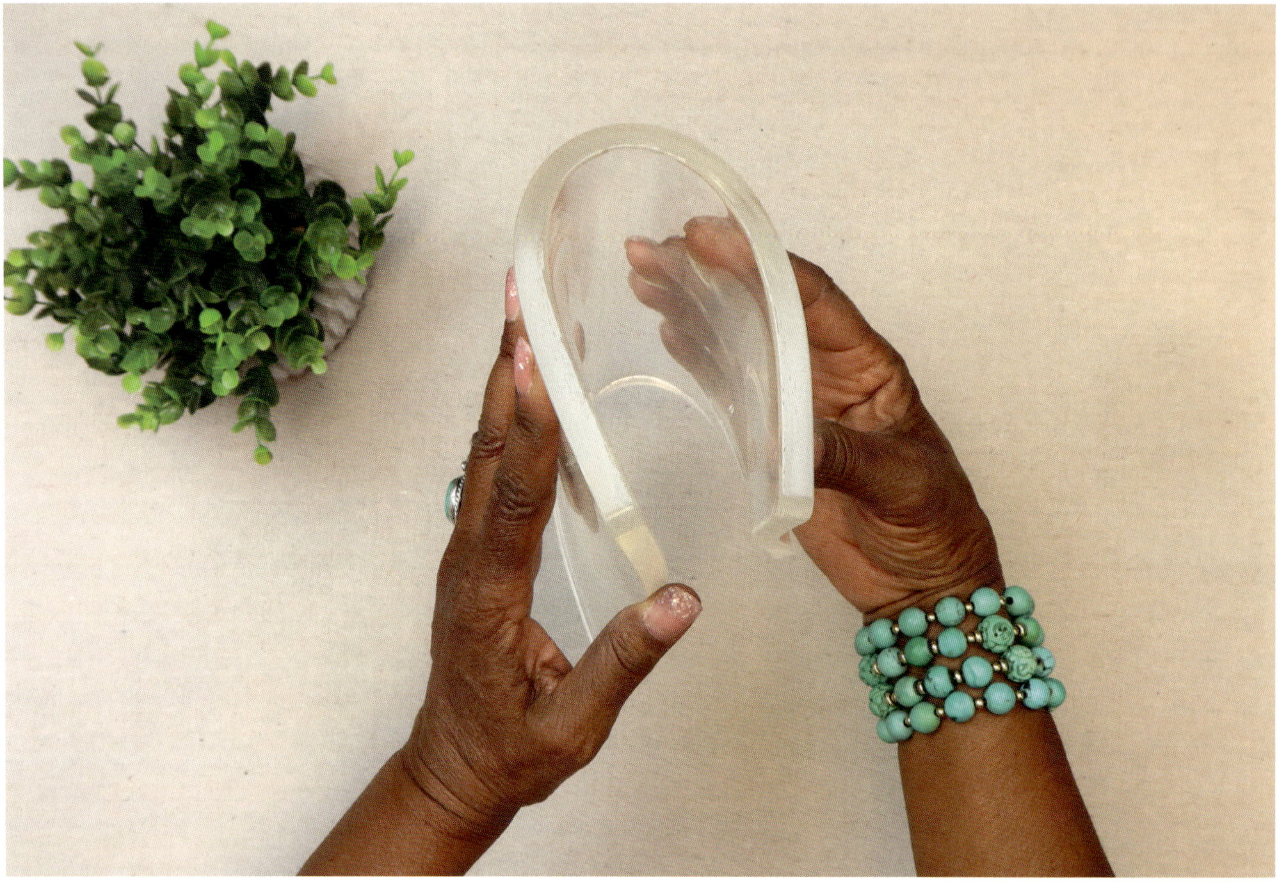

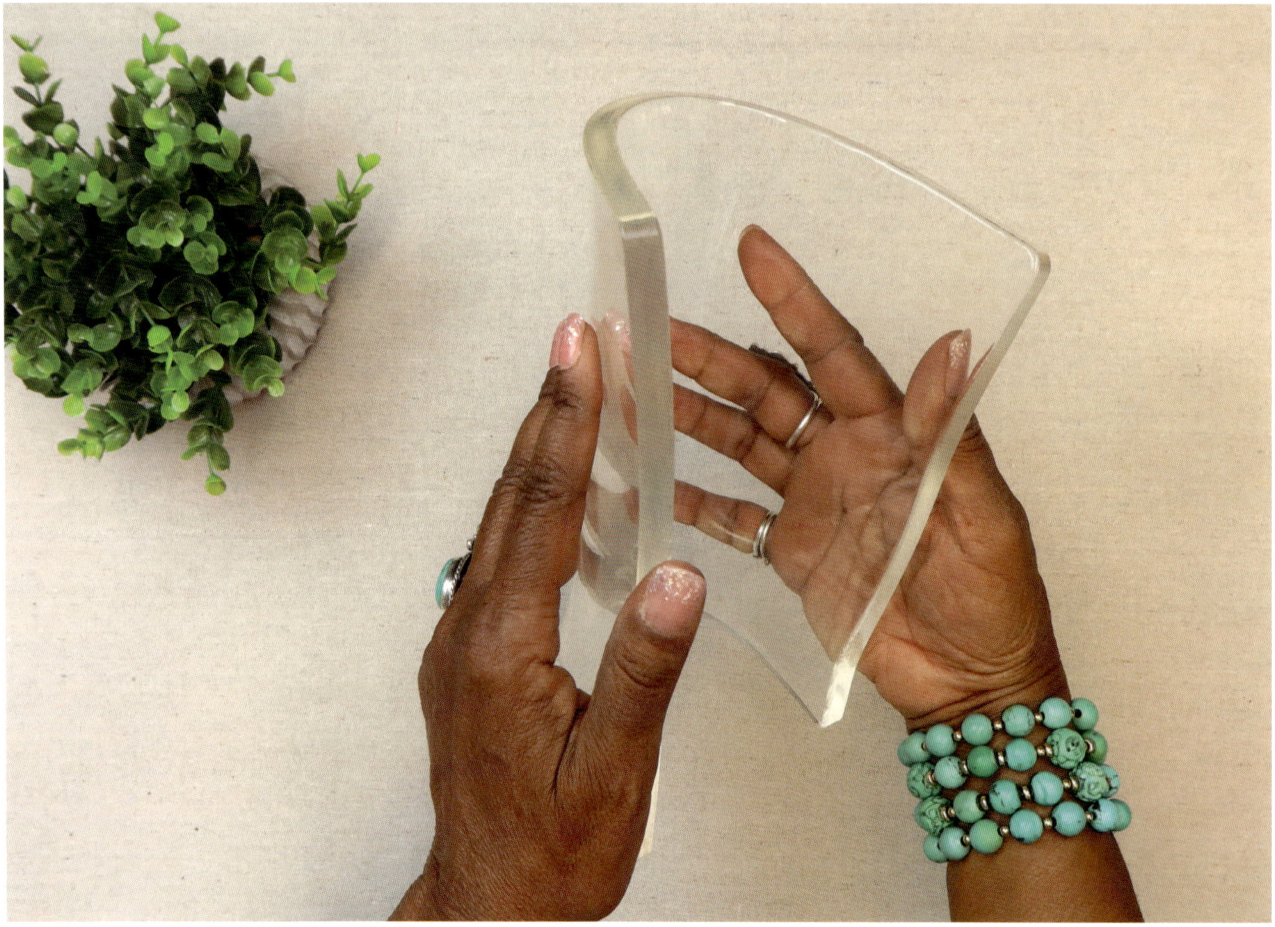

Gel Plate Printing for Mixed-Media Art

What Is a Gel Plate?

The gelatin plate facilitates monoprinting processes and allows them to be easily available to everyone. I use Gelli Arts printing plates. The plates are soft yet firm. They are easy to clean and store, responsive to various mediums, and last indefinitely. Available in different sizes from postcard size to the very large 16″ by 20″, these plates are addictive and versatile!

The Gelli Arts printing plates are flexible surfaces of what looks like clear gelatin, but this gel-like consistency is stable and not water-soluble since the plates are created from petroleum products. They contain no gelatin, no animal products, and no latex.

There are recipes available for making your own plates with gelatin, but for me Gelli Arts' products are reasonably priced, completely reliable, and last virtually forever, so I have not experimented with making my own. From personal experience with them (I've received plates made by artists in my community), homemade gel plates are often not as stable. Especially if left out in the heat, they can melt easily and become wrinkled. I have even traveled with the Gelli Arts printing plates and never had a problem.

History of Gel Plate Printing

Gelatin plate printing was developed in the early 1980s by the artist Fran Merritt, a cofounder and the first director of Haystack Mountain School of Crafts. As a painter, he desired a portable material for monoprinting that could be carried outside the studio "plein air" style, to monoprint without a traditional printing press and its related bulky materials that didn't travel easily.

Over the years he taught his techniques to many visiting artists and students, sharing at length his discoveries with this medium. The plates he created were handmade from gelatin powders, needed to be refrigerated, and degraded with use. (Those who used them favored this deterioration, since it added character and texture that was difficult to re-create.) The plates also would begin to melt with warm air temperatures, making them very unstable. It wasn't until 2011 that Lou Ann Gleason and Joan Bess, the cofounders of Gelli Arts LLC, were able to develop a product that was as sensitive as Merritt's gelatin plates but far more stable and with an incredibly long shelf life.

Setting Up Your Work Area

Of course, you can work in *any* area you have available, whether it be the kitchen table or a little desk or a card table in the corner of your living room. The plate is easy to pack away and store flat. Nevertheless, if you find yourself addicted to printmaking it's nice to have a work area with a few amenities!

Some things to think about as you set up your work area:

1 Try to have a large enough work surface. You'll need your gel plate, a few paints, and brayers. Also allow for a dish of water if you plan to use water-based stains or paints, and a safe surface for sumi ink and brushes.

2 Find a washable surface to set the plate on so that any spills or drips can be easily cleaned. Alternatively, spread a disposable layer of heavy paper over the table to catch drips and spills from the gel plate. A Teflon mat, plexiglass, or butcher paper works well. This also gives you a place to lay your brayer.

3 I keep an old book or spare sheets of paper nearby to roll paint off my brayer when there's too much or when I need to change colors. An old book that you've already torn apart for other projects can be a great way to clean the brayer—just turn the page for a fresh surface! Don't discard these off-sheets, since they become excellent base papers for tea-staining or further printing. Even if they look ugly or useless to you or are covered with muddy color mixtures, you will be continually surprised at how these scrap pieces become beautiful as paint accrues and layers build up on them. I use almost ALL my scrap papers. I set the scraps aside when dry into a stack of "papers to be added to later" and keep them near my work area.

4 Use a table or desk where you can be comfortable whether sitting or standing. You may want to do both, depending on the task.

5 If you become engrossed in your work, you may find (like me) that papers begin to stack up! Wet papers will end up sticking to each other, so it's a great idea to be prepared with multiple drying surfaces. A wire and some clips or clothespins are ideal, but if you are short on space, try a pasta rack or folding laundry-drying rack. Alternatively, work slowly and stack the papers as they dry (luckily acrylic dries fast), using waxed paper between the sheets if needed. Honestly, I have found myself standing ankle deep in beautiful prints and glimmering papers and I have to make myself stop the unleashed creativity for a minute and organize!

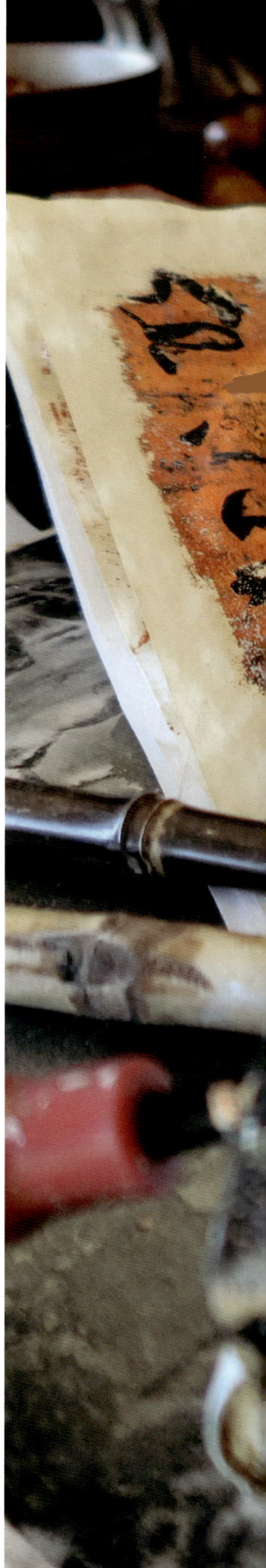

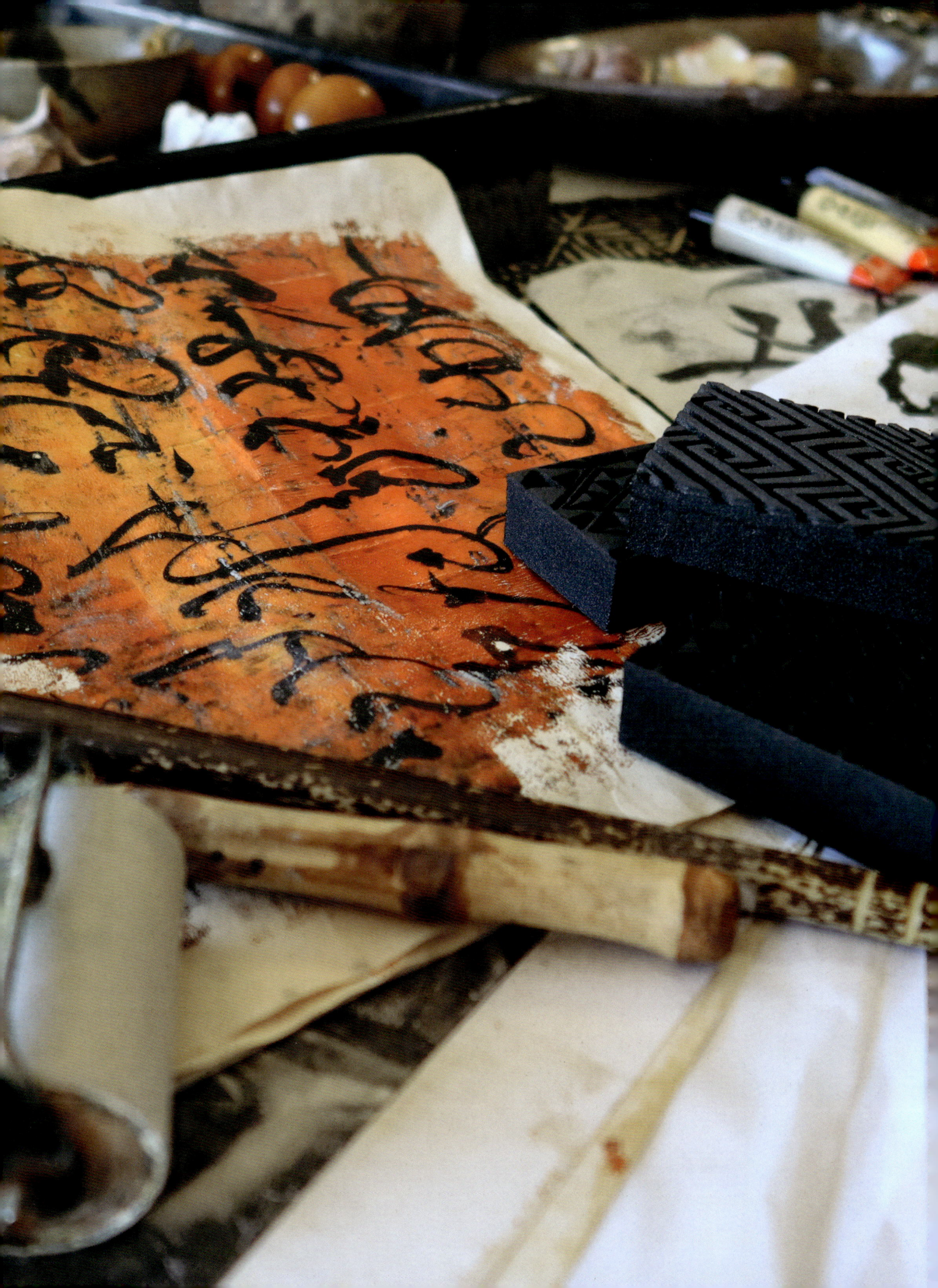

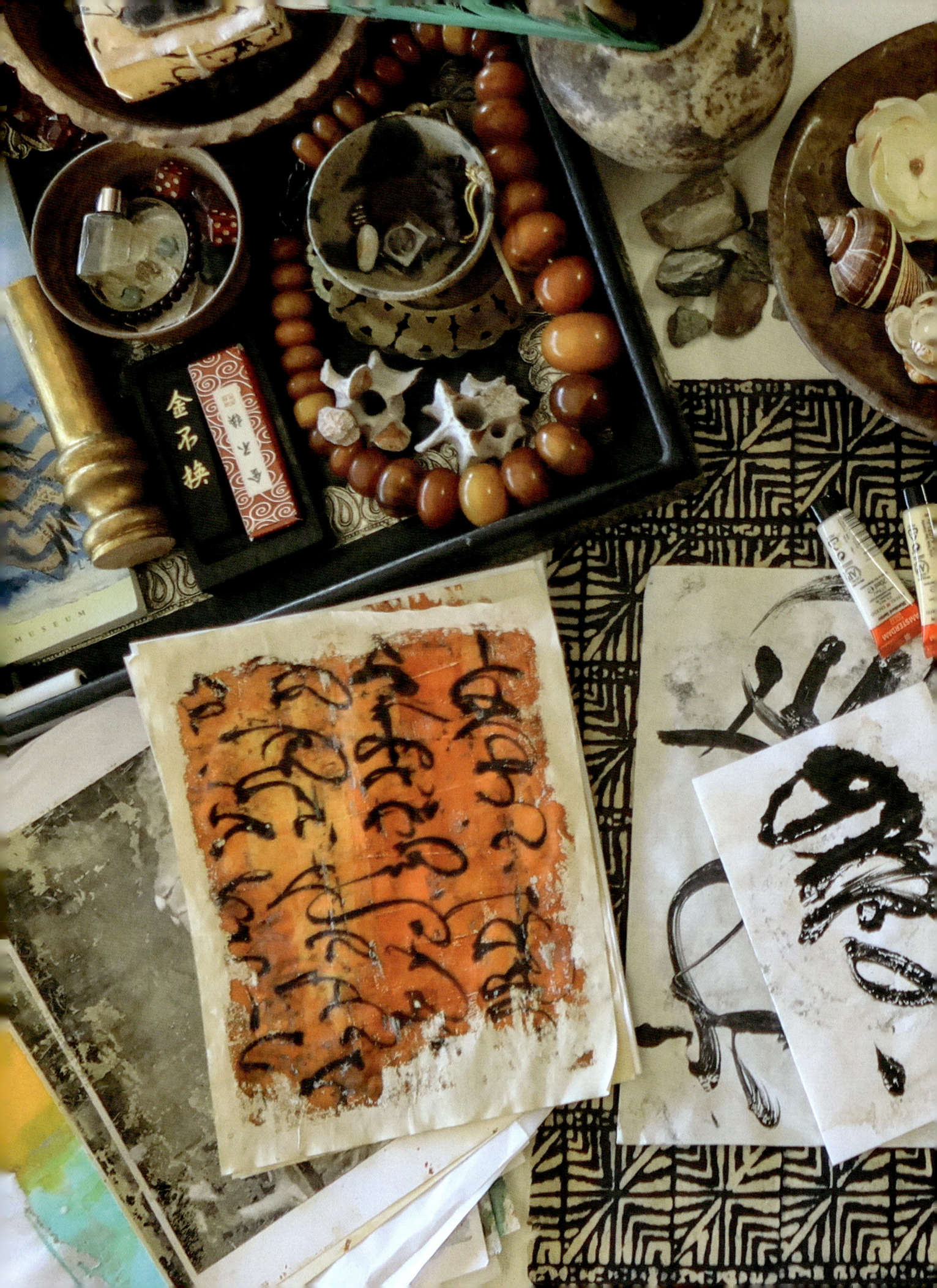

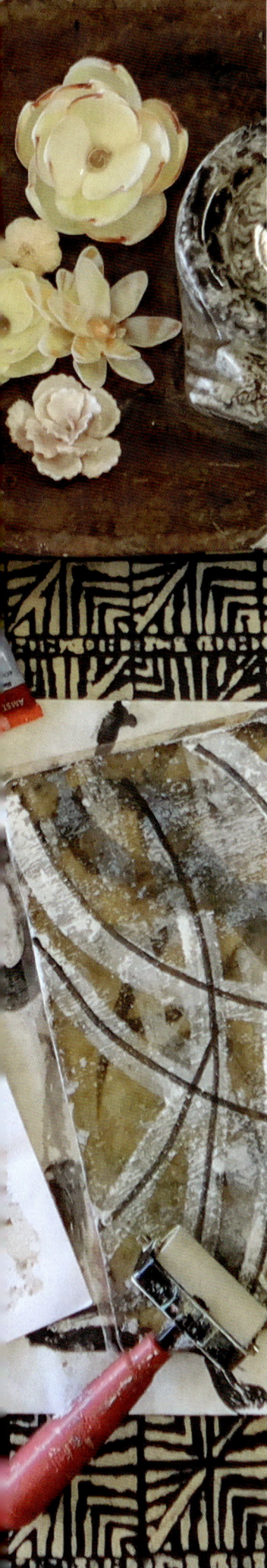

6 I keep a soup-bowl-sized dish of very small scraps on my working surface, where the little pieces end up. That way when I need interesting tidbits for collage, I have them at my fingertips.

7 Stencils, leaves, patterns, and extras—it's optimal to think ahead about what fun pieces you might be using in this particular print session, and to allow some space for them. Perhaps you have a stack of leaves to imprint, favorite stencils, antique wooden stamps, or lacy bits to use in your work; have those at the ready.

8 The concepts of "postconsumer waste" are a motivating factor in my art. So much waste is produced in packaging, for instance, that can be used in amazing and creative ways. With that said, look at your empties differently: various bottle sizes make diverse circular imprint patterns, bubble wrap and other textured packaging materials are tools, and used paper towels from paint cleanup make activated surfaces for gel printing and eco-staining. These are just a few of the ways I use these materials. Gather them up and have them at the ready in your studio!

Tools and General Supplies for Gel Printing

Each technique's chapter will explain any specific supplies needed, but there are a few general tools and supplies you will want to have on hand.

- A brayer. A wider brayer of around 5″ will be preferable to a small 2″ or 3″ size, simply because you will achieve a smoother surface with fewer lines created by the edges of the brayer. I like a brayer with a solid handle, but use whichever kind you prefer or can easily source.

- Cleaning tools: baby wipes, baby oil, packing tape, paper towels or rags.

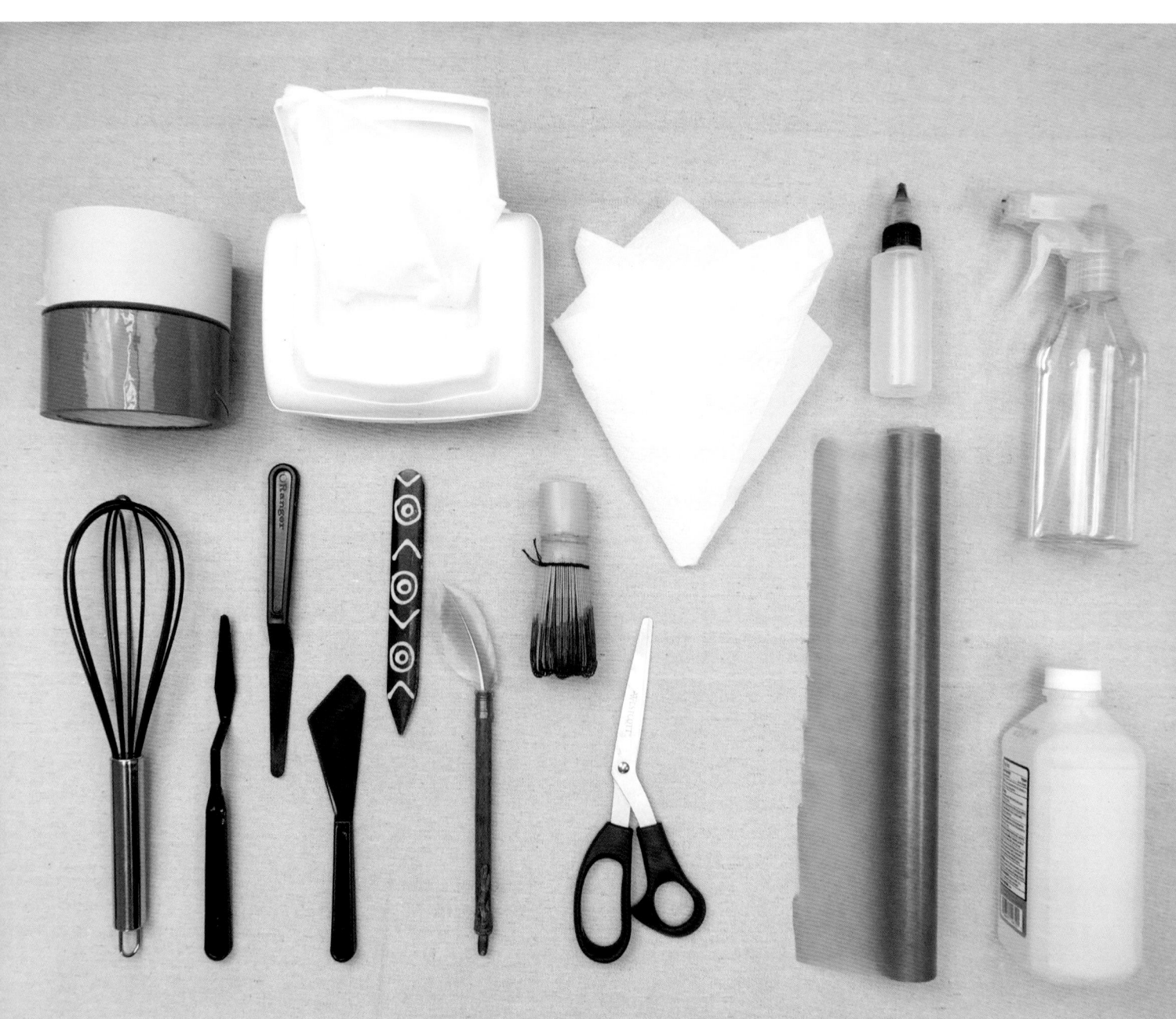

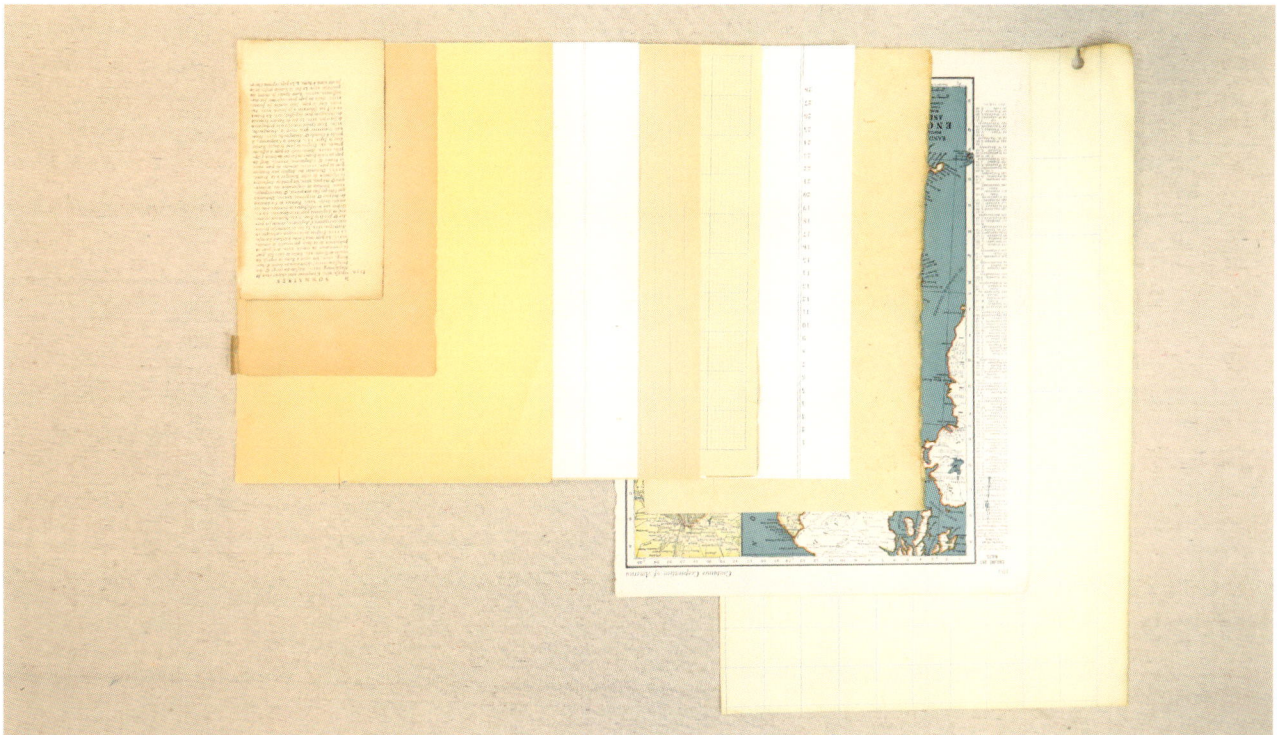

A variety of paints and inks: acrylics, matte/chalk paints, watercolors, sumi inks, acrylic inks, spray inks, alcohol inks, and ink pads

- Scrap paper or an old book for cleaning the brayer between layers (see "Setting Up Your Work Area," above).

- Butcher paper, newsprint, or Teflon mat for protecting your table surface.

- A waxed paper sheet, palette, plastic plate, old dish, or similar on which to set the brayer down between uses.

- A spray bottle filled with water, to create various effects or to moisten the plate surface.

- A couple of large pins or nails to push through the clogged openings of paint tubes or bottles.

- Soft, nonpointy marking tools such as old paintbrushes, cotton swabs, sponges, or eraser tips.

- A variety of papers. See each technique's chapter for additional information, but make this your general approach: don't hesitate to collect all kinds of papers to use with the gel plate. Advertisements from the junk mail pile, anything printed on card stock, windowed envelopes, your printing discards, tissue paper, wrapping paper, cooking parchment, butcher paper . . . acrylic paint covers almost anything, so be creative and experimental in collecting papers for printing!

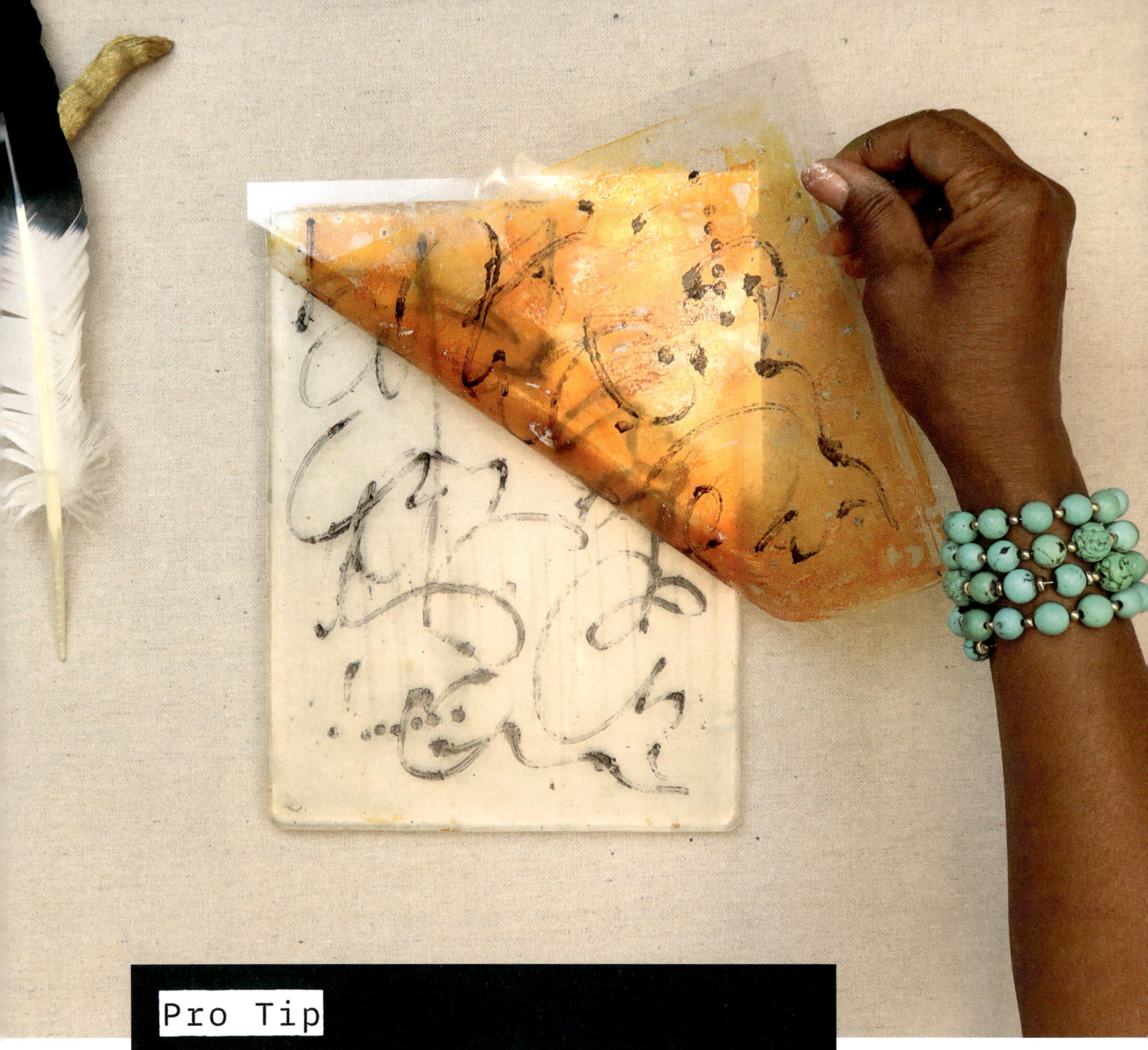

Caring for the Gel Plate

It is easy to care for the plate if you follow a few basic rules.

1. Most important—NEVER USE SHARP OR POINTED OBJECTS OF ANY KIND WITH YOUR GELATIN PLATE.

The only way that the plate is vulnerable to damage is in cutting or breaking its smooth surface. Cuts or gouges on the gel plate will show up forever in printing. Avoid any sharp studio tools.

2. Clean it correctly. Cleaning is easy: a disposable gentle-cleansing wipe (for example, a baby wipe) will clean off most paint residue. Baby oil or mineral oil is a good way to restore the original tacky surface.

Understanding the cleaning of the gel plate is important, but I love to build up paint on the plate and have a tendency not to clean my plate thoroughly after every pull or in between printing sessions. You'll see why as we work with the techniques.

But there does come a time where the plate has so many layers that it needs to be cleaned. There are two main ways to completely clean the gel plate.

The first method is to use baby oil. Rub a thin layer over the plate and let it sit for a few minutes to soften the layers and loosen the paint. Then start to wipe the plate, using baby wipes. You'll find that the paint will begin to come off. You may go through several baby wipes before the plate is clean. (Baby wipes have mild cleaning surfactants, so there are no worries about harsh bleaches that can be found in other cleaning wipes. That said, any disposable gentle-cleansing wipe works.)

The second method goes a step further. Complete the above process to remove as much paint as possible, then use a mild dishwashing detergent or any mild cleaning product. These products are known for breaking up grease and paints while also helping to remove color stains on the gelatin surface. I do this second process only once or twice a year. I find it's not necessary to clean your plates with these products more often than that. After your plate is deep-cleaned, return to the above baby oil method for your regular cleanings, because the oil will restore the surface of your plate, allowing paints to stick to the surface and encouraging beautiful gel plate monoprints.

Cleaning with Tape

For a completely dry plate, another option for cleaning it is by using packing tape. The bonus? It gives you art to use for washi tape or for collage. See chapter 10 for the instructions.

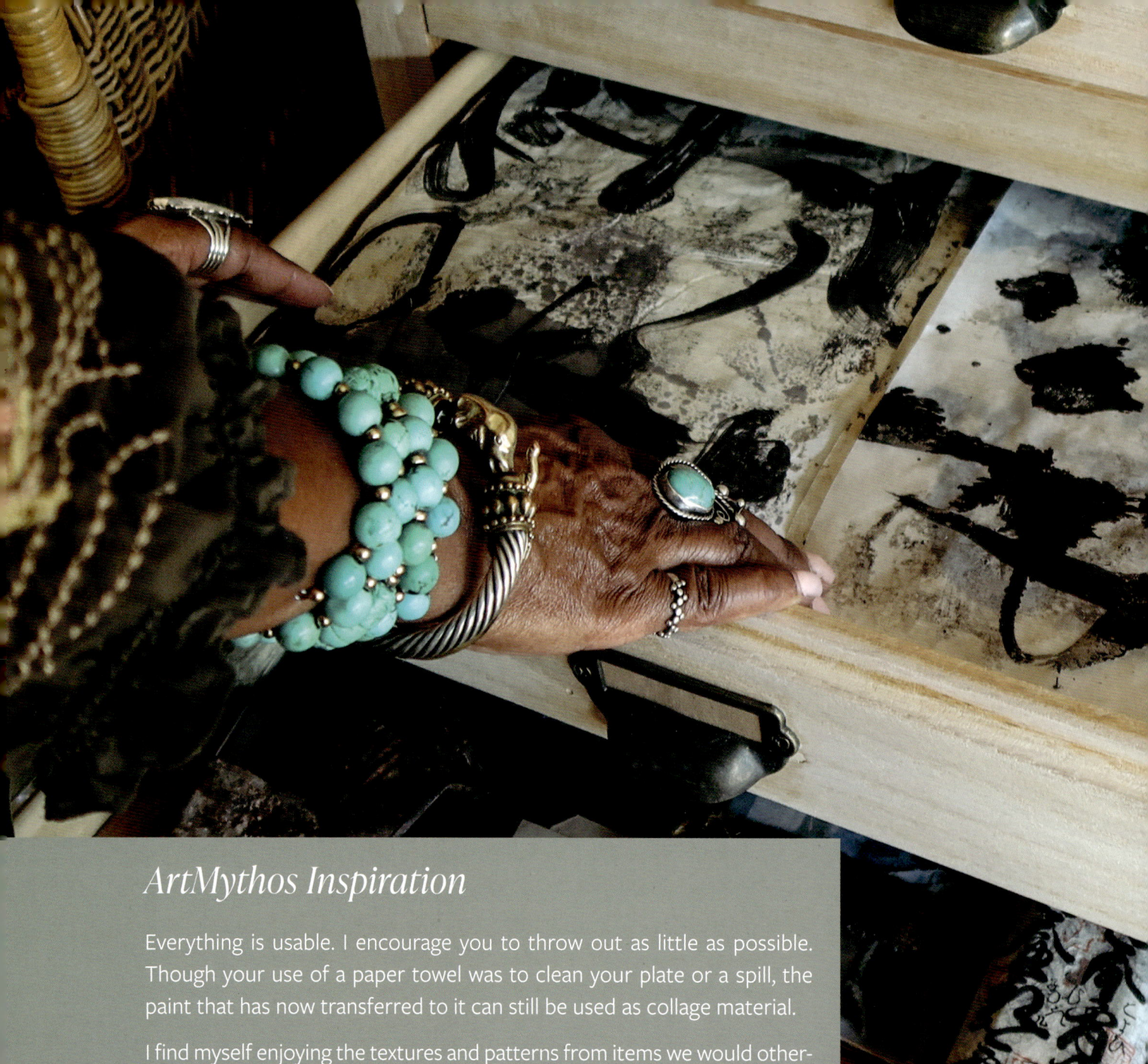

ArtMythos Inspiration

Everything is usable. I encourage you to throw out as little as possible. Though your use of a paper towel was to clean your plate or a spill, the paint that has now transferred to it can still be used as collage material.

I find myself enjoying the textures and patterns from items we would otherwise throw away, and in many cases these items are what is needed to bring diversity to our finished art pieces. Even in the cleaning-up process, challenge yourself to reuse your materials. I spread the used paper towels or baby wipes out to dry, so they are ready to use as collage material. This is about challenging our ideas of what artist materials or mixed-media supplies are. This is also about challenging ourselves to see very little as disposable.

I've begun to label this art movement "postconsumer art" to raise awareness and give ourselves as artists the impetus to reclaim these materials and use them without the fear of them not being archival. I do this in the spirit of Marcel Duchamp, who was inspired by his times to bring awareness to "readymade" art.

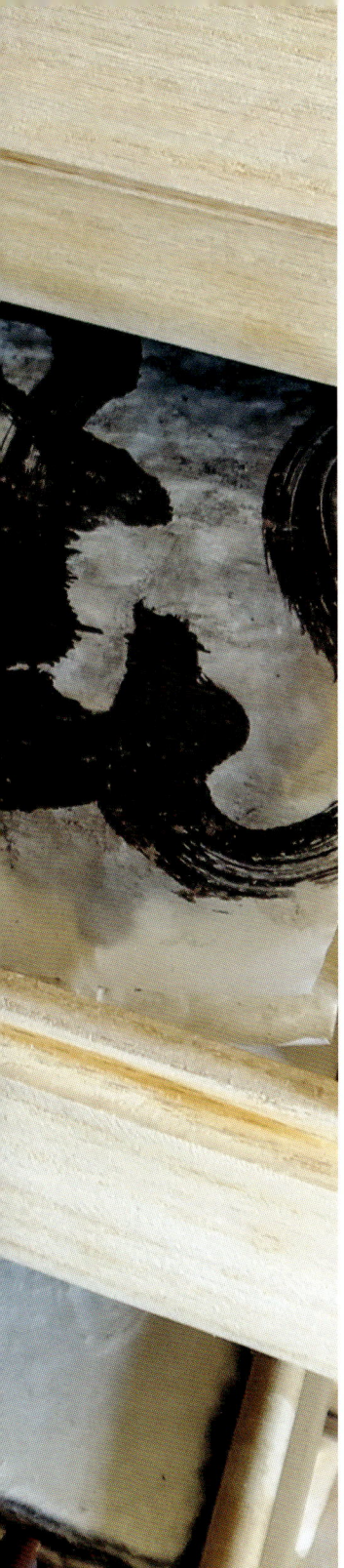

Remember that any color stains occurring from spray inks or oil pigments on the plate will not affect the printing qualities of the gel plate, so avoiding stains is not your goal.

Again, many of my favorite techniques rely on a deliciously messy plate with aging layers, crusty edges, and bits of leftover color. These imperfections in built-up texture and colors bring a sophistication and elegance to the artwork. For this reason, I usually finish a session of work by using my last sheet of paper to pick up the main paint marks or patterns. I put the plate away with some final layers and bits of information ready for my next printing session. The plate is not completely filled with paint, and neither is all the paint off. However, don't leave the plate with a full layer of paint on it. That is not good for the plate.

3. Store your gel plate flat. The clamshell case that it may come with is perfect for storage. The gel plate normally comes sandwiched between two sheets of plastic transparent film. When you finish with a session, put the film back on to protect the plate. Avoid putting other types of thin plastic sheets on your plate, or anything that would create folds or bubbles that will dent or crease the plate when stored.

Gel-Printing Techniques and Philosophy

The possibilities are truly endless when it comes to printing techniques. The list of pigments and supplies that can be adapted to gel printing is limited only by your imagination. Each artist can decide where to begin by thinking about the type of results they wish to achieve and applying their individual preferences to the process. Bright colors and opaque backgrounds? Transparent rainbow images? Shimmer and sparkle? Deep earth tones? Vibrant contrasting patterns? Mysterious fog-like atmosphere? All are easily achievable with some experimentation and practice. As you approach the endless variety of textures and imagery, it also helps to consider how you will be using the prints you are creating—although there is nothing wrong with playing and exploring now and figuring details out later!

Nevertheless, you may already have plans for your designs. You may be preparing papers for collage, or working on creating background sheets for art journals, or perhaps working on a series of monoprints that will stand on their own. Everyone will gravitate toward one technique over another, based on current projects and plans. Often the process itself will lead us into a journey of exploration and discovery as we are inspired by our own work to undertake new and exciting ideas!

You will soon realize that the one theme that sticks out most when we are printing is the idea of layering. Also important is "less is more." Build up small, subtle layers.

2

One-Color Printing Backgrounds

We will begin with printing one-color backgrounds on the gel plate. This is usually the best way to start your printing session. It gets the plate activated with enough moisture. Activating the plate is the first step of each session.

This is extra important if your plate is brand new, because activating it will release the original finish off the plate. Also, if you haven't been using your plate for a while, the moisture will make the plate flexible, pliable, and ready to pull great prints. Keep in mind that it usually takes at least three or four pulls before you start seeing successful prints. For this reason, scrap papers are great to begin with.

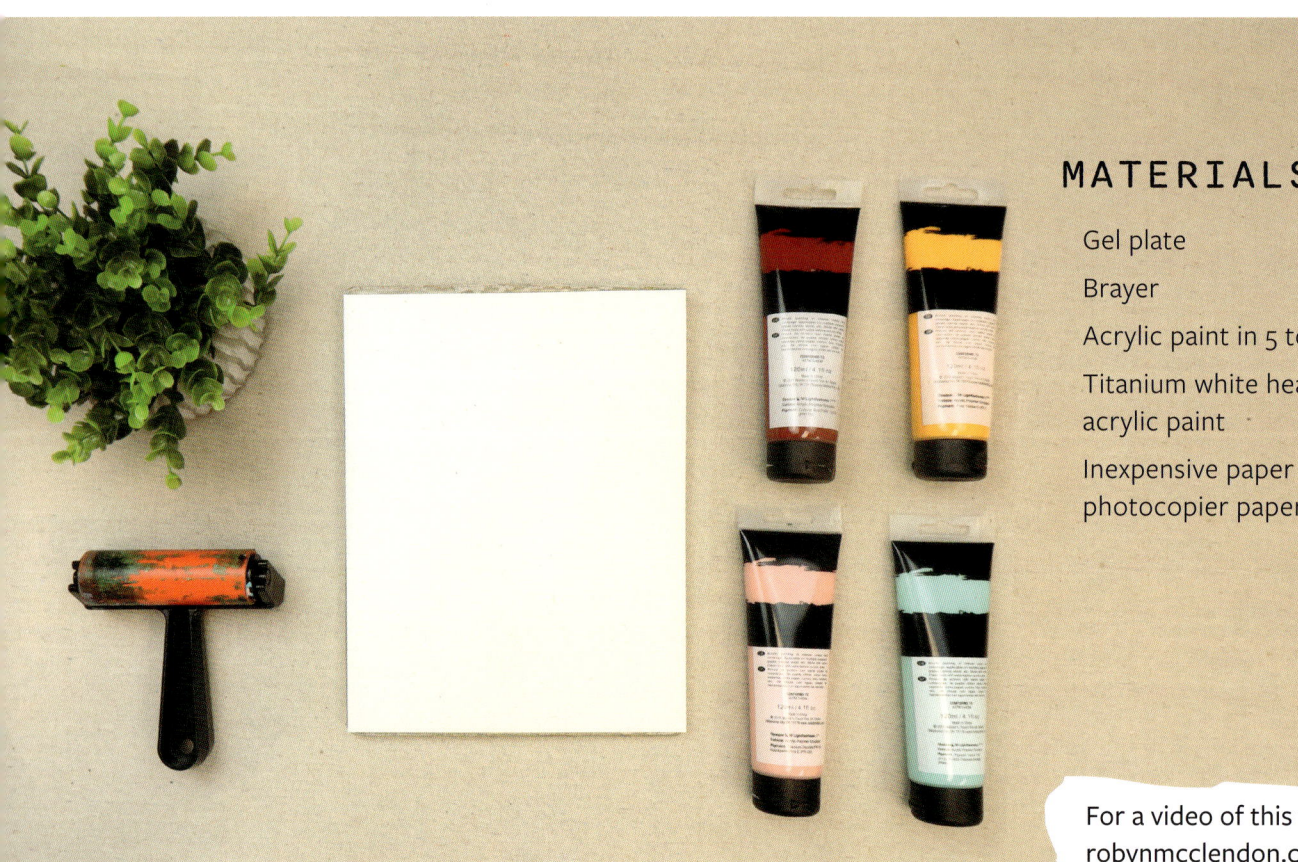

MATERIALS

Gel plate

Brayer

Acrylic paint in 5 to 6 colors

Titanium white heavy-body acrylic paint

Inexpensive paper (for example, photocopier paper)

For a video of this technique, visit robynmcclendon.com.

One-acrylic-paint-color printing backgrounds with added depth from paint buildup on the gel plate

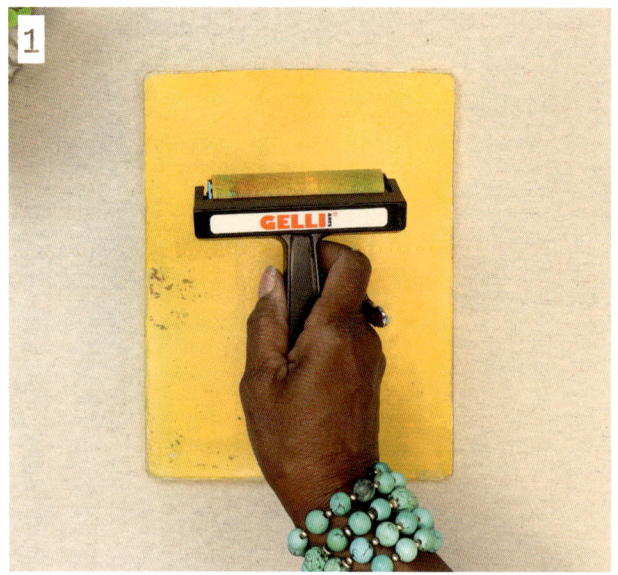

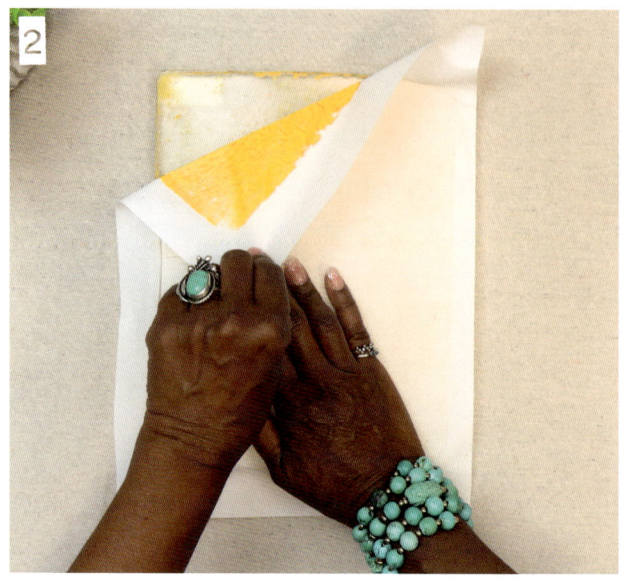

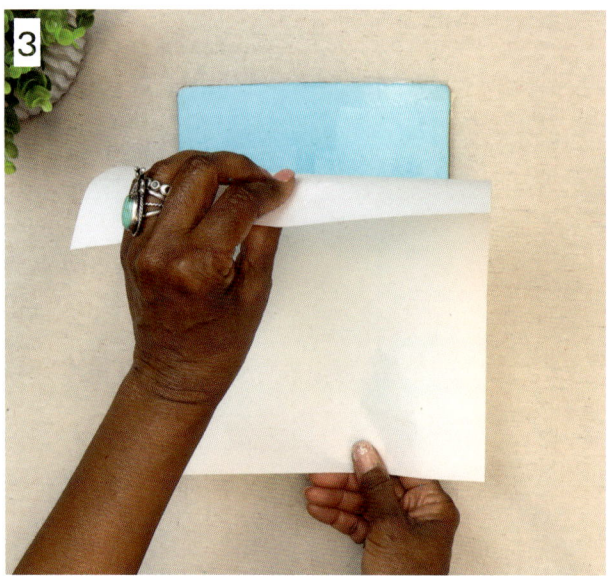

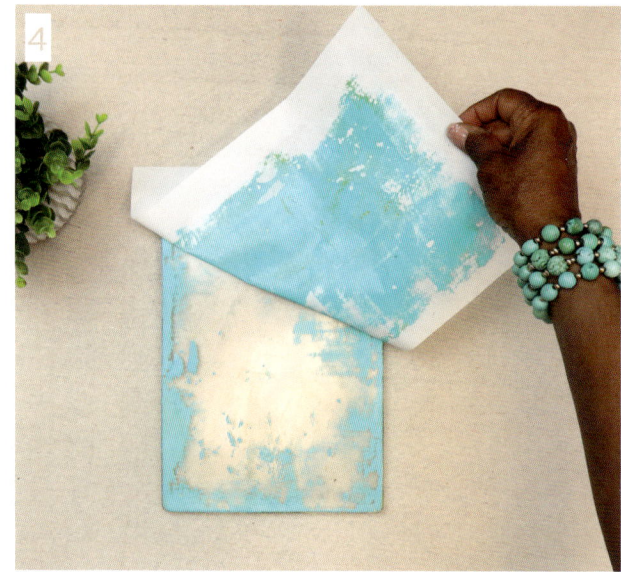

We will start the session by creating a color palette. Choose five to six acrylic paint colors. They can be any colors as long as one of them is a titanium white. Titanium white creates an absorbent layer that allows for other colors to be absorbed into the paint, making it perfect for various techniques on the gel plate.

Any type of inexpensive paper is great for beginning this session. We do not need fancy papers when activating the plate at the beginning of a printing session.

Choose one of the colors from your color palette. We will begin by rolling one color out on the plate. Squeeze out a 1″ long line on the plate. Take your brayer and roll the paint out all across the plate until it creates a thin and even surface **1**.

It is important to always put a thin layer of paint down. Keep in mind that the goal of a monoprint is to pull a thin layer of paint. You don't want to want to create a thick, globby layer because this will prevent you from pulling an even print, and your paper will be oversaturated. If you notice that there is too much paint on your plate once you start brayering (it will make peaks the way whipped cream or icing does), roll your brayer off on an extra piece of paper and then continue smoothing the painted surface.

After you are finished brayering, immediately lay a sheet of paper down on the plate. Using your palms and fingers, rub gently all over the surface of the paper. Soon you should feel the moisture from the paint coming through the paper. Thirty seconds is usually a good amount of time for this step, but adjust according to the humidity in your air.

Next, pull the paper off the plate **2**. Start at the top right- or left-hand corner and peel the paper toward you. Peel it off at an even pace.

Observe your first print and see how it looks. Notice where there is paint and where there is not. Maybe the paint had already started to dry in some places before you pulled the print. This is perfectly normal when you're activating the plate.

Repeat this process, **3**, **4** going through each of your colors except for white. **Do not clean your plate between prints and changing colors.** At the end of the process you should have five sheets with separate colors on each. At this point, we are not worried about image or design. We are activating the plate and getting used to the amount of paint we need on the surface. In the future, you will be able to use the prints that you have created. They are wonderful foundations for stenciling and stamping, and for collage. You'll see that there are so many creative things to do with one of these colored prints.

At this point you have successfully "built up color"

on your plate, a very important part of the process and the reason we've refrained from cleaning the plate between pulls. Building up color on the plate eventually leads to what I call the "Old Wall" technique, which creates beautiful thick-textured prints. If you include chapters 2 and 3 as part of your printing session, you'll notice that chapters 2 and 3 are designed to prepare for the "Old Wall" texture technique in chapter 4.

Before moving on to the next step, look at and study your plate. Notice how there are little bits of residue all over the plate.

Take your heavy-body titanium white paint and brayer out a thin coat, just as you have been doing for the other colors in your palette. Lay a clean piece of paper down and pull another print. This print being your sixth print, you should start seeing the extra colors from your plate transferring onto the white surface.

It is normal for your first prints in this process to turn out a bit spotty. Now that your plate is more responsive, you can reuse some of your first prints and reprint. This is optional; however, whenever you add more layers onto a print, you will be adding more texture to your art.

Look at this technique as just getting started and practicing. Don't hesitate to print over pages that didn't come out completely in this one-color

Paint & Brayer Tips

Start with the light colors and work up to your darker colors. It's easier to put a yellow down first than to try to get a yellow after putting down the dark colors.

Limit your palette to three or five colors. Odd numbers are good because it allows for juxtaposition of balance.

When you lift up the brayer and peaks form, the way they would with icing, there's too much paint. Simply brayer some off onto a scrap piece of paper and keep on brayering to get a thin, even layer.

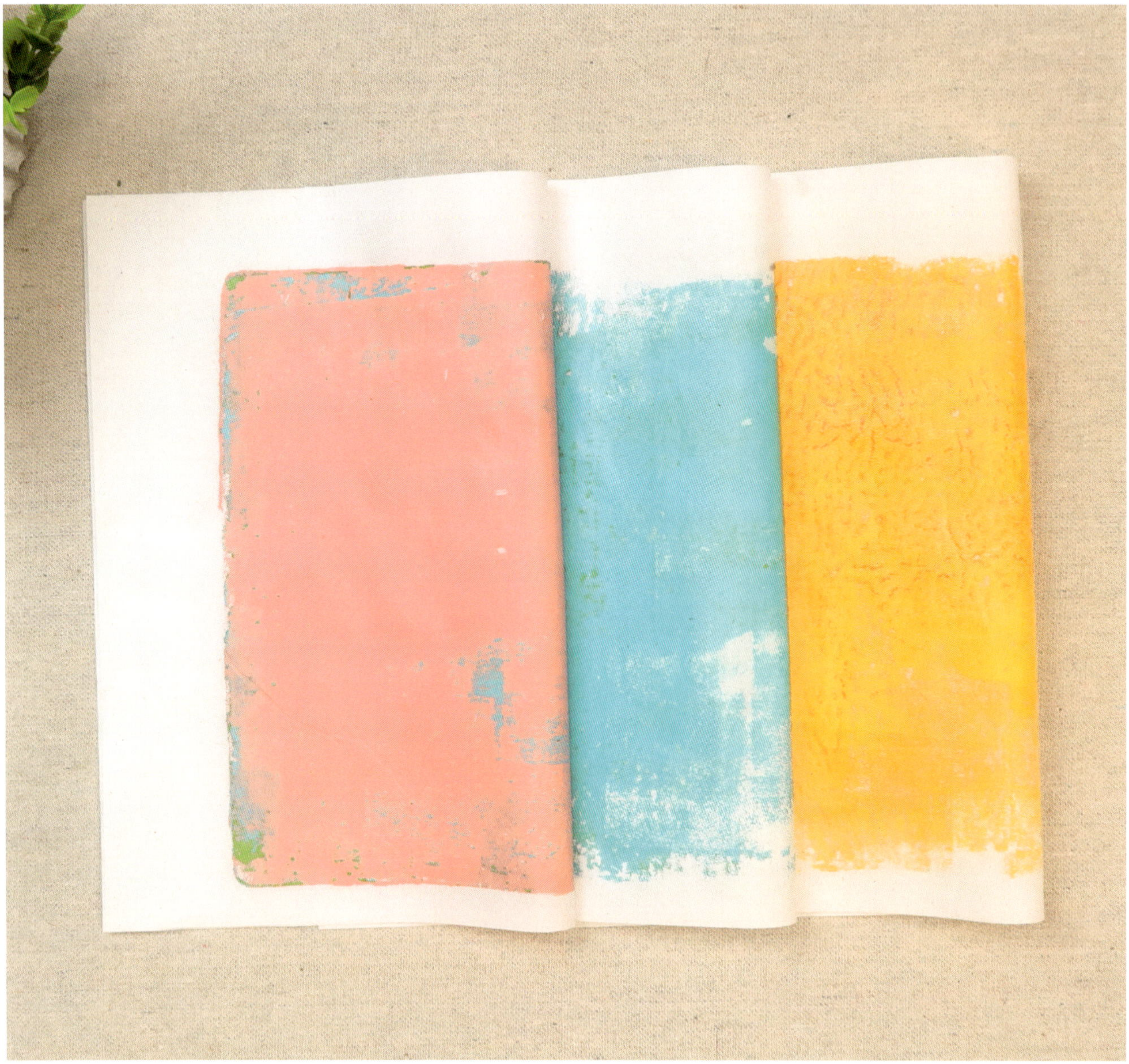

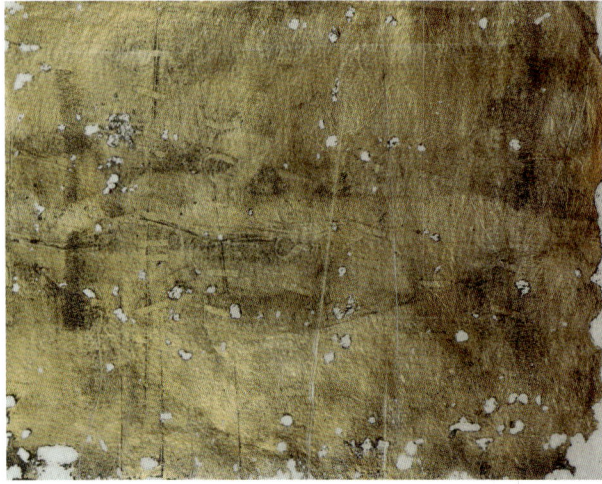

One-acrylic-paint-color printing backgrounds with added depth from paint buildup on the gel plate printed on archival tissue paper

One-acrylic-paint-color printing backgrounds with added depth from paint buildup on the gel plate

technique. You can experiment; there's no right or wrong. Give yourself time and space to get into the flow of this technique.

One-color backgrounds alone can form a complete gel-printing session. You can really make this a discovery session and focus on learning about what paints you like most on the plate. You will find that some paints work better than others. On the backs of your papers, note the names of the paints you used, especially the ones you like. Understanding your paint preferences and how they react on the plate will support you in being comfortable in the future, when you perform more-advanced techniques.

Now that your plate is activated, you can move on to chapter 3, where we'll work on creating background prints with two or three colors.

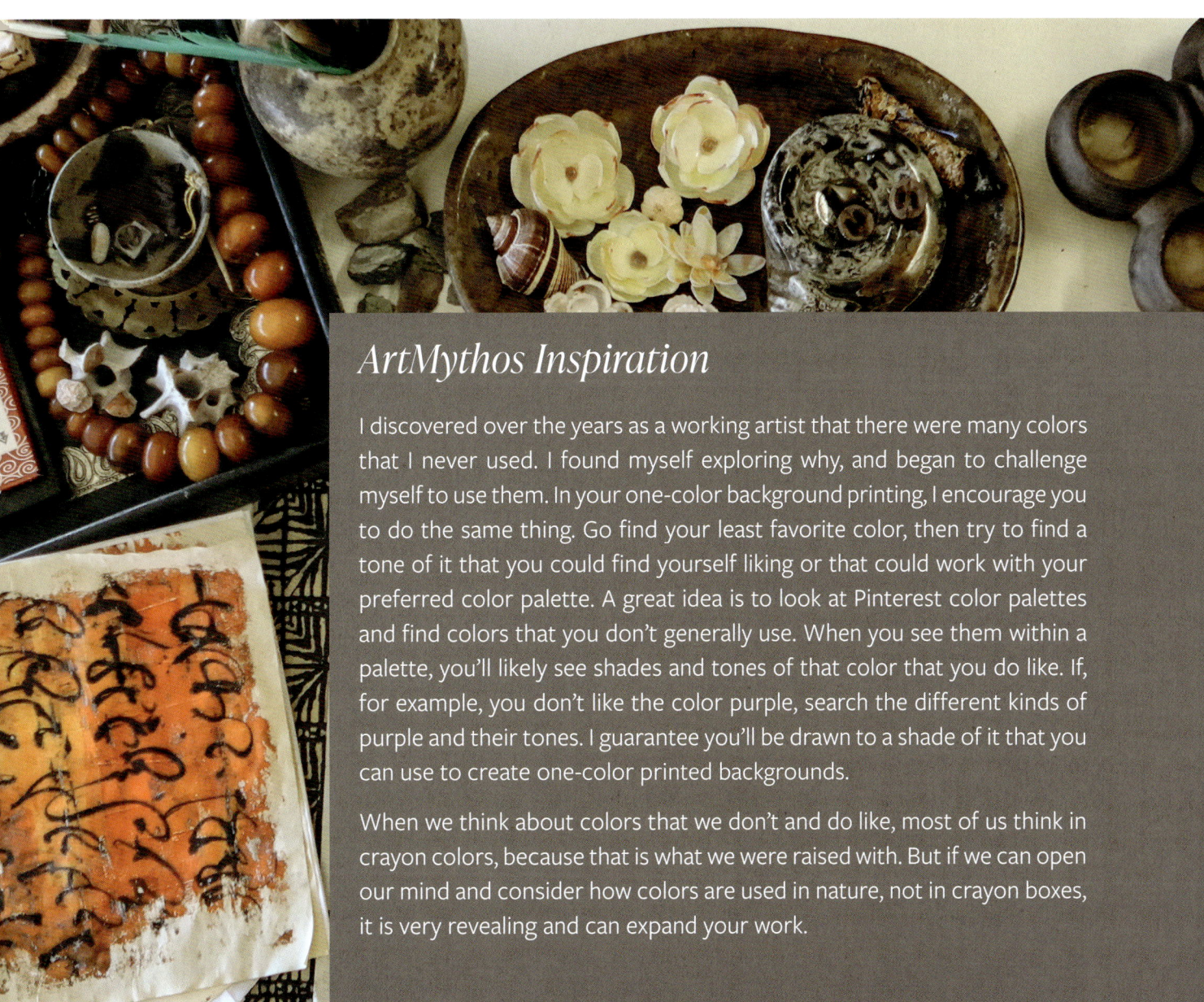

ArtMythos Inspiration

I discovered over the years as a working artist that there were many colors that I never used. I found myself exploring why, and began to challenge myself to use them. In your one-color background printing, I encourage you to do the same thing. Go find your least favorite color, then try to find a tone of it that you could find yourself liking or that could work with your preferred color palette. A great idea is to look at Pinterest color palettes and find colors that you don't generally use. When you see them within a palette, you'll likely see shades and tones of that color that you do like. If, for example, you don't like the color purple, search the different kinds of purple and their tones. I guarantee you'll be drawn to a shade of it that you can use to create one-color printed backgrounds.

When we think about colors that we don't and do like, most of us think in crayon colors, because that is what we were raised with. But if we can open our mind and consider how colors are used in nature, not in crayon boxes, it is very revealing and can expand your work.

3

Two- and Three-Color Printing Backgrounds "Mark Rothko Style"

It is best to begin this session by starting with the one-color backgrounds in chapter 2. Create four one-color backgrounds to get the plate activated. Then you will be ready to do two- and three-color printing.

As mentioned in chapter 2, anytime you sit down with the gel plate, the first step is to get the plate activated. Think of this as priming and seasoning the plate.

Creating two- and three-color prints has similar steps to creating one-color prints.

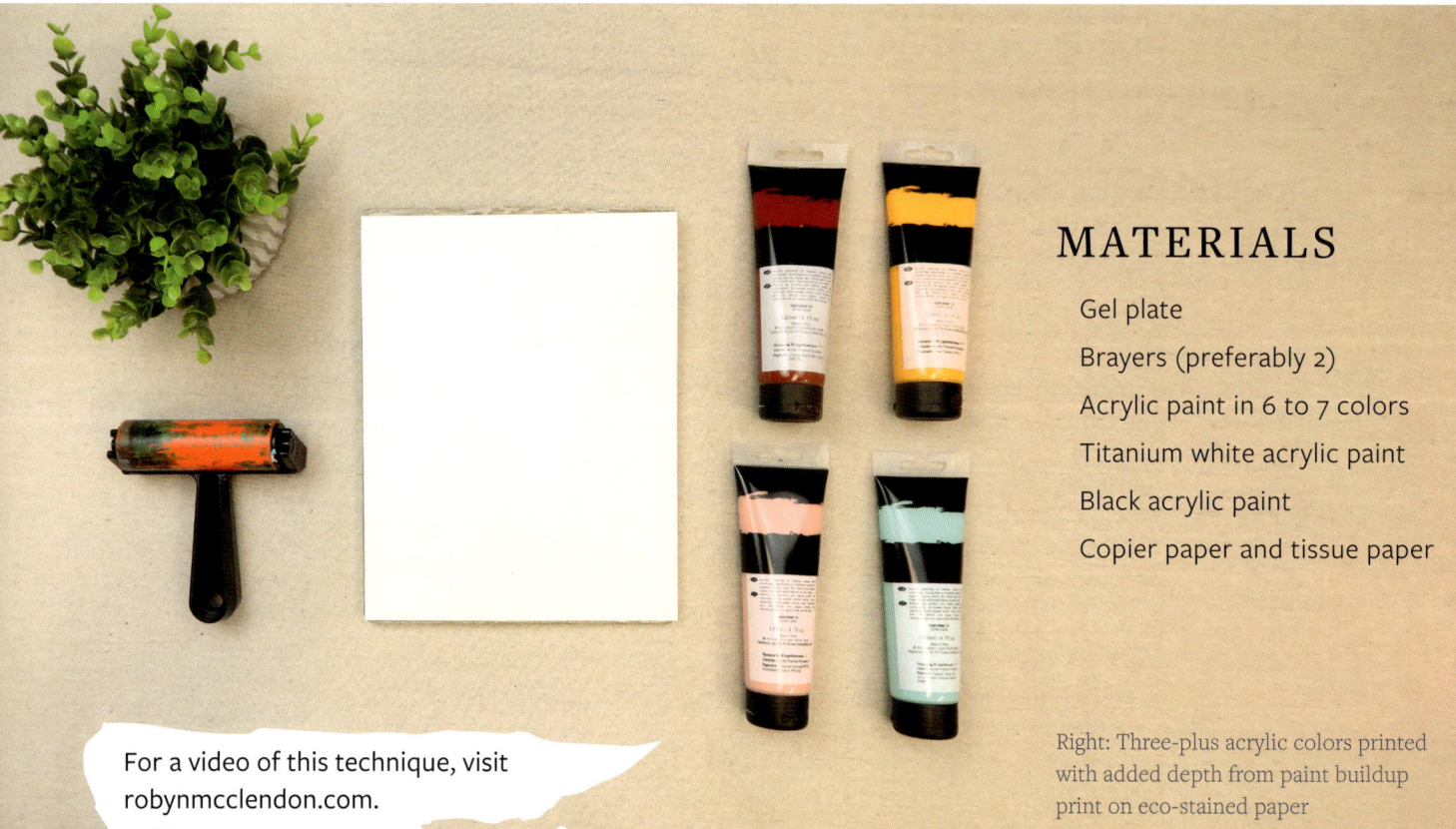

MATERIALS

Gel plate

Brayers (preferably 2)

Acrylic paint in 6 to 7 colors

Titanium white acrylic paint

Black acrylic paint

Copier paper and tissue paper

For a video of this technique, visit robynmcclendon.com.

Right: Three-plus acrylic colors printed with added depth from paint buildup print on eco-stained paper

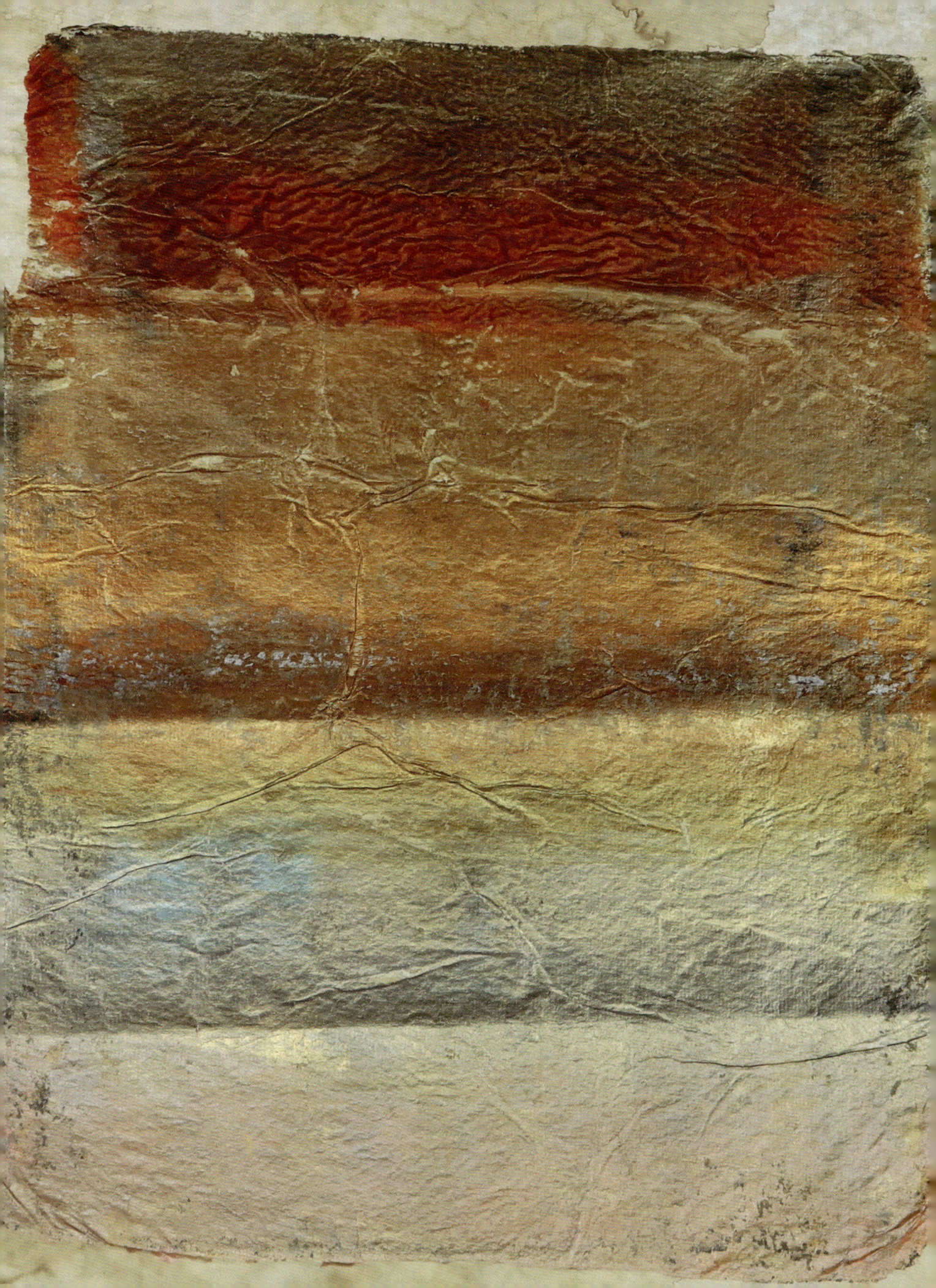

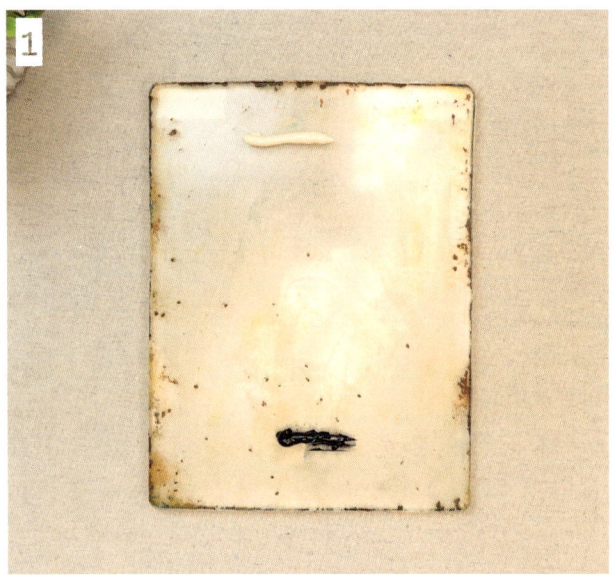

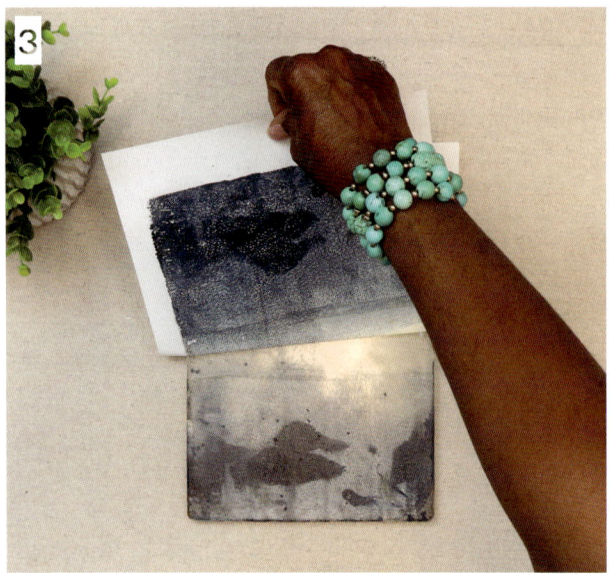

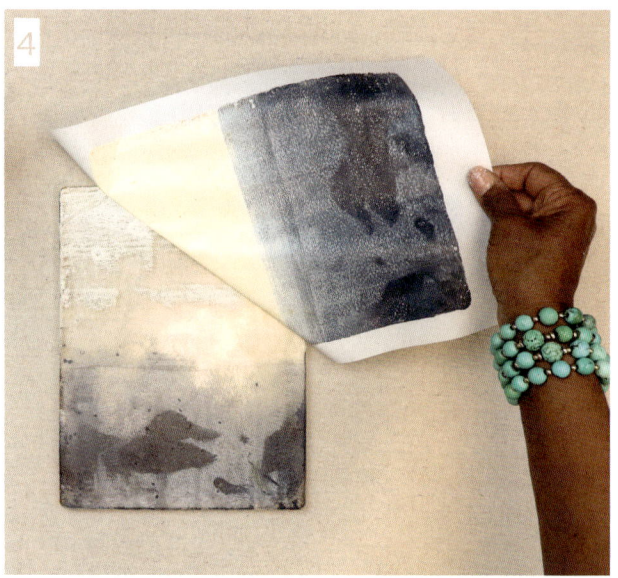

Pick your palette, consisting of six to seven colors. Make sure that titanium white is one of the colors.

I always like to start this process by doing a black-and-white print. It helps to have two brayers. Getting black on the plate is a good idea at this stage because bits and pieces of this color will remain on the plate, so in the future, especially if you are doing the "Old Wall" technique (chapter 4), you will make prints with little splashes and/or hints of black (which I personally really enjoy).

Take the white tube of paint and make a ½″ to 1″ long line on the top of your plate **1**. This once again depends on the moisture factor and humidity in the

air; you will learn how to make these adjustments with practice. Then do the same with the black paint on the bottom of the plate.

First brayer the white. Make side-to-side motions until you cover the upper half of the plate. Brayer off the white on a blank piece of paper. Next do the same with the black paint on the bottom half of the plate. When you're done, half the plate will be black and the other half will be white **2**.

Lay your paper down. Rub the back of the paper with your hands in a smooth motion. Make sure to make good contact. You will begin to feel a cool moisture (this is a good sign). Starting at the upper right- or left-hand corner, peel the paper off the plate.

When you pull the print you should have two colors that blend nicely in the middle **3**, **4**. This is the beginning of the "Mark Rothko" style of horizon line print. Bring your attention to the horizon line. This can be used as a representational painting in the future, such as a mountain, meadow, or beach scene. It can also be an abstract color that you can build on with other techniques that you'll learn in the future, such as mark making and stenciling.

Repeat this process with the same colors for one or more prints. Then move on to other color combinations from your selected palette. It is always interesting if you have a light color opposing a dark color; for example, a yellow opposing a dark pink, or light green opposing a moon-tone blue. This will create a sense of depth at the horizon line.

After you have pulled nine or ten prints, take your titanium white paint and brayer it onto the entire plate, just as if you were doing a single-color pull. Smooth the paper down with your hands. Some people enjoy using a brayer for this part, but your hands will do just fine. I prefer to use my hands because then I can feel the coolness of the paper and know when I have enough moisture on the paper, which lets me know that the print is ready to be pulled and that it's less likely to tear or stick when I do pull it.

In case the paper sticks to the plate, simply peel the bits of paper off. (These small pieces of paper can be great for collaging.) You don't have to stop to clean the plate.

We've now reached the point where you have pulled many beautiful multicolored prints. Next we will work on putting three colors down on the plate: one color on top, one color on bottom, and a small strip in the middle.

Two color acrylic paints using the brayer method on the top and paintbrush on the bottom

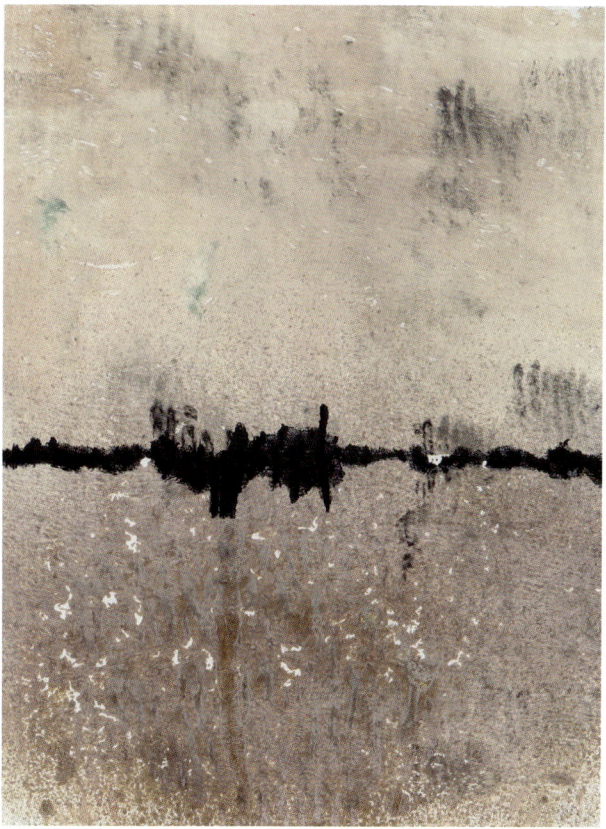

Three color acrylic paints creating a landscape with the technique

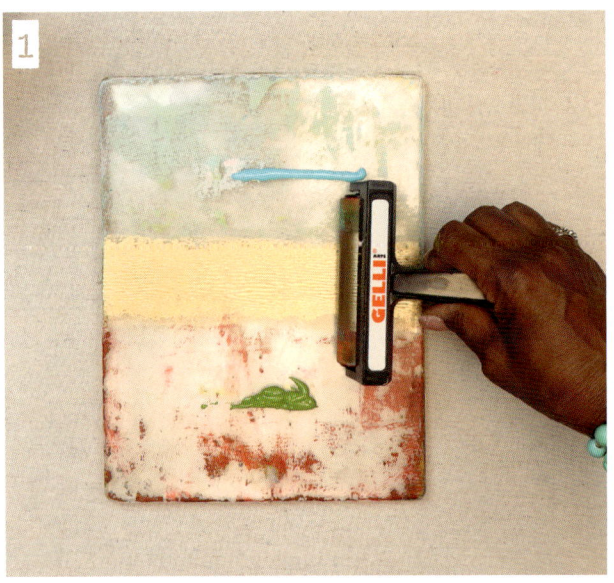

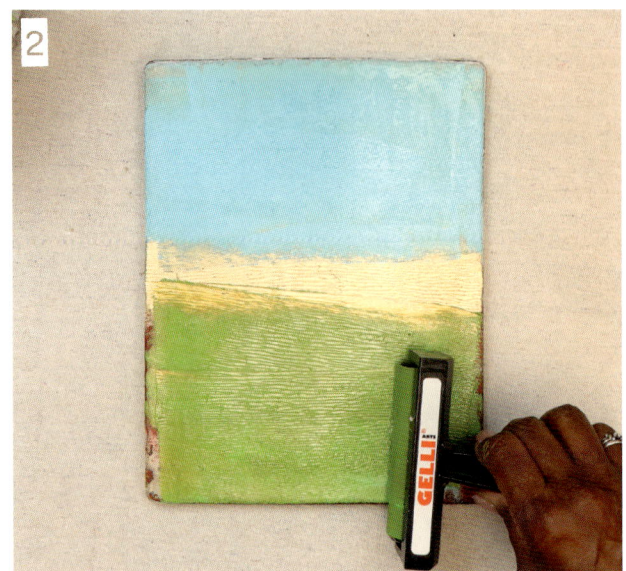

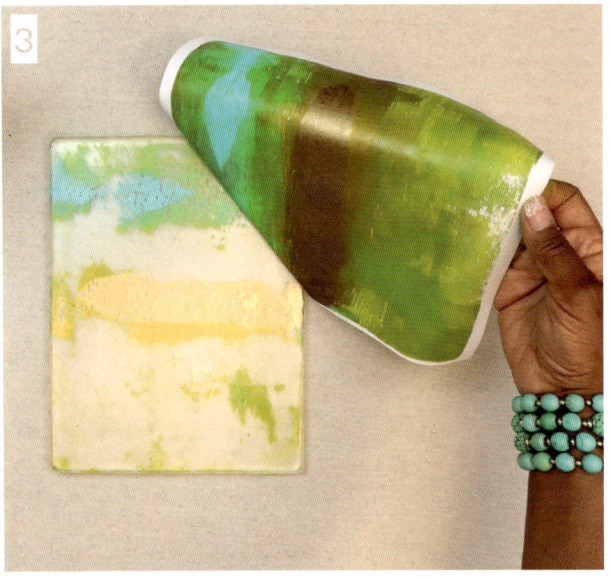

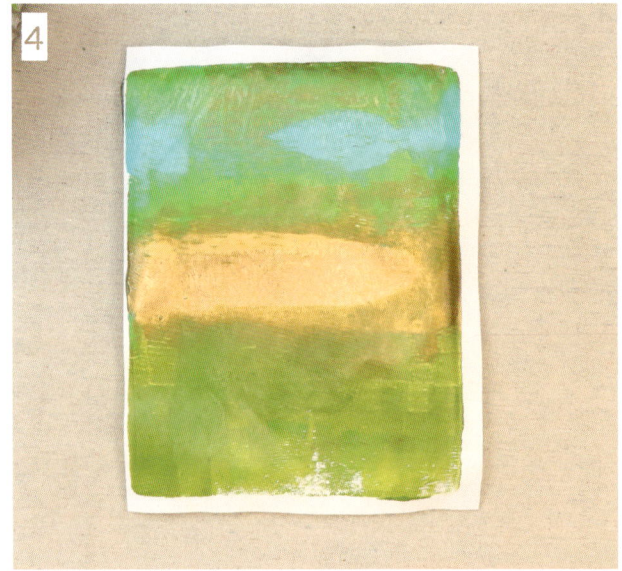

For the middle color, put down only a pea-size amount of paint, as opposed to the ½″ to 1″ long strips that you put down on the top and bottom **1**.

First brayer out the top color, then the middle (this will be a smaller strip), and then the bottom **2**. This way the colors meet and ombré in the middle. Normally metallics, golds, silvers, whites, and creams make great accent colors at the horizon line (middle color). This is another way to create variation in patterning and hence create that little touch of diversity on your plate **3**, **4**.

Congratulations! You have completed another gel-printing session. You can continue making these background color fields or move on to the next technique. We will be using these prints in the future. Of course, you can complete many steps in one printing session; however, it has been my experience that artwork will be more successful if you come back and use stencils or other techniques on a print that is already dry and set. Think of it as giving the paper time to rest.

This session can be a complete session all on its own, or, because your plate is now really activated, you can move right to chapter 4, the "Old Wall" technique. 🎨

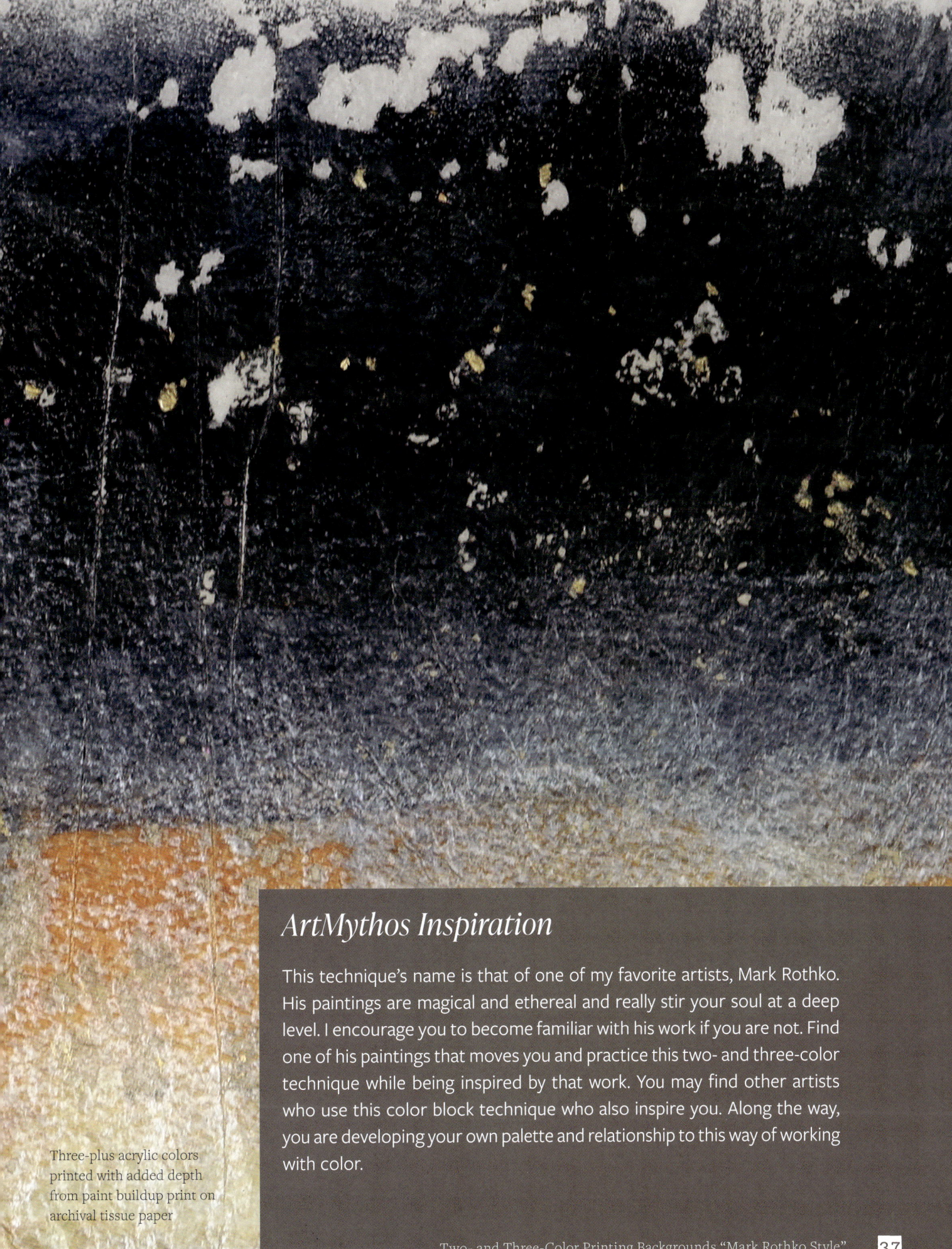

ArtMythos Inspiration

This technique's name is that of one of my favorite artists, Mark Rothko. His paintings are magical and ethereal and really stir your soul at a deep level. I encourage you to become familiar with his work if you are not. Find one of his paintings that moves you and practice this two- and three-color technique while being inspired by that work. You may find other artists who use this color block technique who also inspire you. Along the way, you are developing your own palette and relationship to this way of working with color.

Three-plus acrylic colors printed with added depth from paint buildup print on archival tissue paper

4

"Old Wall" Technique

The "Old Wall" technique is a method I developed to create prints that mimic one of my favorite things: old walls. This technique gives your prints a variety of texture and surprise bursts of color in random areas.

The steps in chapters 2 and 3 are very important for creating a successful "Old Wall" print because your plate needs to be activated and have color built up. Your plate should have a lot of color, bits, and flakes on it, which is why the technique is usually applied at the end of a gel-printing session. It's a great way to create art out of bits and pieces that normally would be cleaned off the plate before storing it away.

MATERIALS

Gel plate

Brayer

Titanium white heavy-body paint

Cream color heavy-body paint

Paper

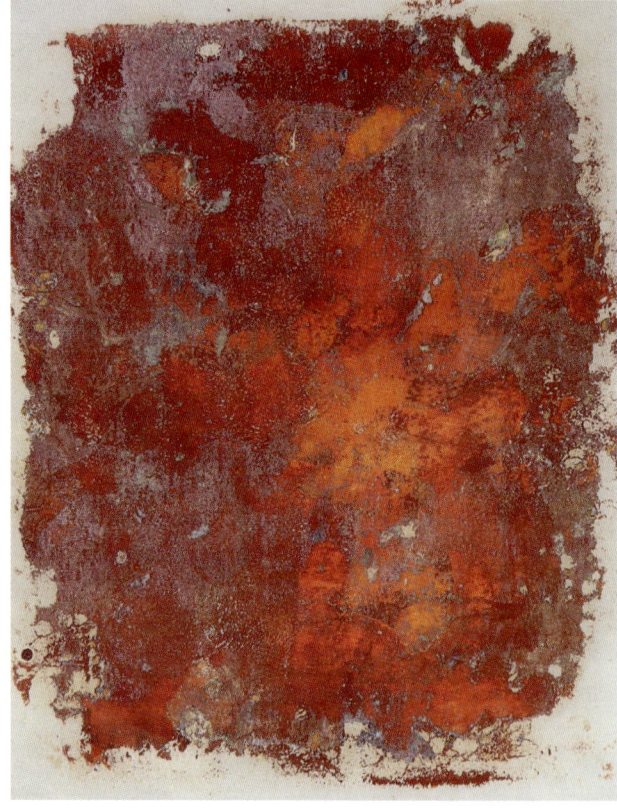

"Old Wall" print

Right: "Old Wall" print on eco-stained papers

For a video of this technique, visit robynmcclendon.com.

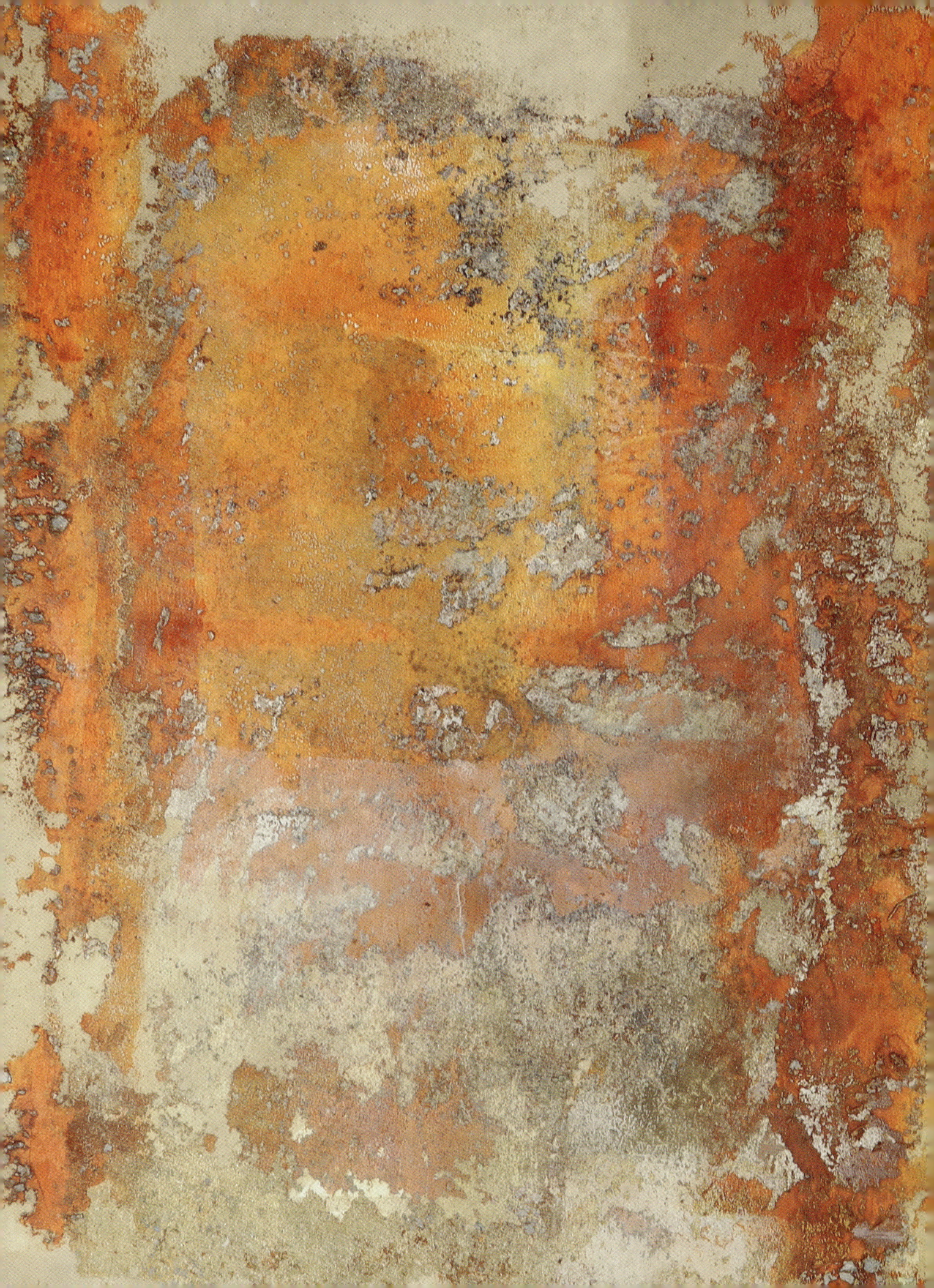

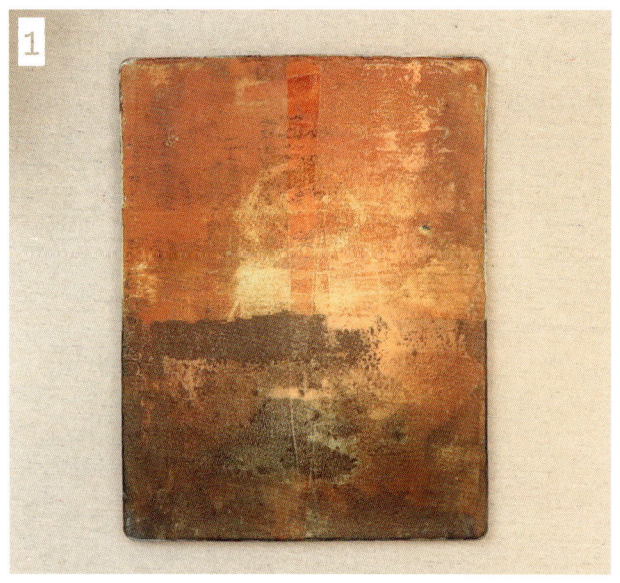

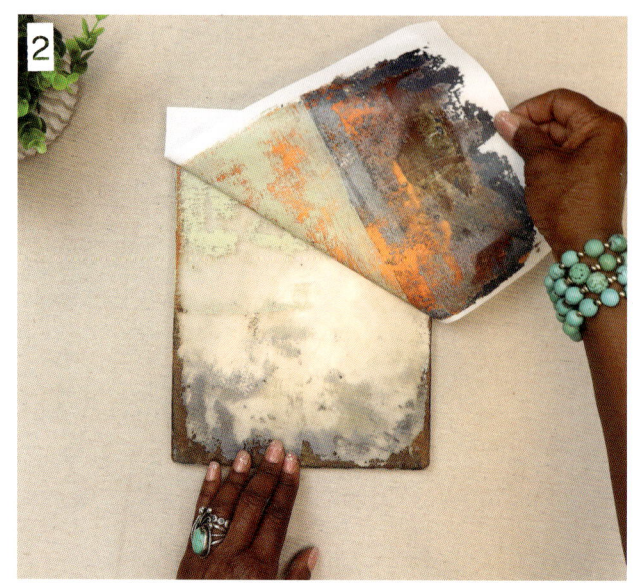

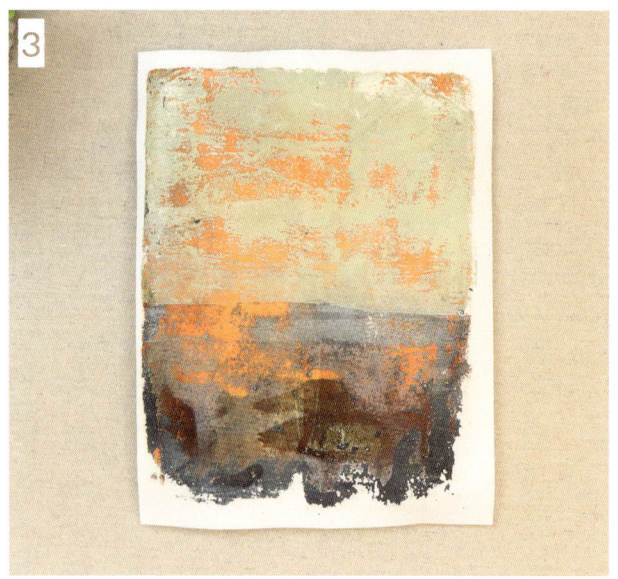

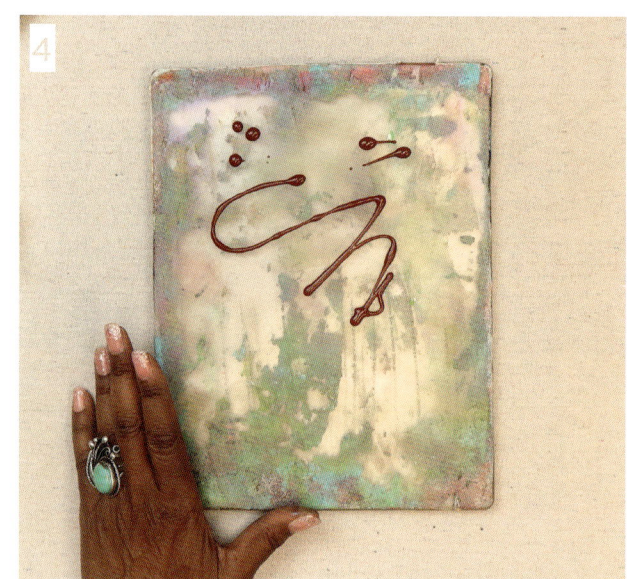

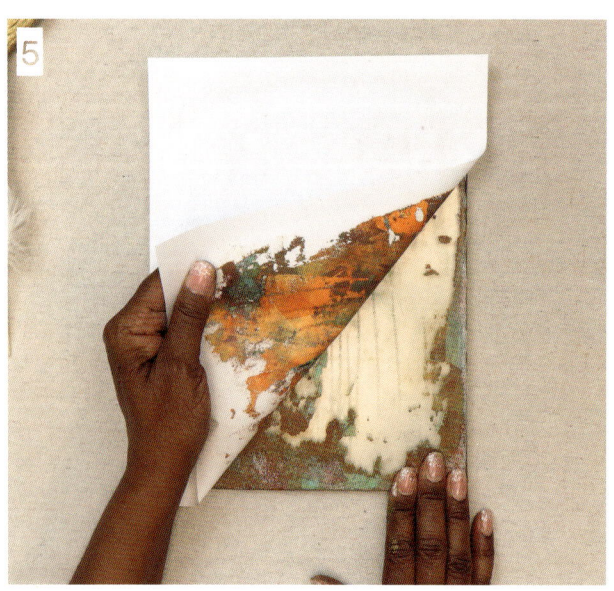

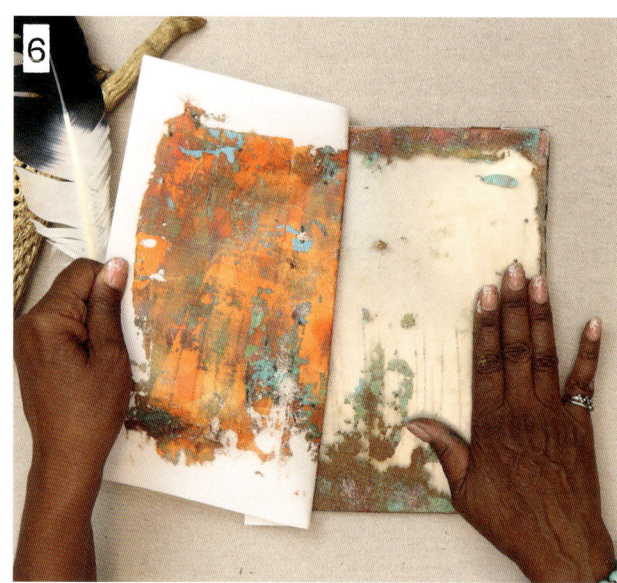

Begin by rolling out your titanium white or cream color on the plate. Pull a print **1**–**3**.

You should notice that the excess color on the plate was pulled along with the white. It looks like bits and pieces come off the plate onto your print. The solid color works like tape; it picks up and releases from the plate the buildup of flakes and residues from your past pulls.

White works really well, but you can use any color. You might find that you can do two or three pulls without adding any more color to the plate **4**. Afterward, if you cover the plate with another solid color, you will be surprised by how much information you're still pulling off the plate **5**, **6**.

Along with its use at the end of each gel-printing session, "Old Wall" technique is also done during other techniques in the chapters to come. Anytime you have a lot of residue and flakes, that's a great time to do the "Old Wall." You'll pull a lot of material that will make wonderful backgrounds for other techniques. 🔶

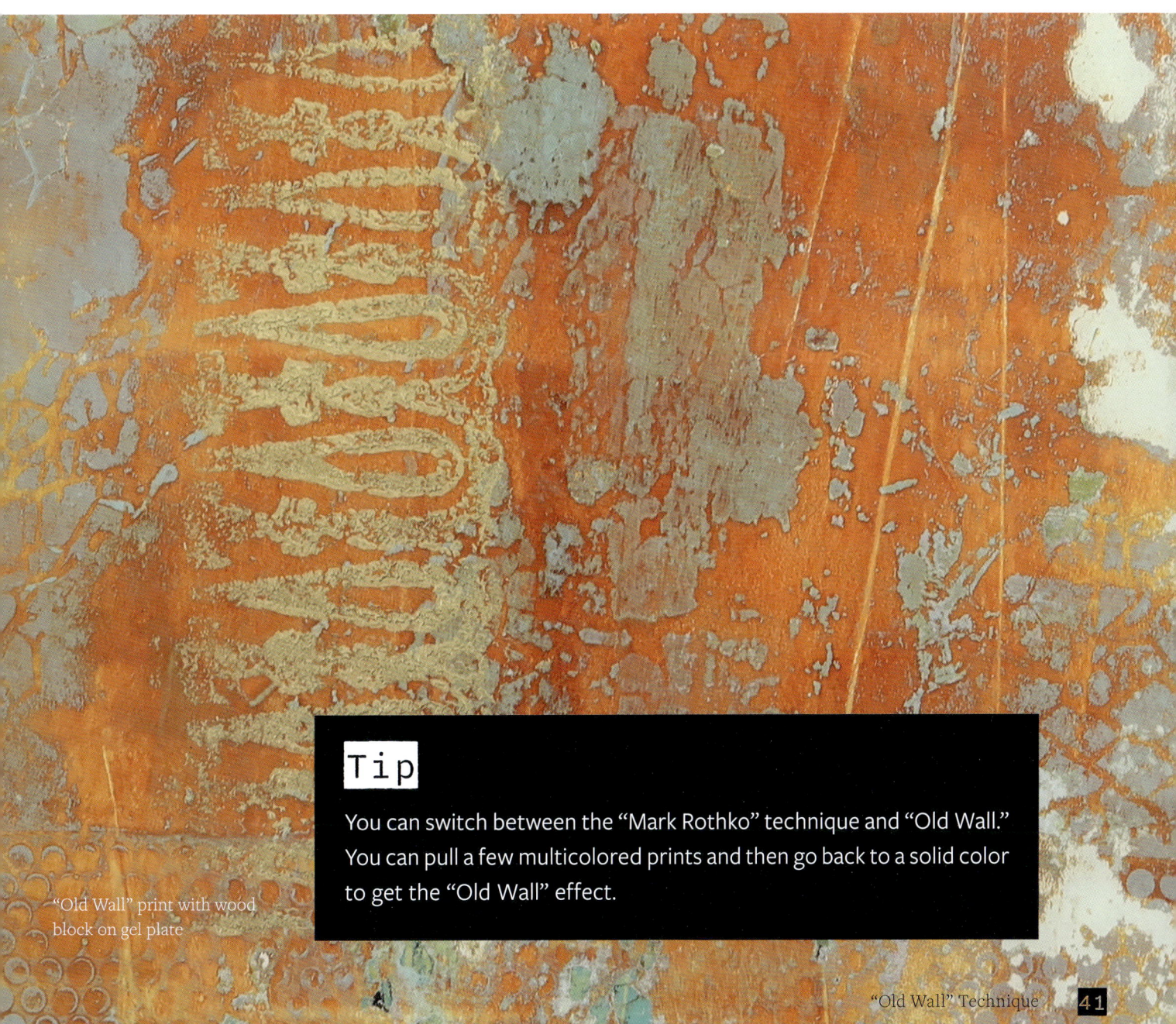

"Old Wall" print with wood block on gel plate

Tip

You can switch between the "Mark Rothko" technique and "Old Wall." You can pull a few multicolored prints and then go back to a solid color to get the "Old Wall" effect.

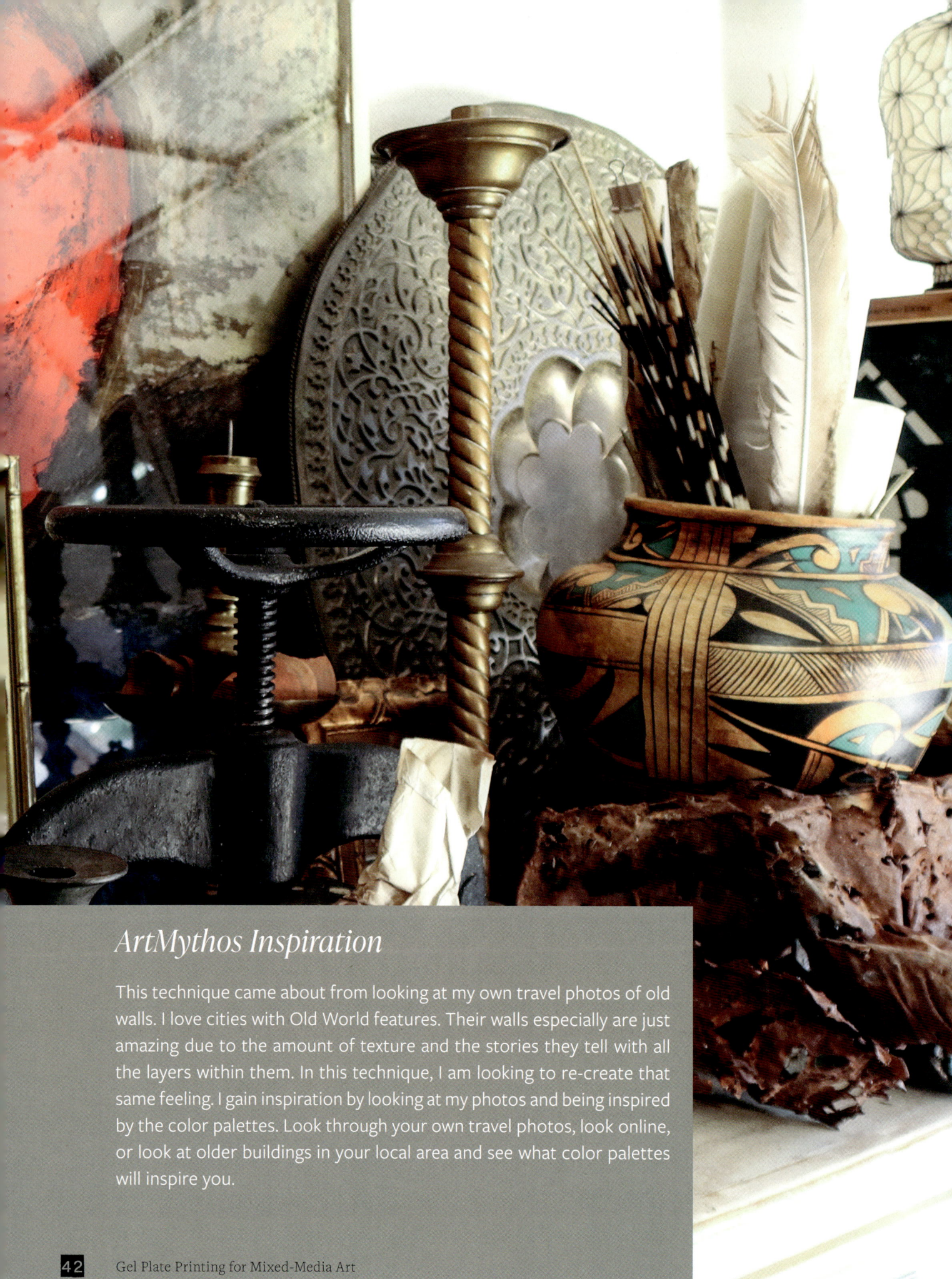

ArtMythos Inspiration

This technique came about from looking at my own travel photos of old walls. I love cities with Old World features. Their walls especially are just amazing due to the amount of texture and the stories they tell with all the layers within them. In this technique, I am looking to re-create that same feeling. I gain inspiration by looking at my photos and being inspired by the color palettes. Look through your own travel photos, look online, or look at older buildings in your local area and see what color palettes will inspire you.

Some color palettes:

Payne's grey, celadon, cream and sky blue
Quinacridone azo gold, turquoise, lime green, cream
Eggplant, pink, leaf-green taupe
Steel blue, light gray, cream, gold

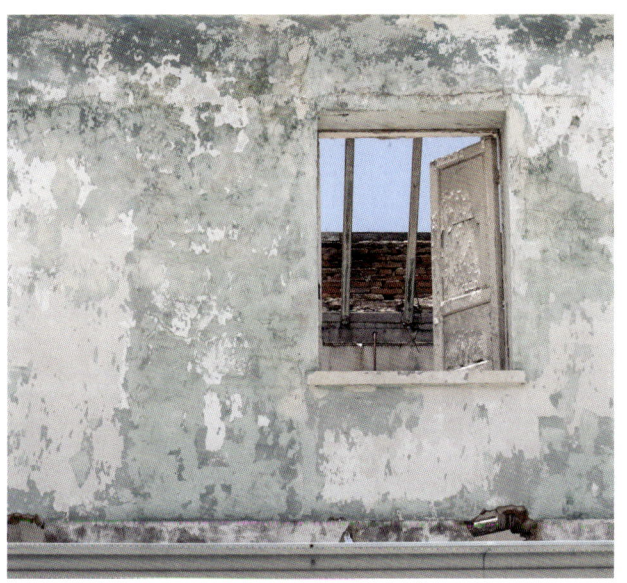

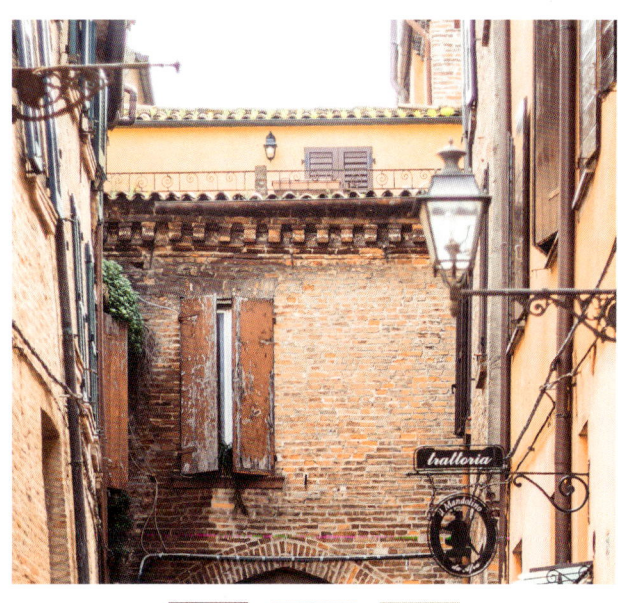

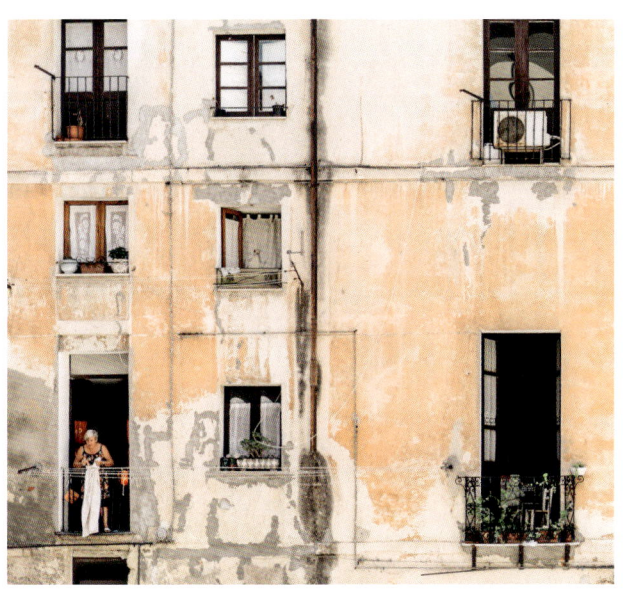

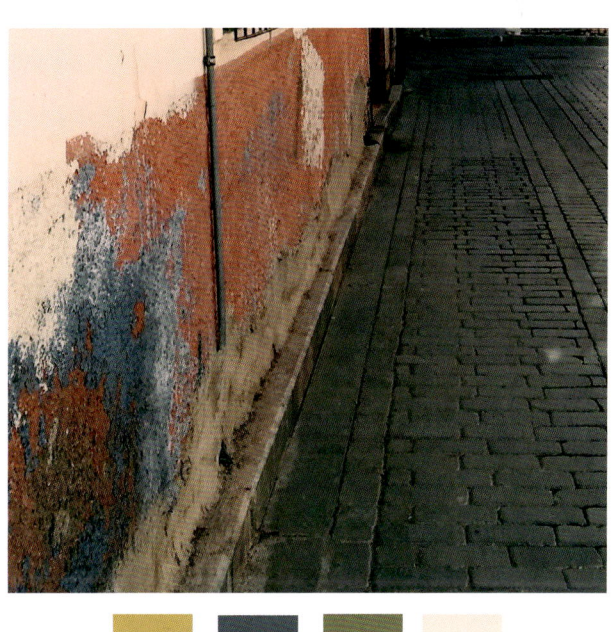

5

Simple Etching and Masking on the Gel Plate

Etching

Simple etching is a way to get organic mark making, images, and symbols directly on the plate by first covering the entire plate with a layer of paint. This is a method for applying pattern and texture.

MATERIALS

- Gel plate
- Brayer
- Acrylic paint in 1, 2, or 3 colors
- Titanium white paint
- Blunt tools, cardboard, packaging, etc. for etching
- Plastic circle shapes for masking
- Paper, your choice (can be previous gel prints)

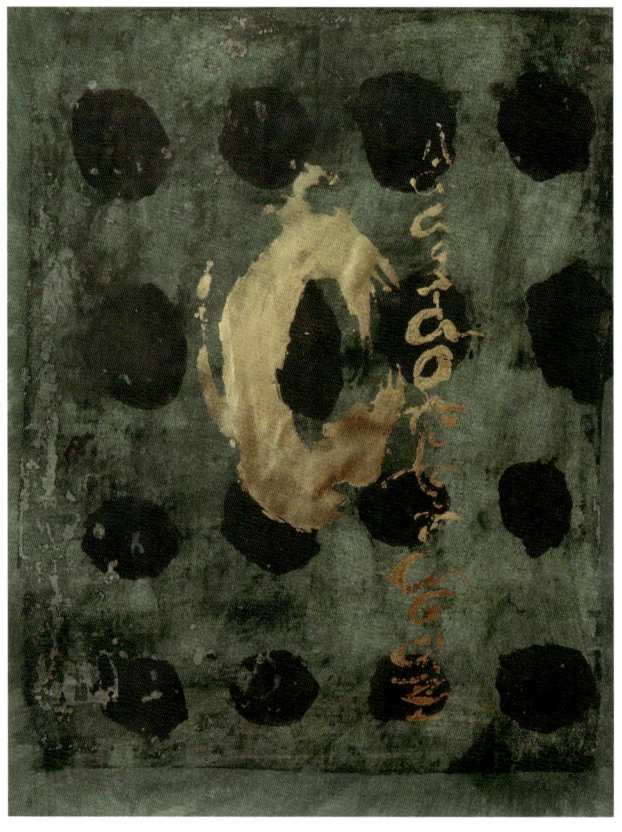

Black circles from handmade stencils on multicolor layered backgrounds with a stencil circle on top

Right: Cream circles from handmade stencils on multicolor layered backgrounds with a stencil circle on top

For a video of this technique, visit robynmcclendon.com.

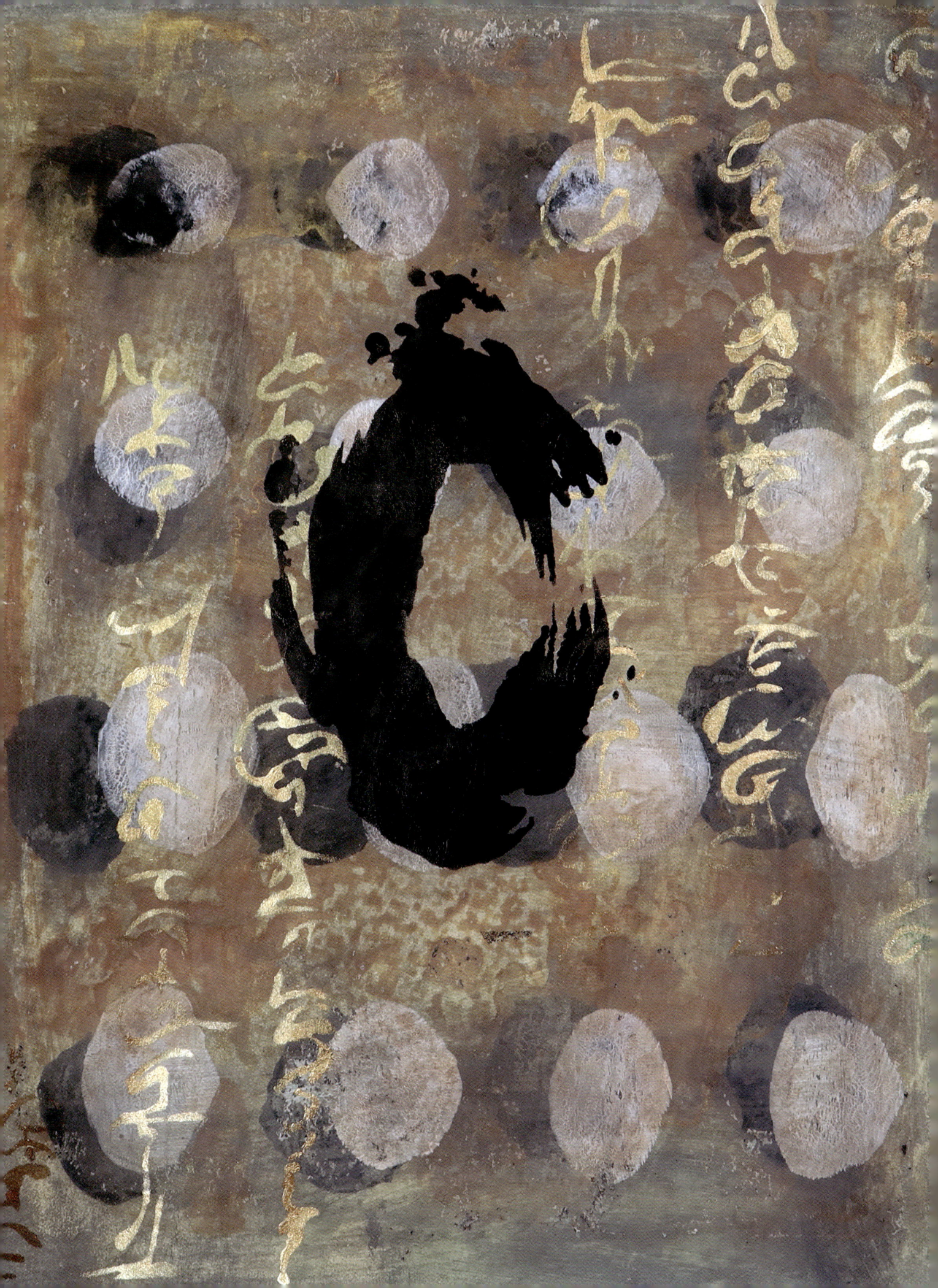

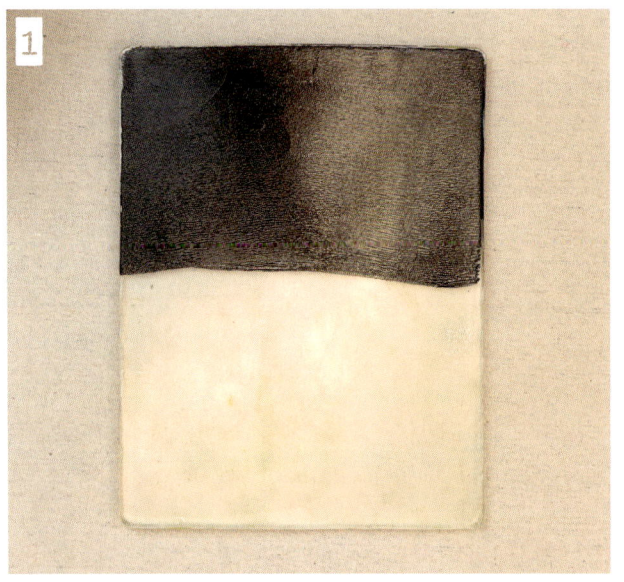

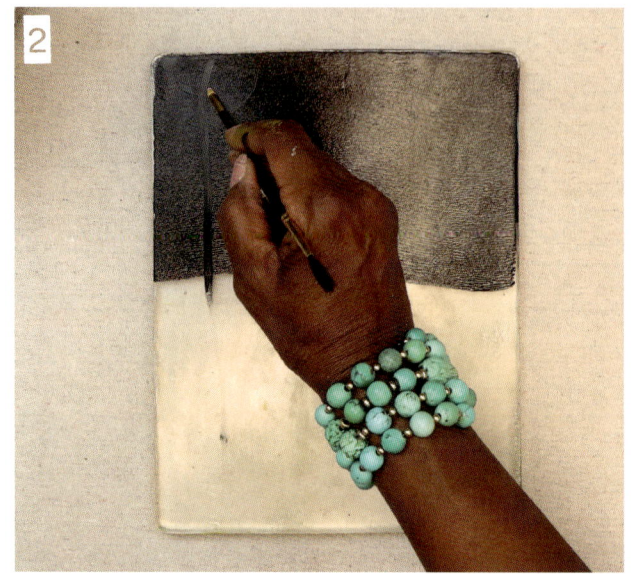

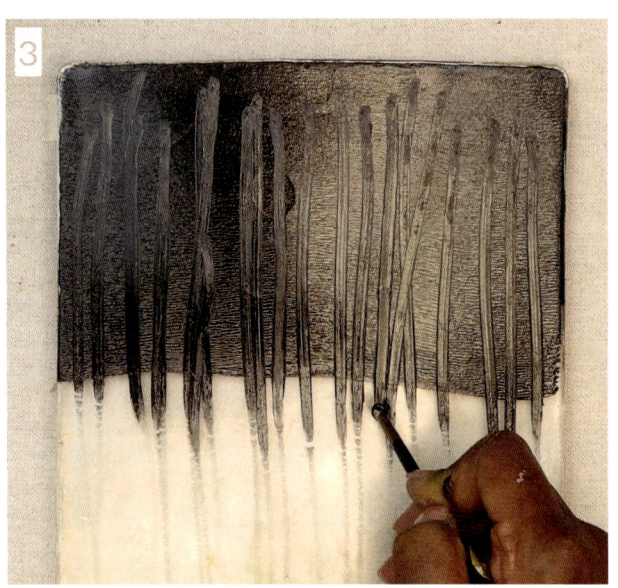

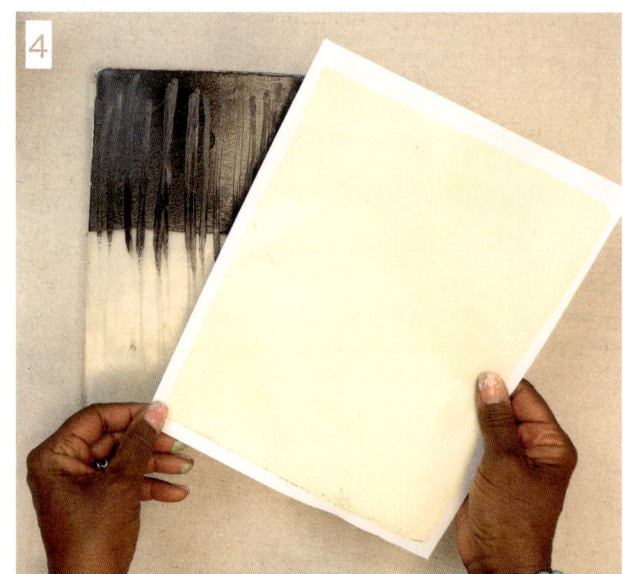

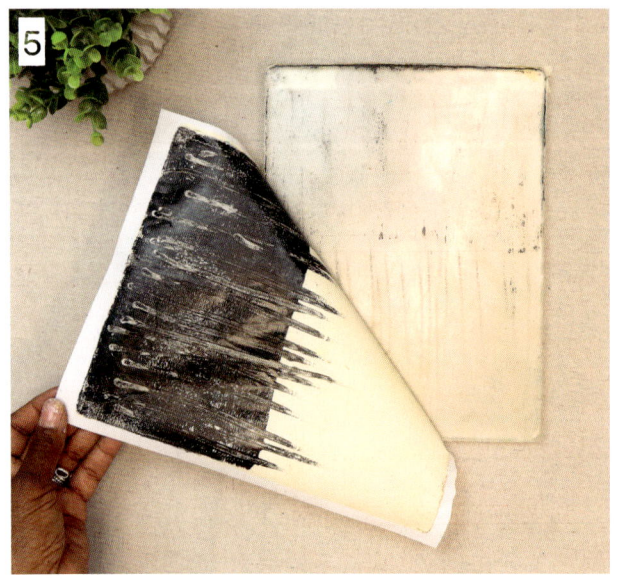

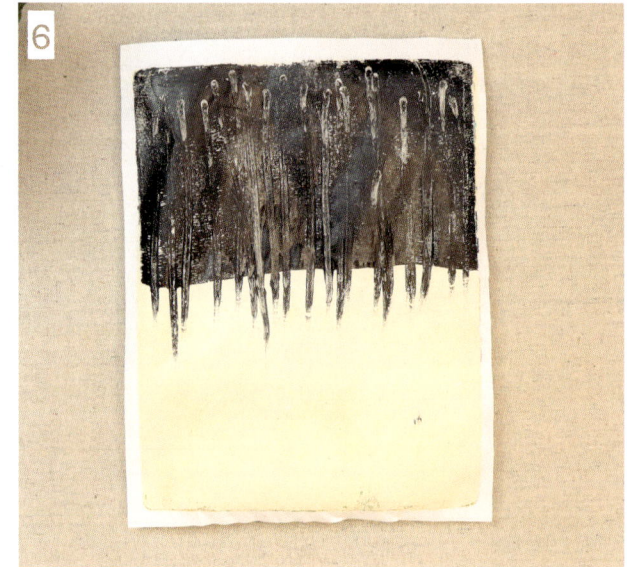

As we did with the one-color and multicolor backgrounds, brayer out one color, or two or three colors "Mark Rothko" style **1** (see chapters 2 and 3).

You're using a reduction method by removing paint. There are a variety of tools you can use to make these marks. Any blunt tool will work. You can use a plastic palette knife to make different sorts of swervy marks and shapes as you remove material. I like to use the back tip of a paintbrush to scribble, scribe, intuitive-script, and make images, floral or fauna patterns, and symbols **2**, **3**.

Other options include flexible card stock, Q-tips, and paper towel rolls. Bottle tops are great for creating circular patterns. Bubble wrap, the bottoms of plastic egg cartons, and corrugated sections of cardboard are some other options. The goal is to manipulate the surface in order to create patterns.

Once you are satisfied with what is left on the plate, lay your paper of choice down on the plate. You can use vintage paper, copier paper, book paper, and other prints that you have gel-printed on **4**. For example, you can roll out and etch into a black paint on the plate and then choose a cream-colored print to lay on top of the plate. After you pull the print, your marks will be cream colored **5**, **6**.

There are many ways you can experiment with this method. For example, you can roll out just a section of the plate so that when you place your paper, you're applying etching on only a part of its surface.

Try using paper that already has writing or images on it, such as dictionary pages or old ledger paper. The technique works best if you already have something on the paper, because the negative space left by the etching will show against something interesting when you pull the print.

Masking

Masking allows you to manipulate positive and negative space to create patterns, shapes, texture, and imagery on the plate. For the masks, you create shapes out of plastic, cardstock, or anything that is sturdy and will hold up to the moisture on the plate. Keep in mind that anything plastic is reusable, enabling you to use your mask shapes for future prints.

Sheet protectors are great to begin with. Start out by cutting out a bunch of circles from the sheet protectors. Then roll out a thin, glaze-like layer of color (**1** on next page). Lay your circles down on top of the fresh paint **2**.

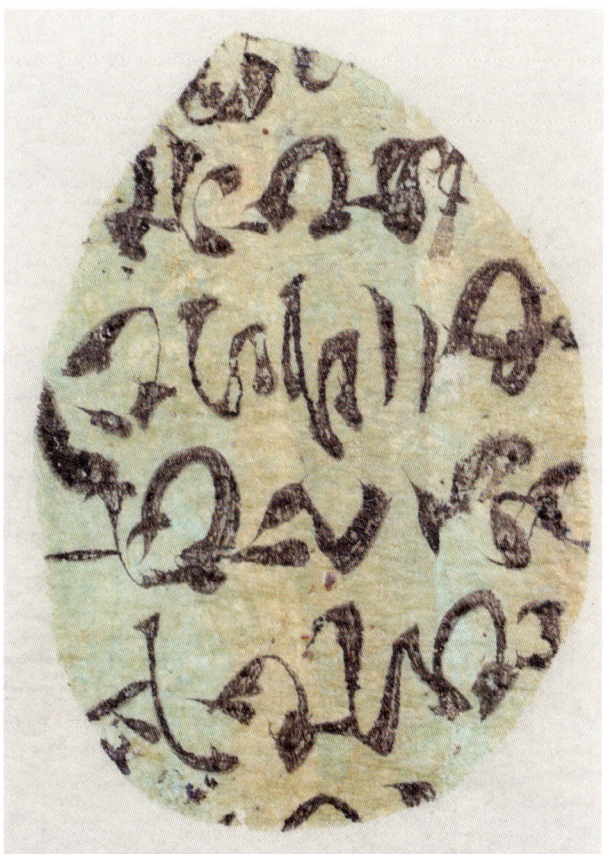

Egg-shaped mask print

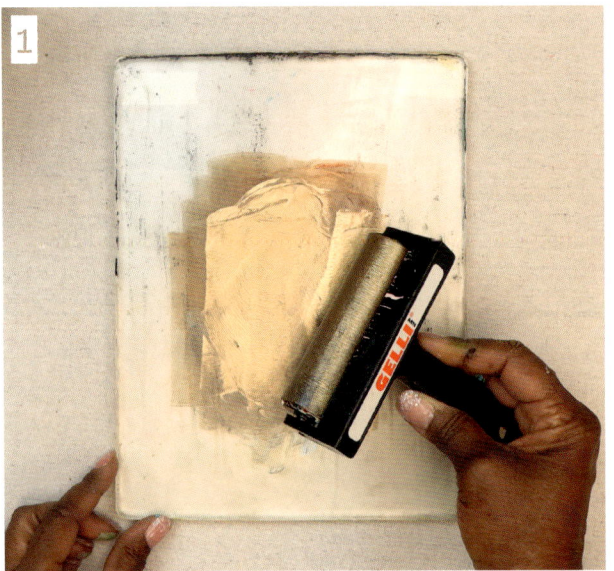

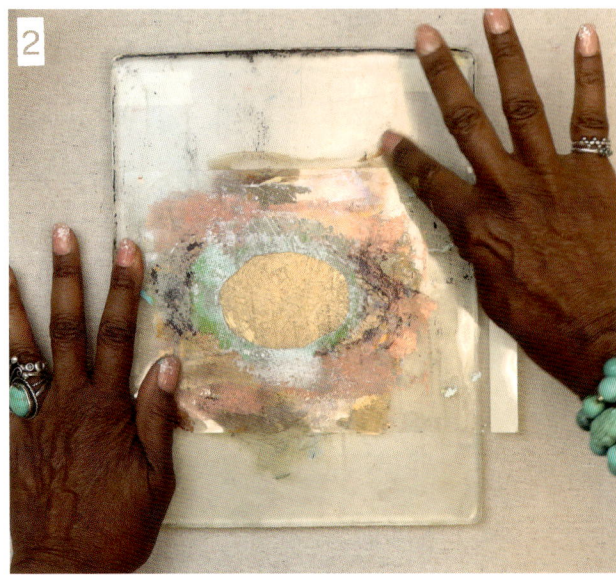

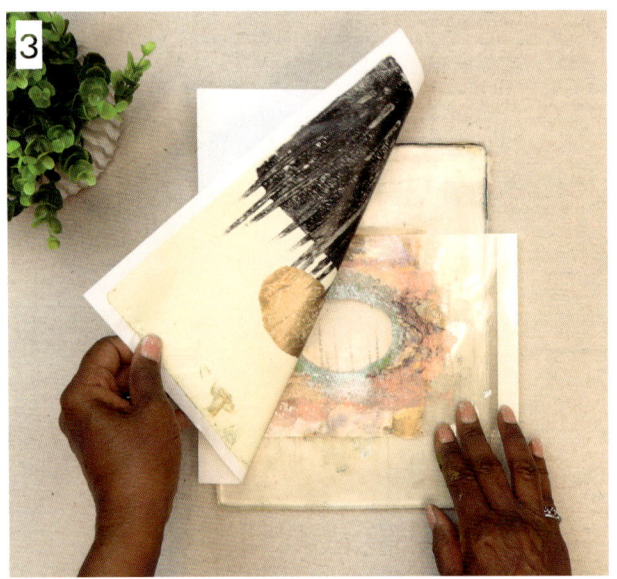

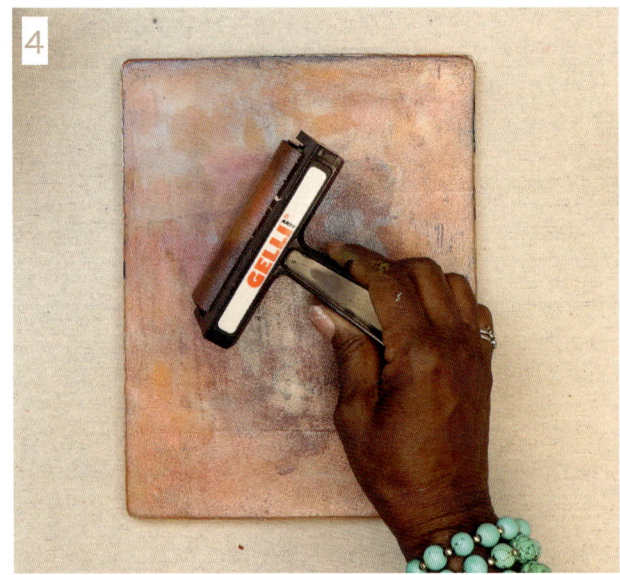

Lay down the paper and pull to apply this layer of images. Try a past print that you want to add interest and texture to. When you pull the print, you'll have a positive space, and the negative space will be underneath the circle masks **3**. This can be done over and over again.

Let's take a moment to clarify negative and positive space. Let's say we make lines on the plate by etching—removing paint. Positive space is what you're printing, the color that will appear on your print. The area that is not showing is considered the negative space. The circles used for masking are similar to the lines. They block out or "mask" certain spaces on the plate **5**–**7**.

After you do circle masks you can create ghost prints. When you remove the little circles, there's often still paint left behind. Go over the plate with titanium white and pull that **8**, **9**. Now you'll have a white background, and, whatever color those circles were, they will now come out as a positive space **10**.

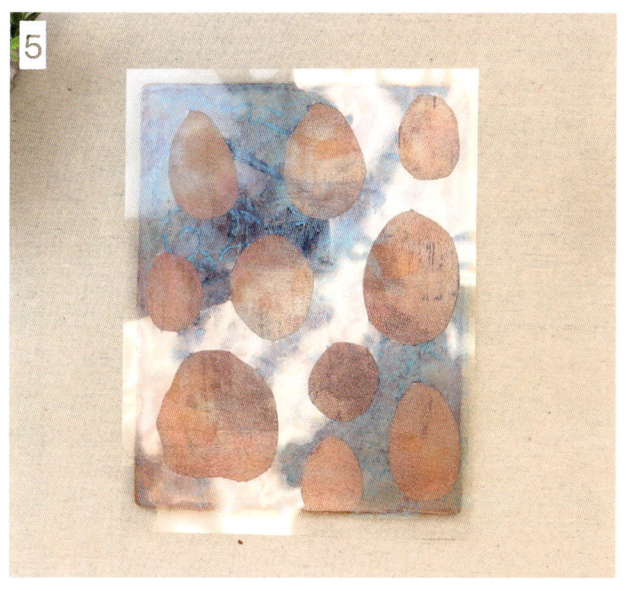

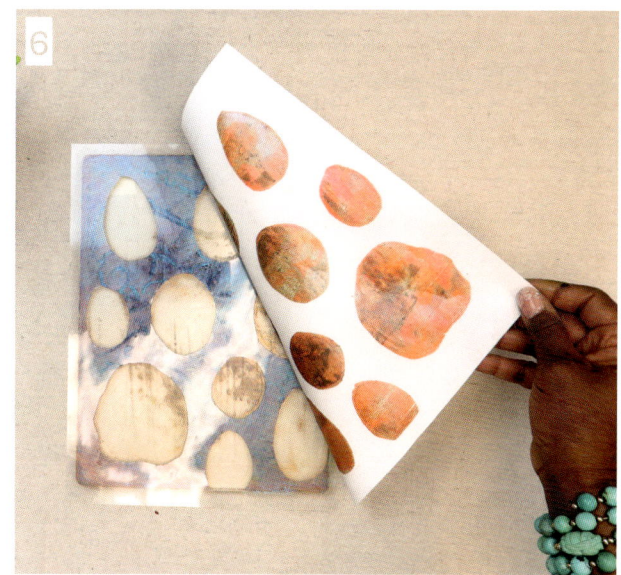

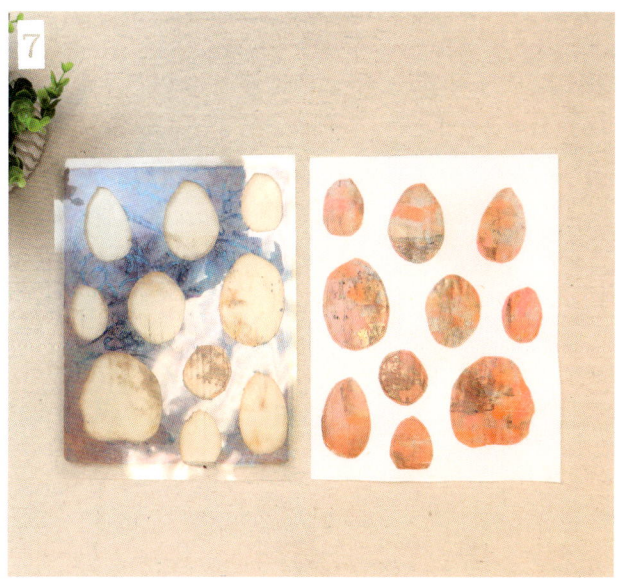

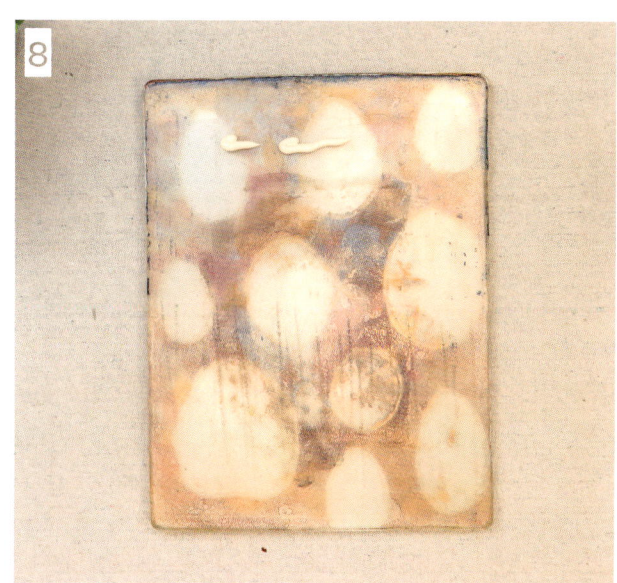

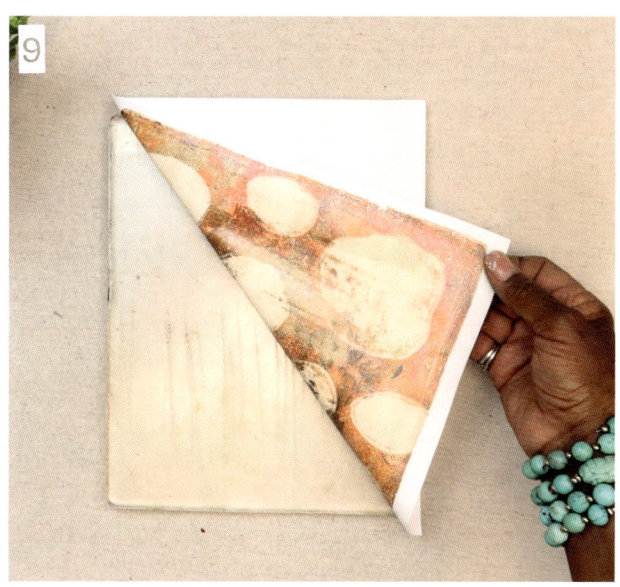

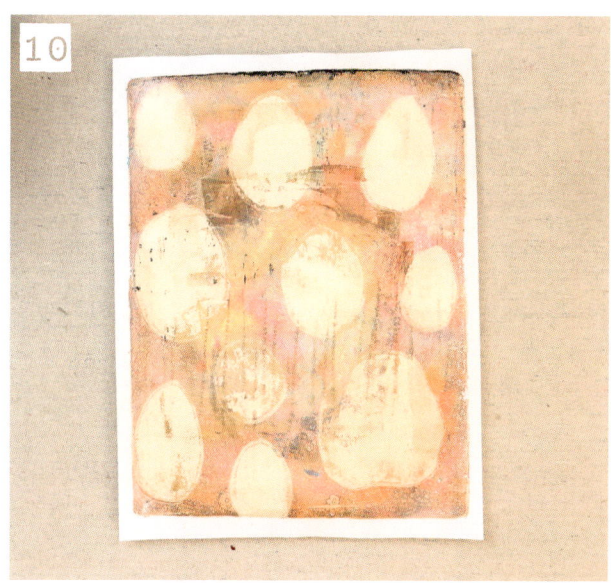

6

Patchwork Technique

Patchwork is a way to overlap thin layers of color to create a woven-like pattern. This technique is wonderful for creating interesting color and texture combinations in an overlapping style. All the papers you have created up until this point with techniques mentioned in previous chapters can be used for patchwork.

For patchwork it really helps to use sheets of paper that are larger than your gel plate. I normally use an 8½″ by 14″ sheet with my 9″ by 12″ or 8″ by 10″ or smaller gel plate. It's a perfect size to fold into a book format. You can do this technique on any size paper. Don't worry about any white space that you may have left over; this will look beautiful when you eco-dye your prints.

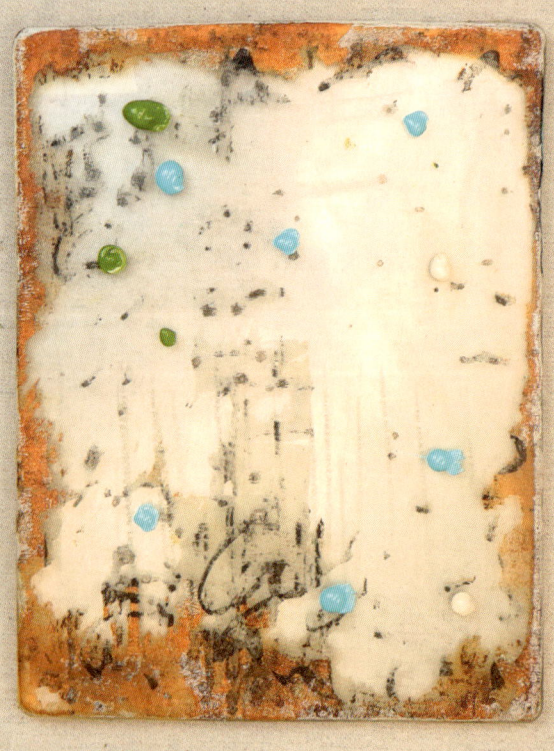

MATERIALS

Gel plate

Brayer

Acrylic paint in celadon (or any midtone color, not too light and not too dark)

Green acrylic paint (optional)

Quinacridone acrylic paint (optional)

Translucent blue acrylic paint (optional)

Stencils (optional), preferably 3 different patterns that cover the entire plate

4 sheets of paper (can be previous gel prints)

For a video of this technique, visit robynmcclendon.com.

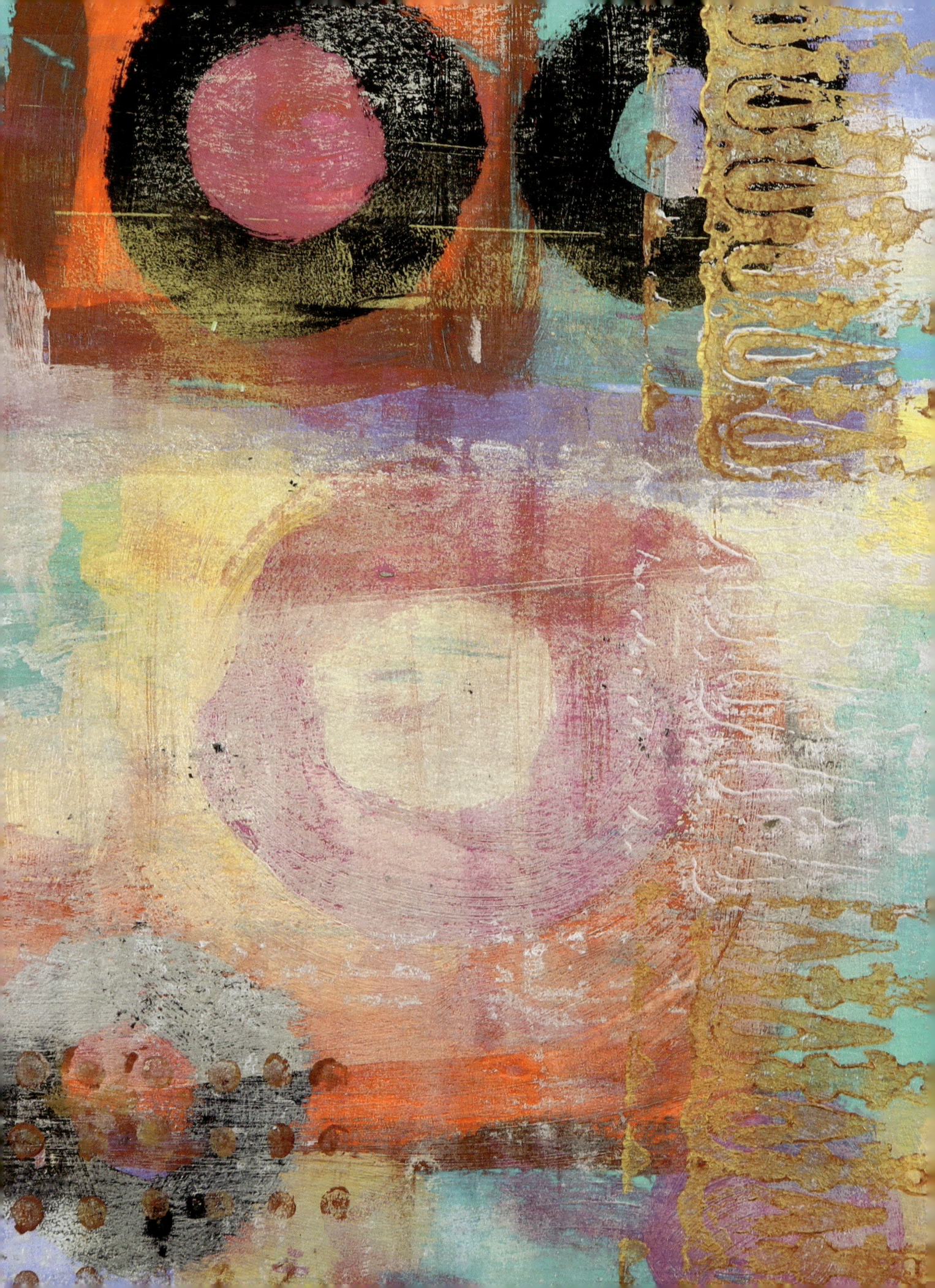

In this technique, it is great to start with four sheets of paper, but you can work with any amount that you'd like. In this example, we will be using both sides of each paper so that after you are finished, you can fold them in half and create a "mini journal." However, you can definitely work only one side of your paper.

Start out with a color that is not too light or too dark, and brayer it out on your plate. I like to begin with a color that has some depth to it, such as an acrylic celadon. It is a lighter color, but it has a matte quality to it. It creates a chalky surface that other paints work with very nicely. It is also not too dark a

color, and that allows me to keep working over the top of it 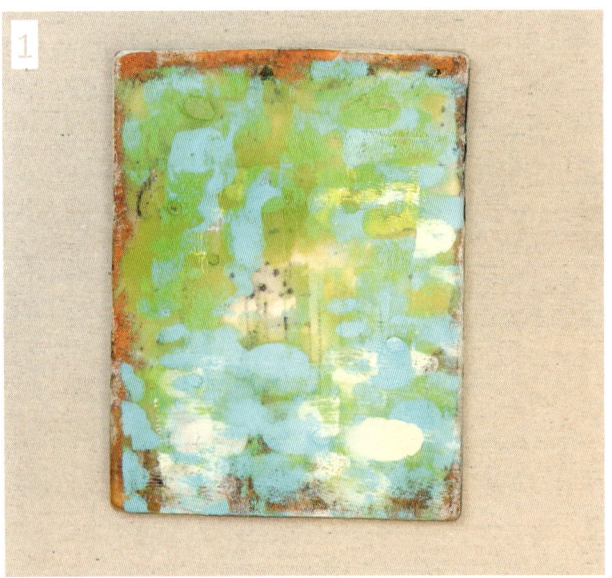, 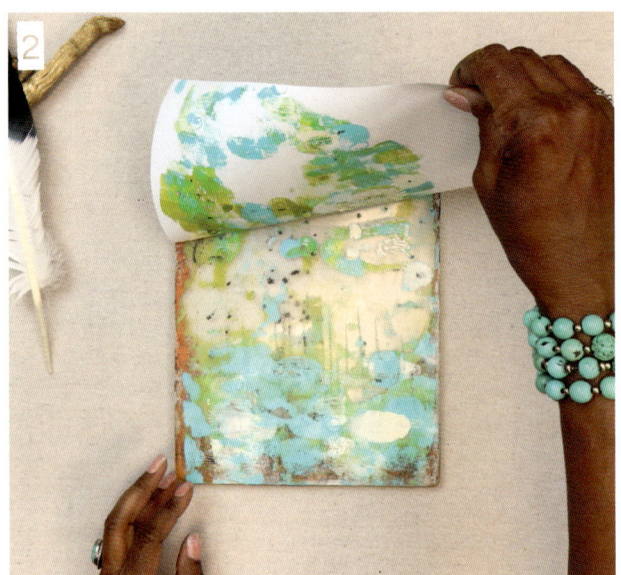.

Experimenting with matte acrylics at this stage will be helpful for bringing depth to your layered images. The mixing of various paint formulas in the printing process (e.g., matte, fluid, heavy-body acrylic, and metallic) provides a richness of buildup in textures that translates into dynamic layers on the monoprinted surface.

Next, add your midtone color 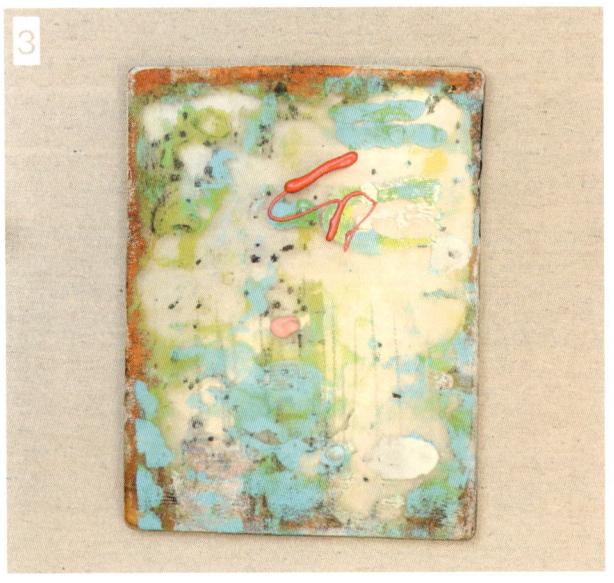. I don't use stencils in the project seen here, but if you'd like to use them, now is when to begin. Put a stencil on the plate,

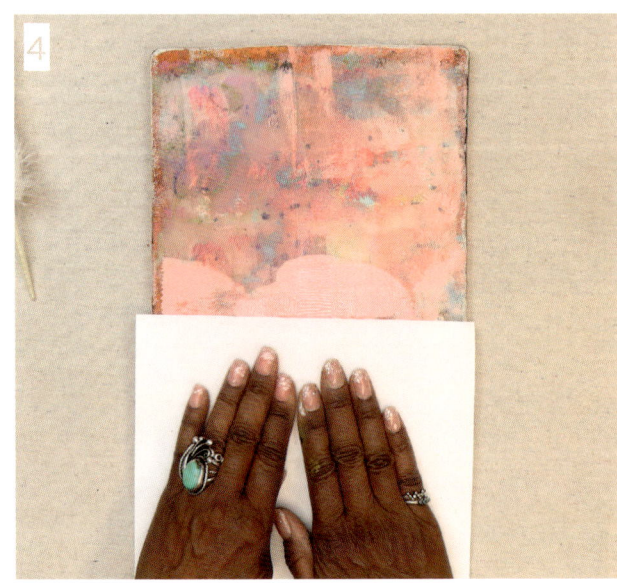

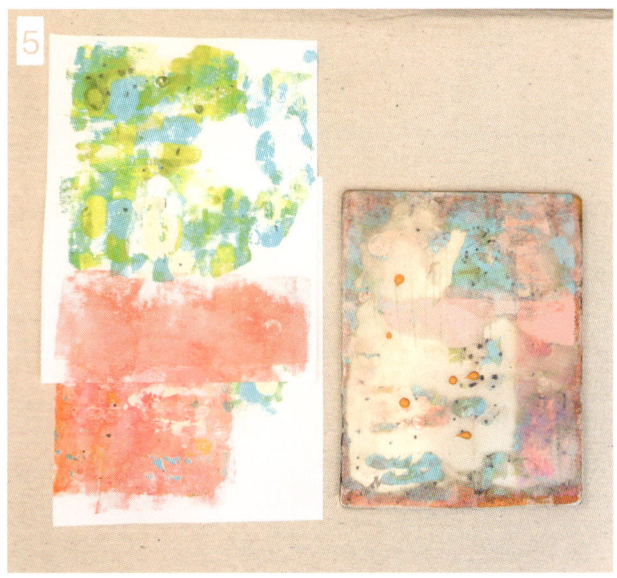

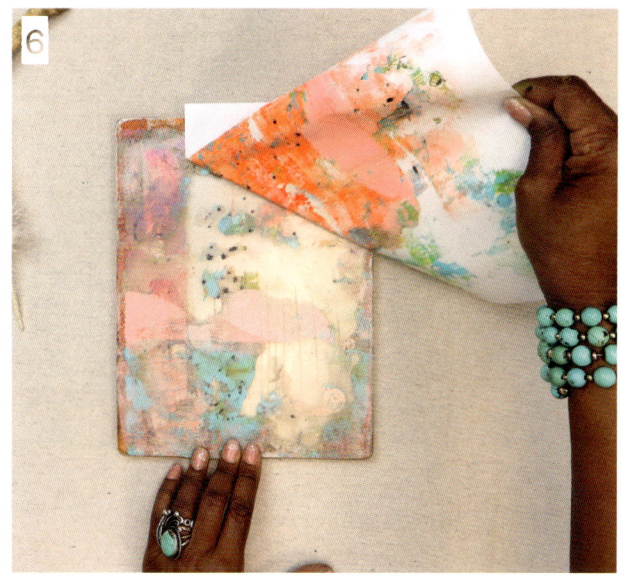

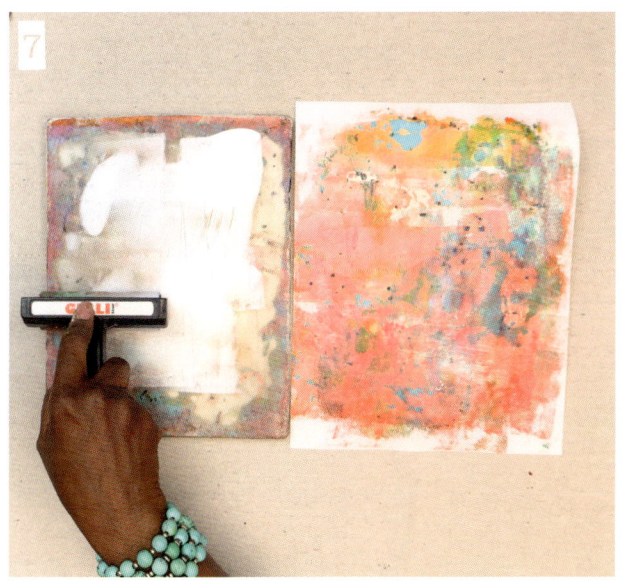

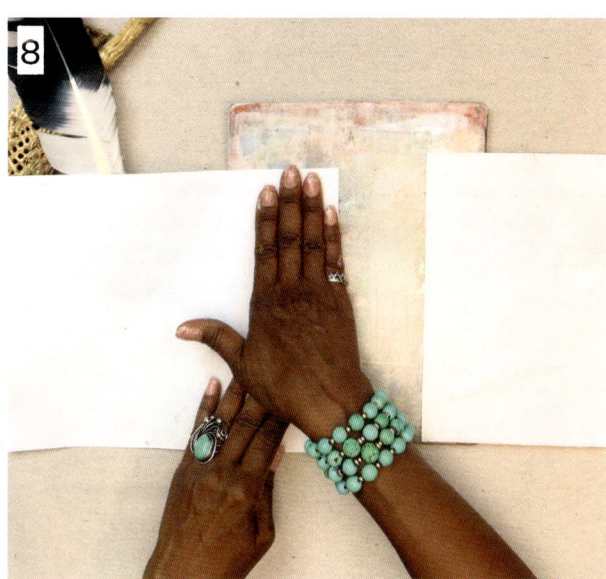

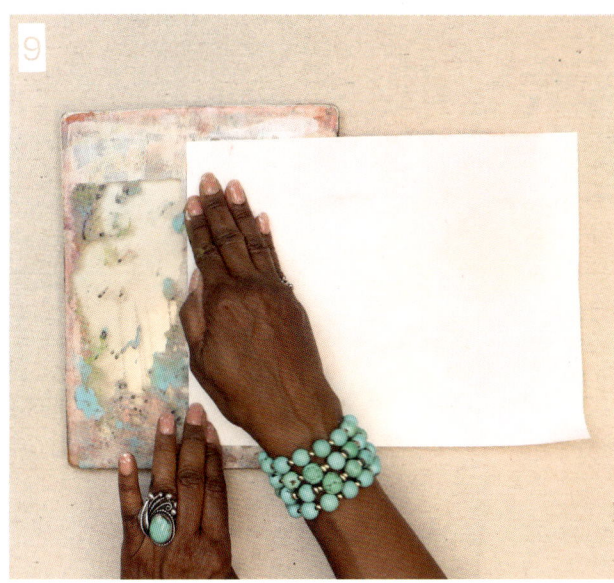

preferably one that covers the entire plate. (One of my favorites is a dollar store plastic bathmat turned stencil that I particularly enjoy for patchwork. When I'm at the dollar store, I often visit the kitchen and bath sections to find patterns I like that can be used as stencils.) Put your sheet of paper over the entire plate and smooth your hands over it. Pull the print and set it aside. Take the stencil off and get your second sheet. Put this sheet on the plate, smooth your hands over it, and pull it off the plate (this is to pull what was left on the plate from the first stencil pull).

Now it's time to put down more color; for example, a translucent green and quinacridone. I put a drop of each on the plate and then mix them right on the plate.

Take your first print from this session and put the back (unprinted) side of it down horizontally on the plate. The bottom of the plate should be exposed. Take your second print from this session and lay any section of it on the plate, so that the exposed bottom part of the plate will transfer onto your second print. Smooth your hands over both pieces of paper and pull the prints **4**–**6**. Set them aside.

Now it is time to put another color down on the plate, such as a translucent blue. Any translucent paint will work well for this step because the texture from some of the remaining colors from your previous prints will transfer. Lay your third sheet of paper down over the entire plate, smooth your hands over it, and pull the print.

On to the next step. Apply your next color of paint and brayer it out over the entire plate **7**. Take one of your three prints and lay just a portion (you decide) over the plate. For example, here we use several inches of the right edge of the print. After you pull, rotate the paper and decide on another portion of the paper to lay down. Repeat this with the other two prints. Two or three random places on each print should be sufficient **8**–**9**.

Take your fourth sheet (the one that hasn't been used yet). Lay it down on the plate in a way that leaves the bottom half of the plate exposed. Take one of your other already-printed sheets and choose a portion to lay down over this exposed bottom part of the plate. Smooth your hands over both sheets of paper and pull both prints.

Continue in this style and experiment with different colors (and stencils) as your put your papers down in random sections. Remember that your goal is to overlap squares and sections of your paper. Continue to overlap until you get a dense page that is full. There are many different ways that you can "disrupt" the surface. Using bubble wrap is a great example. You can combine masking, etching, and the "Mark Rothko" technique on the plate. The more you do on the plate, using overlapping, the more texture and interest you'll create. 🖌

Translucent paints (including fluid acrylics and metallics) allow you to cover the plate with a thin layer of paint and pull a print as you have been doing, but will also allow the plate layers beneath to be seen on the pulled print.

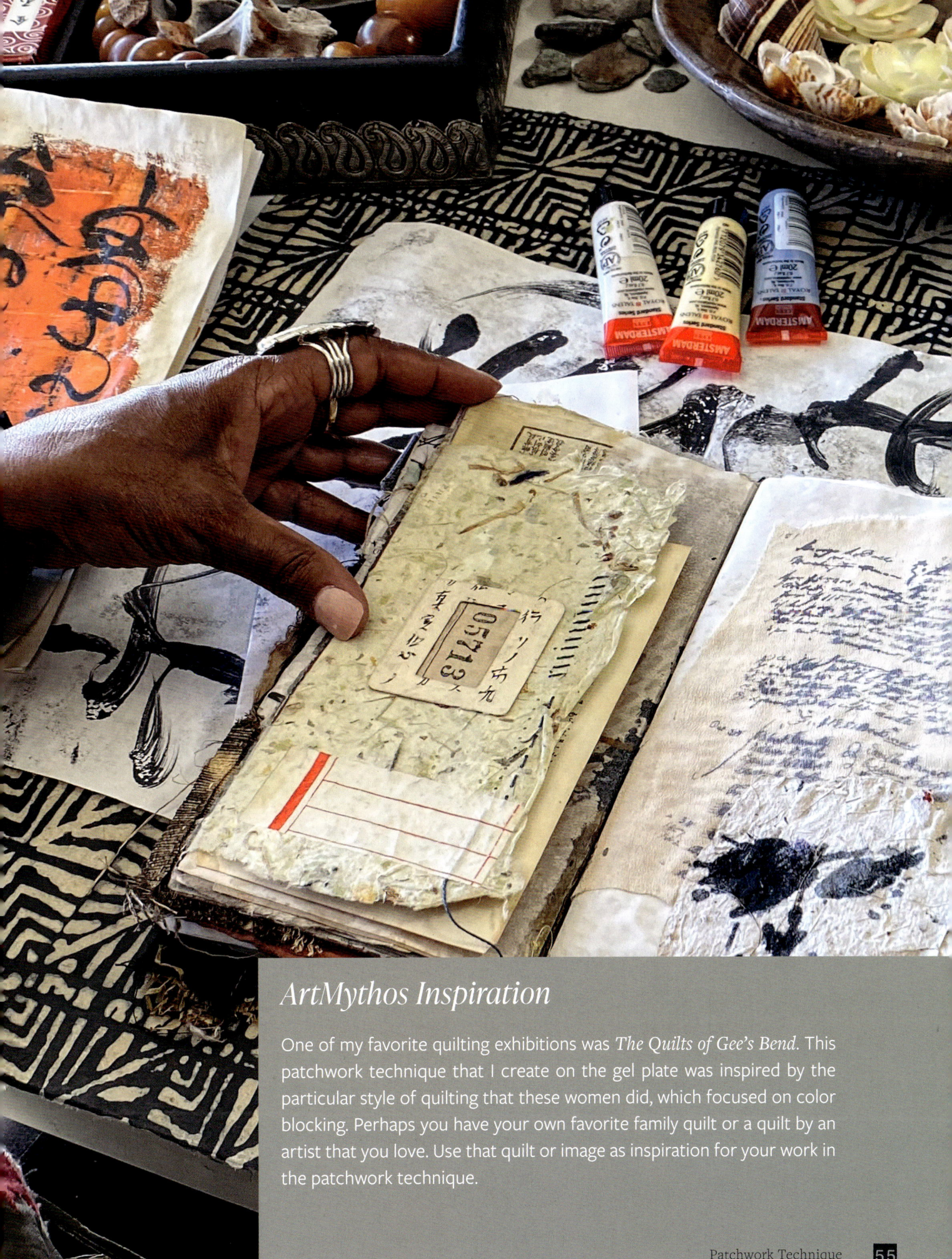

ArtMythos Inspiration

One of my favorite quilting exhibitions was *The Quilts of Gee's Bend*. This patchwork technique that I create on the gel plate was inspired by the particular style of quilting that these women did, which focused on color blocking. Perhaps you have your own favorite family quilt or a quilt by an artist that you love. Use that quilt or image as inspiration for your work in the patchwork technique.

Intuitive Collage

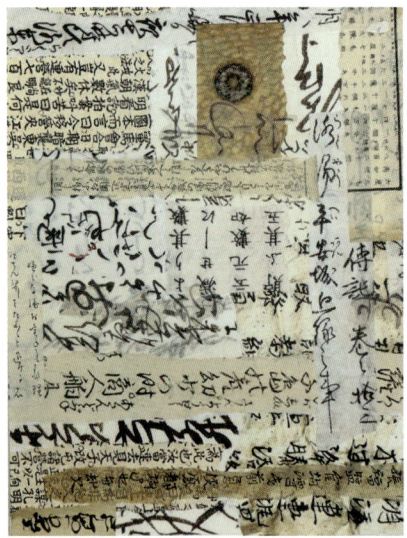
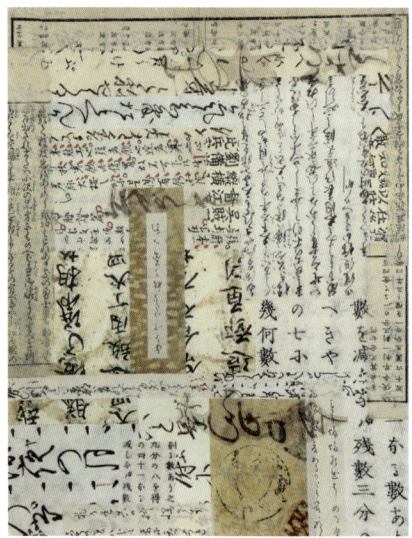
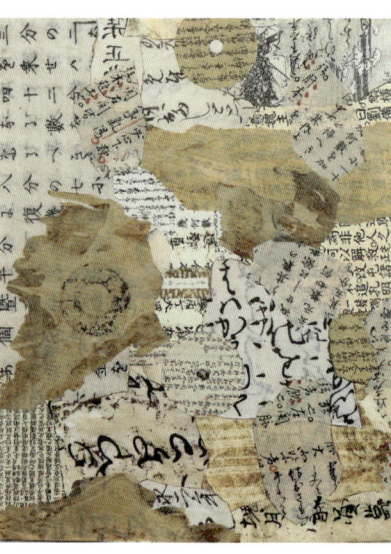

Intuitive collage using the block method

Intuitive collage using the linear-strips method

Intuitive collage using the amorphous-shapes method

The intuitive-collage technique allows me not to spend a lot of time thinking about the elements I will be using. This is a great way to use the gel prints that you have created. You can tear or cut them into different shapes. The idea is not to do a lot of editing. Whatever you pick up, you glue down and trust the process; you trust that the creative mind knows what it's doing. You will be surprised at how many beautiful collages you'll create.

This is also a great time to use fragments (see chapter 15).

To get a variety of shapes, it is great to start out getting familiar and building a relationship with specific shapes. Take your prints and punch or cut out circles. Then collage only with circles. What this does is force you to really see the shapes and how they come together, and the different techniques to apply to work with a specific shape. Next try cutting only triangles, squares, rectangles, etc. and collage only with that shape.

Once you have collaged several pages of just one shape, create a page using a variety of these shapes.

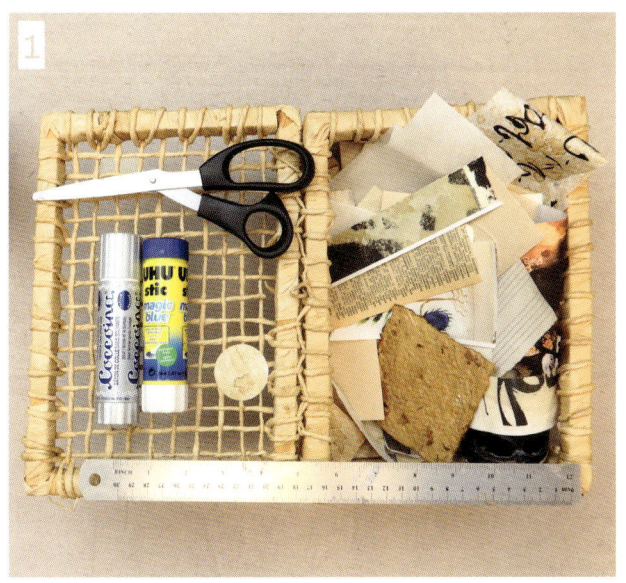

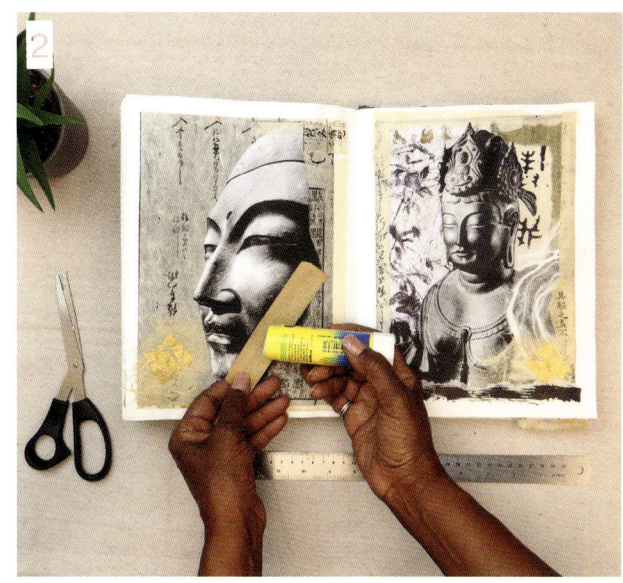

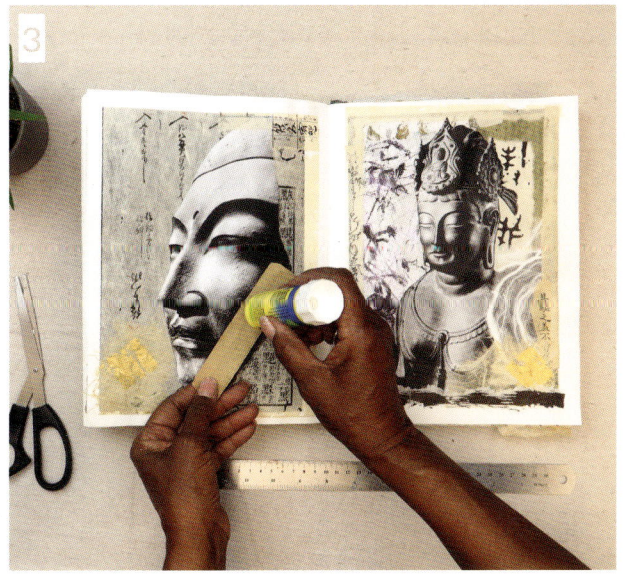

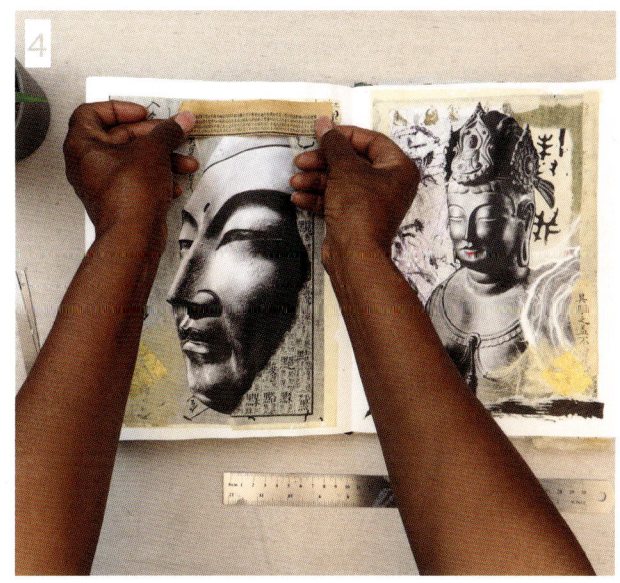

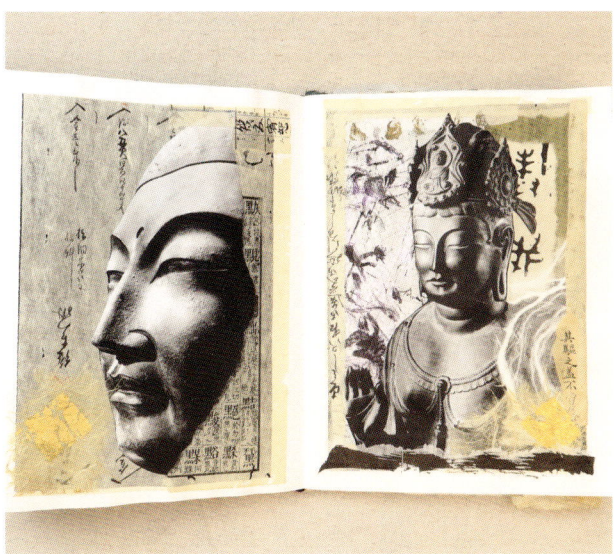

You can apply this technique to create a master board, which you can use to apply repeat images for coordinated items such as cards or journal pages. Make a full collage on an 11″ by 14″ sheet of paper, Take a picture of the master board and print out multiple copies. Use these to apply the image on your related projects.

Ink Blot Printing

7

Ink blot printing is one of the easiest and most dramatic ways to use the gel plate. Ink blot monoprints are strong images and can be used as main elements in journal spreads, collage, and other artwork.

I like to approach ink blots from the standpoint of Rorschach. As a kid, I was always fascinated by ink blots. They seemed to be a popular topic in cartoons and old movies. I was fascinated with the idea that various test subjects could look at the same ink blot and see different images in it. As a kid, I could spend hours just making ink blots. I've carried out that same basic practice in my artwork over the years, since I like the contrast of black and white and use a lot of ink in my work. Naturally, when I came across the gel plate, I had to continue this exploration of ink blots.

MATERIALS

Gel plate

Sumi ink (or other acrylic or india inks)

Inexpensive sumi brushes in varying sizes, large to small, for moving ink around

Papers of your choice, such as printer paper, mulberry paper, sumi calligraphy paper, scrap or vintage papers, and tea-stained papers

For a video of this technique, visit robynmcclendon.com.

Right: Collage on large eco-stained papers with ink blot, white paint swirls with brush on gel plate, fragment at top (black brushstroke line on archival tissue paper), a strip of kraft colored archival tissue paper with gold acrylic paint stencil print as washi tape, a paper next to it using a "grunge" photo transfer of a woman's face, another fragment (one of my symbol stencils in gold), bottom glassine paper with black Post pen print on gel plate, and ivory Post pen scripted over the print, and vintage Asian papers

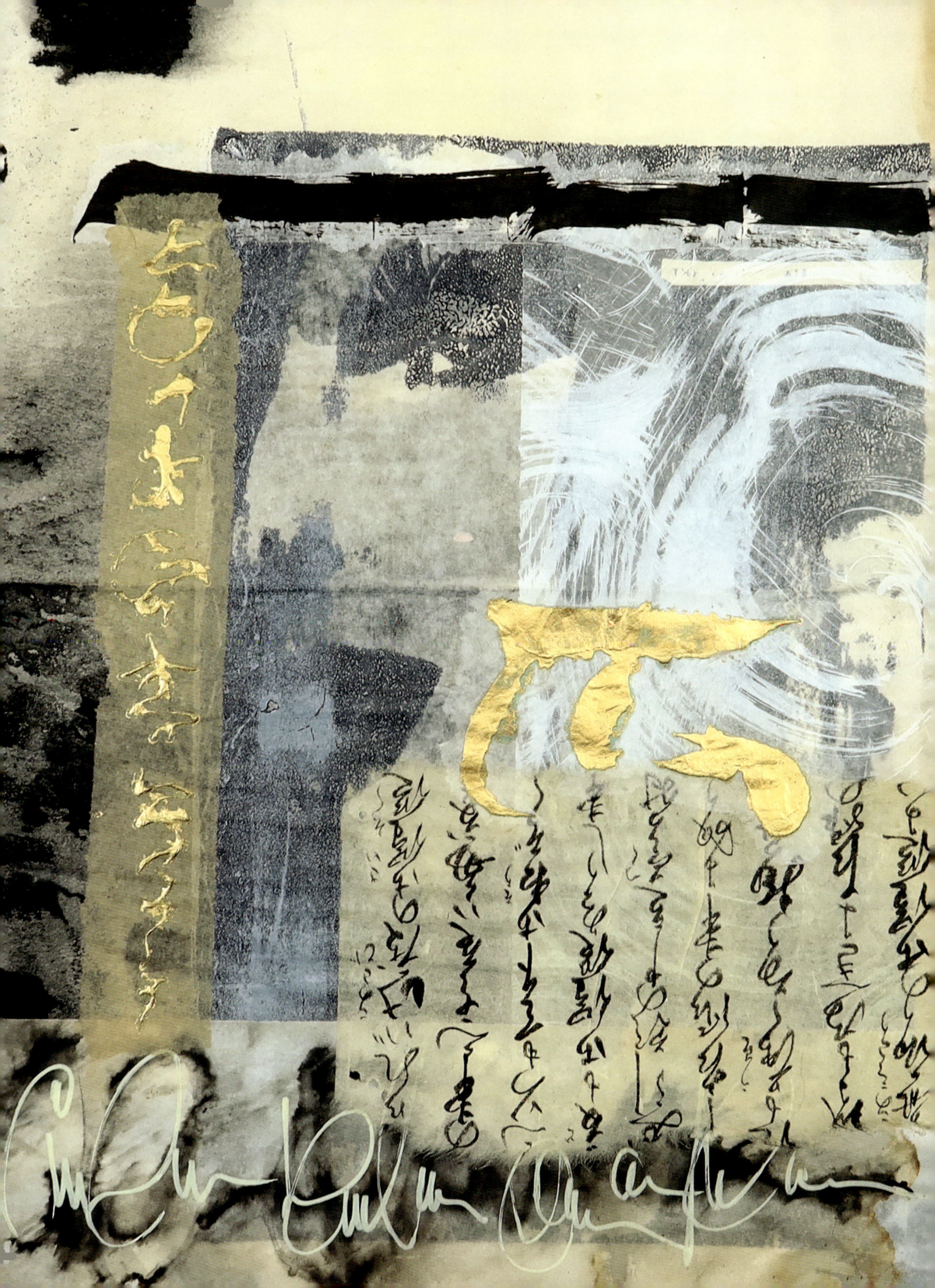

Because the sumi ink is relatively thin and less sticky than acrylic paints, lighter papers with less strength can be used, but note that after the first pull, as the paper picks up more moisture, it must be set aside to dry. This is a great time to remember all the aforementioned reasons that papers can stick to the plate.

Different papers provide different effects. Calligraphy and mulberry papers, for instance, are soft, sometimes fibrous, and absorbent and will create softer outlines and deeper pools of color. On the other hand, papers with a shiny coating will repel the ink in some areas and create interesting patterns and crisper edges.

Sumi ink is a carbon-based ink that is indelible. In its liquid form it comes in convenient bottles with a small opening, unlike many other kinds of ink that come in "inkstand"-shaped bottles with a large opening designed for easily refilling fountain pens or for use with a dip pen. Due to the small opening, you can apply the sumi ink directly from the bottle onto the plate, squeezing, dripping, or drizzling the ink in whatever pattern you like.

Directly from your sumi ink bottle or with a tool, create random drop patterns on your gel plate **1**, **4**.

To create a myriad of patterns, use mark-making tools such as feathers, grass bundles, and other various found objects dipped in ink and distributed over the plate in a random way.

The ink will spread out of its own accord to an extent but can also be pushed into patterns with a brush.

Lay your paper on the plate. The inks are very quickly absorbed so I generally will put a waste sheet on top of the printing paper to avoid bleed-through onto my hands.

When paper is applied to the plate surface, even the thinnest of lines melt into broad areas of pigment, creating an ink blot effect **2**, **5**. This freshly pulled piece of paper will be very wet and should be laid on a blotting paper **3**. There will be plenty of ink left on the plate to create a second or even a third print, but these will already come away with a slightly different look than the first wet print; this randomness and the shifting edges is part of the delight of the process.

Remove the paper from the plate and lay it to dry.

There is generally more ink on the plate, so picking that ghost print up can be rewarding.

Ink blots on archival tissue paper to use as elements in collage

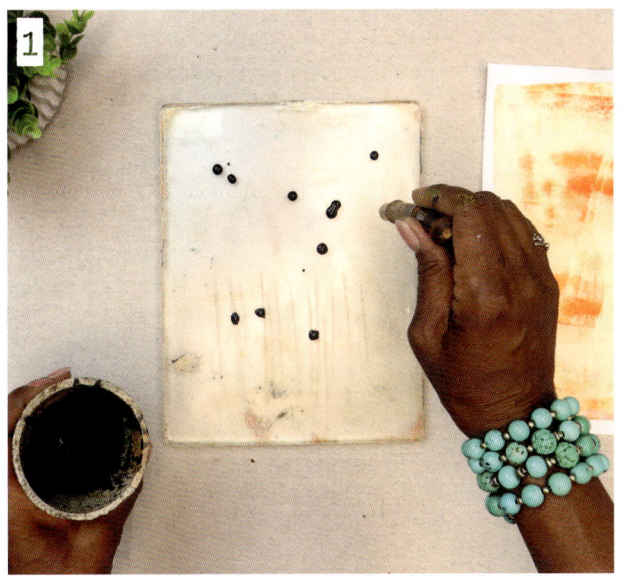

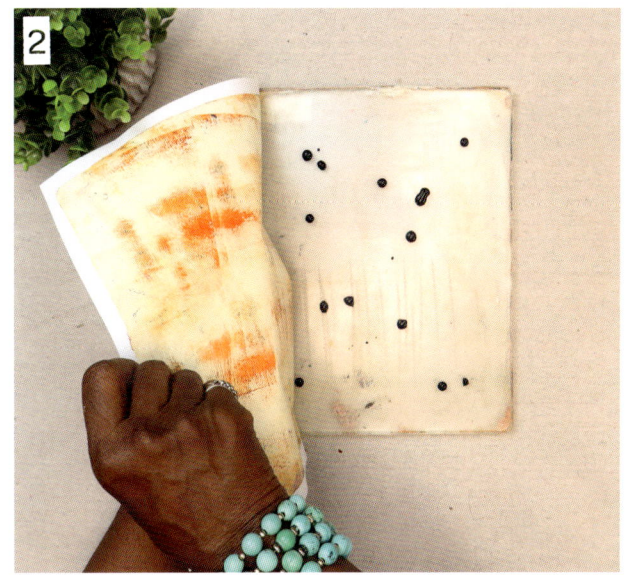

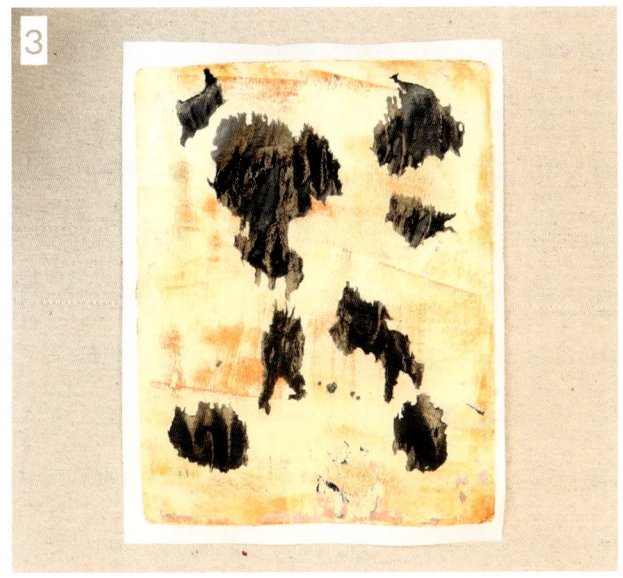

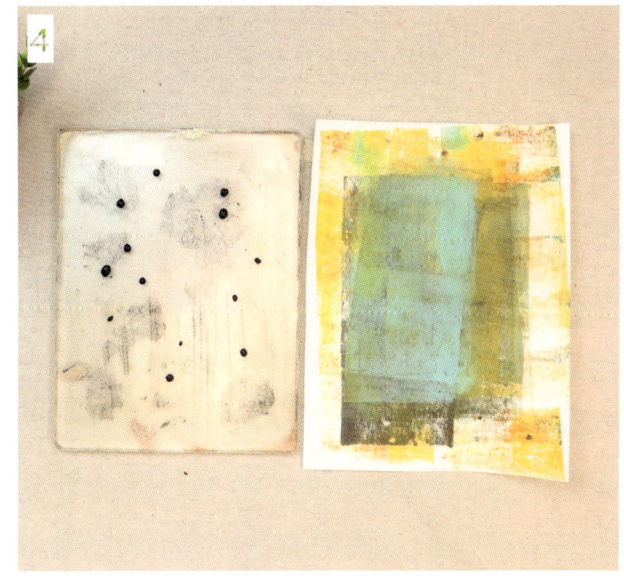

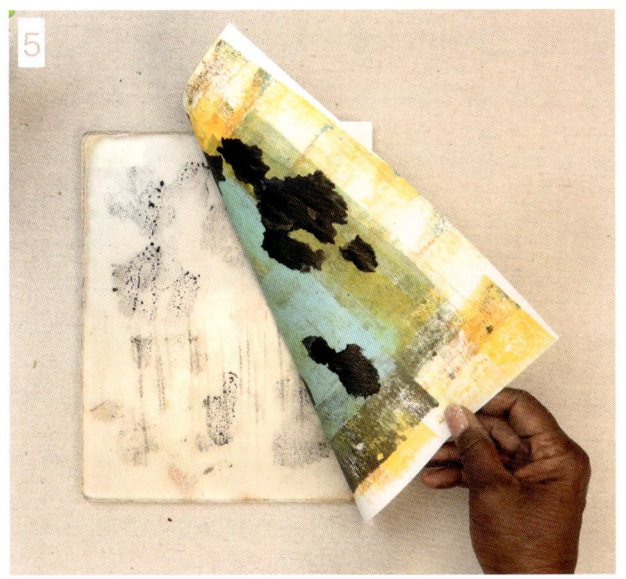

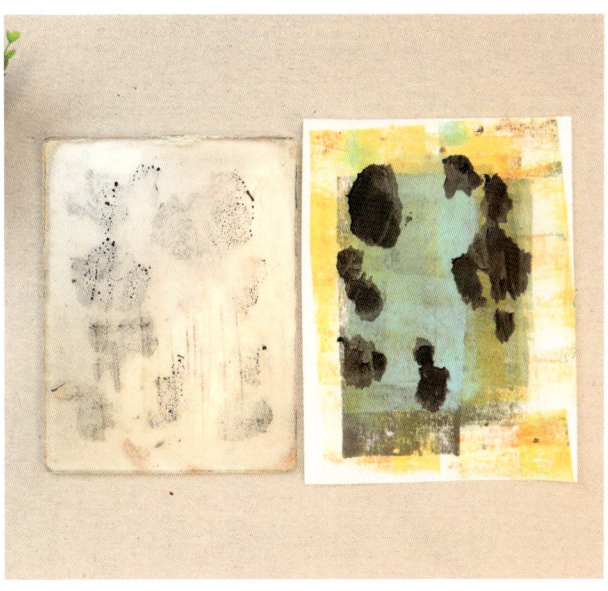

Glazing and Vintage Photo Silvering Technique

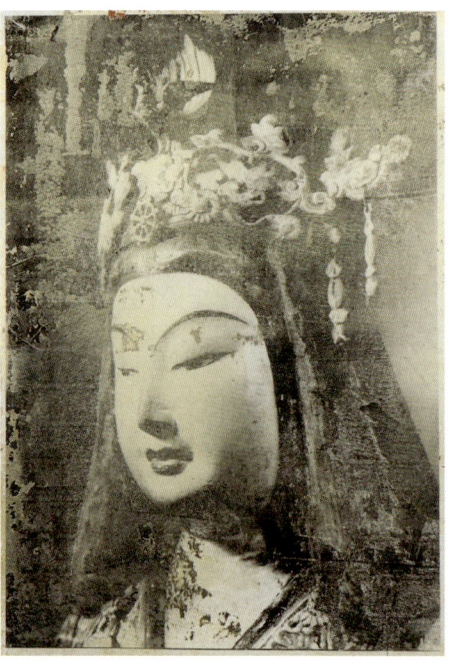 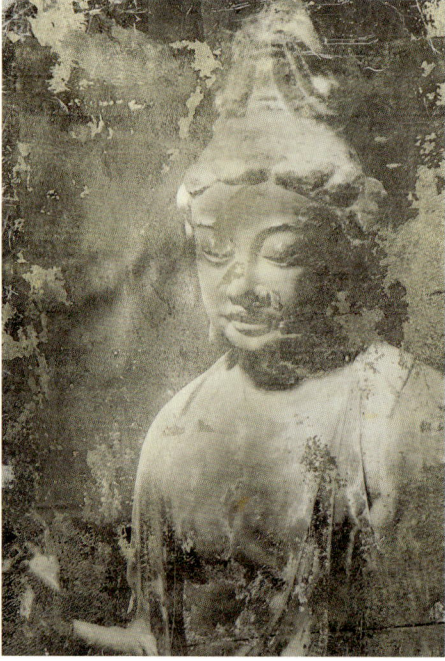

Left: Glazed laser print of a vintage photo with glazing technique

Right: Glazed laser print of a vintage photo with glazing technique

This is a way to use the gel plate as an external application. Up until this point we have been creating artwork with the plate. With the glazing technique, we take something that is already finished **1**, **2**, such as an already-completed gel print, a magazine page, photocopy images, or "grunge" photo transfers (see chapter 14), and use the plate to add an additional layer of diversity to it.

I discovered glazing by creating very thin metallic layers of paint on the gel plate. This technique works especially nicely with photo images and creates a vintage sort of "Old World" look. The colors that work best are champagne gold, ice blues, pale golds, and pewter silver. These colors will affect the mood of the photo image and elevate an image or a print.

Here's how. Select the type of glaze that you want to use. Brayer out a thin layer **3**. Lay your paper down. Smooth the paper down, using your hands, and then pull the print **4**, **5**. This is a very simple technique.

Think about the color and the texture you created; glazing usually adds a dreamy film. How can you use glazing to add mood to other images?

For a video of this technique, visit robynmcclendon.com.

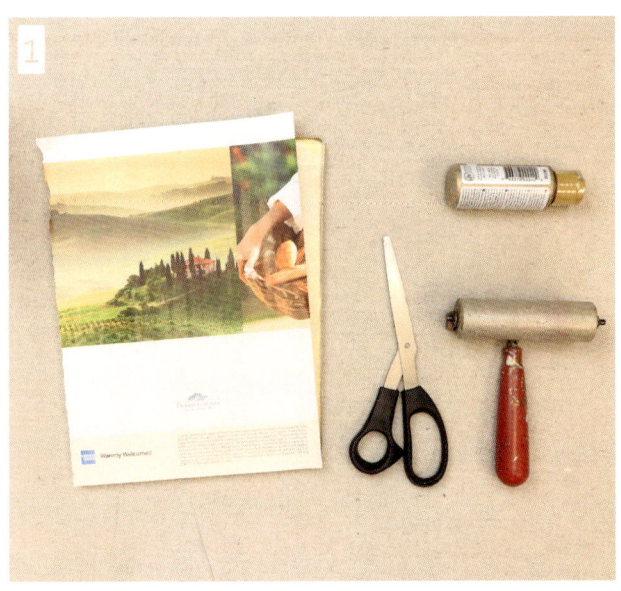

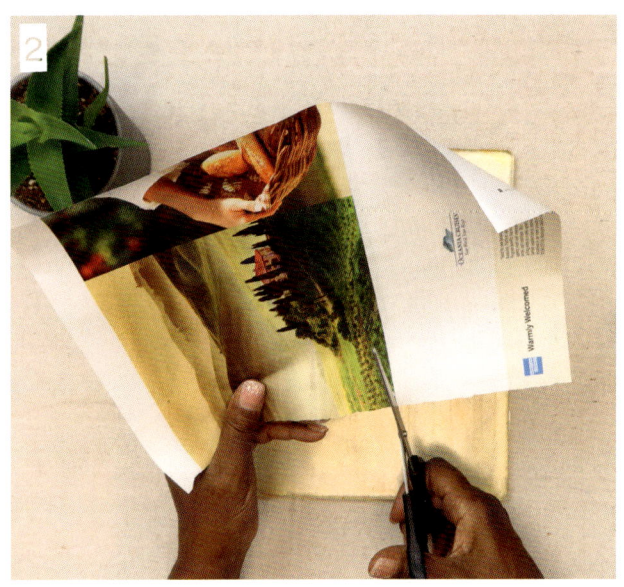

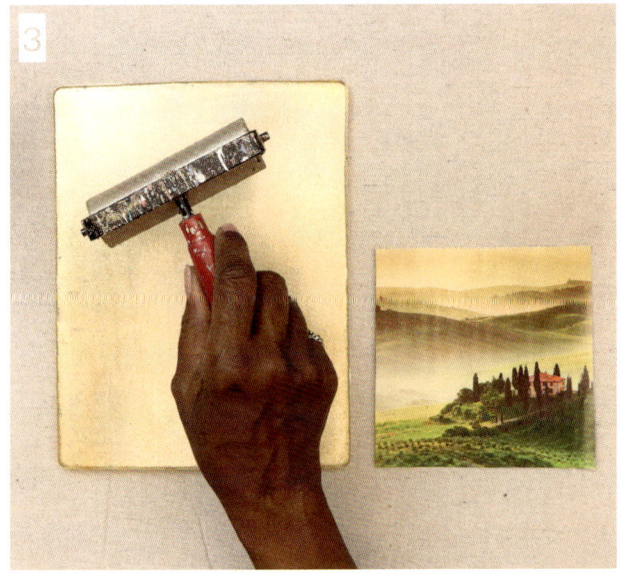

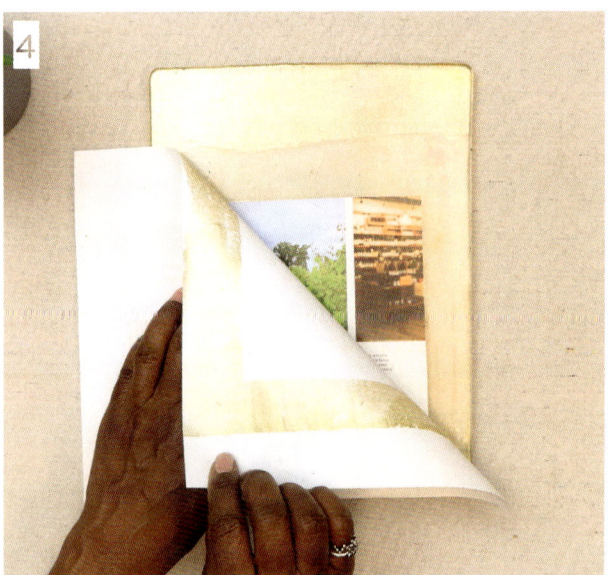

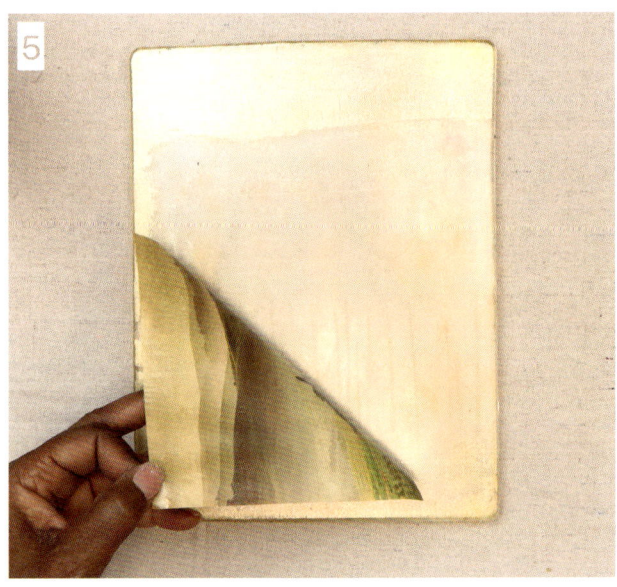

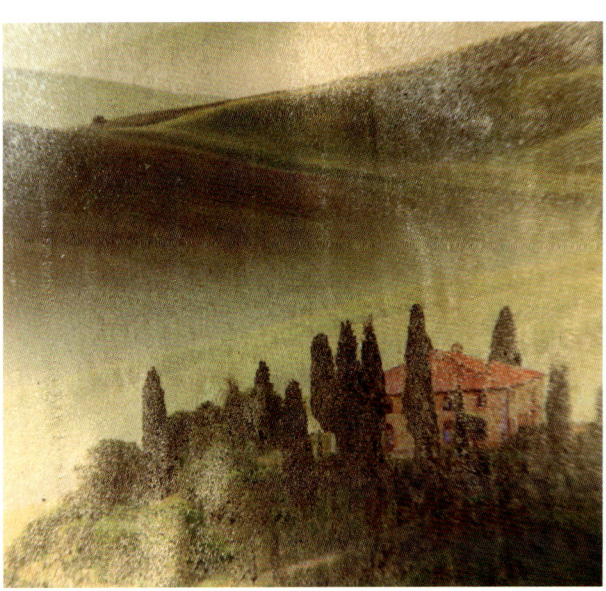

8

Sumi Ink for Intuitive Scripting and Mark Making

Here's why sumi ink painting is presented right after the section on glazing: because you can intuitively script or mark-make with the ink on a glazed print, and then you can sandwich the scripting or mark making between another glaze layer once the ink dries.

Intuitive Scripting

This is a good place to talk about what my intuitive scripting is. Unlike scripting that's asemic, which means "without the smallest unit of meaning," intuitive scripting has much intention and meaning. It is an intuitive and natural response. It comes out of a very old practice. It is a sister to *kana*, which was a set of characters that, for hundreds of years, aristocratic Japanese women used for writing; they could exchange messages, letters, and literature that men could not understand.

Intuitive scripting at first appears simple and direct, yet it takes connecting to a silent voice within, one that rarely speaks, to foster its natural and instinctive occurrence. Intuitive scripting, or "soul writing," not only adds an inimitable personal touch to your work, it instantly creates an ever-available portal to your creative voice. Whether you are using it as a mindful exercise of inner attention or applying it as an artistic practice, this graceful dance of brush and ink can become a rewarding and soothing addition to your creative work.

Many of us, especially women, were taught to be careful about "leaving a mark." Where we long to create boldly, we remain tentative and careful, often stifling the seedlings of our emerging style. The very act of confident mark making serves as a vital breakthrough—it helps us access that infinite pool of individual creativity.

To start, lay out a thin layer of metallic glaze or matte medium on your plate **1**.

There are two ways of doing this intuitive scripting. You can let the first layer dry. Then do

For a video of this technique, visit robynmcclendon.com.

Right: Mark making on the gel plate with eco-staining

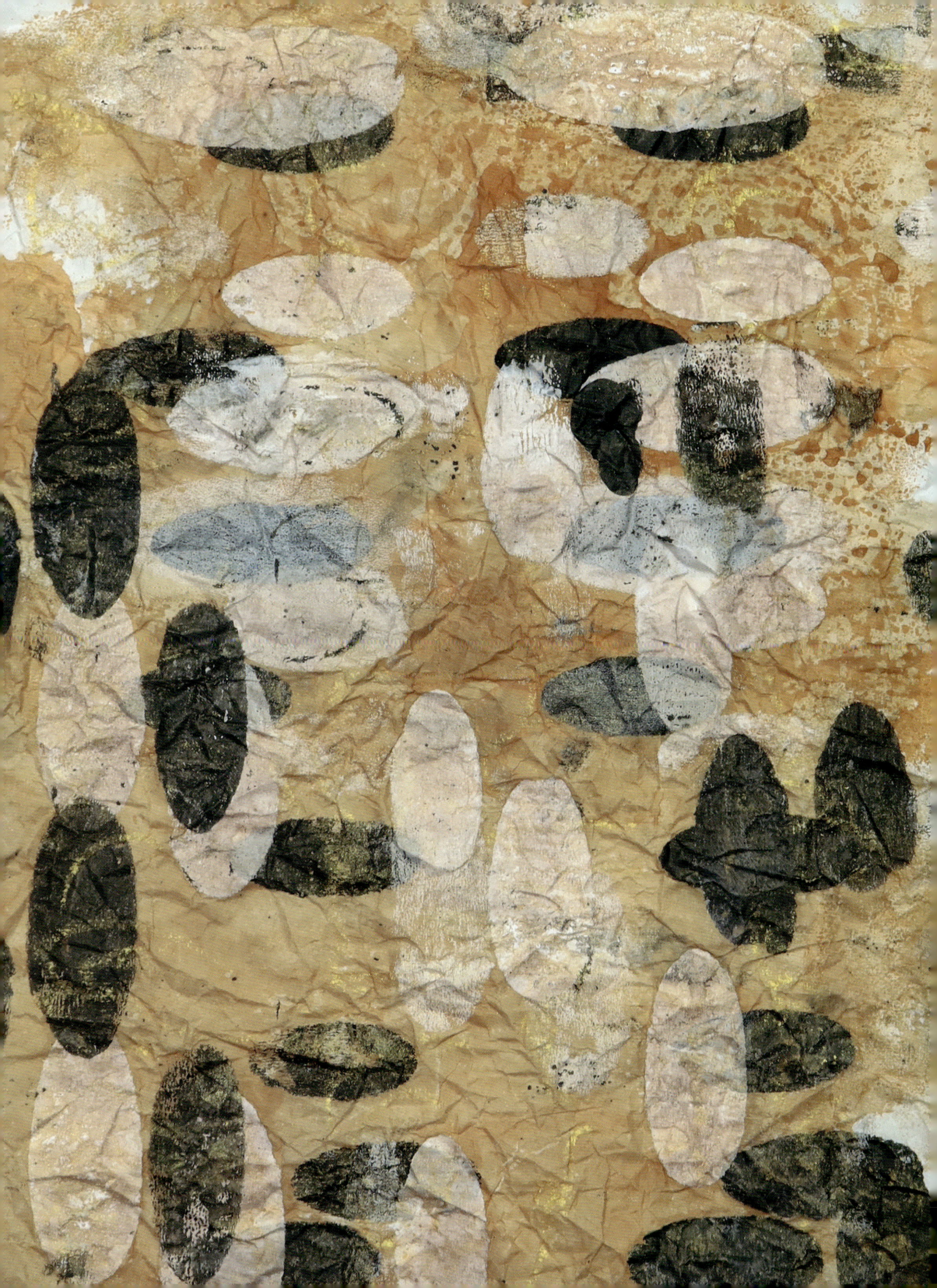

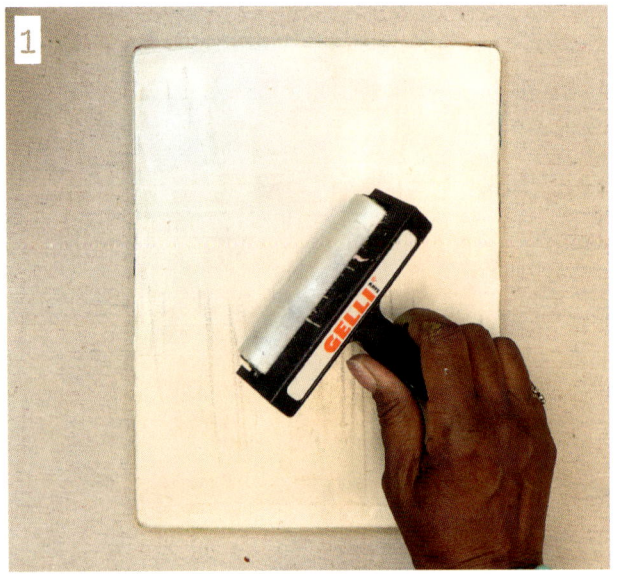

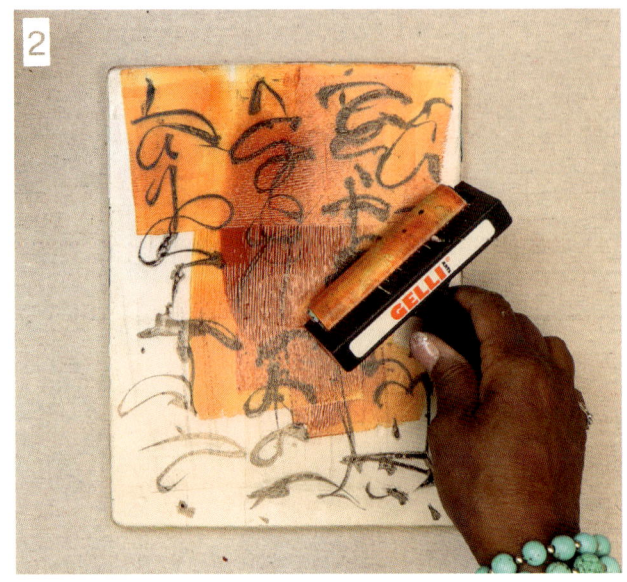

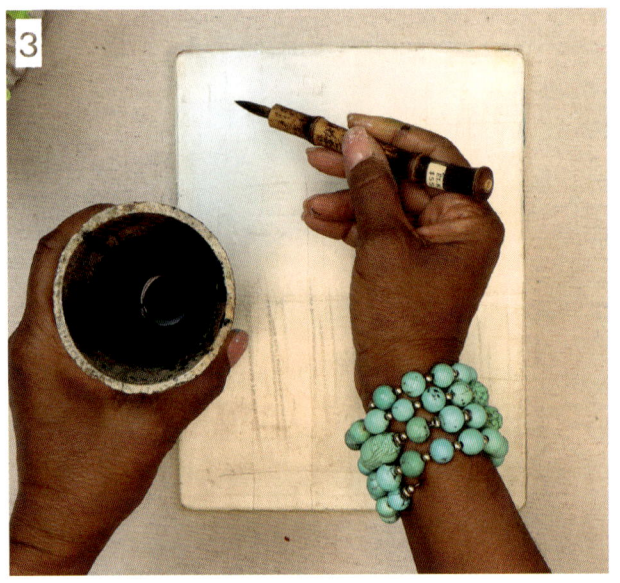

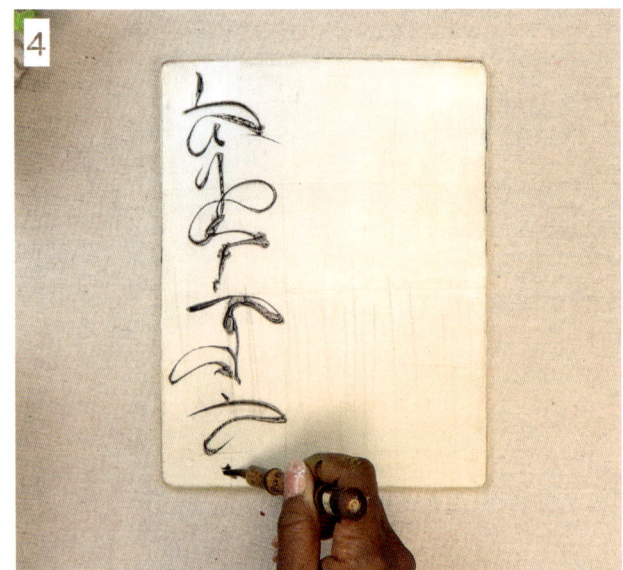

some scripting on the plate, using the sumi ink. Let that dry completely (at least fifteen minutes), so that when you add another layer of glaze on top, the ink won't bleed. Pull the print immediately, and all the scripting will transfer onto your paper **2**.

For the second way, put the glaze layer down and do not wait for it to dry. Script on it immediately **3**, **4**, then lay the paper down immediately and pull the print **5**.

In the first method you can pull a really nice clean print—everything will be crisp. In the second method the print is more painterly and watercolor-like; the inks will bleed more and you get a grunge or ethereal vibe.

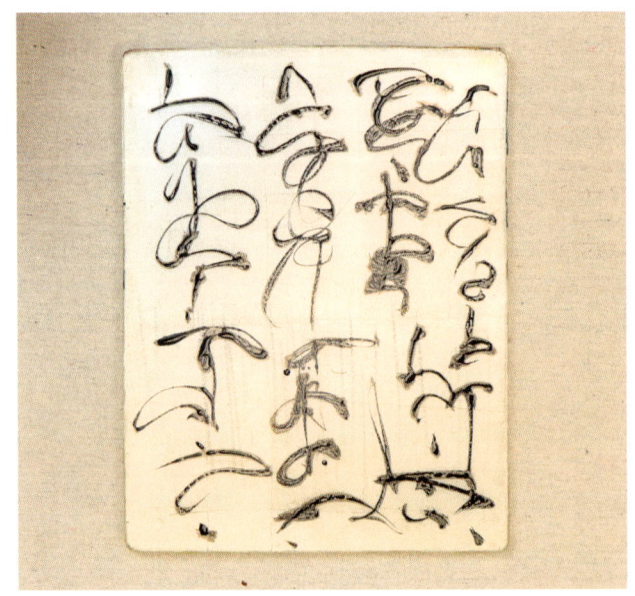

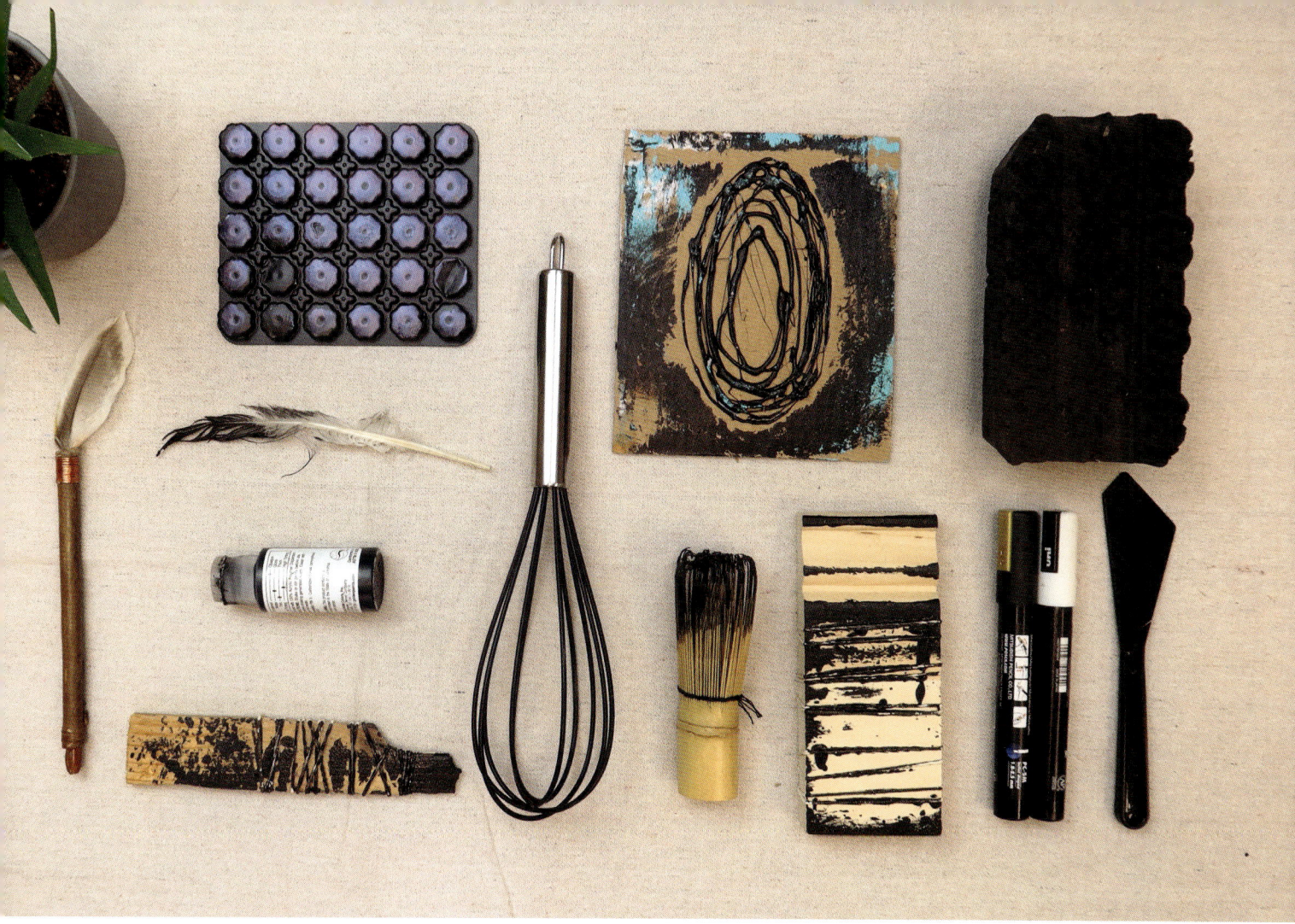

Mark Making

In mark making we basically follow the same process as in intuitive scripting. In this case you will be making random marks. The idea is to make very natural marks, using just about any object.

Think about all the different types of objects that can make patterns and marks on the gel plate. You will be surprised at the number of everyday objects that will expand your image vocabulary for printmaking. Search for a variety of things. Try bottle tops/bottoms; textured papers; cardboard; plastics; bubble wrap; potato mashers; plastic basting brushes; other kitchen items; grasses, leaves, sticks, and seed pods; and other found objects, both natural and man-made.

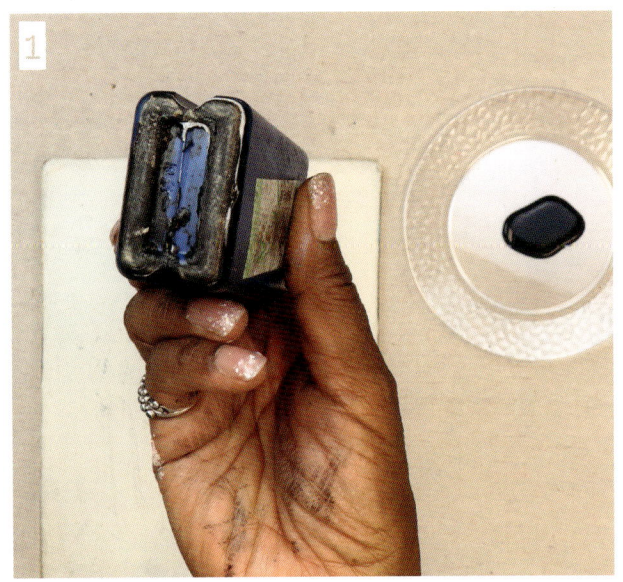

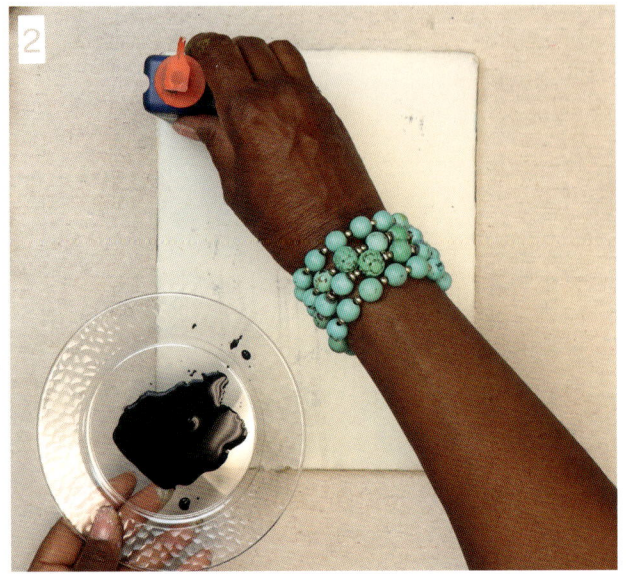

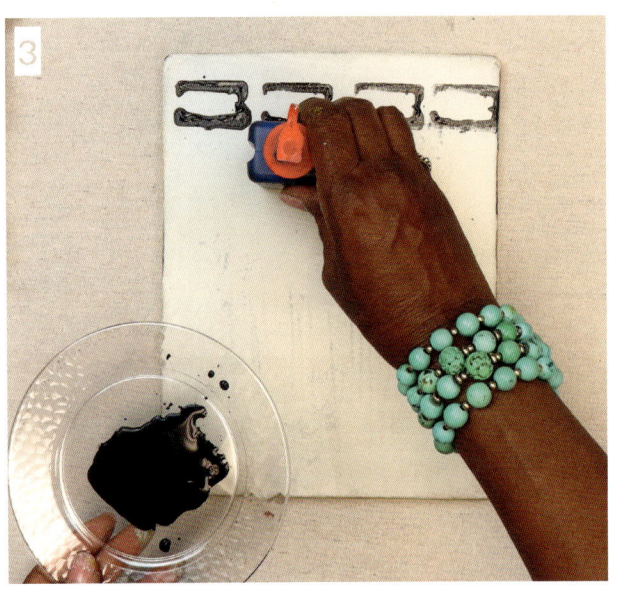

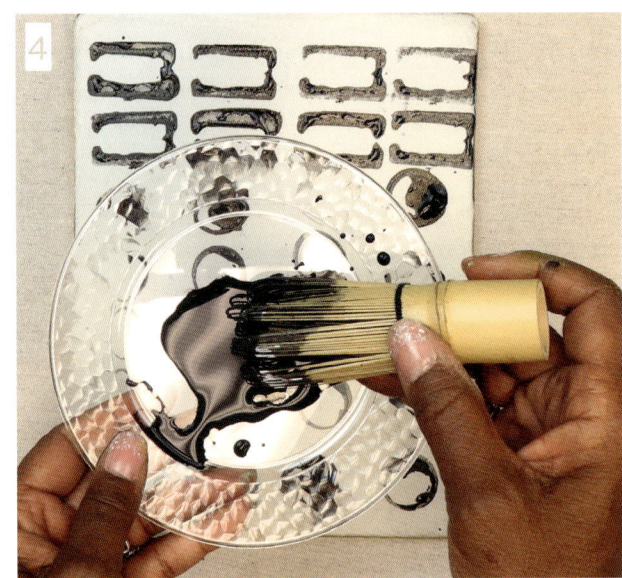

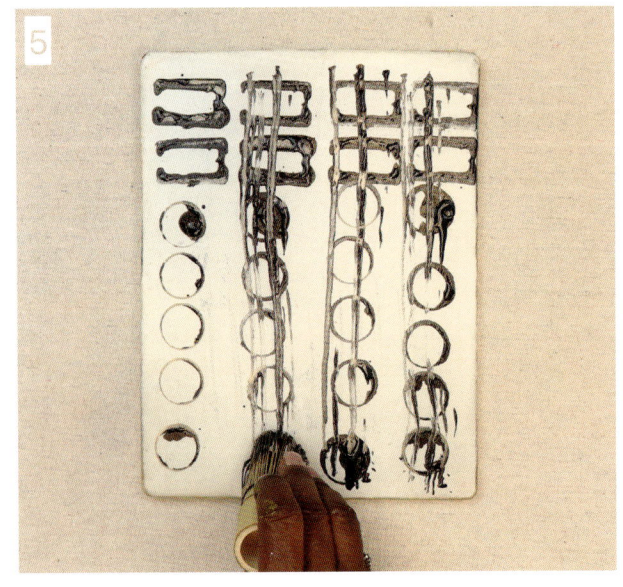

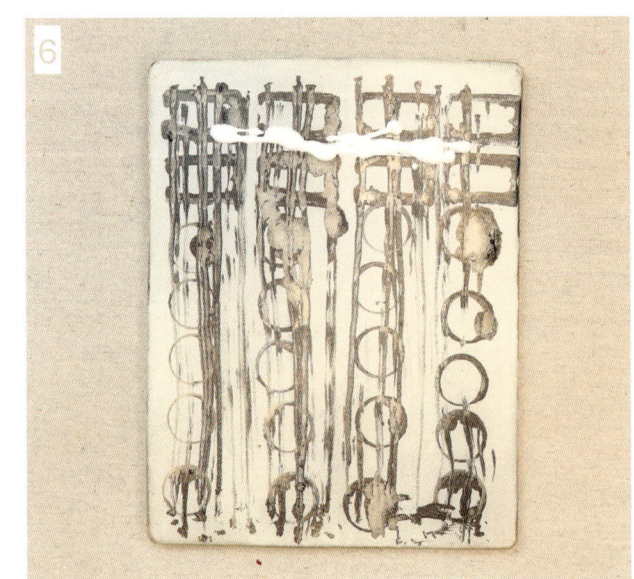

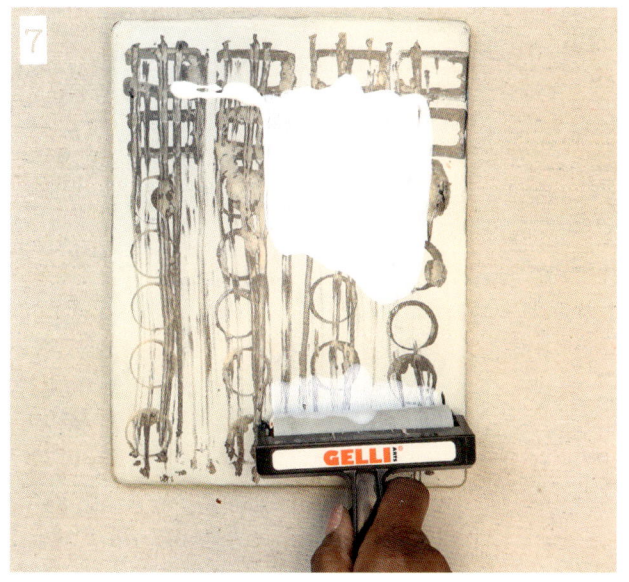

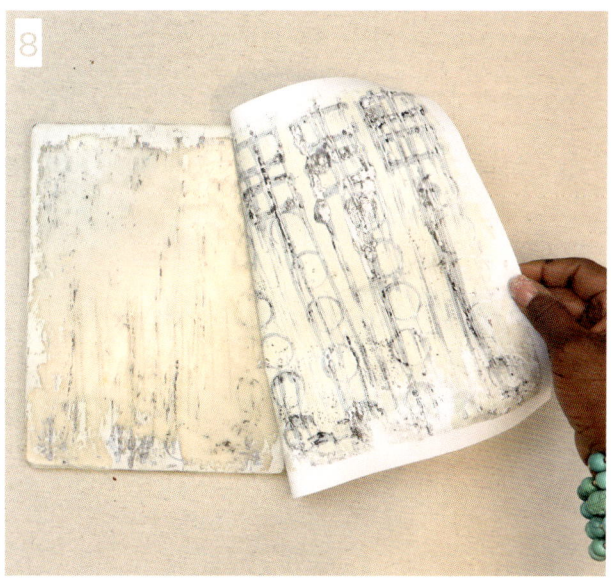

Repeat the process of layering as described above, now applying marks rather than intuitive script. Mark making too can be done with sumi ink. For example, fill a bowl with your sumi ink and dip in your stamps **1**–**3**. Next, add some circles: dip a bottle's opening into the ink, then stamp it on the plate. You can use a brush on your marks **4**–**5**, if you like, before pulling a print **6**–**8**. 🟡

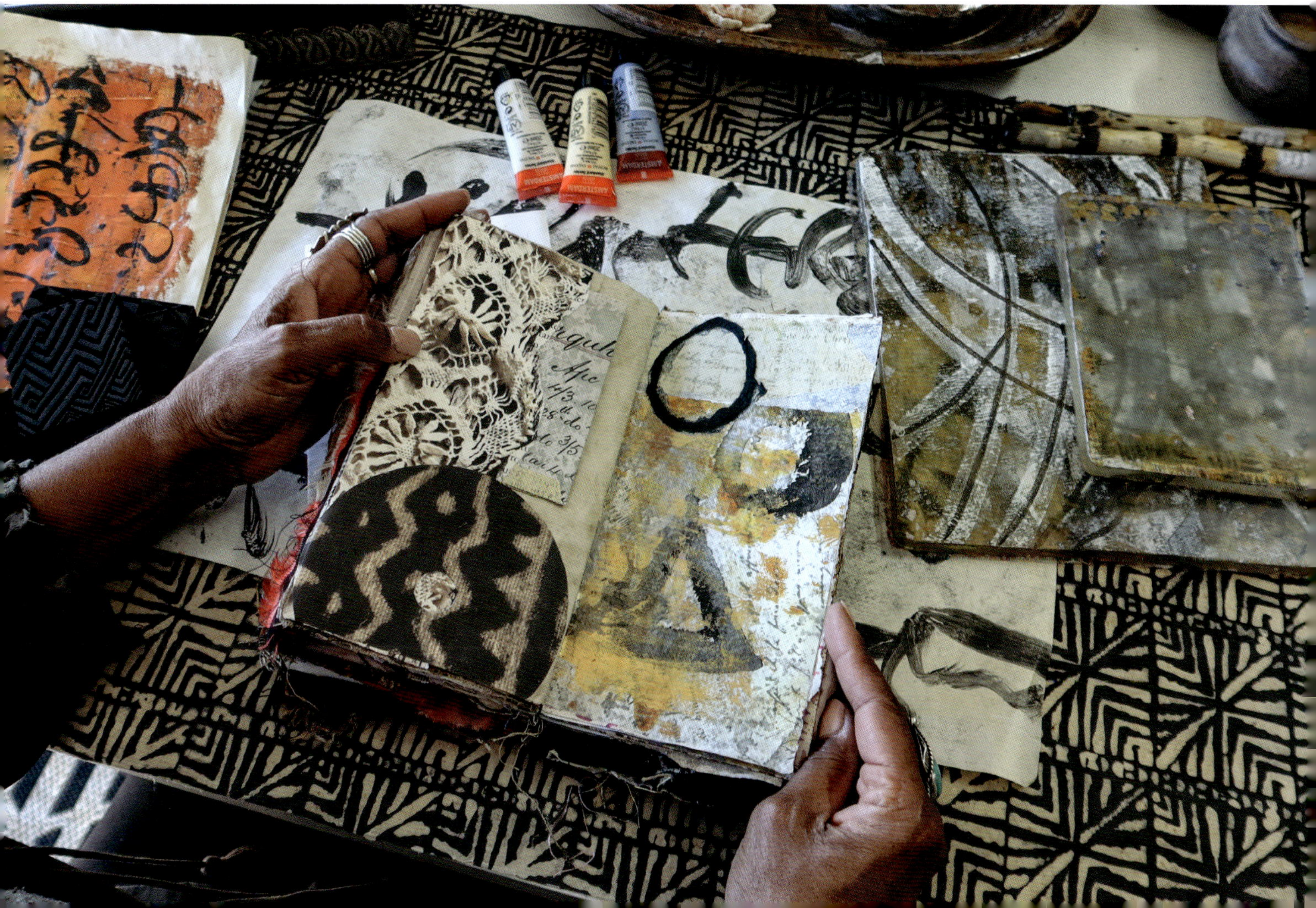

If you want tools to create line spacing, you can make them out of cardboard. You need cardboard that's thick enough so that it can be used over and over again. This is great for making marks on the gel plate.

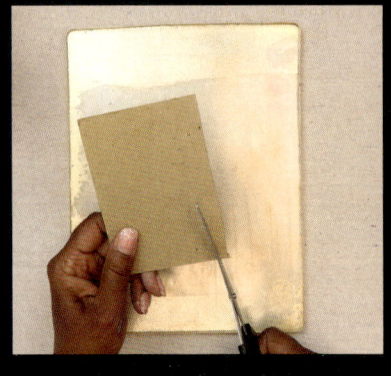 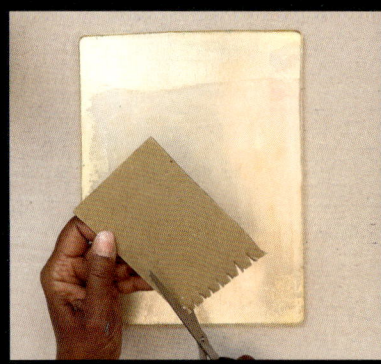 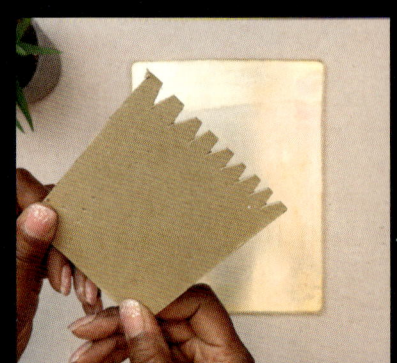

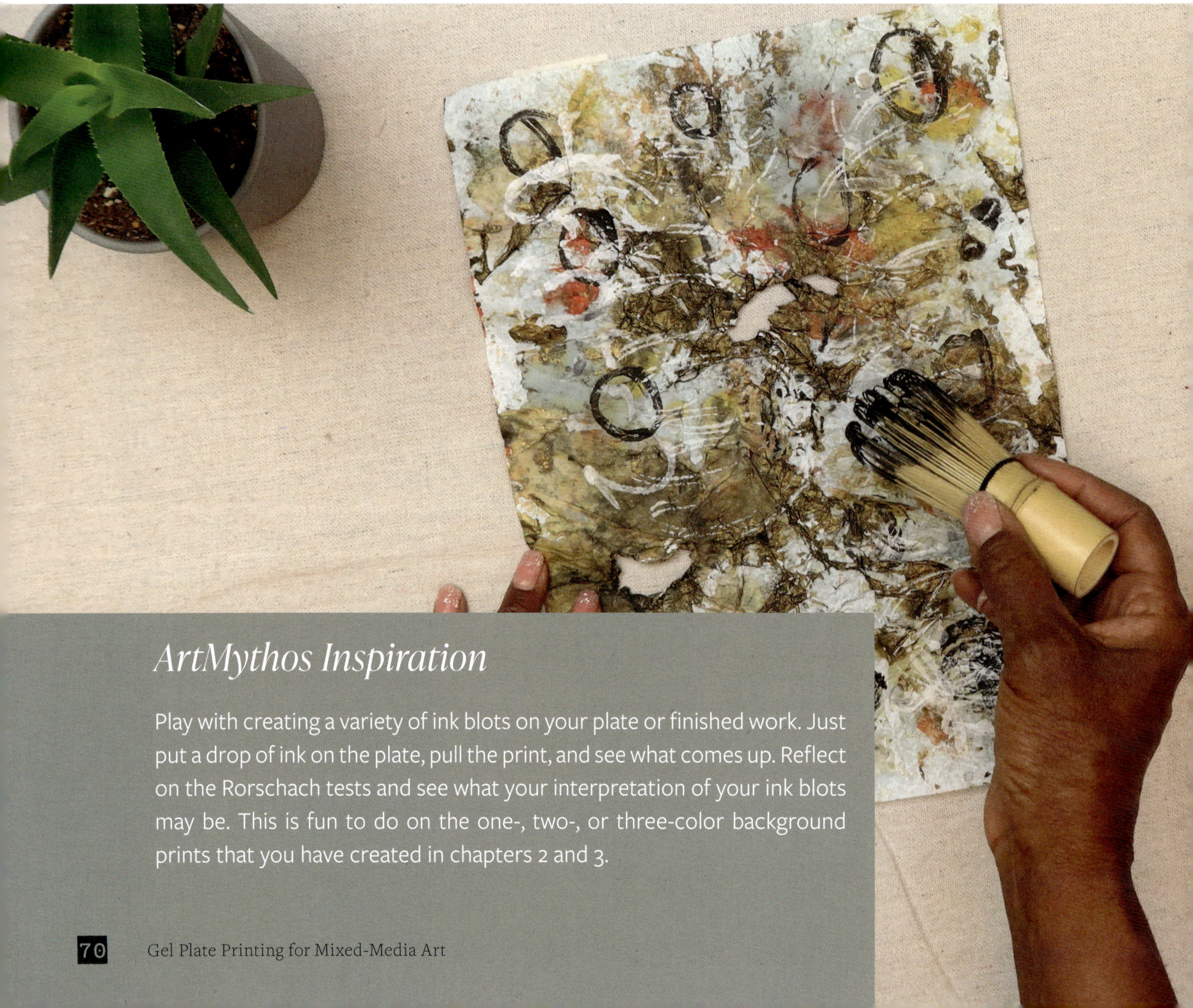

ArtMythos Inspiration

Play with creating a variety of ink blots on your plate or finished work. Just put a drop of ink on the plate, pull the print, and see what comes up. Reflect on the Rorschach tests and see what your interpretation of your ink blots may be. This is fun to do on the one-, two-, or three-color background prints that you have created in chapters 2 and 3.

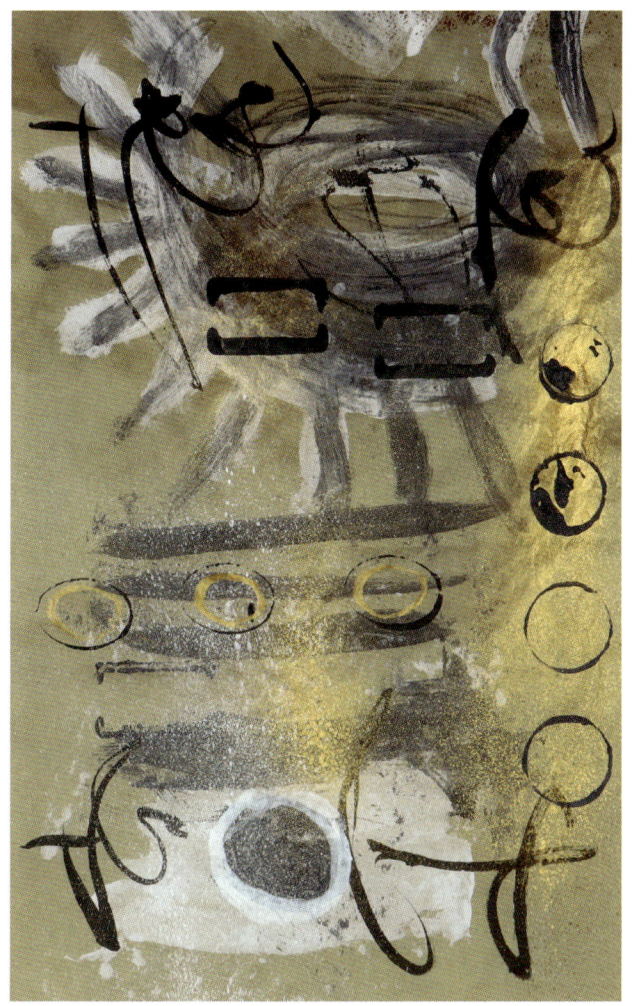

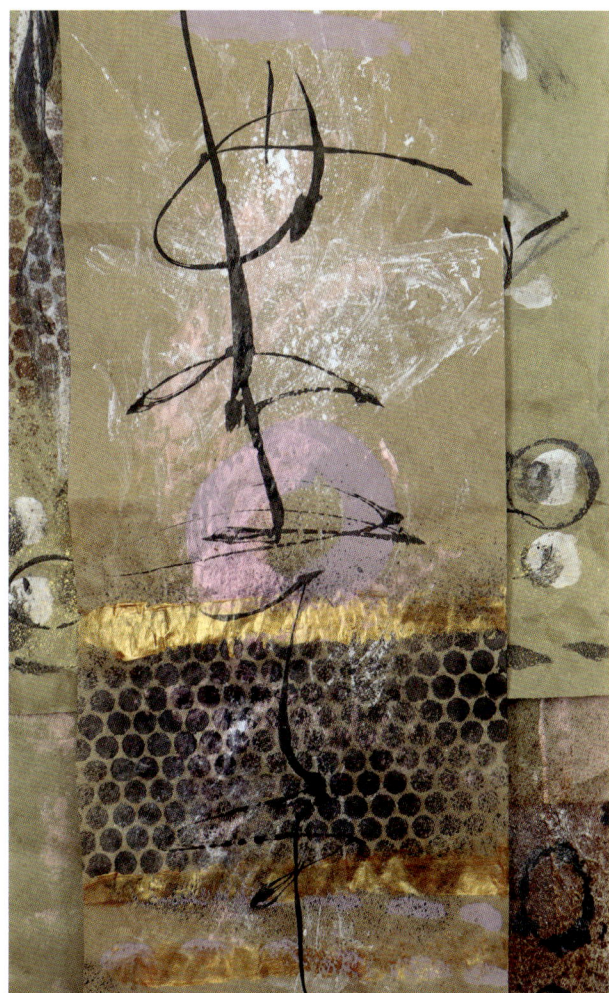

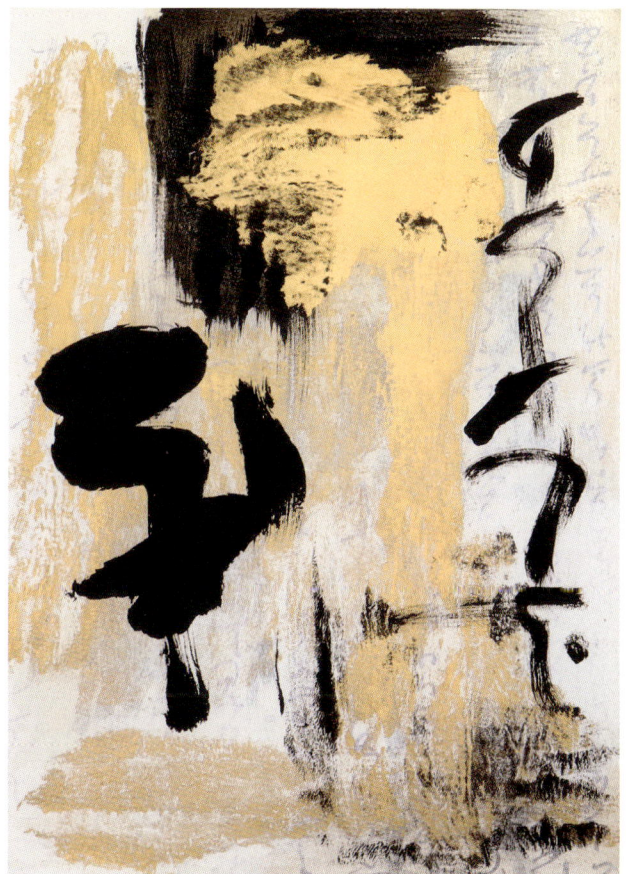

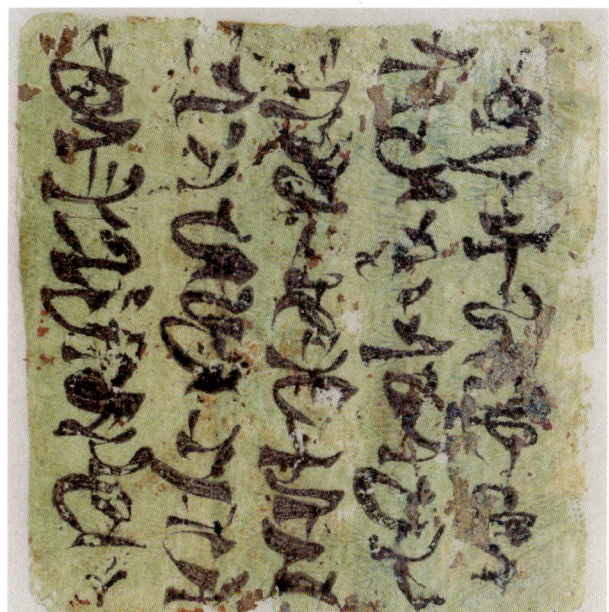

Clockwise from top left:

Mark making on stained paper

Mark making with the gel plate and found objects

Intuitive scripting on gel plate

Sumi brushstrokes on gel plate

Sumi Ink for Intuitive Scripting and Mark Making

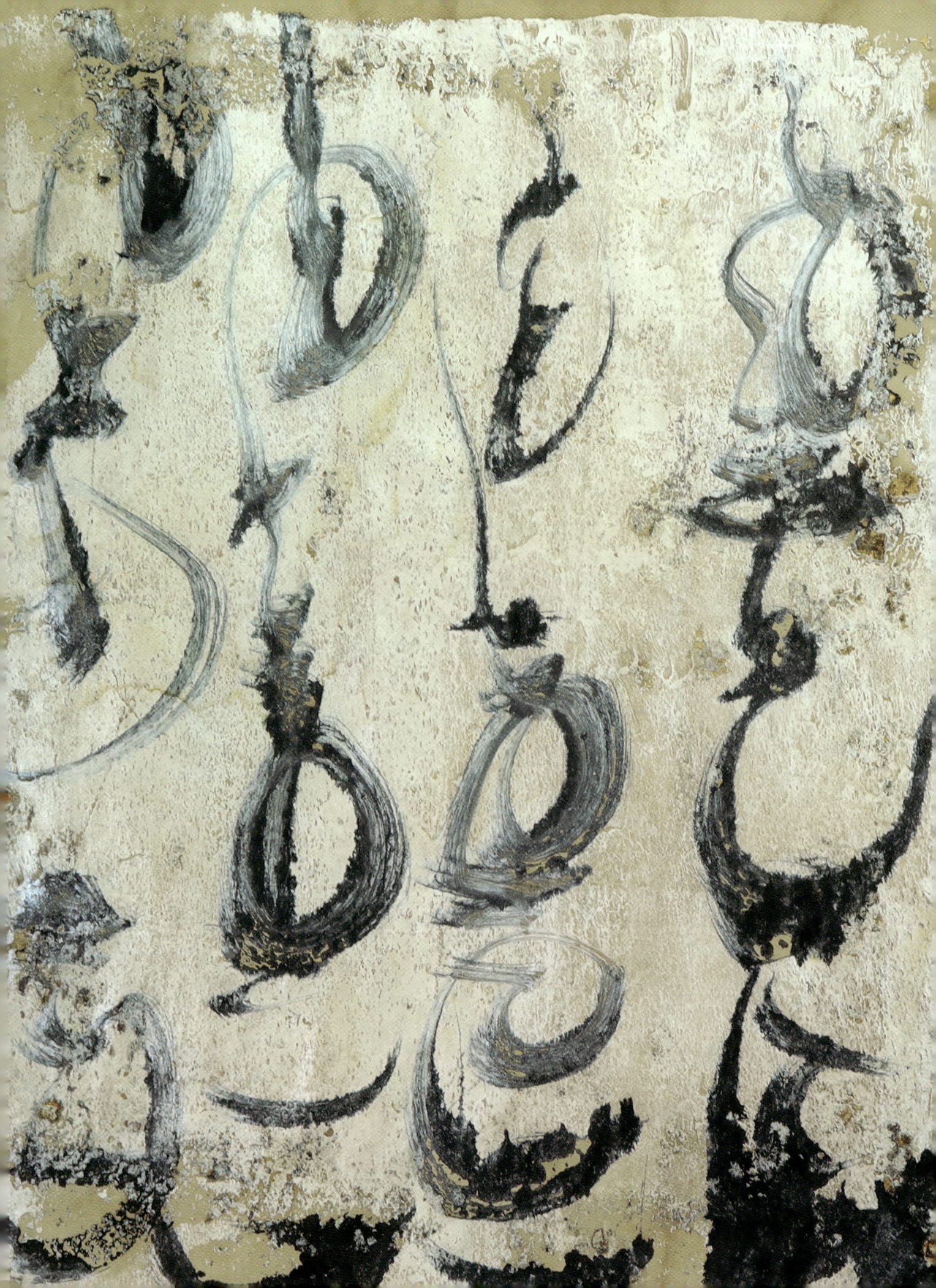

Printing on Transparencies

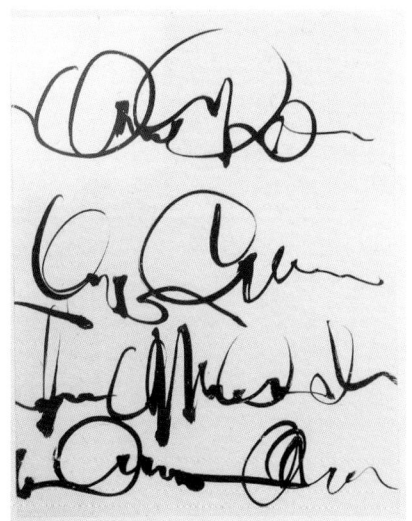

Sumi ink intuitive scripting on transparencies

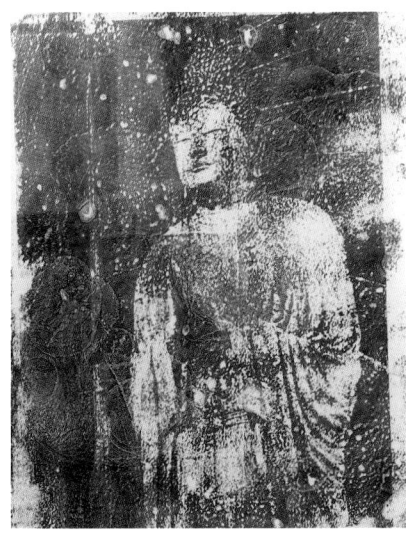

"Grunge" photo transfer on transparencies

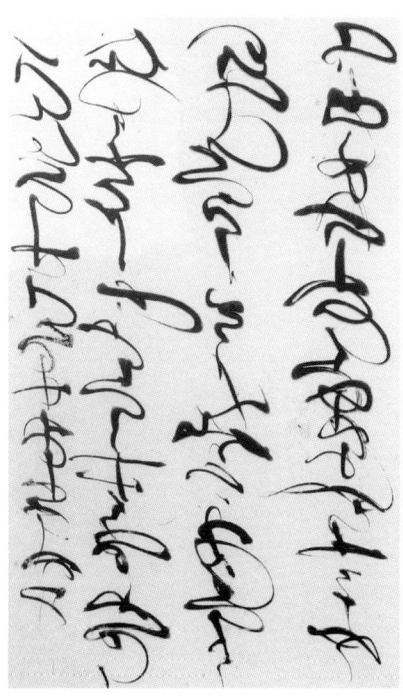

Sumi ink intuitive scripting on transparencies

Any of the techniques that have been offered in this book (except oil paints, since they will not dry) you can use on transparencies. A different kind of substrate, a transparency gets you some really interesting effects because you can layer it over other gel prints, and it creates extra-interesting layers in collaging.

You can also do mark making with markers or Posca pens to create organic patterns to collage on top of your prints as a layer. And you can also glaze after applying that mark making. Here you can really play with all the techniques.

Steps **1**–**8** repeat the brayering of paint on the gel plate, mark making, and pulling of monoprint images onto transparency film, instead of onto paper as we have been doing.

Left: Sumi brushstrokes on gel plate

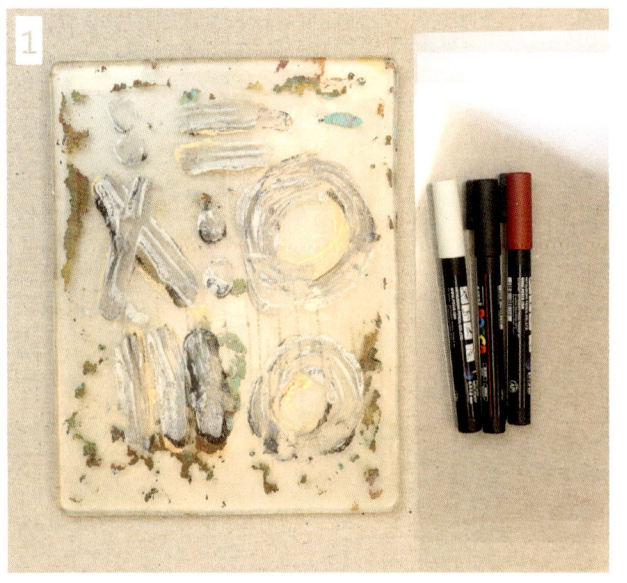

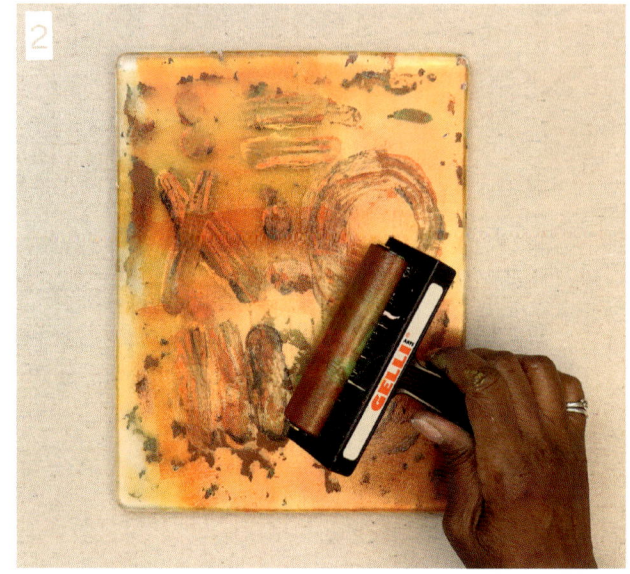

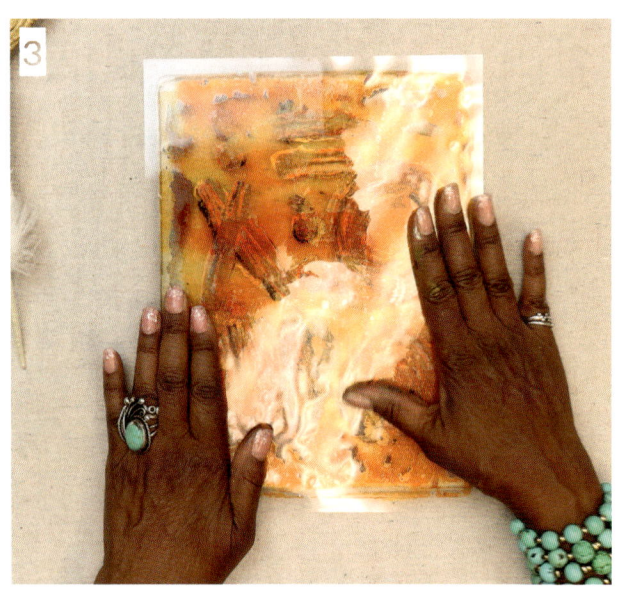

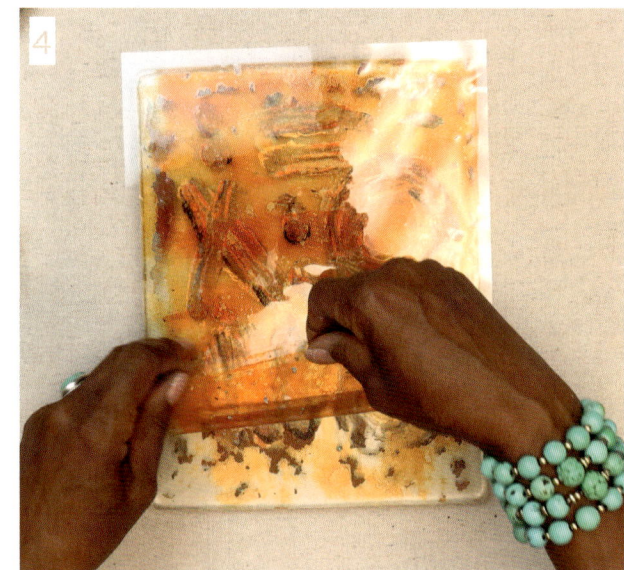

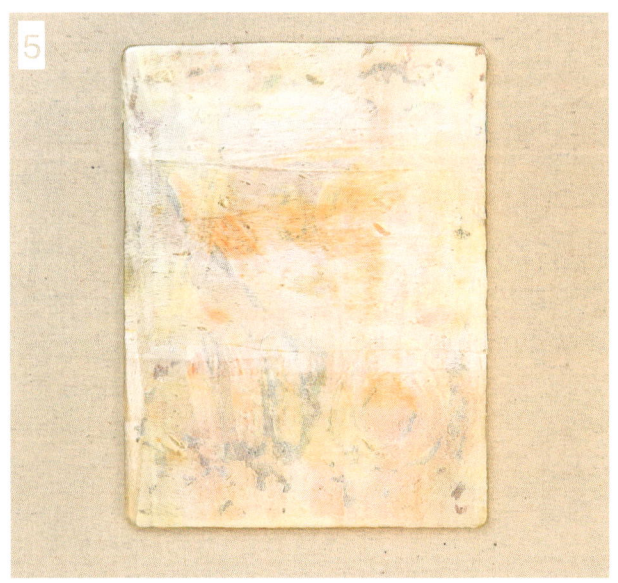

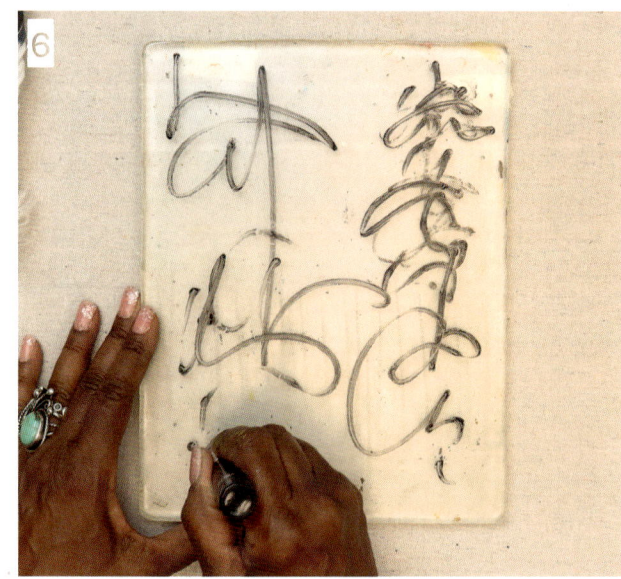

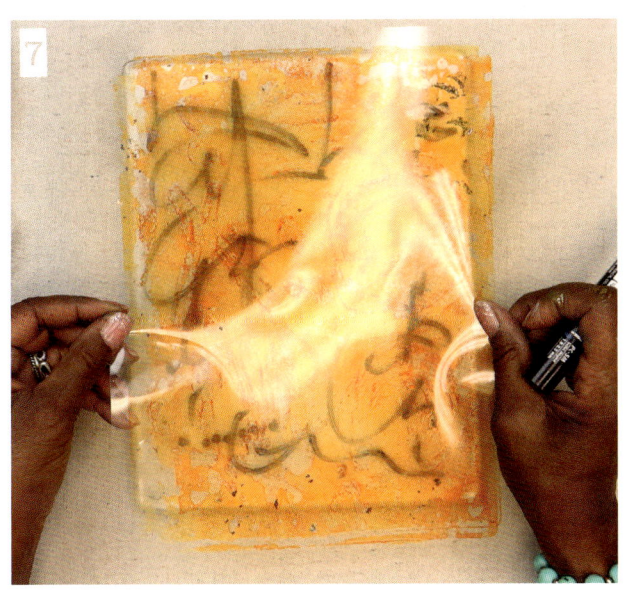

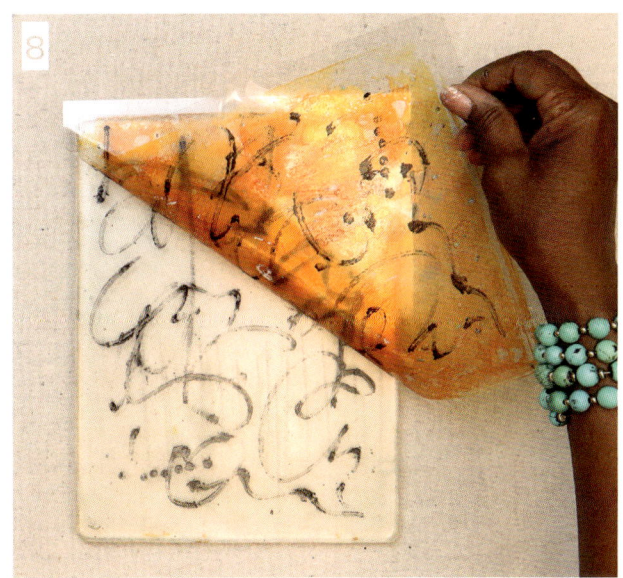

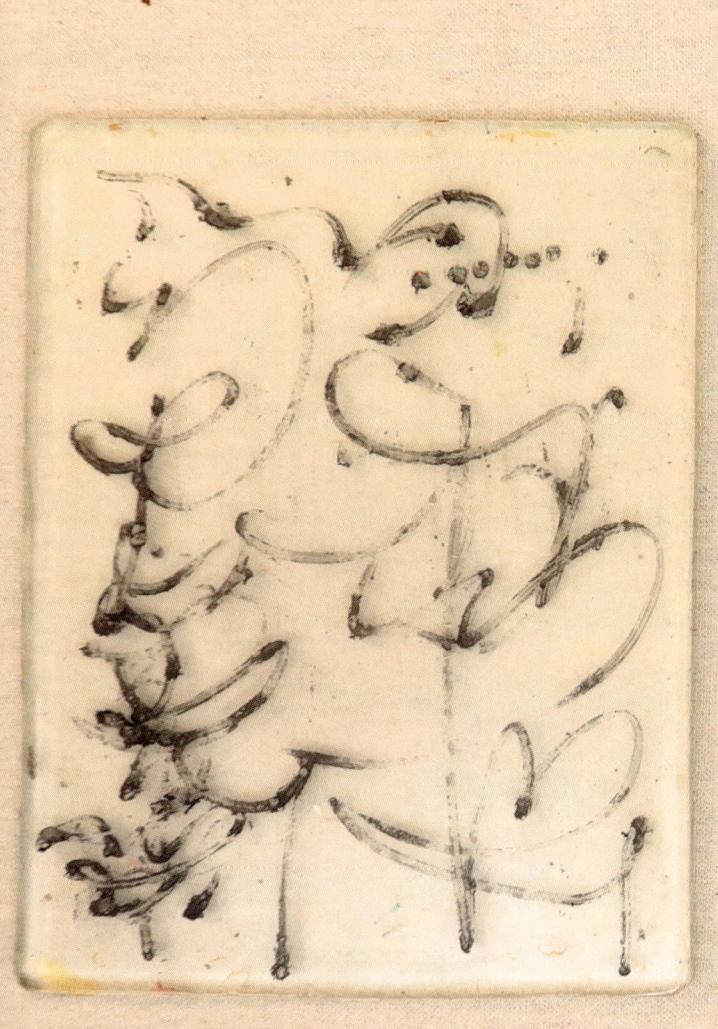

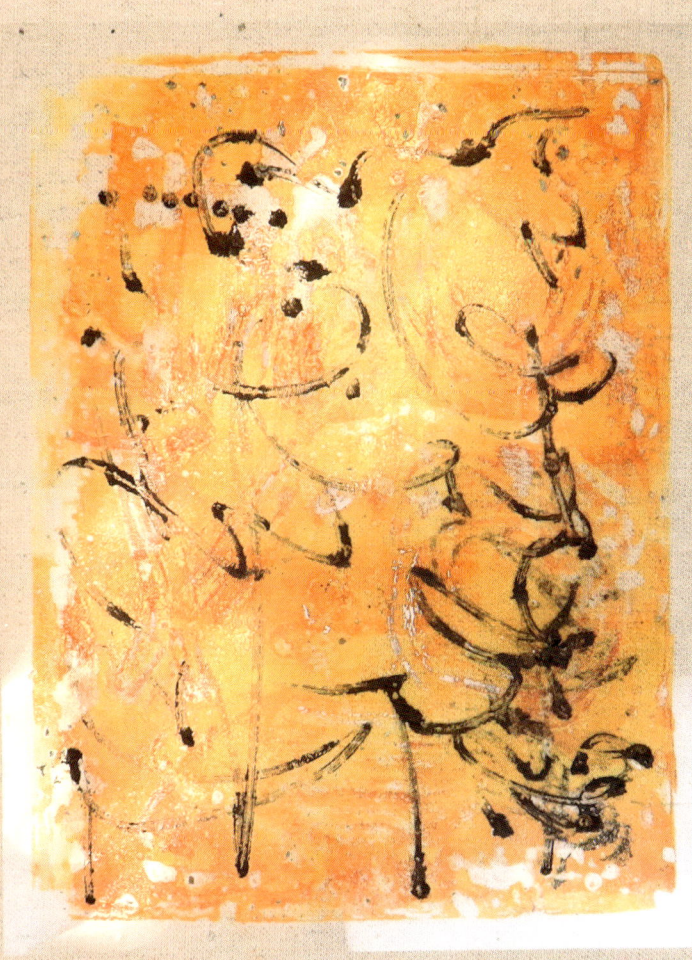

9

Stencils on the Gel Plate

While I enjoy using purchased stencils, I also love to create or find my own. Stencils and patterns are everywhere once we learn to see them. Imprinting these found patterns in our work is a way of incorporating physical elements from our world, and of embedding our tactile experience into our work. You may find that certain patterns and imprints have deep personal meaning for you and appear over and over again as you create. Others that appear may surprise you.

My approach for stenciling is layering. Yes, the idea of picking up a stencil and stenciling all over the gel plate is an obvious choice, but it isn't necessarily going to give you a complex and interesting approach to creating prints. We have already looked at simple etching and masking (chapter 5), patchwork (chapter 6), glazing (page 62), and sumi ink painting (chapter 8). I like to think of the stencils as another layer that can be added to all of these techniques.

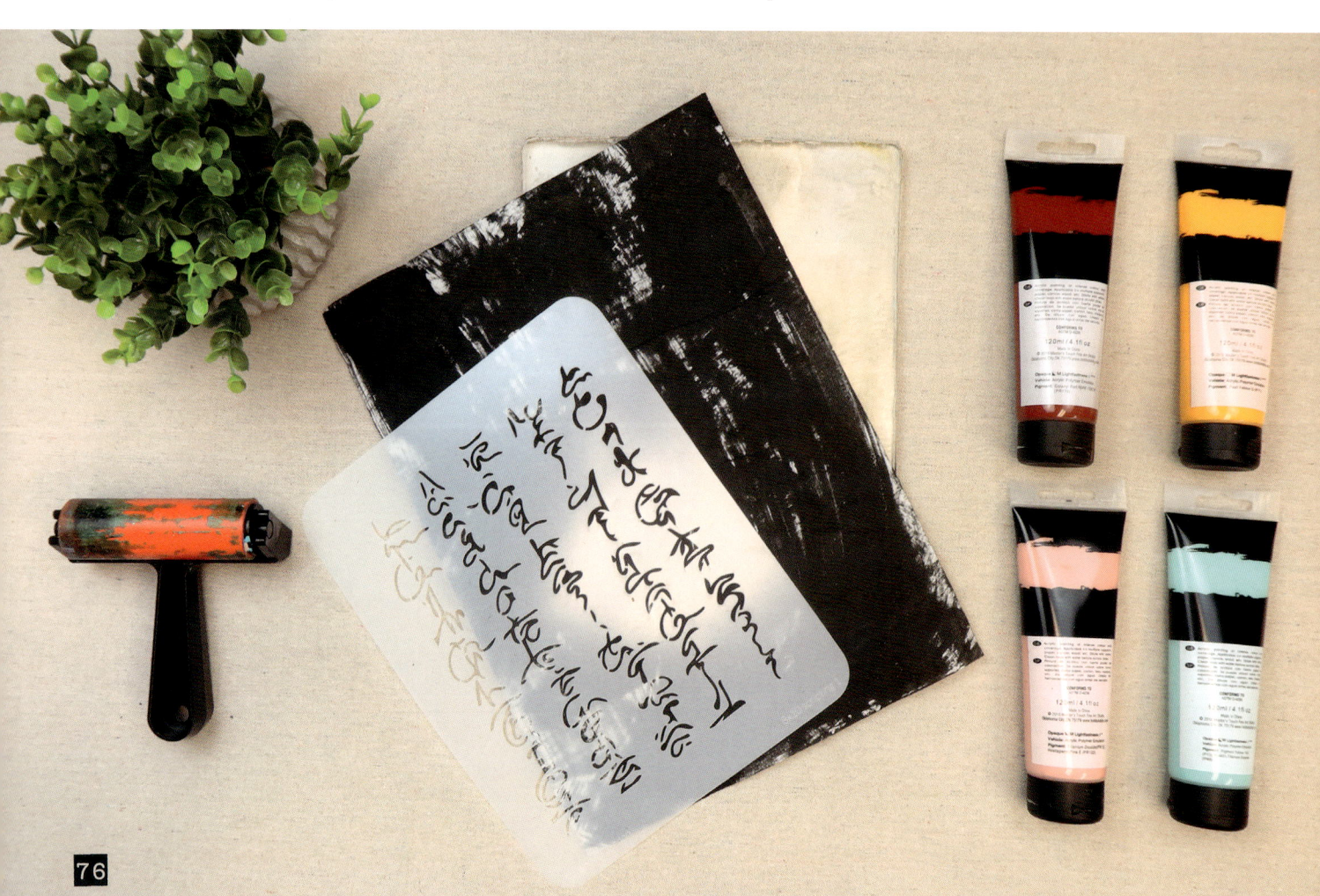

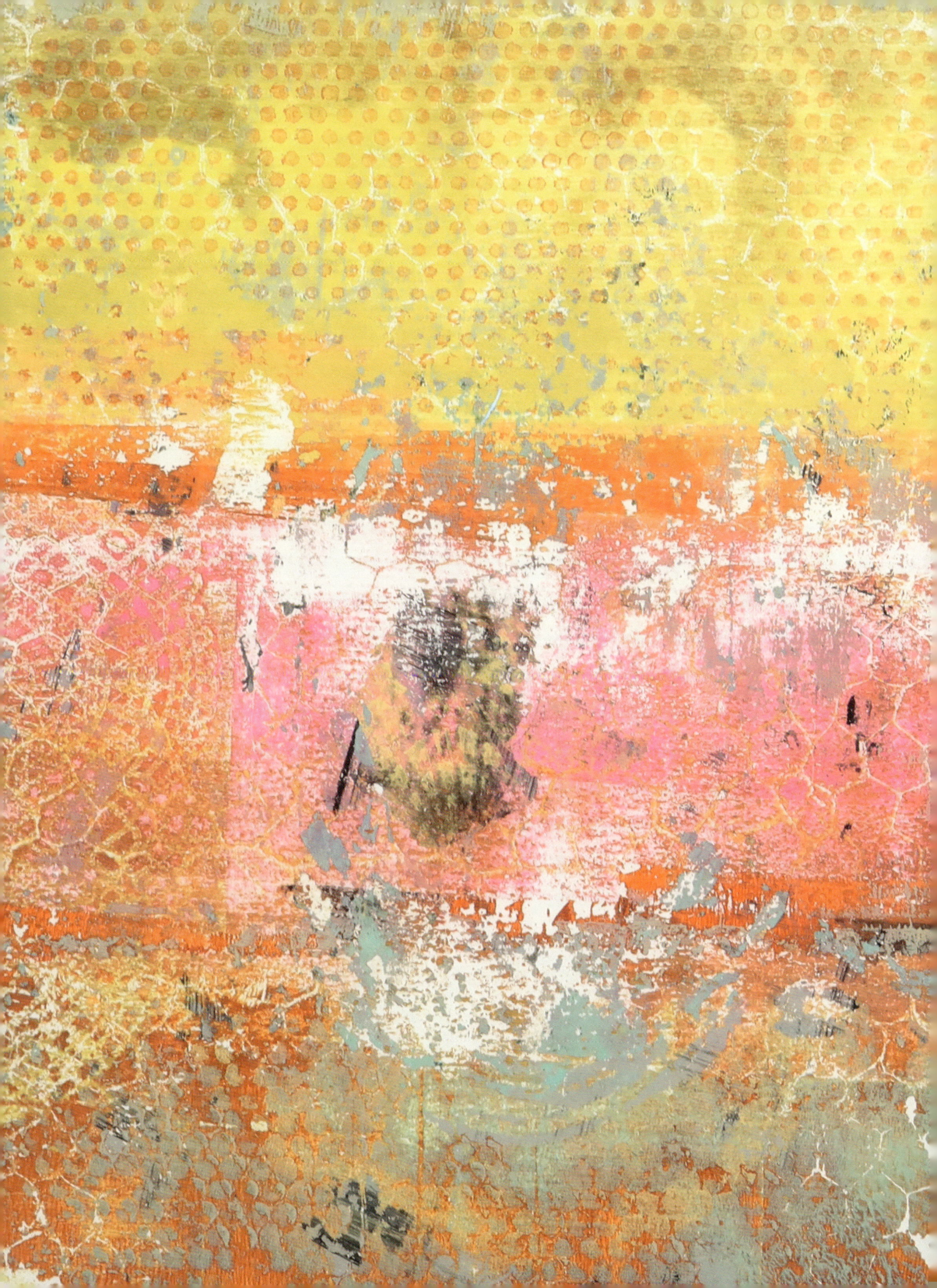

Every stencil will give you options. Do you want to roll paint out on the plate, lay the stencil down, pull it up, and take a print? Or lay out the stencil and add another layer of paint, taking a first print before pulling up the stencil? Does the stencil have enough paint on it to be useful for making its own print? Do you want to overlay the first stencil with a second pattern before pulling . . . ? The possibilities are endless, fun, and addictive!

Using the paint that is on the top or on the underside of the stencil (or both) gives us a variety of looks in the positive and negative space of every pattern.

Before you get started, remember to keep a large stack of "waste" paper beside you, on which to clean your stencils and your brayer. These offprints are as useful as the prints themselves, so "waste" paper isn't a very accurate description. I reprint, stain, glaze, and experiment with almost all my extra papers, often using both sides. The randomness of these extra pieces can be inspiring in itself.

Stenciling on the gel plate involves using the positive or the negative (or both) from the stencil, as well as using the stencil for mark making.

Using the Stencil as a Positive Imprint

This involves putting paint on your plate and brayering it out into a smooth, even layer, not too thick and not too thin.

Lay your stencil down **1**. Note that unless your stencil covers the entire plate, the print will pull the extra paint outside it, adding a "frame" to your print **2**. When you lay your paper down, the image that you will pull is the positive (as seen in **2**).

Gently lift the stencil and lay it on scrap paper—does the wet side of the stencil create a pattern?

Depending on how much paint you used and the relative humidity, you may be able to get a second print.

Before moving on, try rolling out a second thin layer of paint in a different color or in a metallic, then pull another print **3**–**8**. Are you able to see any of the original stencil print still visible in places? Becoming aware of the "leftovers" on our plate is part of the fun of the process! Soon you will have a feel for the moisture and receptivity of the plate and instinctively know that there are still patterns and bits waiting to come up, or, on the other hand, when it is time to start fresh.

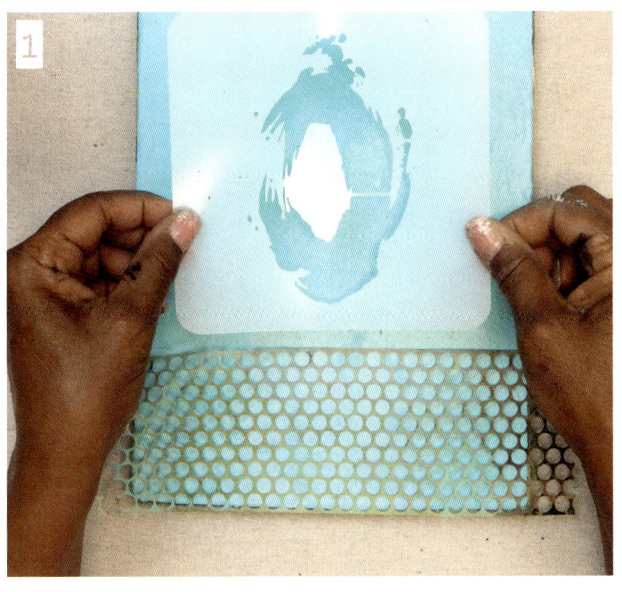

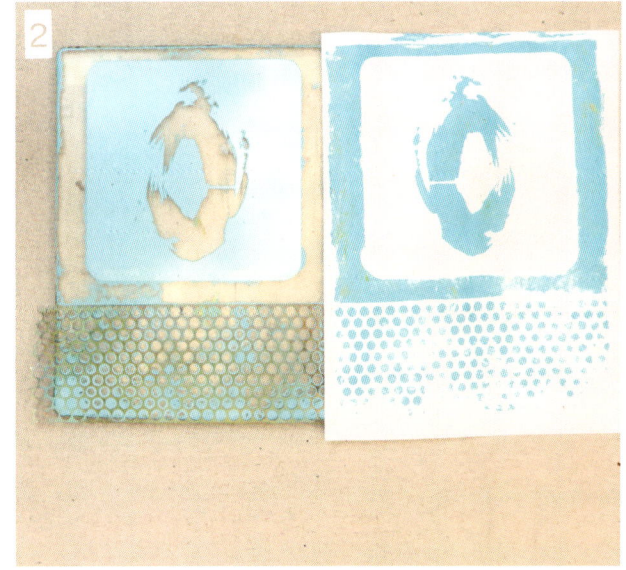

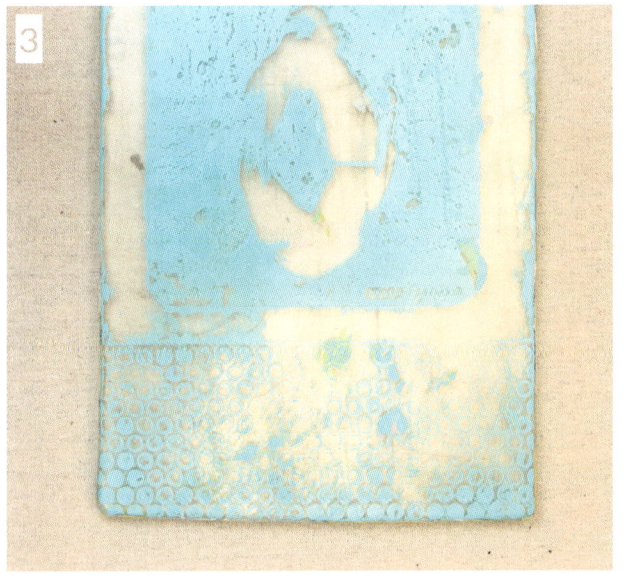

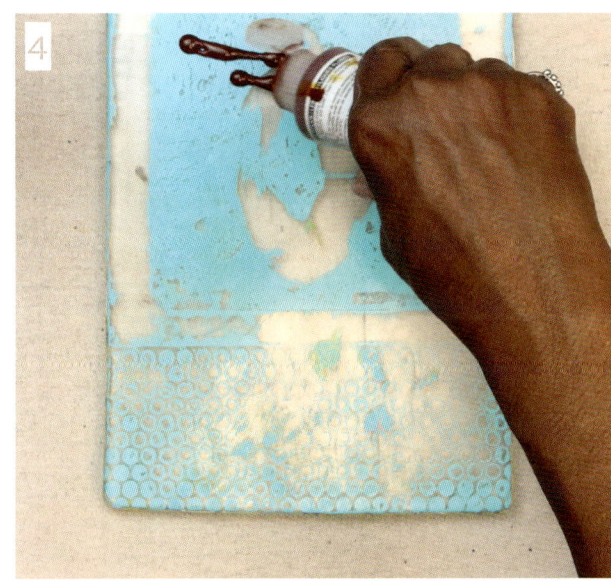

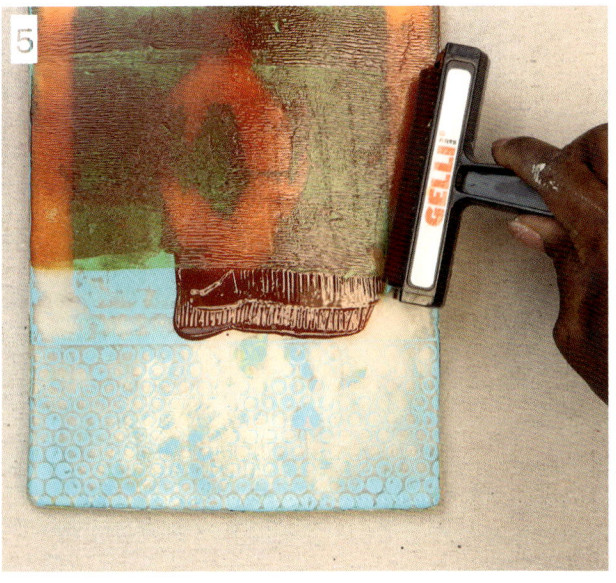

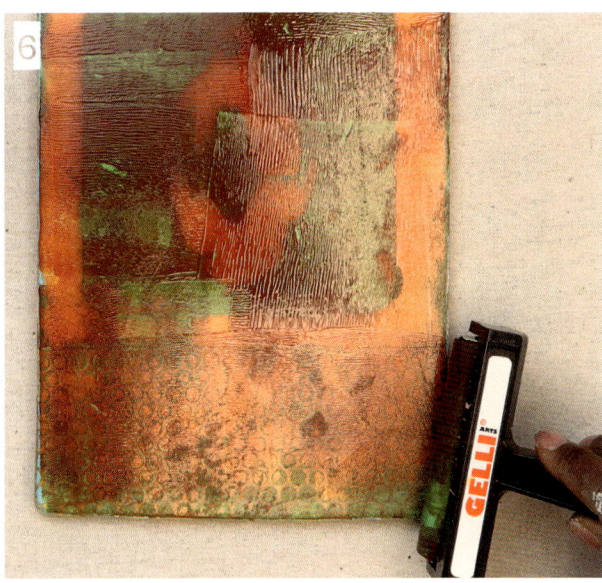

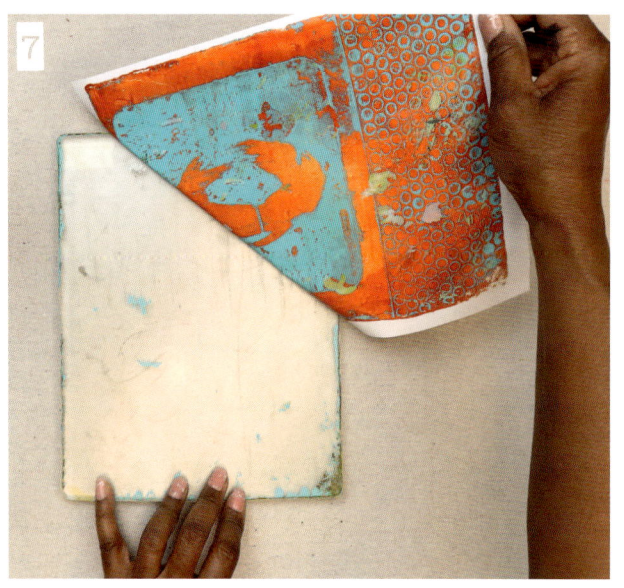

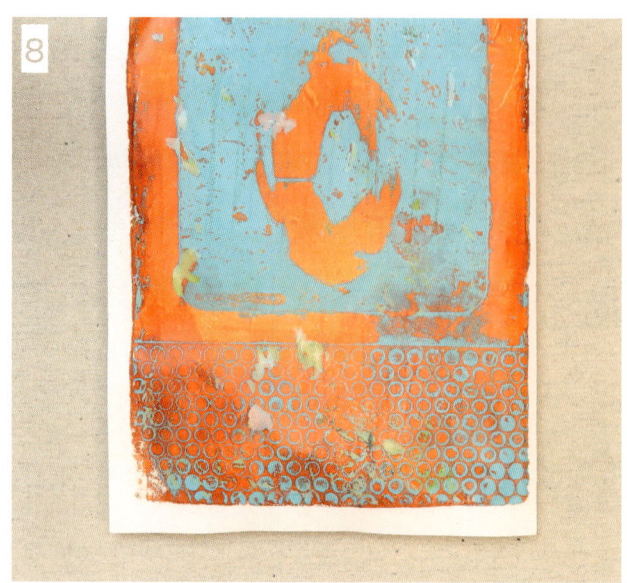

Using the Stencil as a Negative Imprint

After you pull your positive print, allow the paint to dry. Remove the stencil. What is left on the plate is considered the negative of that stencil. This can also be pulled off the plate as a print.

On another sheet of paper, you may want to see what this looks like. The trick here is to use a contrasting color. So if you had a dark color on the plate, you want to lay down a paint that is opposite or light.

Let's say you used black on the plate. You will want to put a white down to pull this print. If you had a white or light color down, you instead want to use a black or dark color to pull this print.

Once again you lay out a 1″ line of paint (over the dried paint from the negative print). Roll out an even layer of paint as above, lay your piece of paper down, and pull the print. This will give the negative of the stencil.

Play around with the negatives and positives of your stencils to see what they will do. Everything is an experiment when it comes to gel printing.

A third way you can use a stencil is by laying it directly on a gel print on which you've been building texture. Using a sponge, such as a makeup sponge, pick up paint and dab it onto your stencil directly. This method **1**–**7** is also creating a positive print.

Working with a Variety of Stencils

What you are trying to do is integrate your patterns as if you were weaving a tapestry. Altering the size and placement of your stencils, and overlapping different sizes and placements to break up the pattern, will give you something that is more interesting. Overlapping will ensure that you are touching on different parts of the print. You can do this with two different stencils or reuse the same one—just turn it in different directions or alter the placement.

If you are looking to break up a bold pattern, choose a stencil that has smaller repeat patterns, such as a series of holes, diamonds, or squares. It's important that they be small.

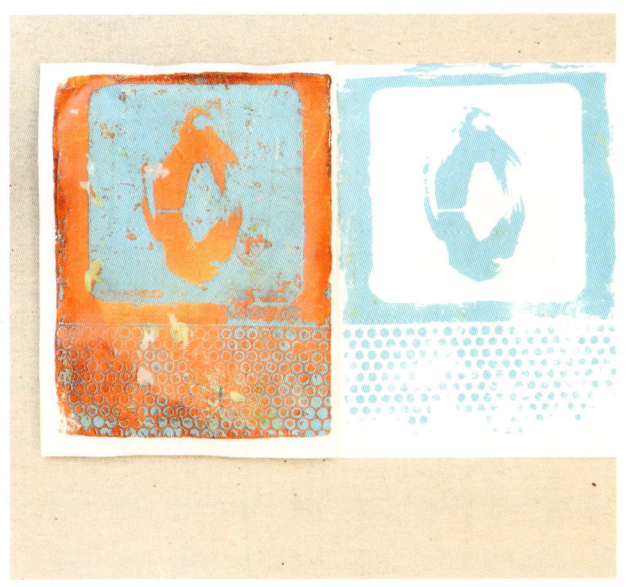

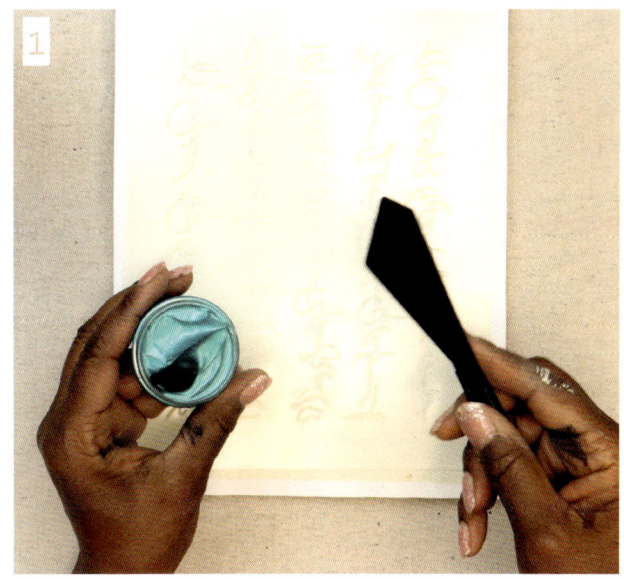

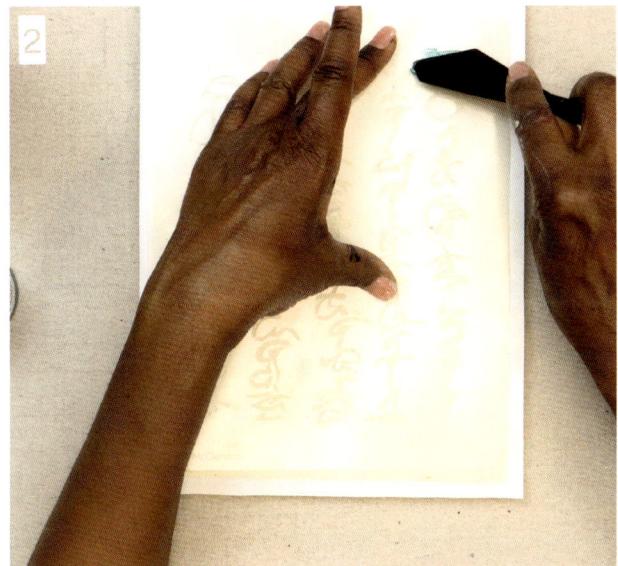

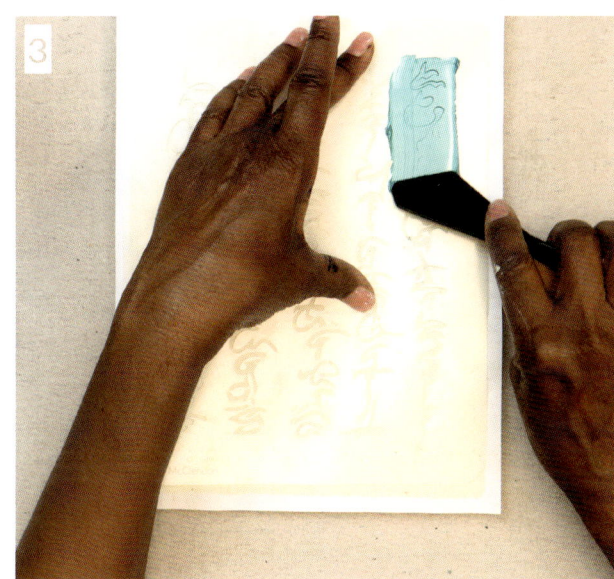

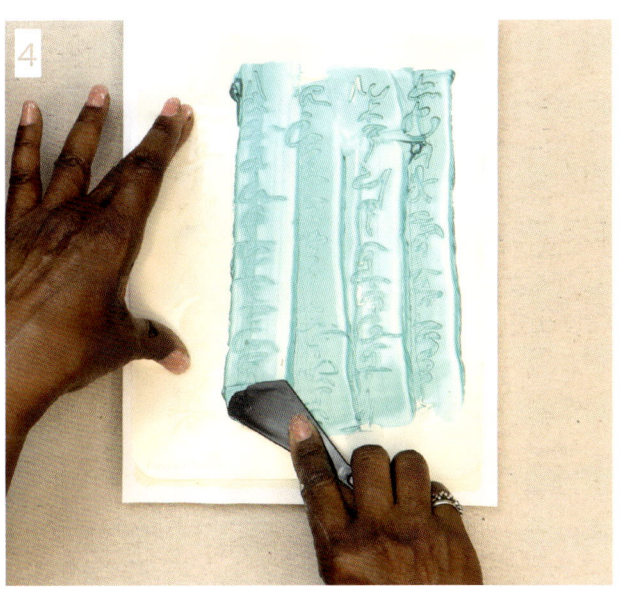

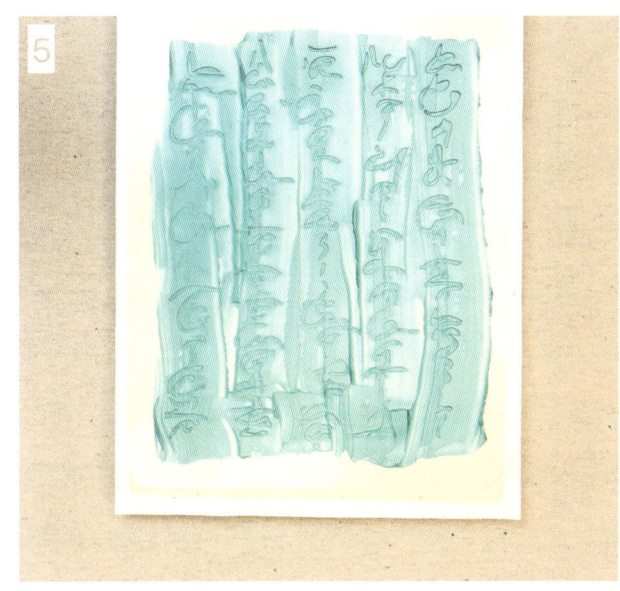

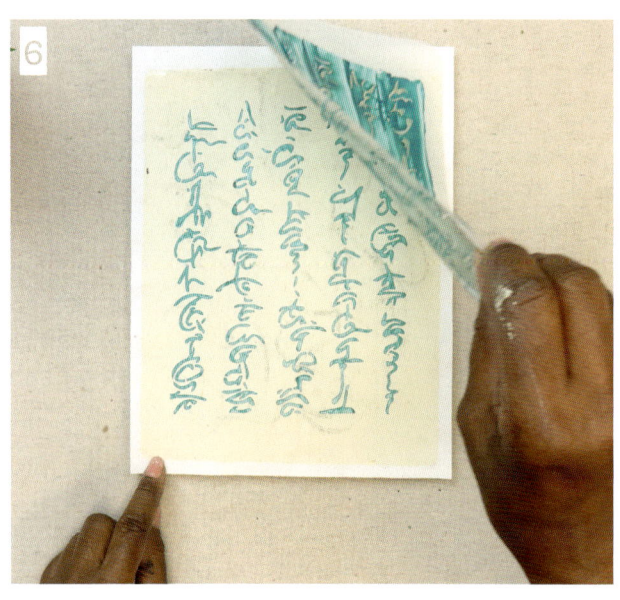

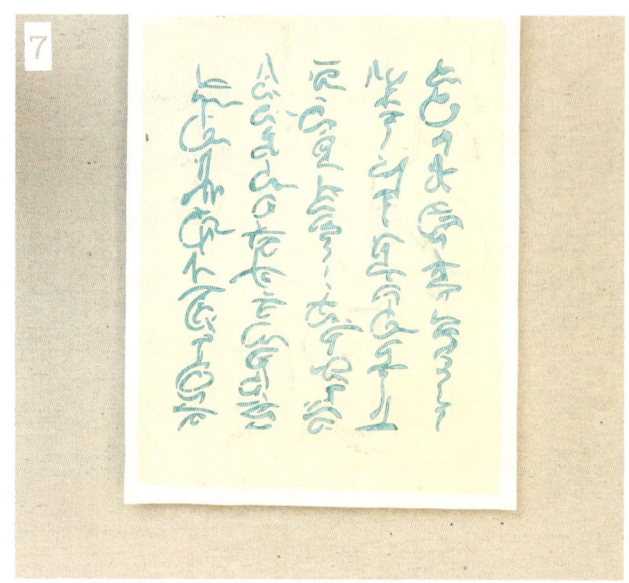

Patchwork Stenciling

It's easy to get used to seeing our tools in the same way as we use them time and again. Remember that you can use small parts of your stencil and stamps in interesting ways, as well as using the entire pattern. This is also a great chance to elevate throwaway sheets. Using the brayer, lay out any one color of paint evenly across the gel plate. Too much paint will give a thick base, and the pattern of the stencil will be lost. Stay fairly thin but with an even, moist coat.

Lay your stencils across the plate in overlapping layers. Allow some of the stencils to go off the plate, using only a portion of the pattern on the active plate.

ArtMythos Inspiration

I challenge you to create your own stencils. Use any disposable plastic (try a sheet protector or packaging or transparencies). Maybe cut a repeat pattern of circles, or squares. Perhaps cut out some shapes that intuitively come to you. You can even use hole punchers and other shape punchers. Just think outside the box. Make it simple. You will be surprised at how responsive the gel plate is to laying down these simple stencils and the effects that will come from using them.

You can make stencils of your own preferred images, those that you are inspired by, to begin infusing your prints with your own signature iconography.

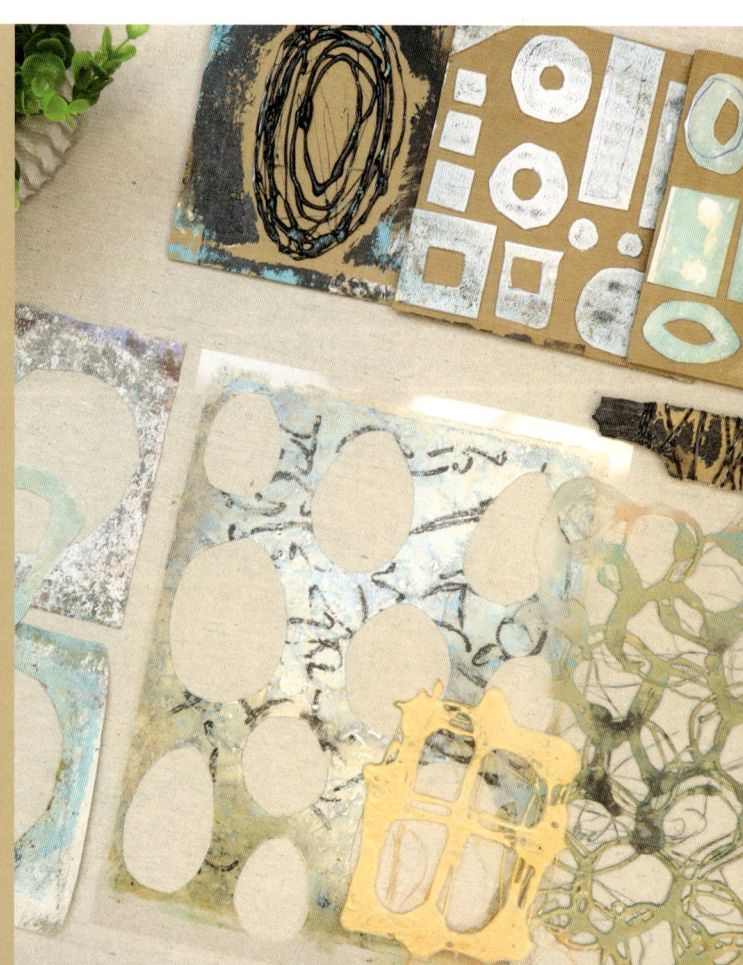

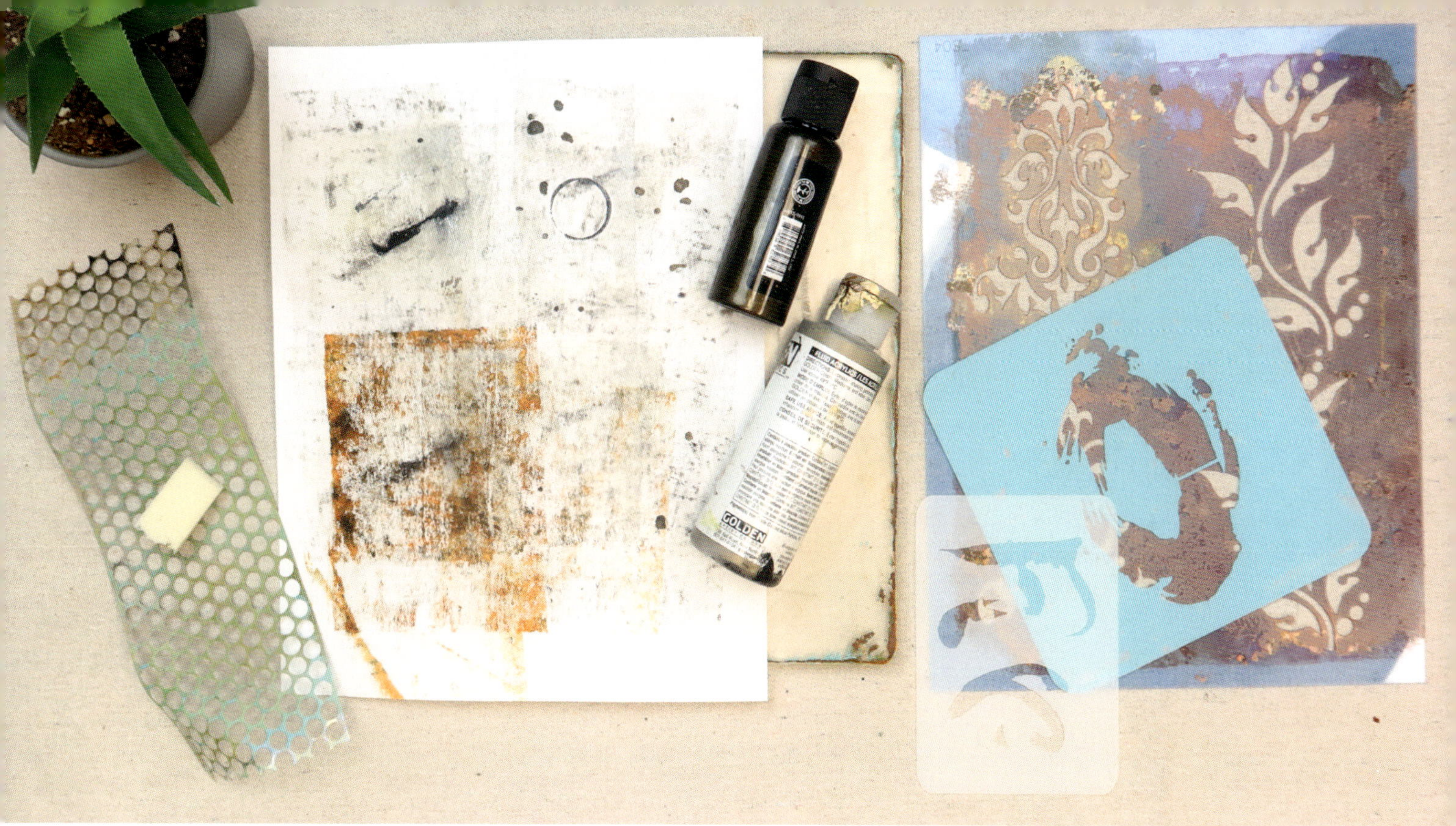

You can cover the whole plate with various patterned stencils or leave an open place where you can press in a stamp or pattern **1**–**8**.

I like to use waste paper to press across all the stencils, lifting paint from the spaces as possible to provide a more distinct pattern and interesting effects on the final print. But this is optional.

MATERIALS

Gel plate

Brayer

Acrylic paints, 2 or 3 colors

Stencils or stamps, 3 or 4

Scrap sheet from brayer cleaning

Printing papers

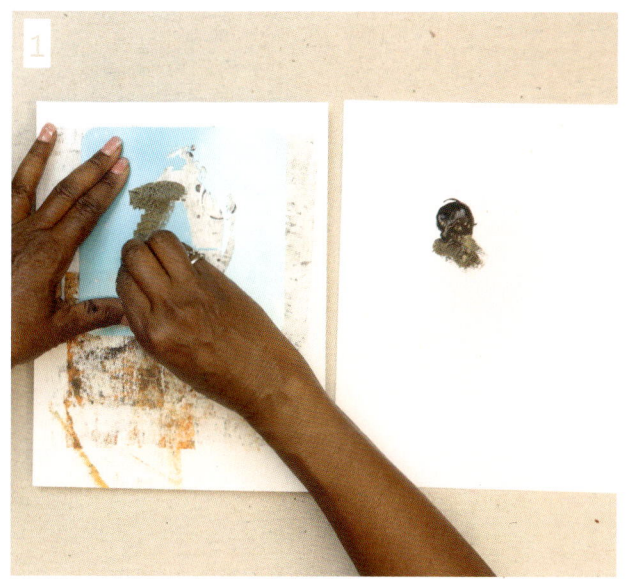

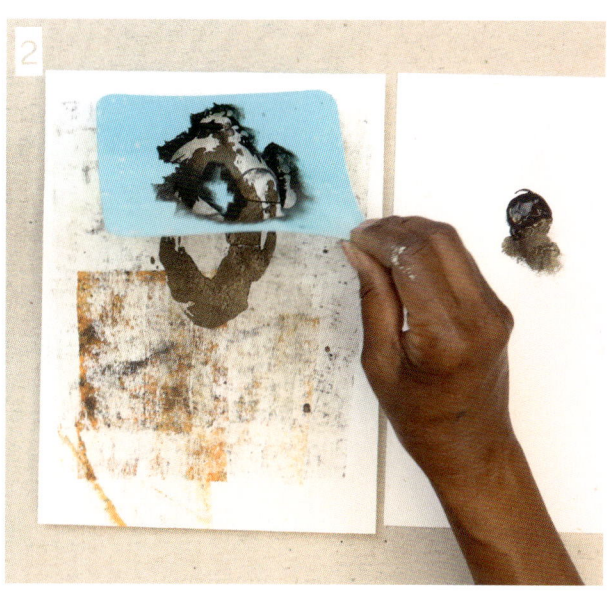

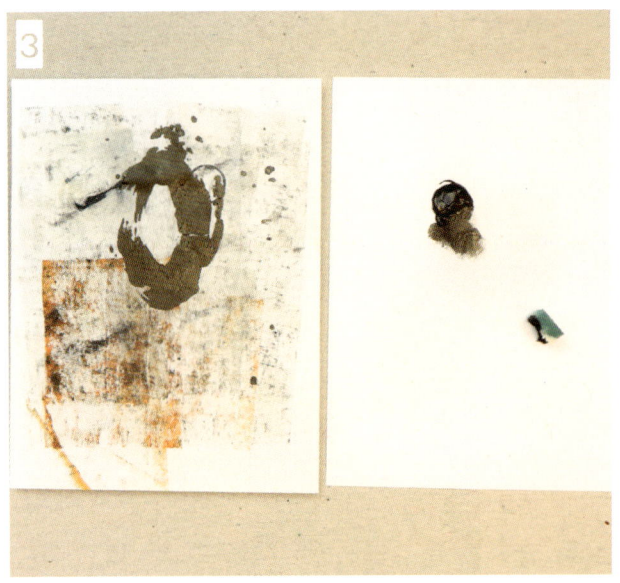

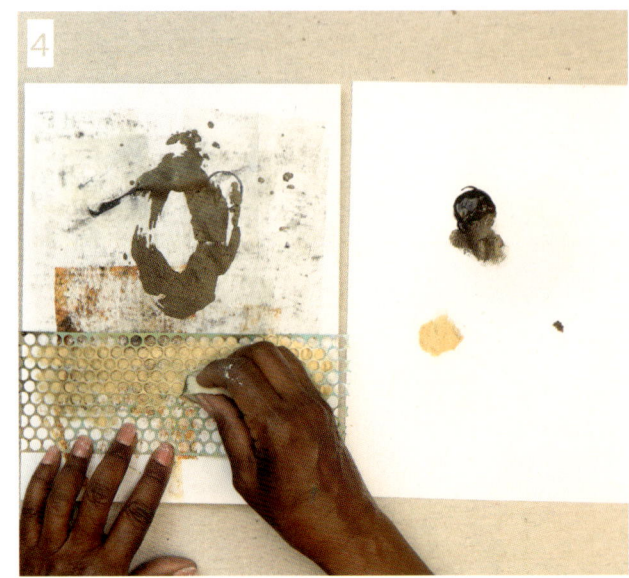

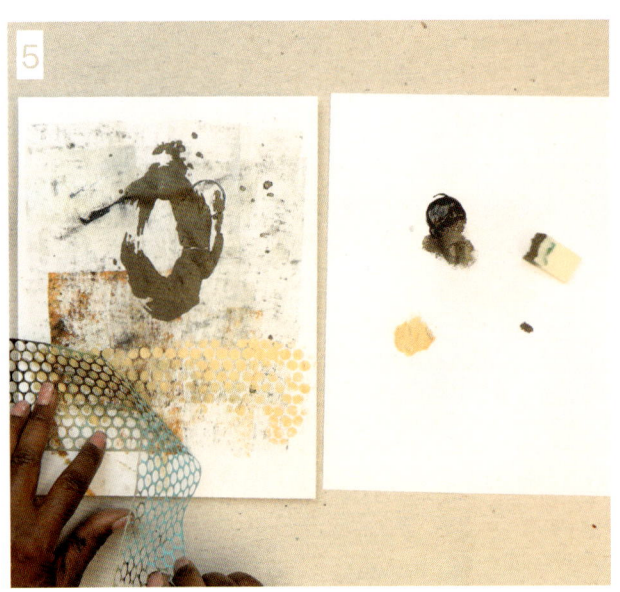

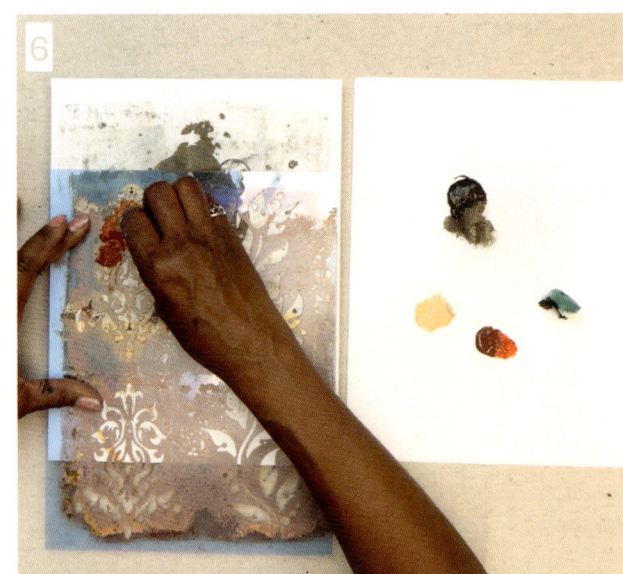

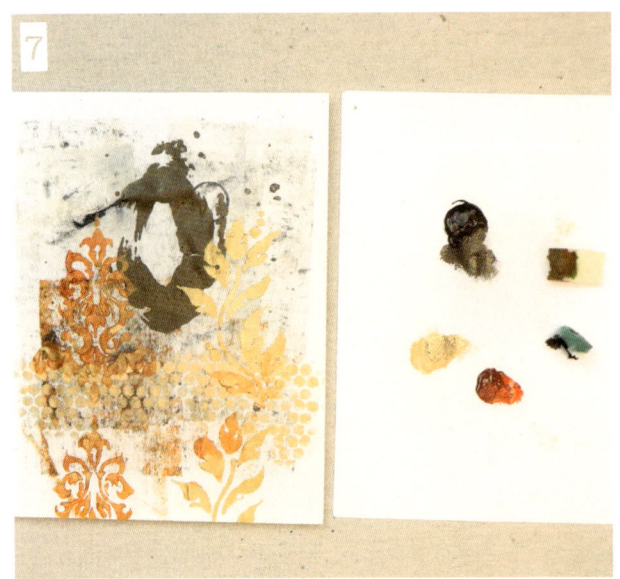

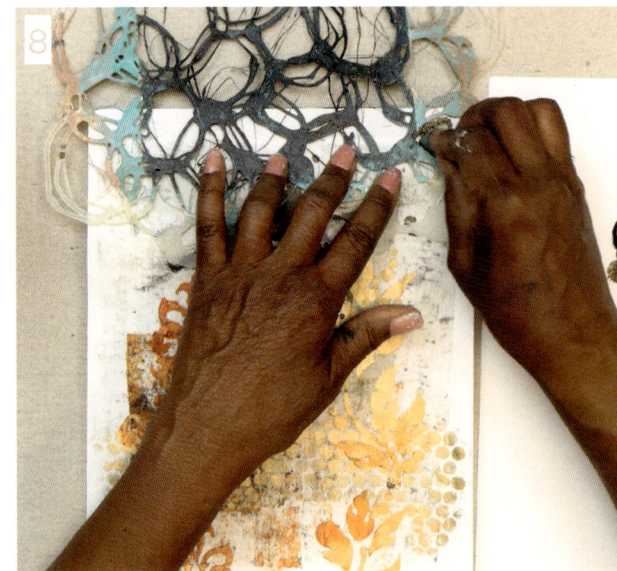

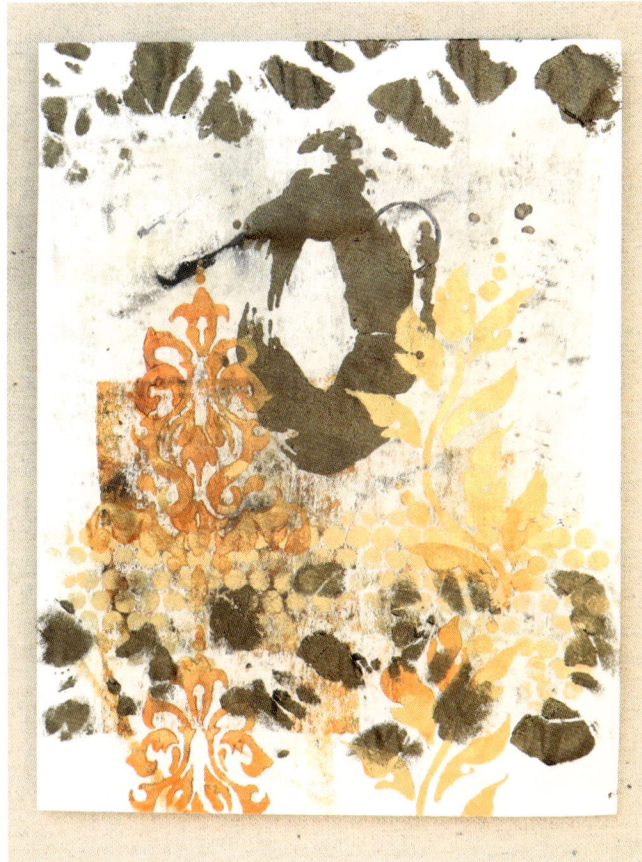

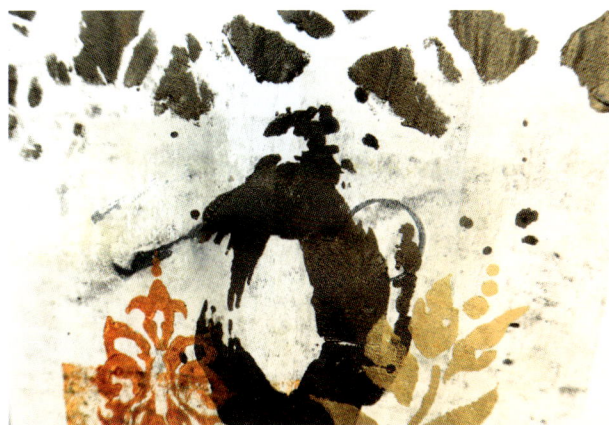

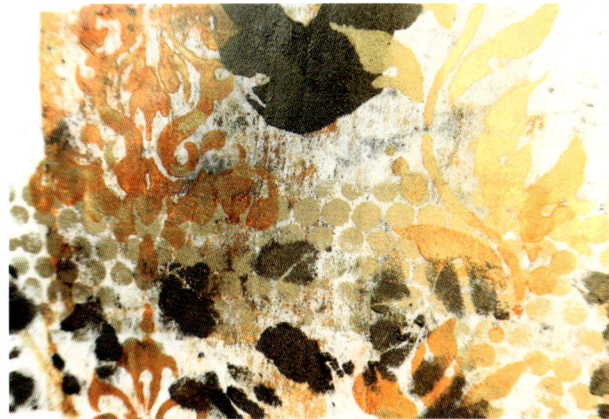

At this point a second layer of paint can be added and a quick print pulled from the top of the stencil patchwork while they're still in place on the plate.

Gently lift the several stencils, placing them on scrap paper to capture any designs.

Now place your paper gently across the plate, press firmly, and allow the warmth of your hands to infuse through the paper to the plate. Catch the edges. Peel up the patchwork print.

Lift a second print, if possible, or add another thin layer of paint in a contrasting color (cream or white can be interesting, and the opaqueness of the acrylic paint will adhere well to the remaining faint patterns on the plate) and pick up the whole thing, incorporating multiple layers of paint and texture.

Keep trying different variations of your patchwork patterning.

Don't be afraid to add layers to the prints you have already made, using only parts or interesting bits of larger stencils and choosing how to place these pattern pieces into your finished product.

Finding and Making Stencils

I see possible stencils everywhere I go. At resale shops or the dollar store, I find endless troves of ready-to-use fascinating patterns. Place mats, plastic tablecloths, sink liners, shelf paper, packaging backgrounds, cutout cards, sponges, lace pieces, old netting and curtains, fruit bags, corrugated cardboard, bubble wrap... these along with dozens of other materials create distinctive patterns. Many of these items I cut up into smaller pieces and use over and over again to make my own stencils and mark-making tools. When you begin looking for patterns, you will see possibilities everywhere.

In addition, you can cut your own patterns out of thin cardboard (think cereal boxes) or, as in the ArtMythos Inspiration earlier in this chapter, out of plastic sheet protectors. These and other fun office products are often available for very little at recycle centers or resale shops. Even cardboard stencils become quite tough and reusable after they acquire a few layers of acrylic paint and literally become plasticized.

Cleaning Stencils, a.k.a. Ethereal Washed-Out Prints

One of my favorite ways to clean my stencils is to lay them down on a clean sheet of paper or on top of a gel print that perhaps has only a background on it. Using baby wipes, begin to clean the stencil from the edges toward the center so that the paint is being pushed into the positive spaces of the stencil. This will create a very washed-out print: a fascinating ethereal, stained look. Sometimes the print will blur and have irregular undefined edges, which gives it a completely different look compared to pulling a crisp print from the stencil.

You can also use a soft cloth or a paper towel dampened with alcohol instead. The alcohol will move the paint onto the paper and create a bit of bleeding. Some of the results from this technique are amazing. It's a great way not to waste paint.

Once you have taken the opportunity to create these washed-out watercolory prints, lay your stencils in a shallow pan with water and Murphy's oil soap. Just let them sit and the oil soap will dissolve whatever paint is left, leaving the stencils nice and clean. Leave them to air-dry and then you can begin again.

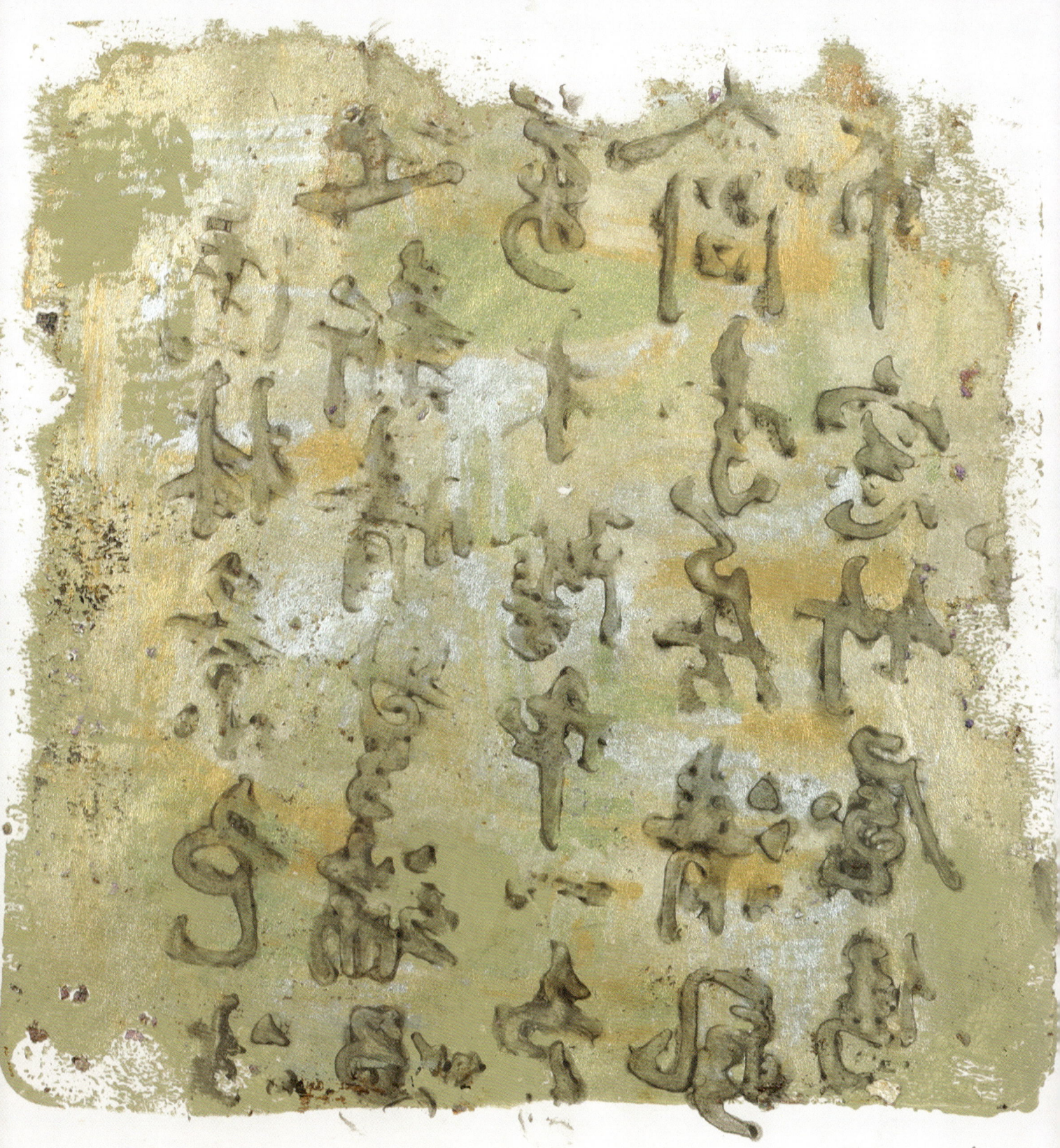

Cleaning a stencil on an "Old Wall" gel print

10

Making Washi Tape from Gel Prints

As artists, individuality is an important aspect of our work. Thanks to the gel plate, we can create some of our own supplies, items that many often purchase commercially and that result in look-alike creations. Washi tape, popular among artists and crafters of all kinds, can easily be re-created in original and endless patterns by using the gel plate.

Scor-Tape is a high-quality, double-sided, adhesive, acid-free, and heat-resistant tape originally designed for the scrapbooking community. It is perfect for this technique and is available in several widths, from ¼" strips to 1" and even 2" rolls. For making washi tape, widths of ¾" and ½" are good since they closely mimic the sizes of washi tape.

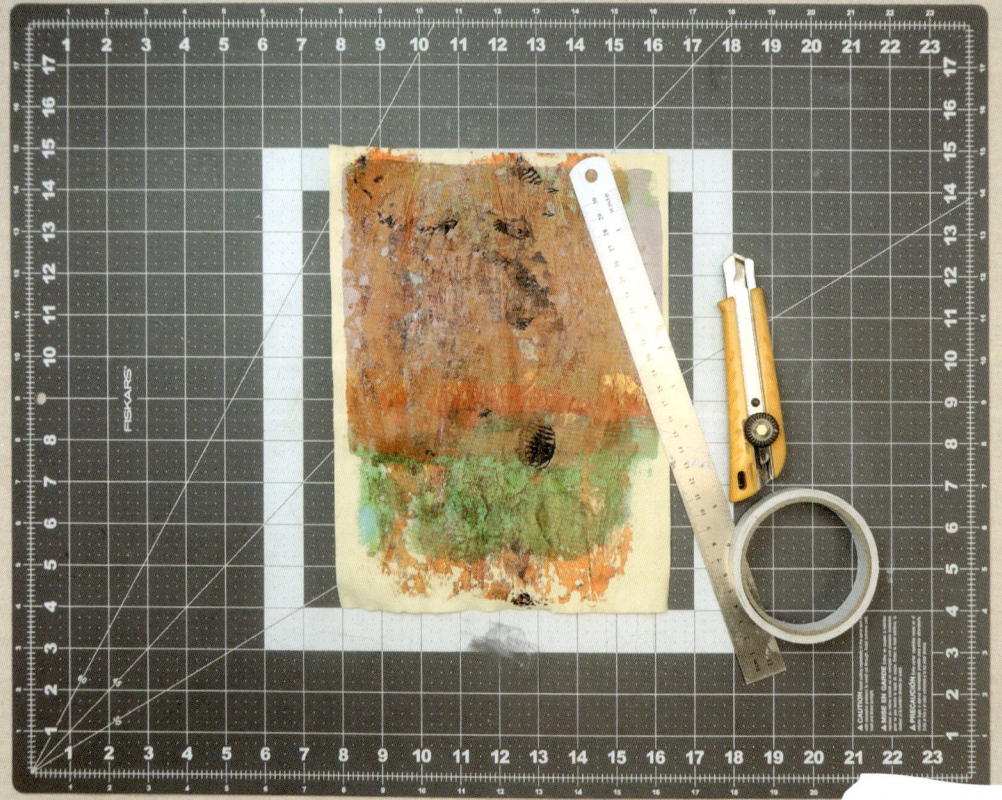

MATERIALS

Gel plate

Scor-Tape or any similar double-sided tape

X-acto knife or other cutting tools such as a rotary paper trimmer

Metal-edge ruler

Self-healing cutting mat

Prepared gel prints and other specialty papers

For a video of this technique, visit robynmcclendon.com.

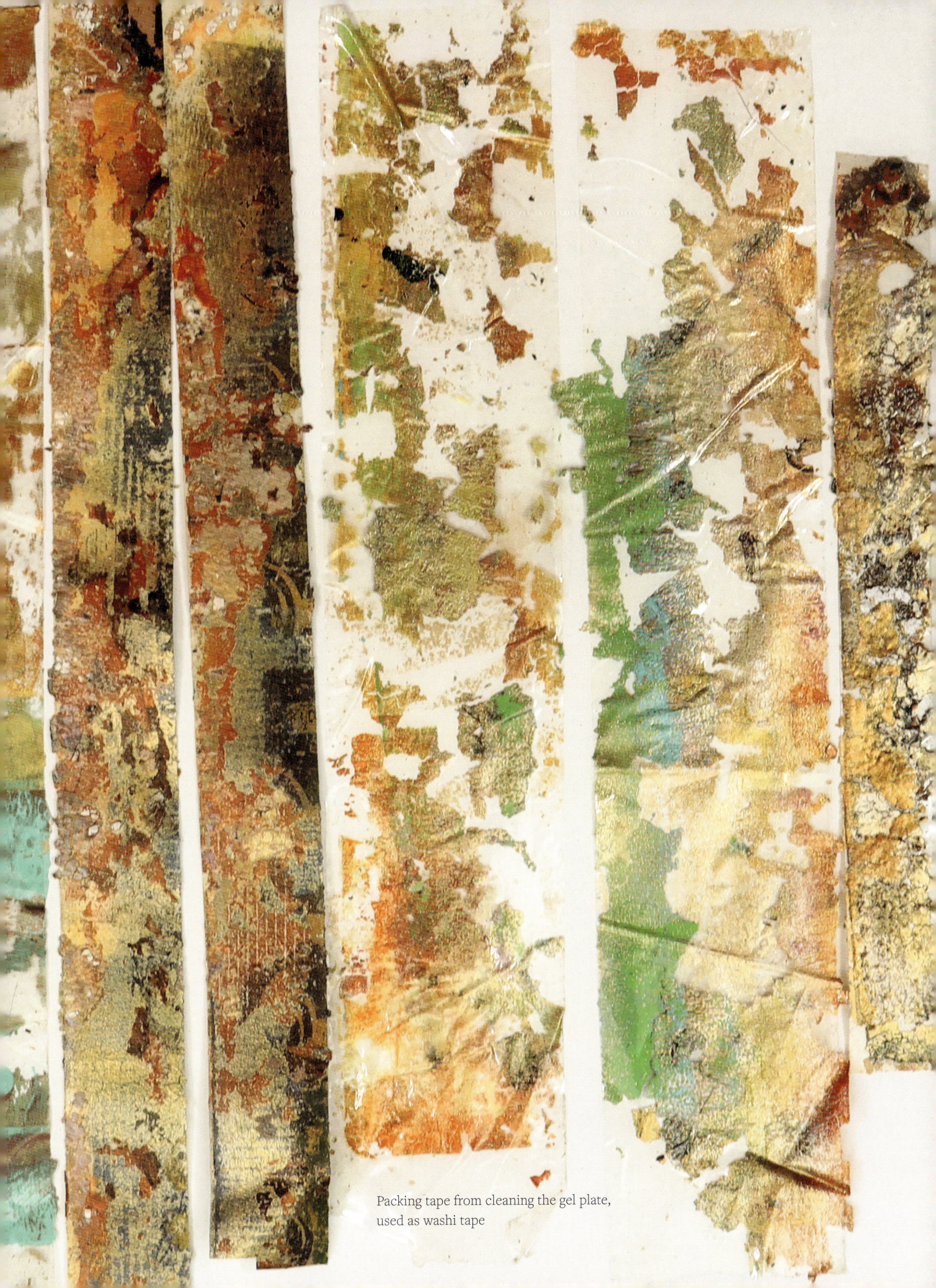

Packing tape from cleaning the gel plate,
used as washi tape

There are several questions you can answer while you're selecting and creating gel prints for your washi tape. How will pattern size translate onto ¾″ strips? How are colors repeating across your gel print? Would you like to have more texture on your strips? You may not yet have answers to some of these questions, but thinking about them as you work will add value to your printing process and usher in the magic of discovery.

You can use various kinds of paper, including very thin tissue paper. I typically use photo copier paper, vellums, glassine, and machine- and handmade papers with cotton content. One paper that works particularly well is Japanese sumi ink paper, which is used in Japanese calligraphy. This traditional paper is long fibered. It is in the same family of papers that is used to create washi tape, thus making it perfect for our project!

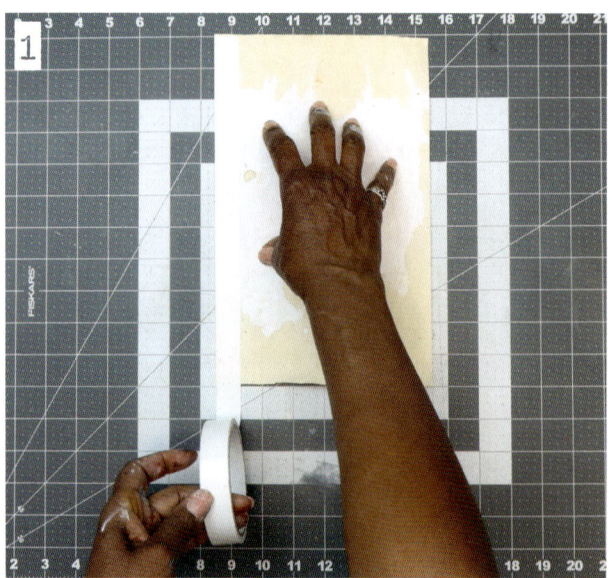

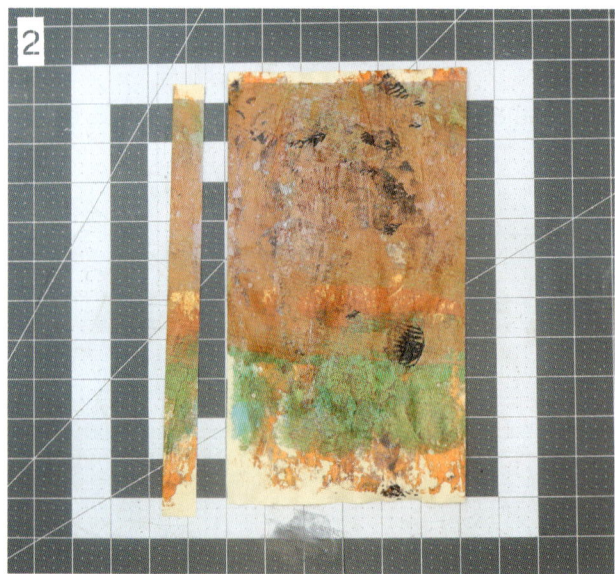

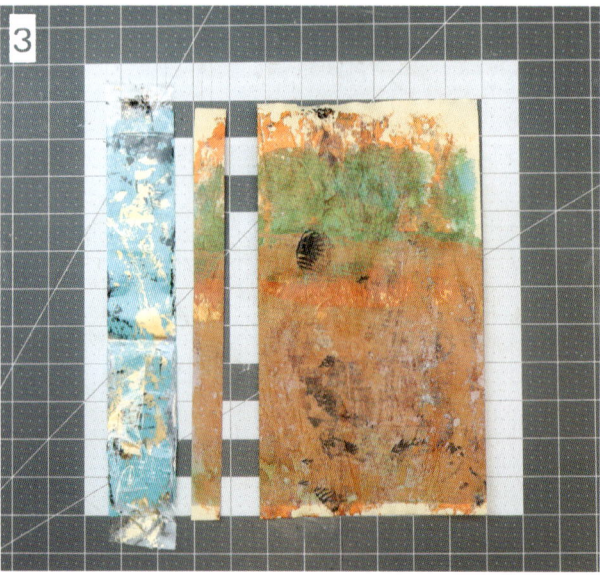

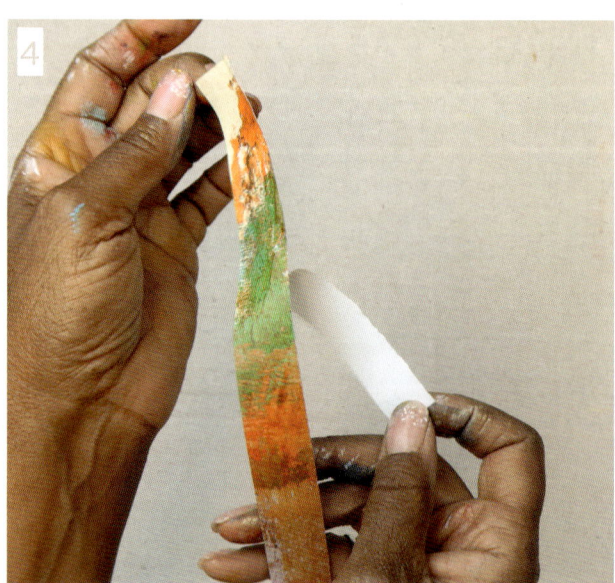

Bring your selected papers together into a stack. Then TURN THE ENTIRE STACK UPSIDE DOWN. You will be applying the sticky Scor-Tape to the BACKSIDE of your prints.

Unroll your Scor-Tape, laying the sticky side down in neat rows on the backside of your prints **1** (left). It is important to lay each strip out straight in successive rows. You'll find it is best to keep the strips very close together, so that later you don't have as much trimming to do. Don't worry if they end up at somewhat of an angle—the finished strips will work beautifully in your art. You will have a collection of elements that you will be able to pull from for future projects.

Put the papers on a cutting surface, such as a self-healing cutting mat. Work on the backside of the papers. Lay down a metal ruler to guide you, and cut along the edge of the Scor-Tape. This will leave you with strips of paper displaying gel prints on one side and the plastic backing of the Scor-Tape on the other side **2**–**4**.

You now have fabulous washi tape patterned with your own designs! Use it by removing the backing strip to reveal the adhesive strip. The washi tapes can be stored until you are ready to use them in your art.

When you have a completely dry plate containing some paint, it's an opportunity for another washi tape making method. You will need a good-quality, clear packing tape **1** (below). Lay the tape down on the plate **2**, burnish it with your hands or a credit card so it is making good contact, and then remove the packing tape **3**. The paint will come along with it.

Try putting the same strip down repeatedly to capture more information from the plate **4**, **5**. You can add some new paint **6**, perhaps brush it out **7**, then reapply the tape strip **8**.

The tape strips can then be used to create a washi tape of sorts by laying them on double-sided tape as above, or they can be laid directly onto a collage or used as a collage medium. You can also cut shapes out of the tape for use as collage pieces. 🎨

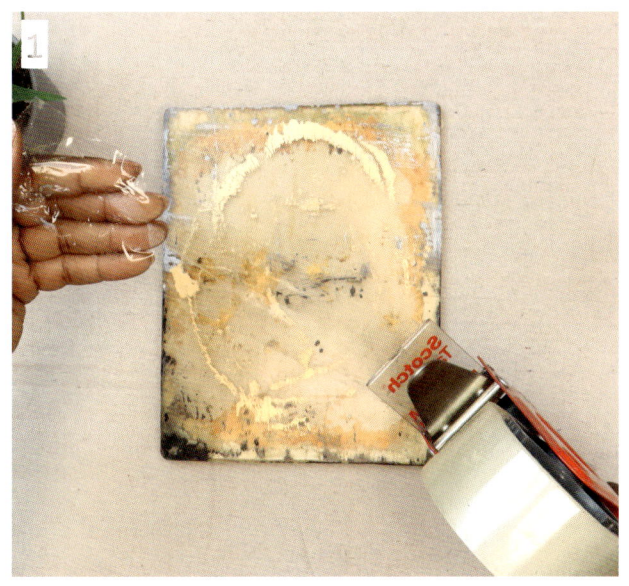

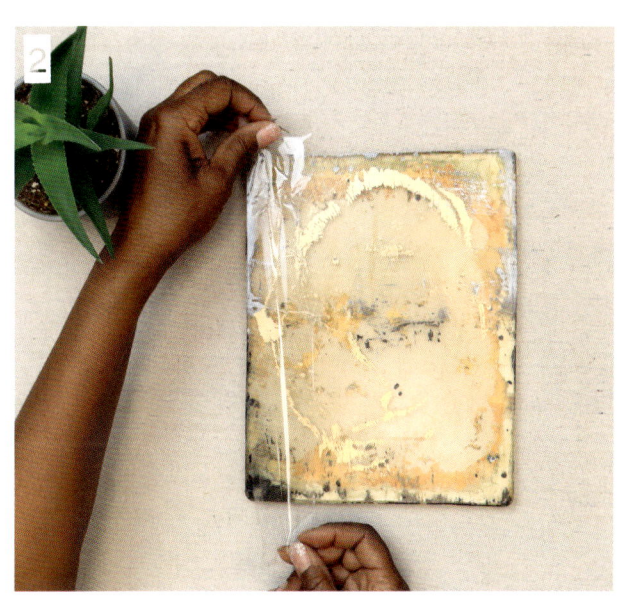

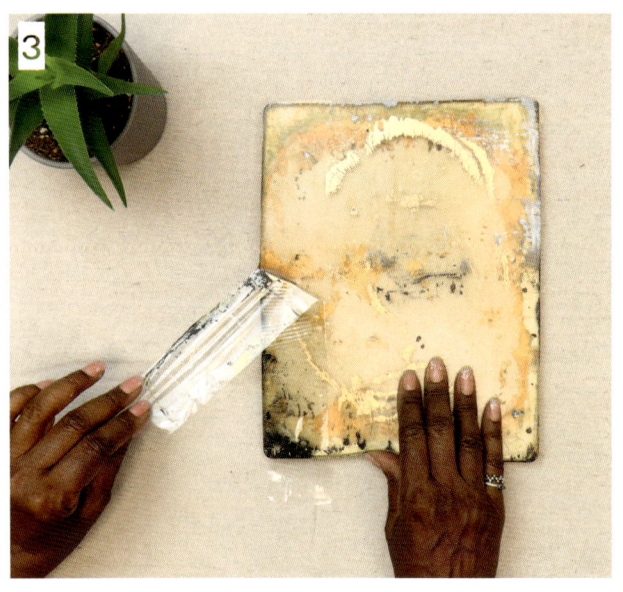

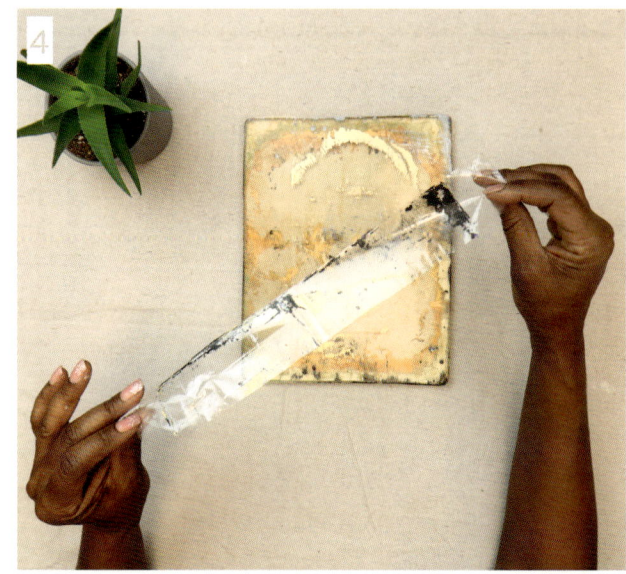

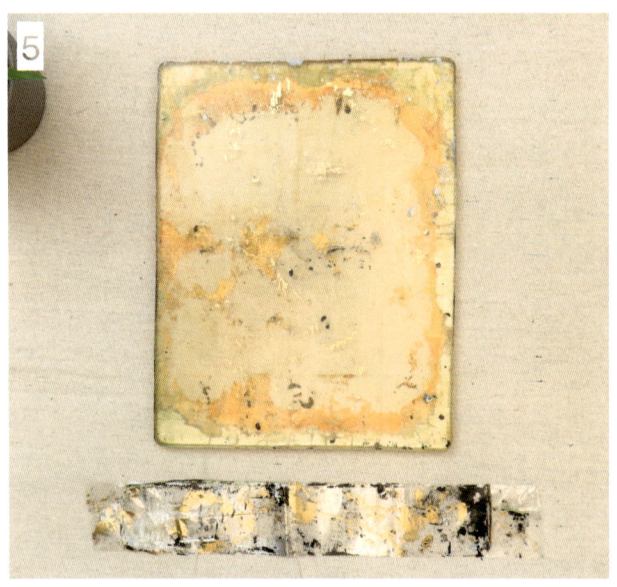

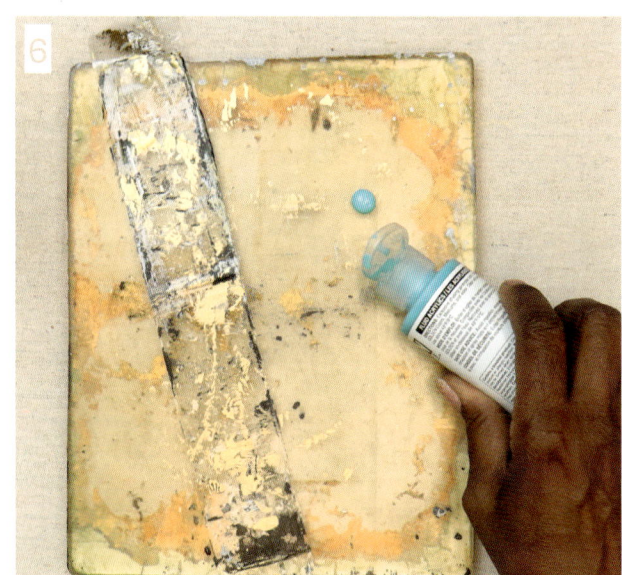

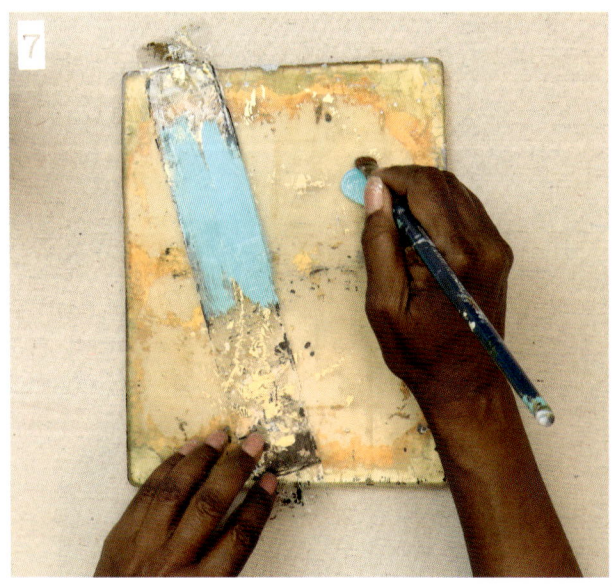

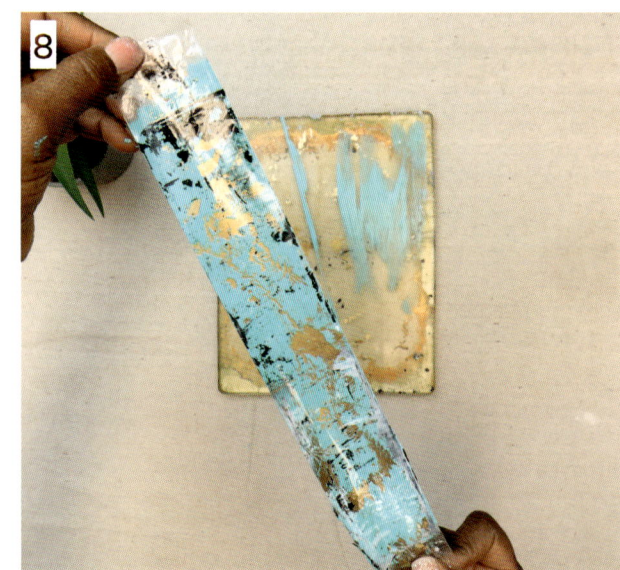

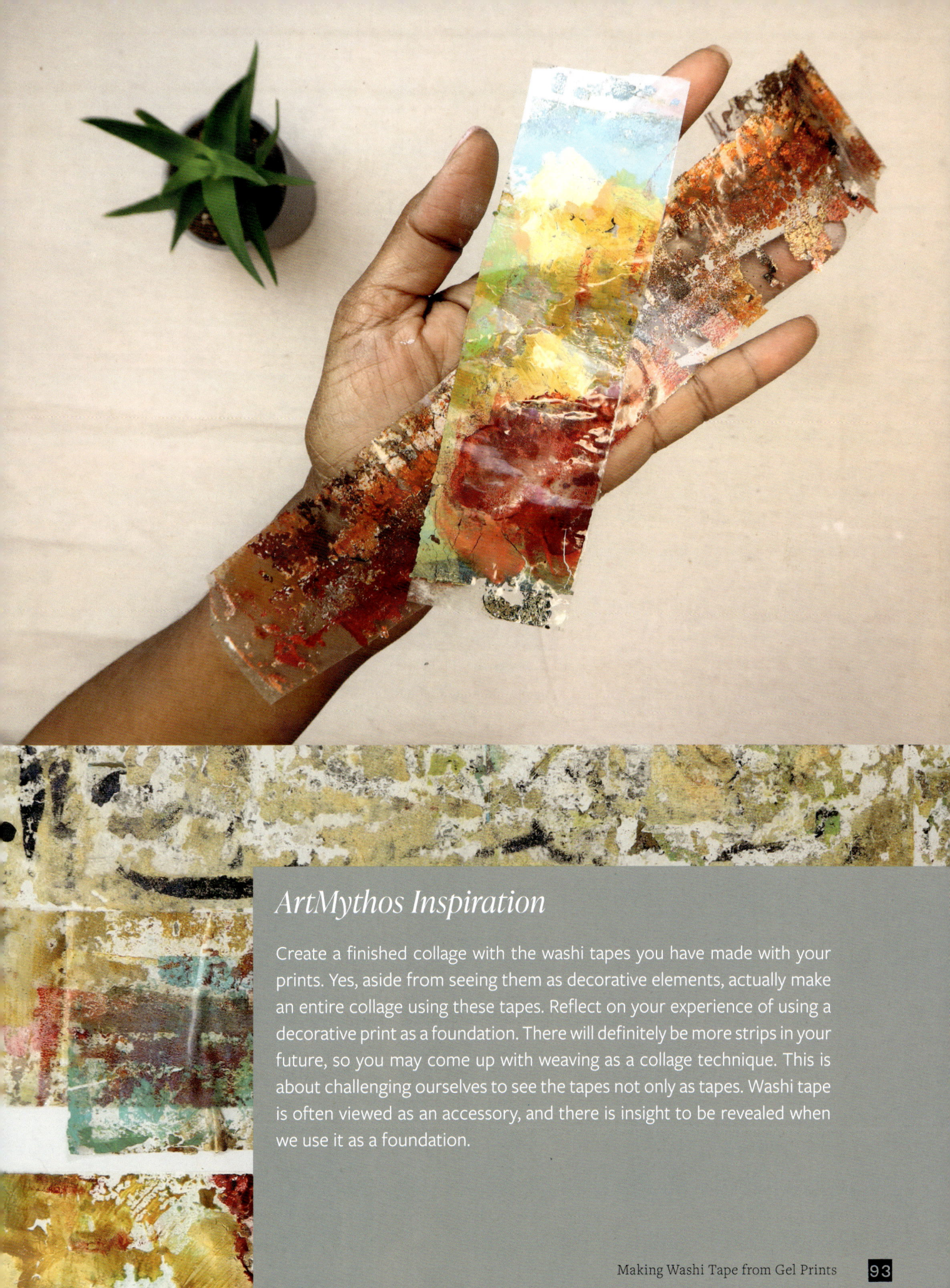

ArtMythos Inspiration

Create a finished collage with the washi tapes you have made with your prints. Yes, aside from seeing them as decorative elements, actually make an entire collage using these tapes. Reflect on your experience of using a decorative print as a foundation. There will definitely be more strips in your future, so you may come up with weaving as a collage technique. This is about challenging ourselves to see the tapes not only as tapes. Washi tape is often viewed as an accessory, and there is insight to be revealed when we use it as a foundation.

11

"Venetian Plaster" Technique

How did I come up with the name for this technique? Venetian plaster and Fortuny silks. Fortuny was a fabric designer who manufactured the most-incredible silks. He was known for his technique, and nobody has been able to truly duplicate it.

Once when I was in my studio, I was working with spray inks, distress inks, and chalk paint on the gel plate. This combination really started reminding me of Fortuny-like textures and colors. When I thought about these subtle, chalky, ethereal colors and finishes, I was reminded of old Venetian palazzos; hence the name.

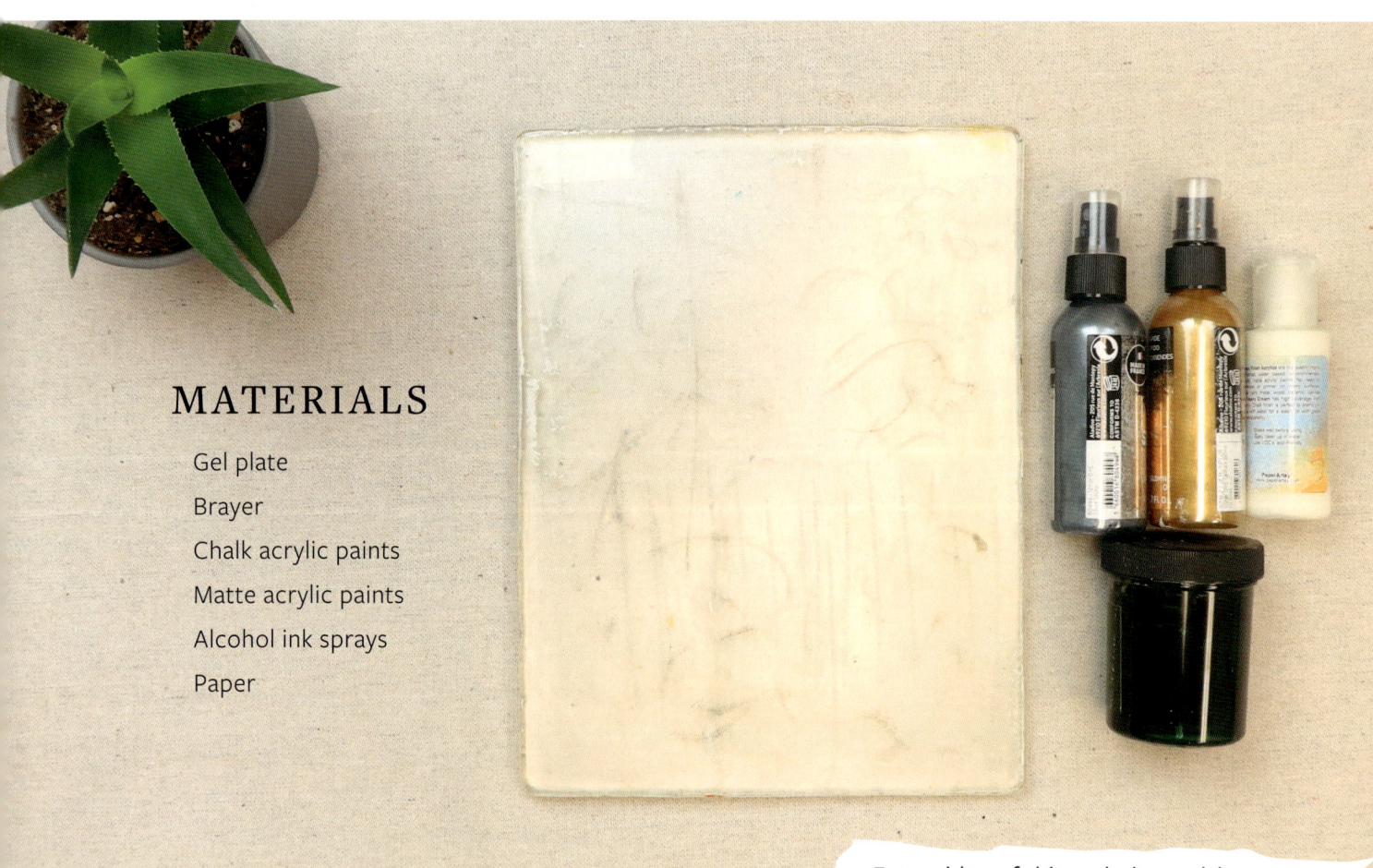

MATERIALS

Gel plate

Brayer

Chalk acrylic paints

Matte acrylic paints

Alcohol ink sprays

Paper

Right: "Venetian plaster" technique in turquoise

For a video of this technique, visit robynmcclendon.com.

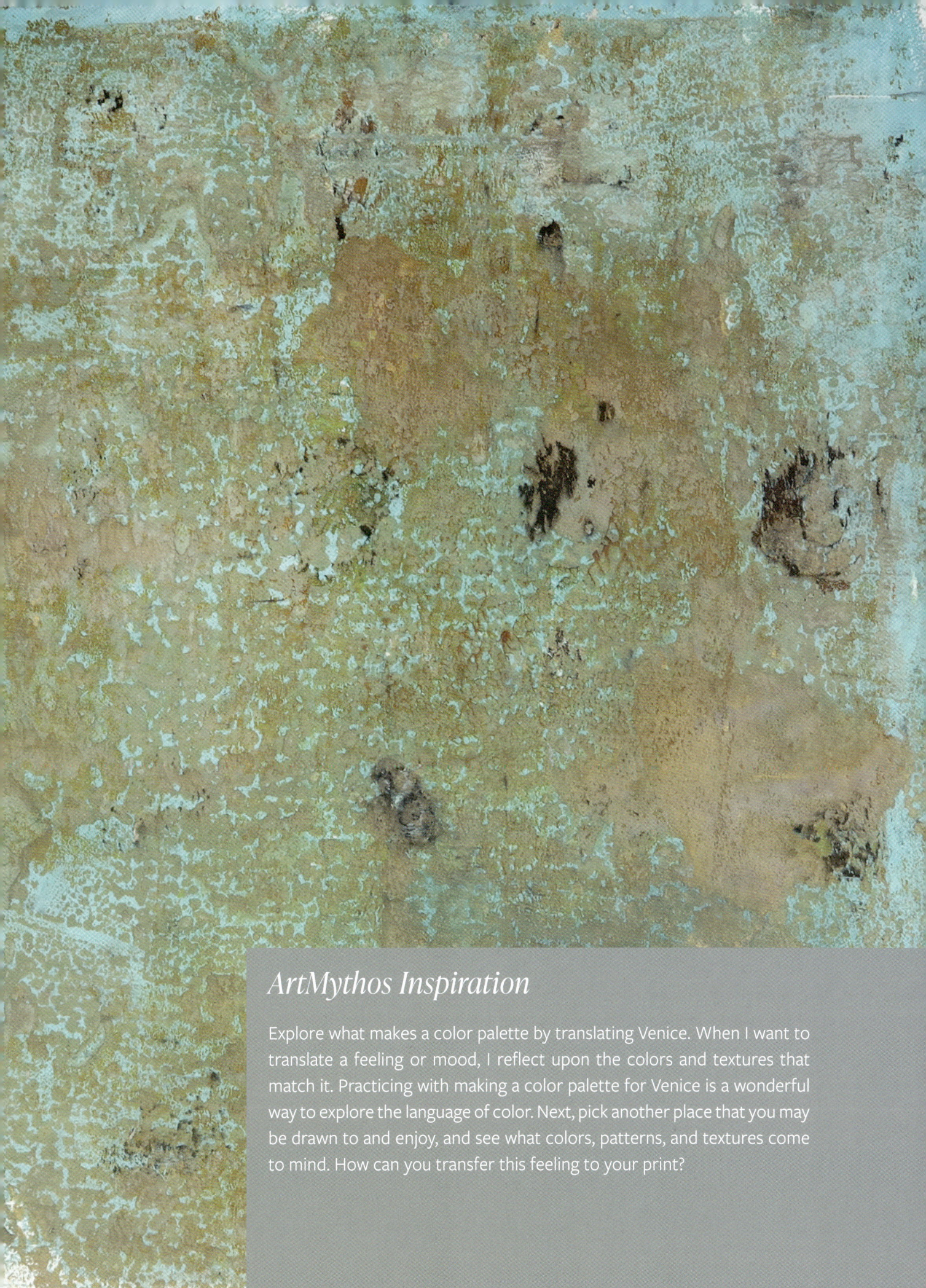

ArtMythos Inspiration

Explore what makes a color palette by translating Venice. When I want to translate a feeling or mood, I reflect upon the colors and textures that match it. Practicing with making a color palette for Venice is a wonderful way to explore the language of color. Next, pick another place that you may be drawn to and enjoy, and see what colors, patterns, and textures come to mind. How can you transfer this feeling to your print?

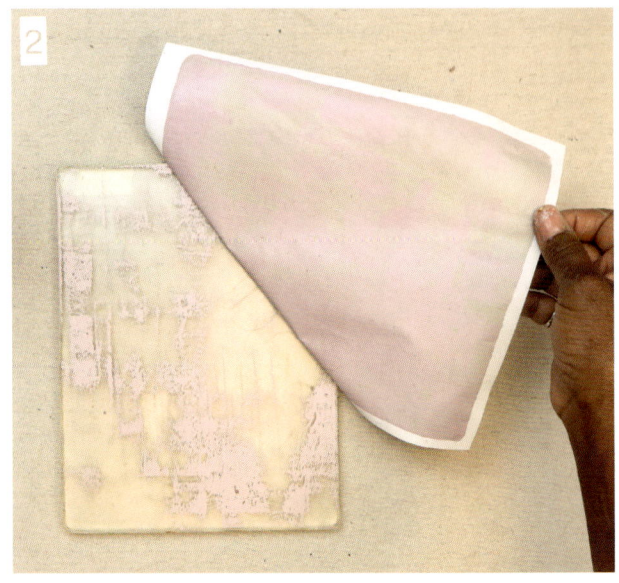

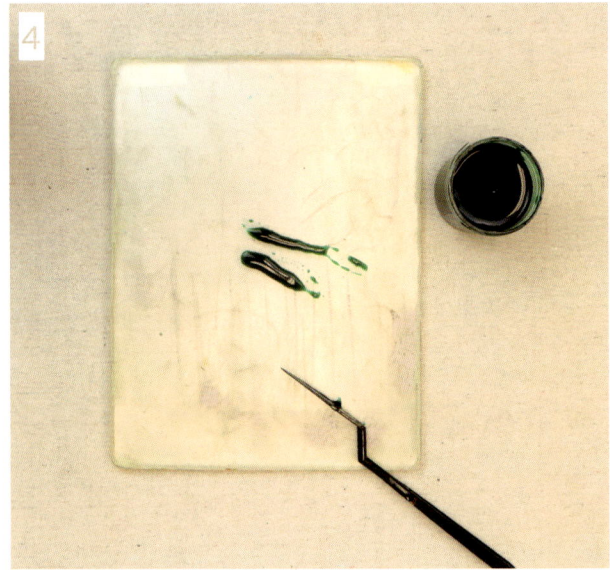

For this technique you will need a selection of chalk and matte paints. Choose one color, roll it out on the plate, and pull this one-color background. Repeat this process for several more prints **1**–**3**.

Patricia Viramontes has her own finish that I have used in this technique, and it works beautifully. Her product is called Stainz, and its consistency is similar to a syrup. I put a little of it on the plate and sometimes mix it with a "distress ink" (this is what Tim Holtz calls his products of this type). A distress ink gives an aged look, one that is different from alcohol inks.

Once you have pulled a number of these **4**–**7**, spray the gel plate with metallic alcohol inks (such as Seth Apter's gold Izink) **8**. I sometimes brayer out the alcohol ink a bit. It will puddle and retract, of course—it won't lie flat on the plate. Then, take one of your dried prints and lay it back on the plate. Pull your print **9** and notice this Venetian plaster / Fortuny look. You can do a combination of alcohol inks and distress inks.

Any kind of alcohol spritz is worth experimenting with here. But NO acrylic glossy paint for this technique. You want to use a matte acrylic or a chalk paint acrylic because it creates that chalky plaster-like finish, and it absorbs the alcohol inks nicely.

As a final step I spray the plate with a gold or bronze—anything metallic—alcohol ink.

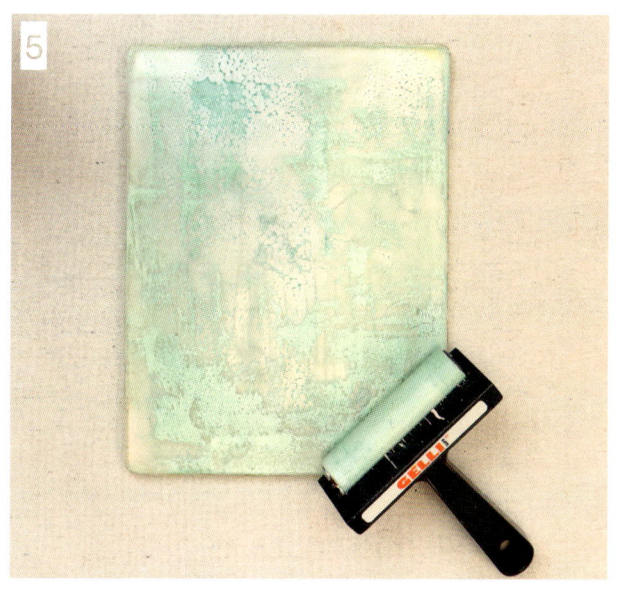

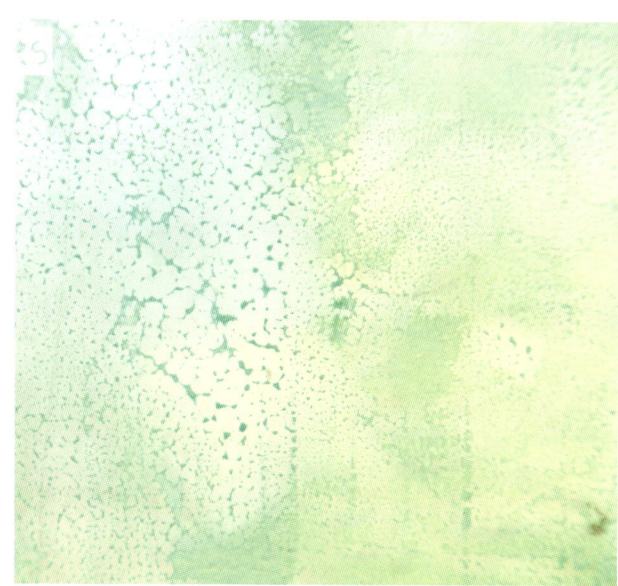

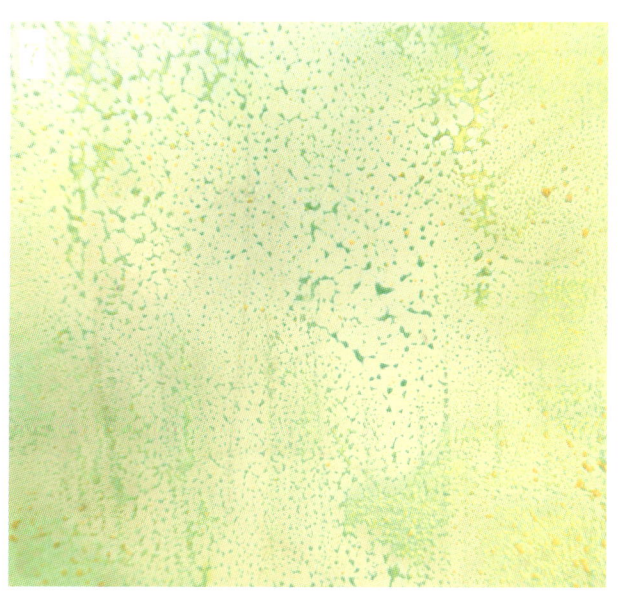

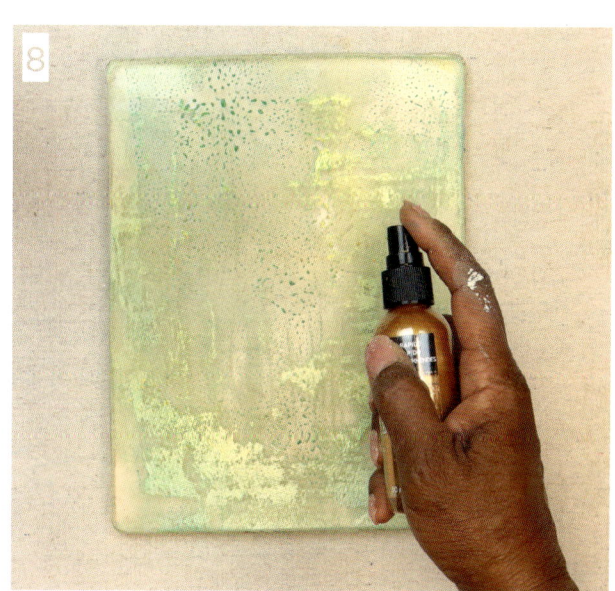

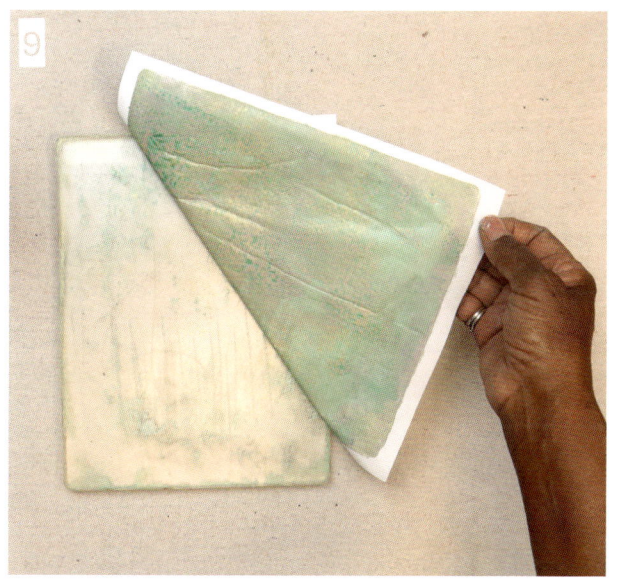

12

Watercolor + Alcohol with Stain Sprays on the Gel Plate

You will often hear it said that you can't use watercolor or alcohol inks or anything water based on the gel plate. Well, that's just not so! What you get when you use various mediums on the gel plate outside of the traditional acrylic paints is simply different effects. In the case of watercolor or any water-based, very loose, flowing mediums, the results are active patterns with distinct shapes and textures on the plate. The images created are organic and very unpredictable, creating an element of surprise.

My principle of layering is definitely in full effect here, because we can work on base layers of acrylic, chalk paints, and matte mediums and then layer with the watercolor and spray stains on top. This creates amazing patterns and decorative papers.

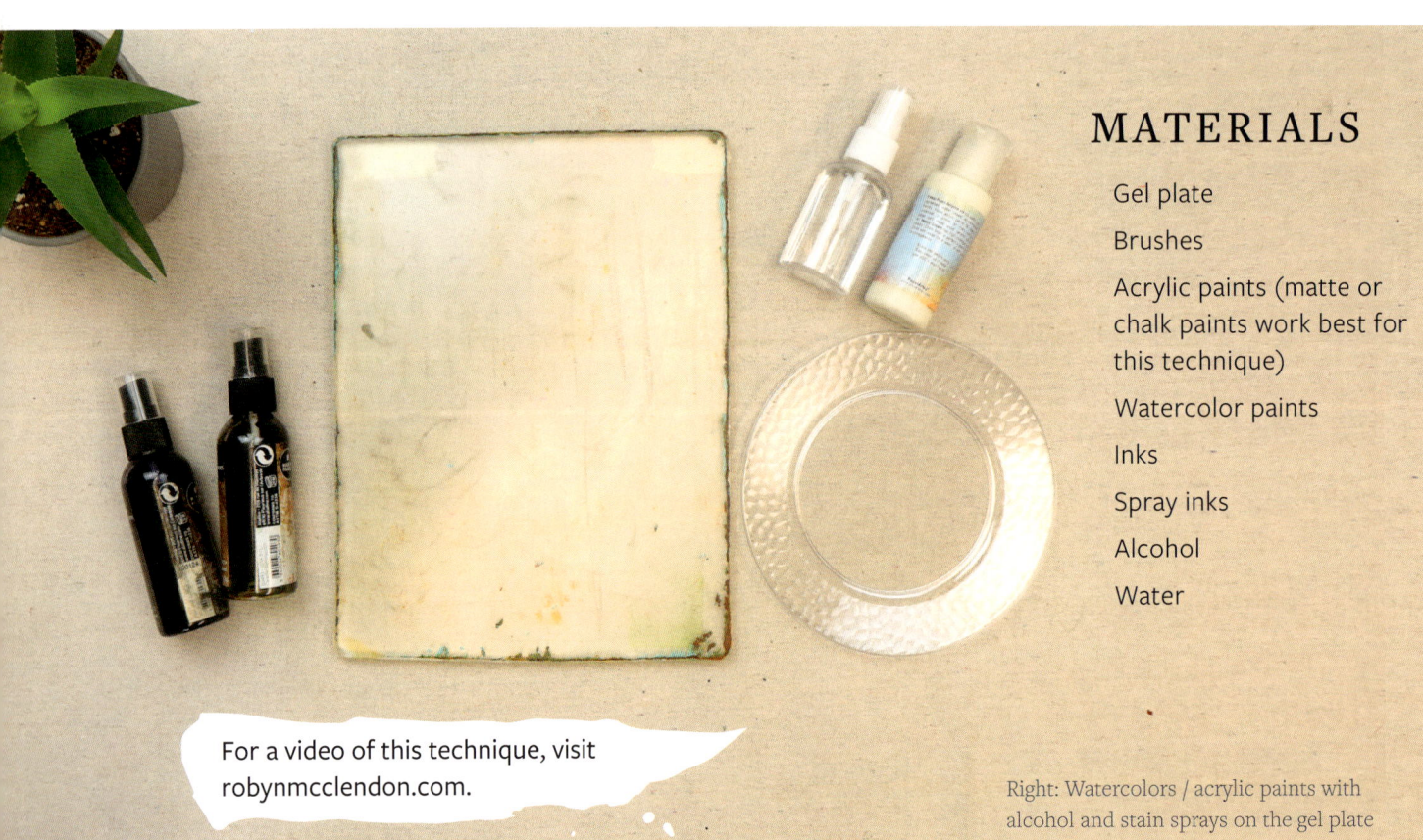

MATERIALS

Gel plate

Brushes

Acrylic paints (matte or chalk paints work best for this technique)

Watercolor paints

Inks

Spray inks

Alcohol

Water

For a video of this technique, visit robynmcclendon.com.

Right: Watercolors / acrylic paints with alcohol and stain sprays on the gel plate

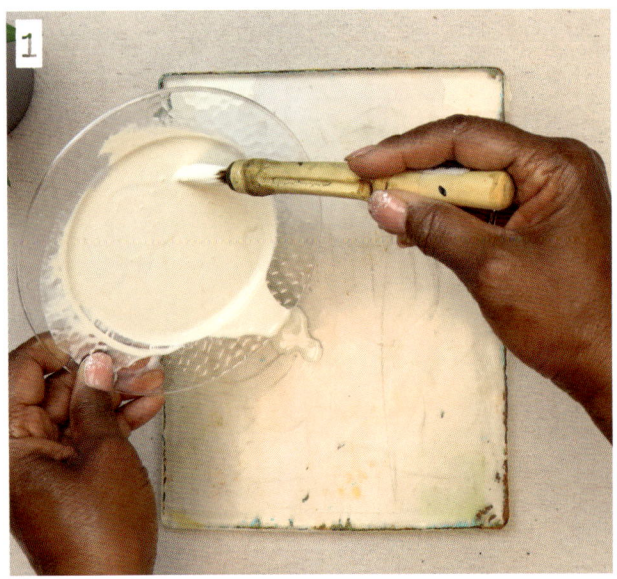

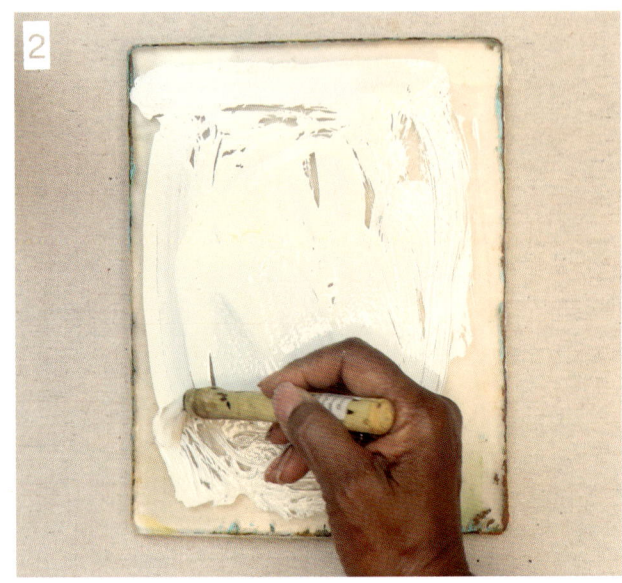

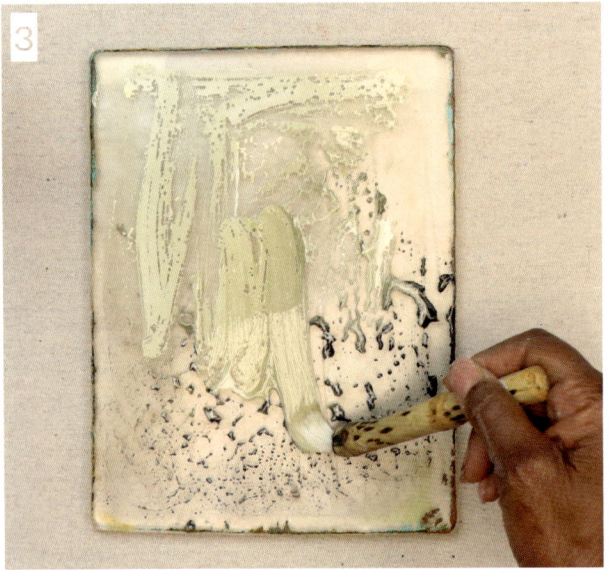

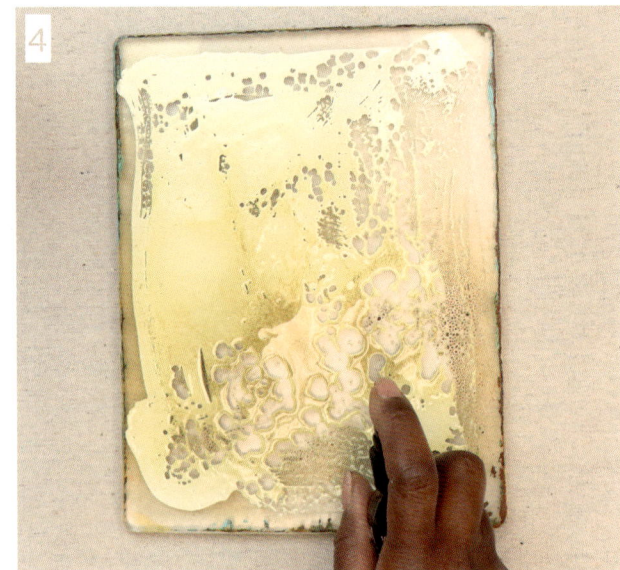

This technique creates a washed, pebbly stone pattern effect. It is fluid, ethereal, and watercolor-like. The areas that you spray, in particular, will create a stone pattern. The technique is very dense in texture. I love to use it to create backgrounds for my collages. Try this technique on tissue paper and use those prints as collage material along with other ephemera.

Take a mixture of acrylic paint that has been very watered down with alcohol. It's best to use a matte acrylic or chalk paint. The ratio is anywhere from 75% paint to 25% alcohol, up to 50/50. Before you start mixing, put a few drops of water in your acrylic paint **1** to begin loosening it up. This breaks the binders

down in the paint so that when you add alcohol to it, it will continue to flow. Some paints have a tendency to clump if you pour alcohol straight into them.

Brush the solution onto the plate **2**, then move it around to create patterns. At this point you will notice that the paints will flow. Keep working **3** until you reach a visually pleasing pattern. Try having three colors already prepared in your color palette so you can create three different color fields.

Once everything is laid out, take the spray stains and spray them into the loose mixture on the plate **4**. You will start seeing the stone patterns right away. Place your paper down and pull the image **5**.

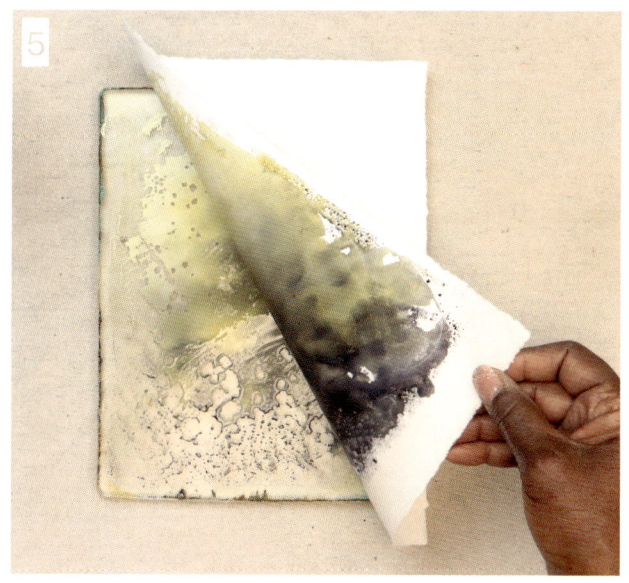

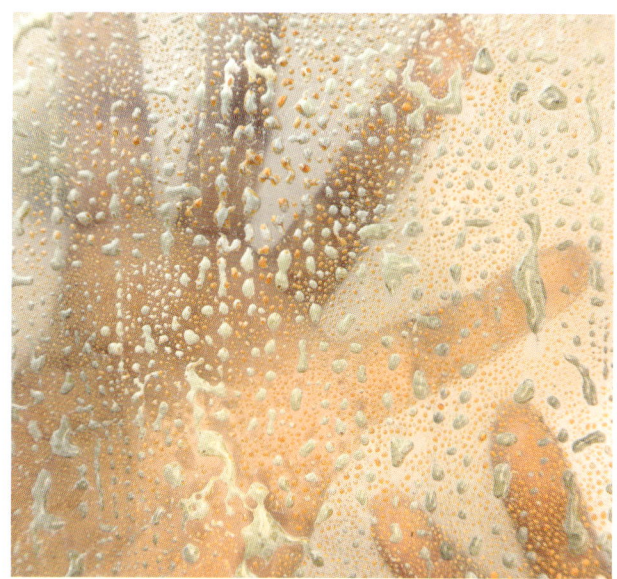

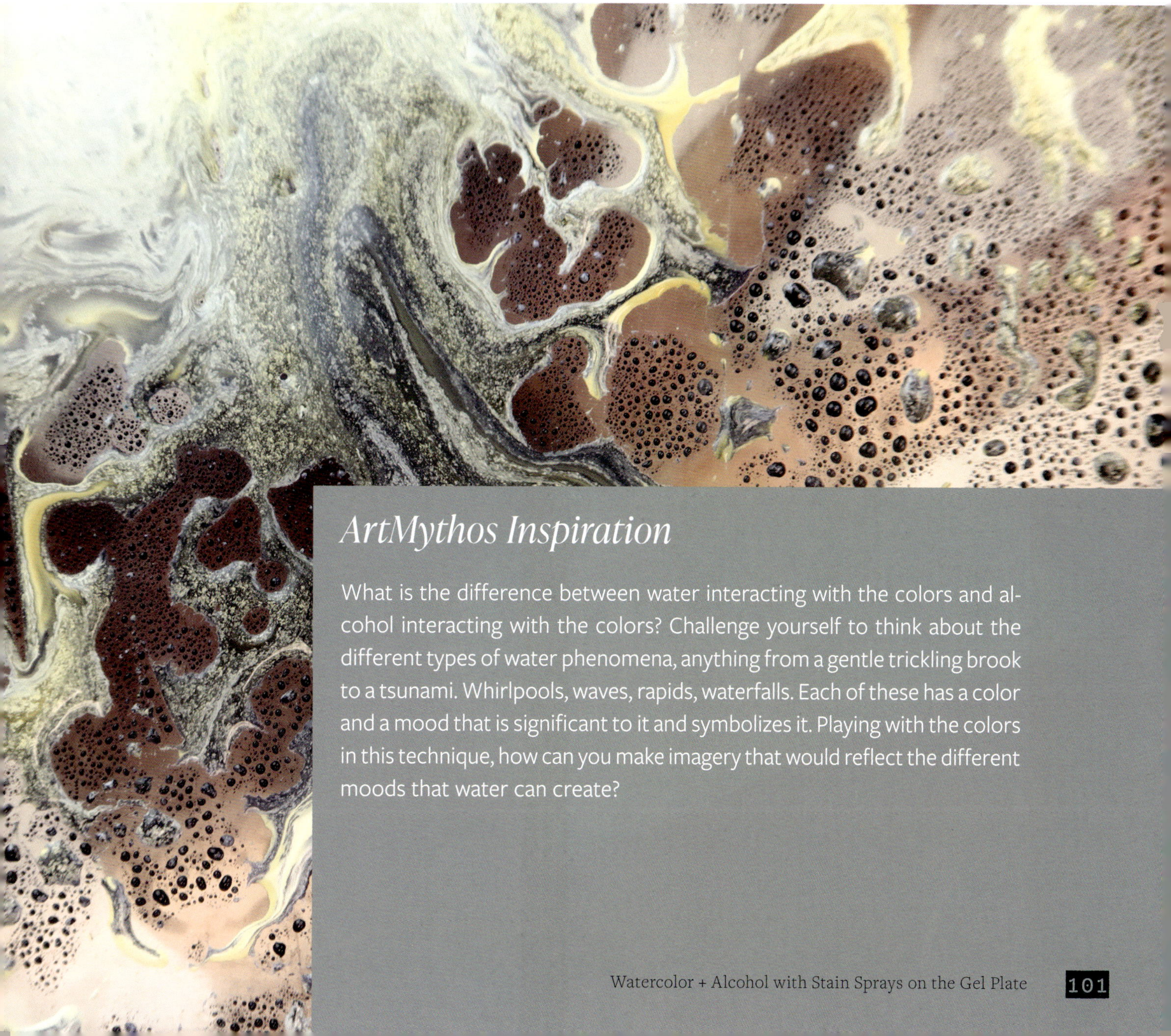

ArtMythos Inspiration

What is the difference between water interacting with the colors and alcohol interacting with the colors? Challenge yourself to think about the different types of water phenomena, anything from a gentle trickling brook to a tsunami. Whirlpools, waves, rapids, waterfalls. Each of these has a color and a mood that is significant to it and symbolizes it. Playing with the colors in this technique, how can you make imagery that would reflect the different moods that water can create?

13

Ink Pad Backgrounds with Alcohol

The techniques here are wonderful for creating a very thin film and adding detailed texture on previous prints to which you'd like to add layers of interest.

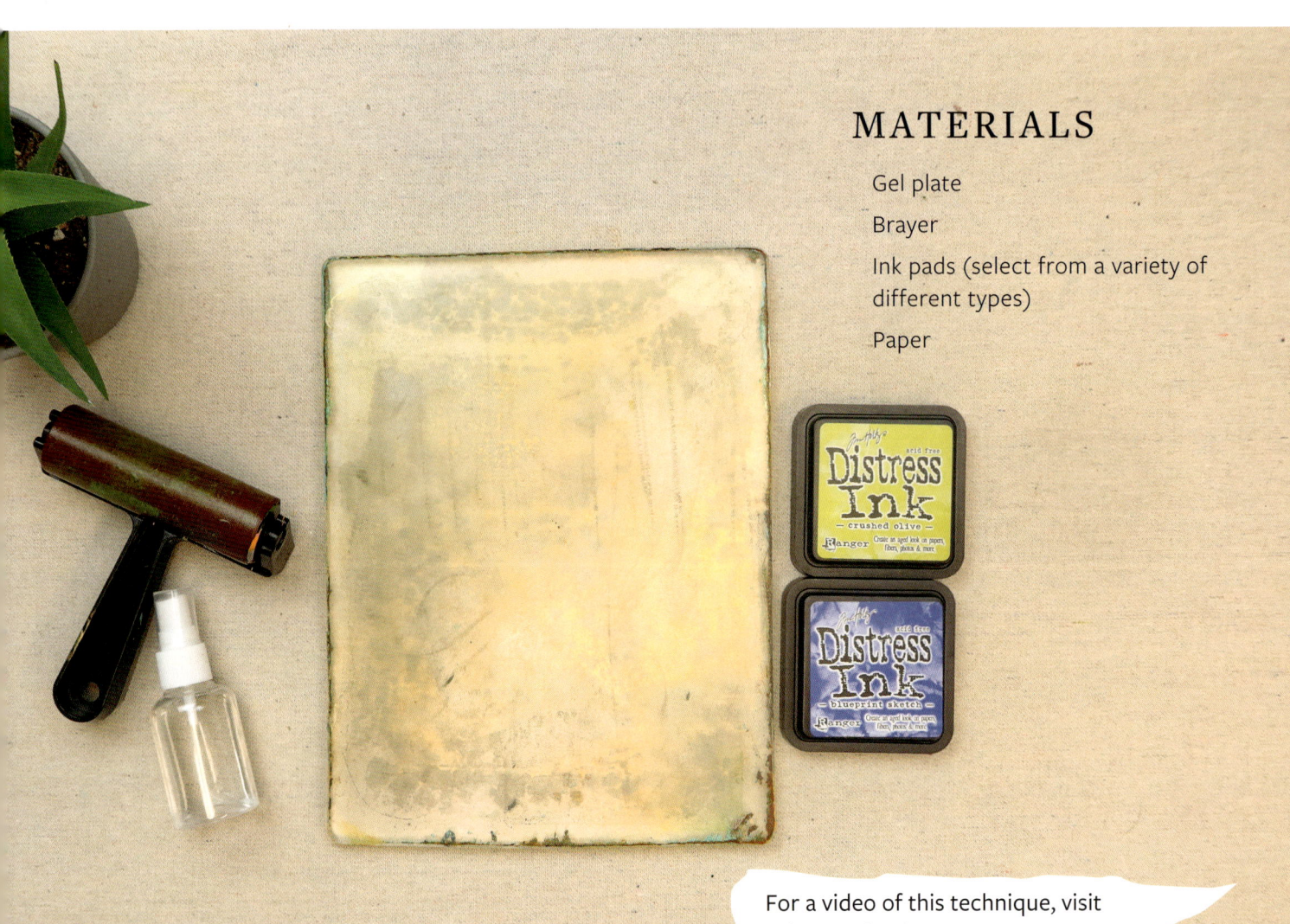

MATERIALS

Gel plate

Brayer

Ink pads (select from a variety of different types)

Paper

For a video of this technique, visit robynmcclendon.com.

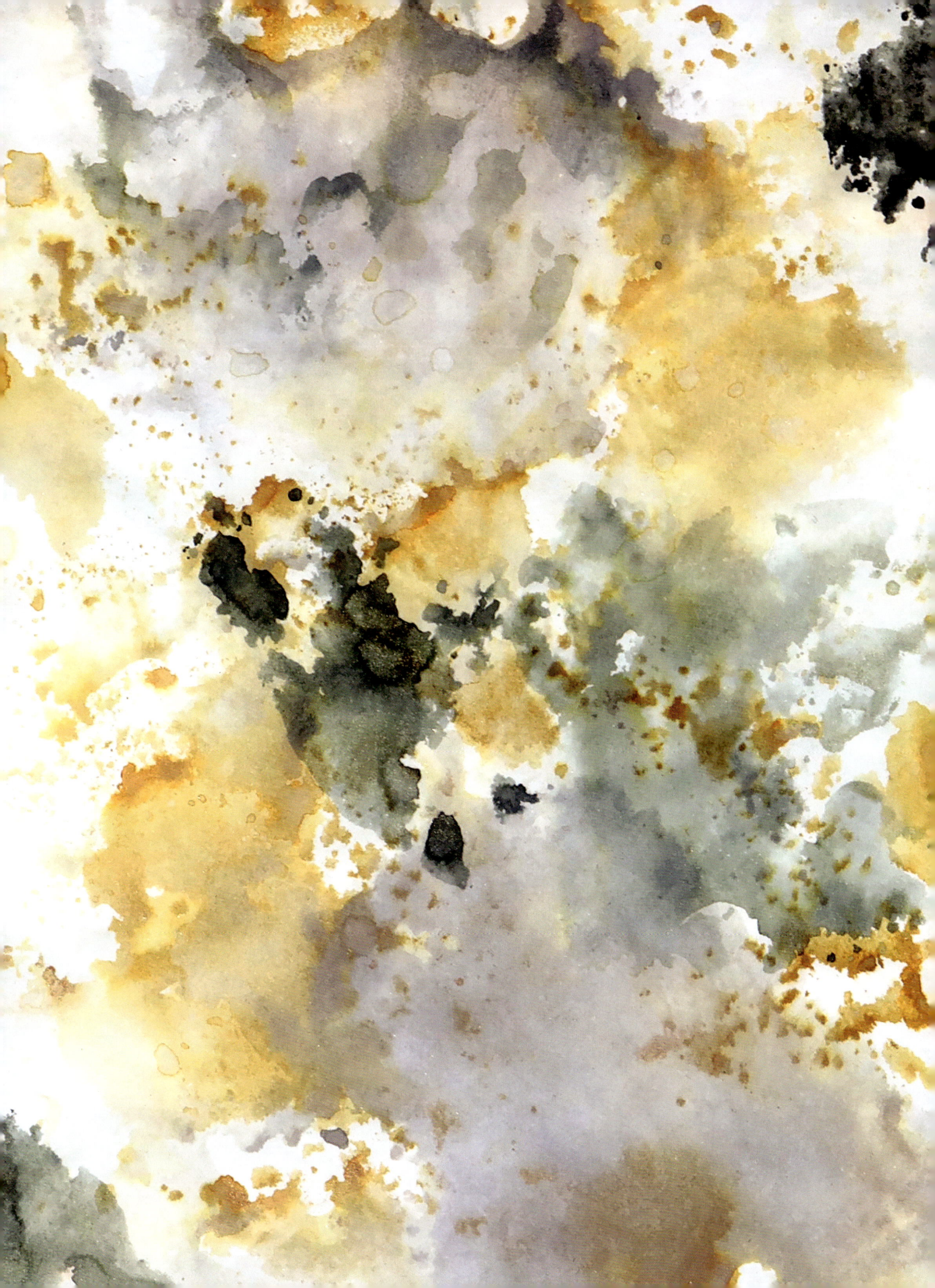

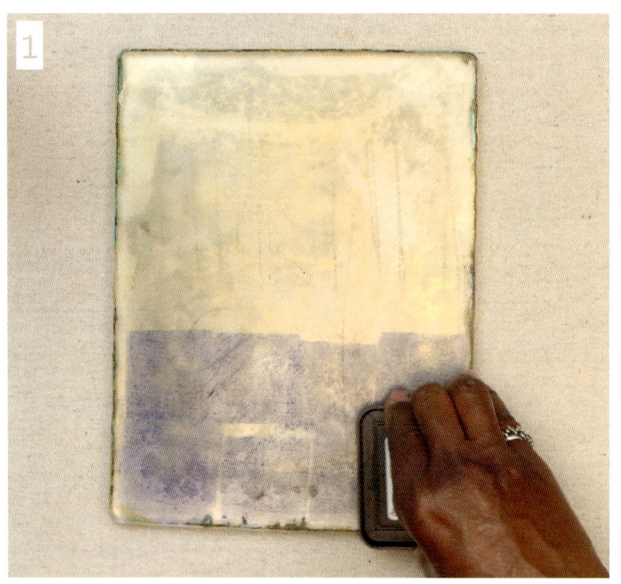

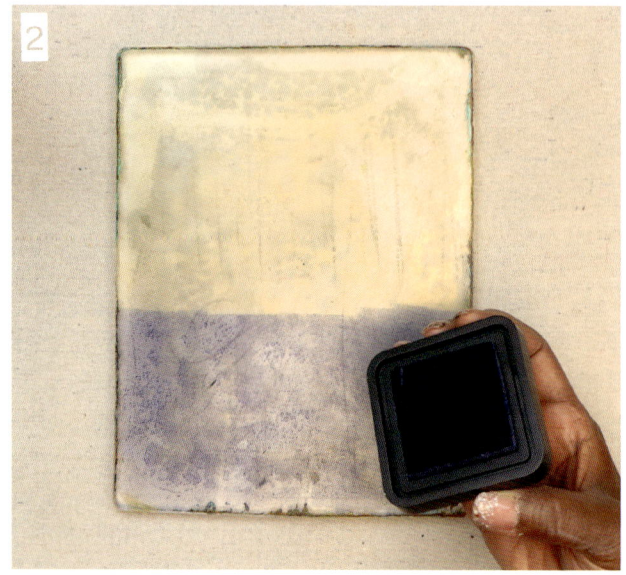

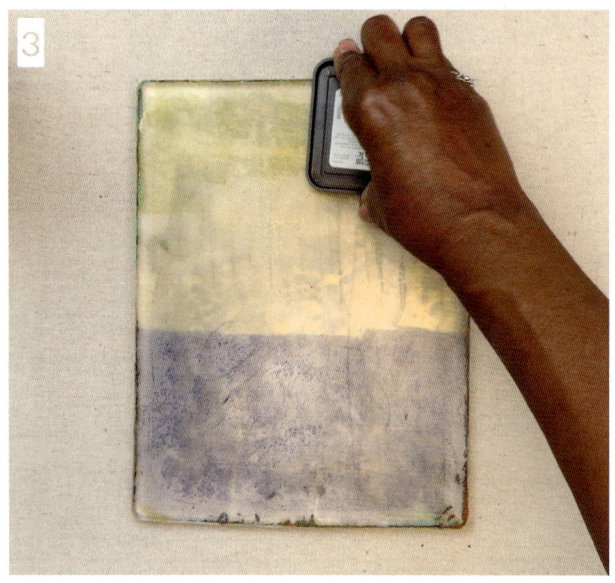

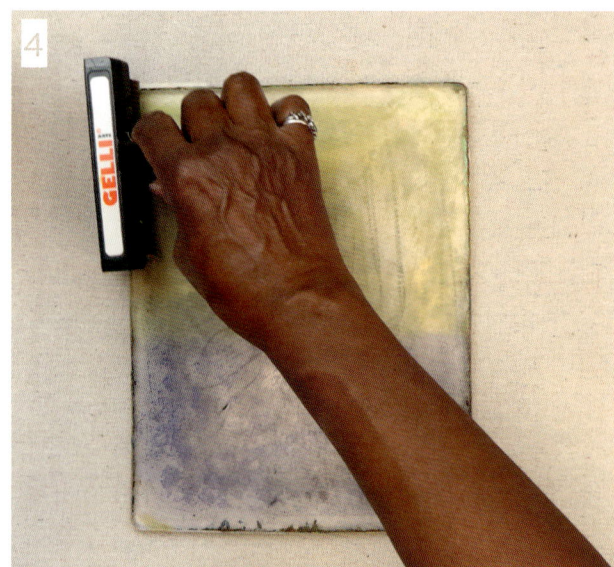

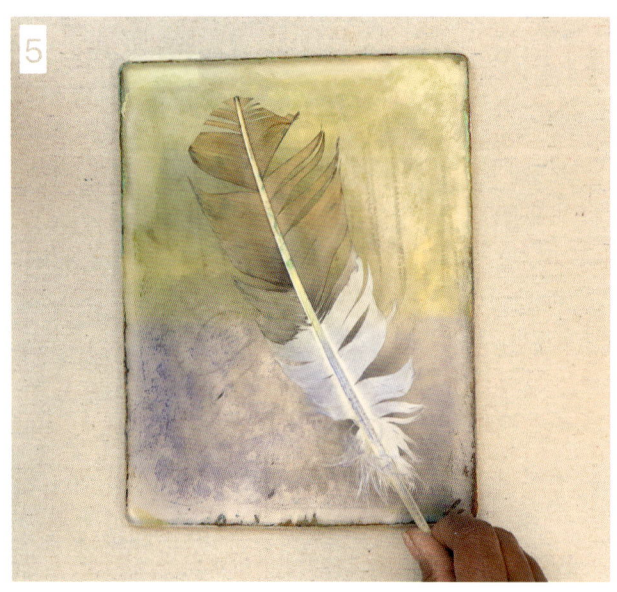

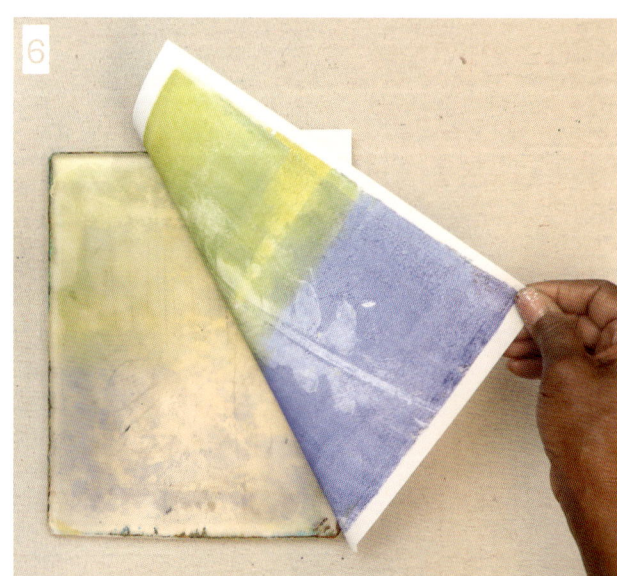

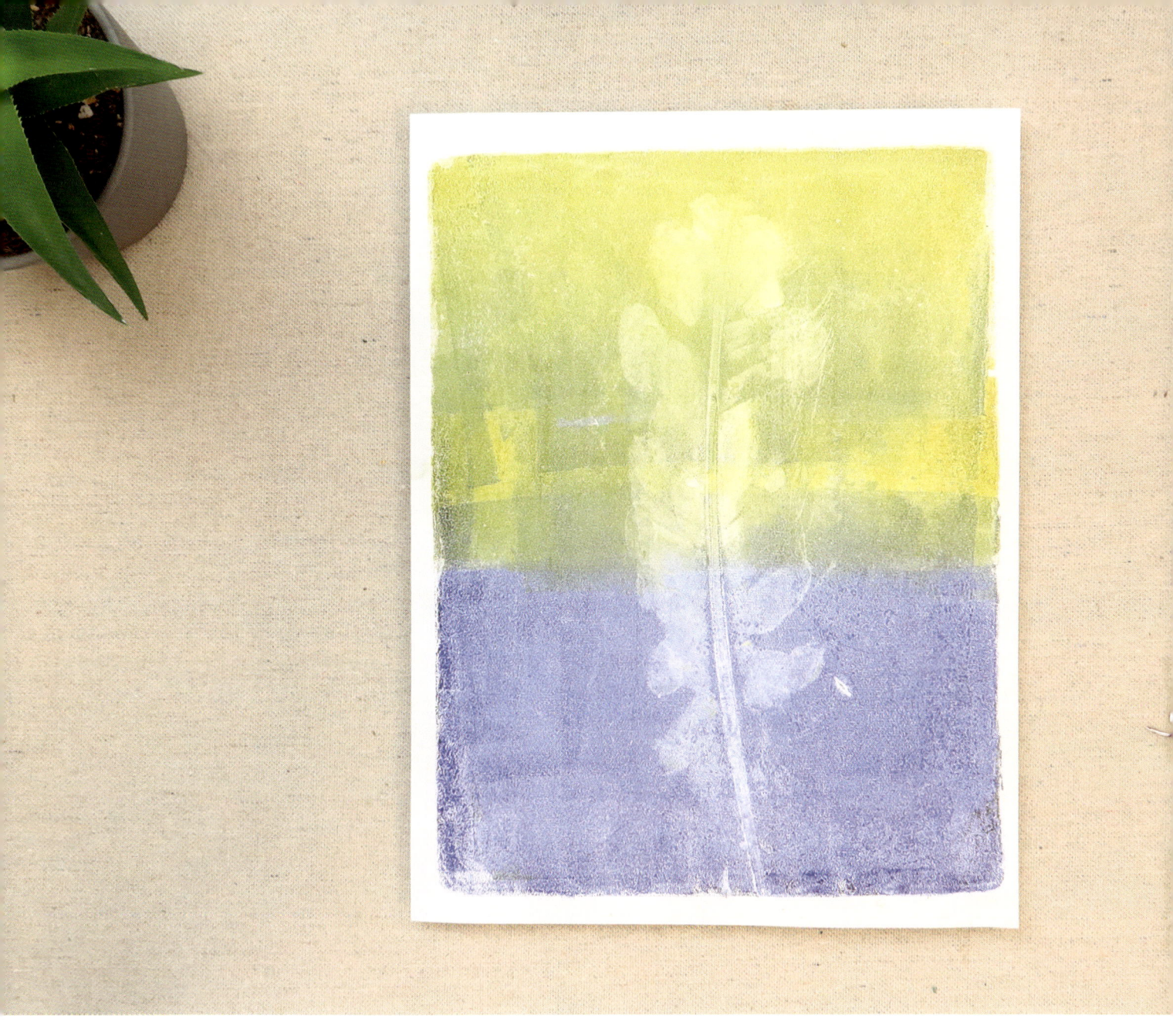

For this technique, any ink pad will work. Two I really enjoy using are Tsukineko Versafine ink and Tim Holtz Distress ink pads. By taking the ink pad, you can literally stamp it right on the gel plate and then brayer it out **1**–**4**. It makes a very thin layer. You can do this several times on the plate. If you want to create more color fields you can also manipulate the surface by stamping or laying down a feather **5**.

Lay the paper down and pull a print **6**. This can be the first layer of color. This technique is best if you want to create a very thin layer. It will make a solid film of color and look like an ink wash. Afterward you can double-print.

Repeat on the same image if you want to build up layers and add intensity. This building up of layers works well with this technique because the ink pads create thin, translucent layers. You can also put more ink on the plate and use a brush and other mark-making tools to create patterns.

This works beautifully with the watercolor and "Venetian plaster" techniques. It's also great for creating an aged-paper look. The following photos **1**–**8** show various options for stamping and manipulating the surface to create variety on the gel plate surface.

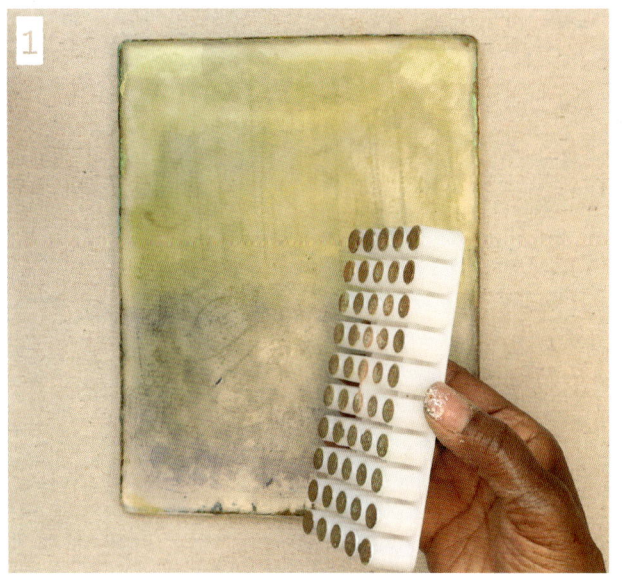

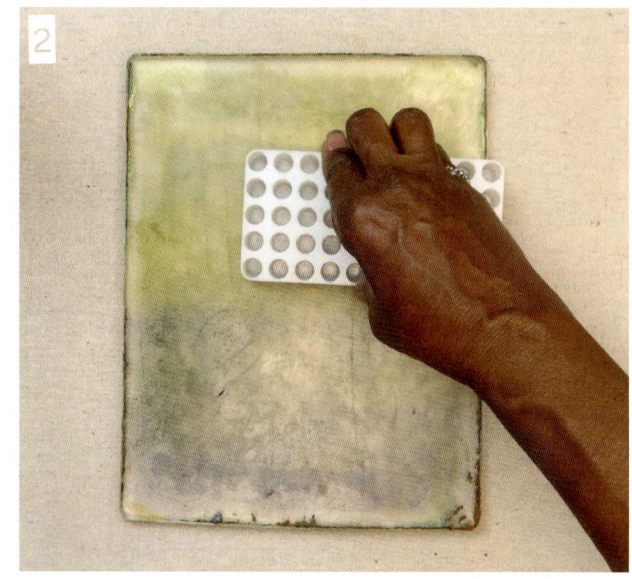

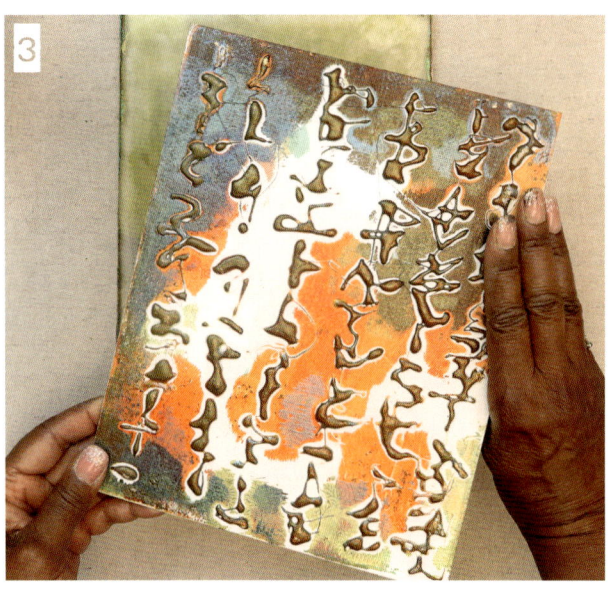

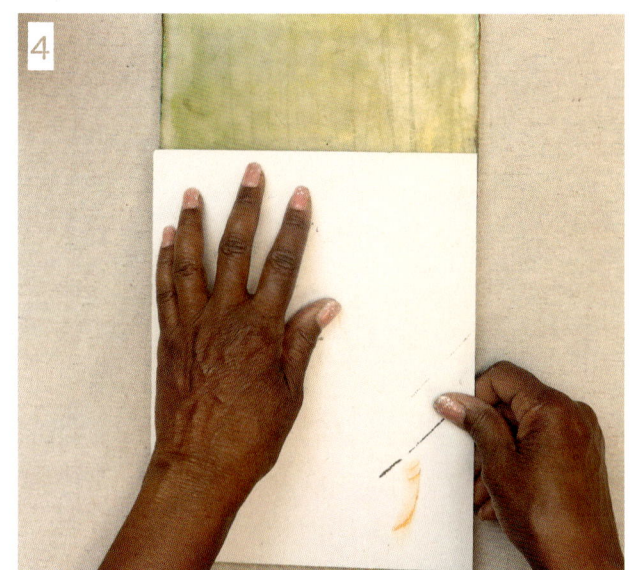

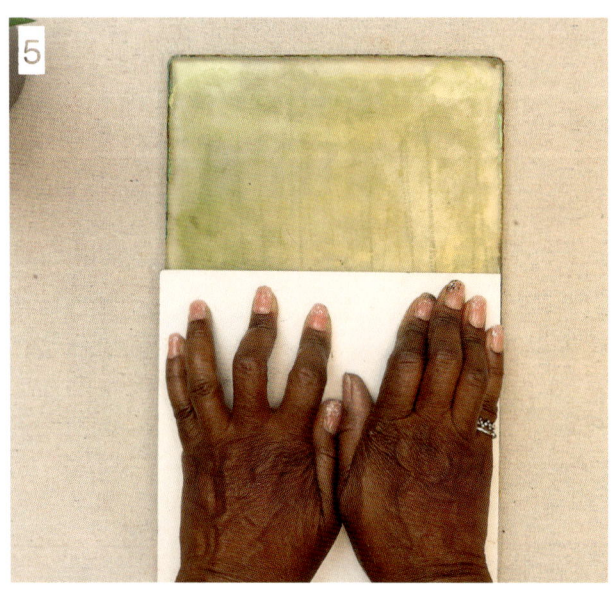

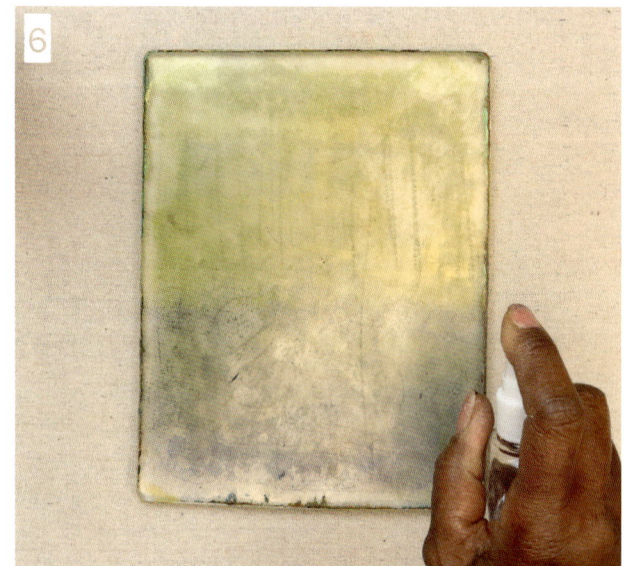

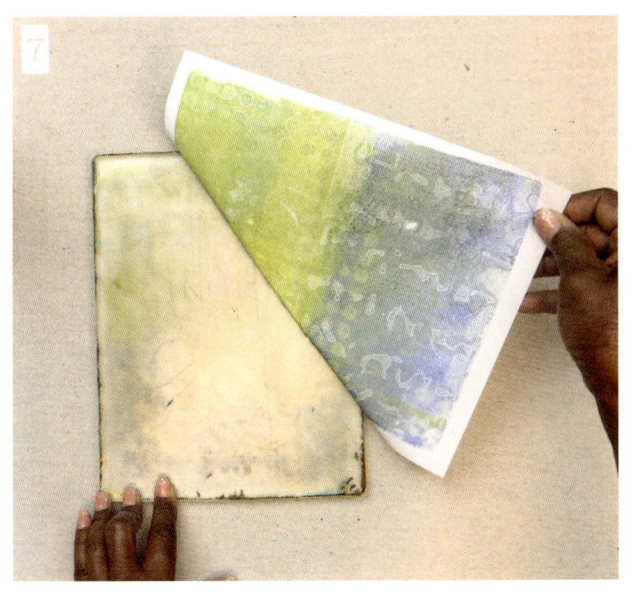

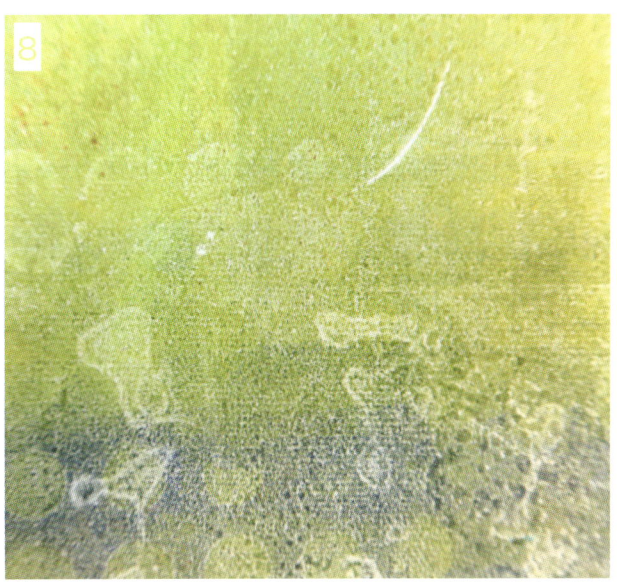

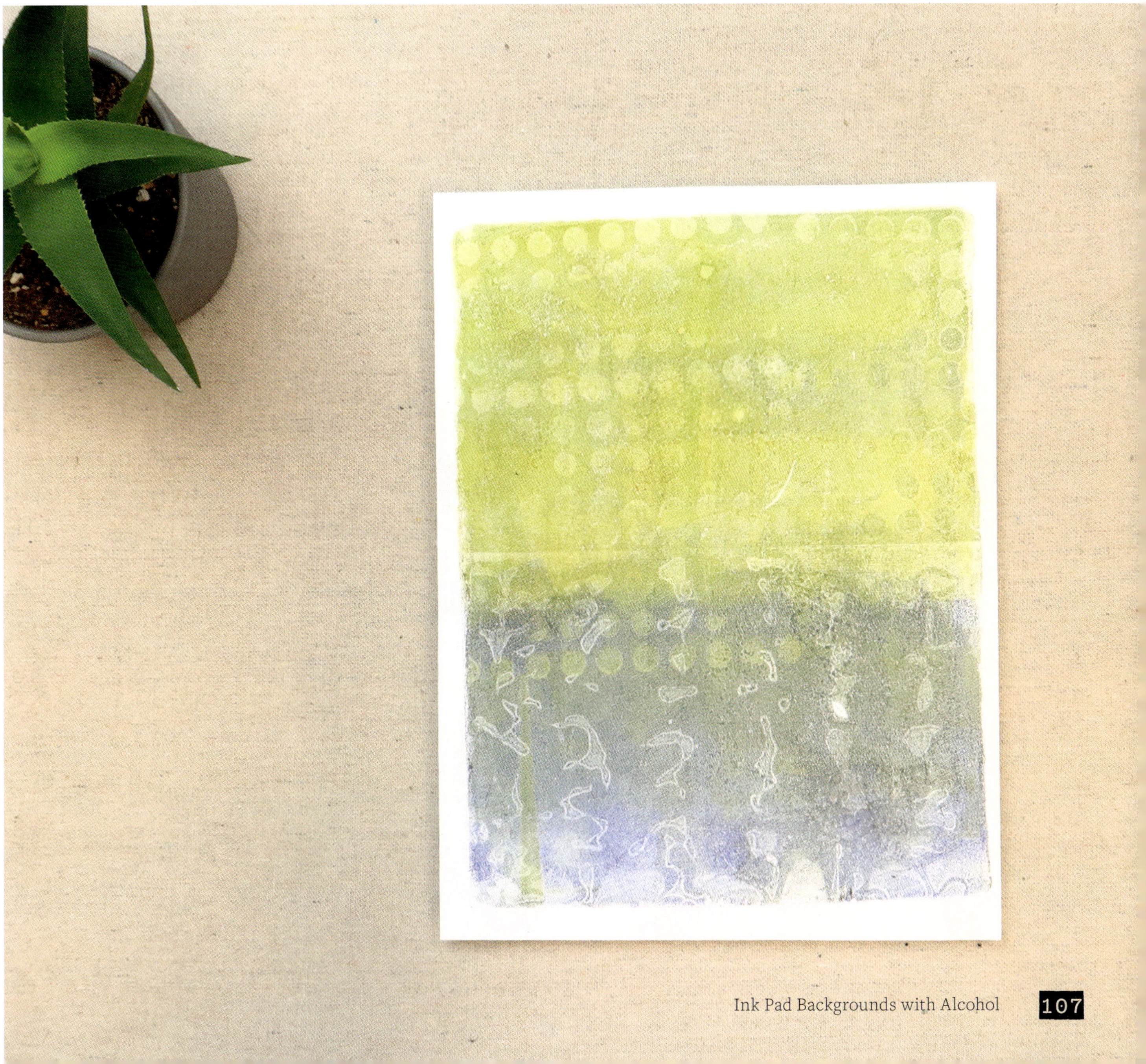

Other Variations to Try

1. Brayer out another layer and then spray a fine mist of alcohol. This will pebble and stone the ink just as we learned in the previous chapter. This adds texture—a.k.a. another layer of interest—to your existing gel prints.

2. You can also use the paint left on your plate after previous techniques to add interest to specific areas of your prints that call for more embellishing. As opposed to placing the entire sheet on a freshly prepared gel plate, try pressing small sections of the print onto the plate, picking up areas of additional paint and images to enhance the print.

3. To create an aged-paper or old-ephemera look, you can use distress ink pads. The technique will work best with a Tim Holtz Distress Ink Pad. My go-to colors are browns, grays, and earthy greens, because of their subtle, natural hues. Bright blues, oranges, greens, and yellows are also available, and the colors mix beautifully together—so don't be afraid to blend shades to get the exact look you want!

4. Tea and coffee staining and eco-staining, which will be covered in chapter 20, provide gorgeous layers to add to our work, but there are situations when you don't want to immerse a particular delicate paper, or you may be working on a project that is time sensitive, so you don't have time to go that route. These distress stains can be used to create quick and lovely layers in just a few minutes.

5. Put some ink on the gel plate and then spritz it a bit. Add more water if it looks too dark, or add more stain for a bolder color. Then take a print that you would like to create an aged look for. Lay it on the plate and gently tap it on random places.

6. Don't forget the edges! Sometimes we concentrate on the center portions and neglect the edges. Having patterns move off the paper is one way to give a more interesting look to your work in general. Our eyes move around the page, and you want to create interest all over the page. Working with edges creates movement and can include your imagery moving off the page in various places.

ArtMythos Inspiration

Think about the different colors that aged papers take on. Not all old-looking paper is a dusty brown or sienna color. Some old papers have a blueish color to them, or a gray. Some have red/browns and a smoky quality to them. Things get an aged patina resulting from the soil of a particular region. For example, if you were to find aged papers in a French chateau, they may differ in tint because of the local soil. When you stain and age your papers, think about all the different regions you could be in. Not all papers age brown.

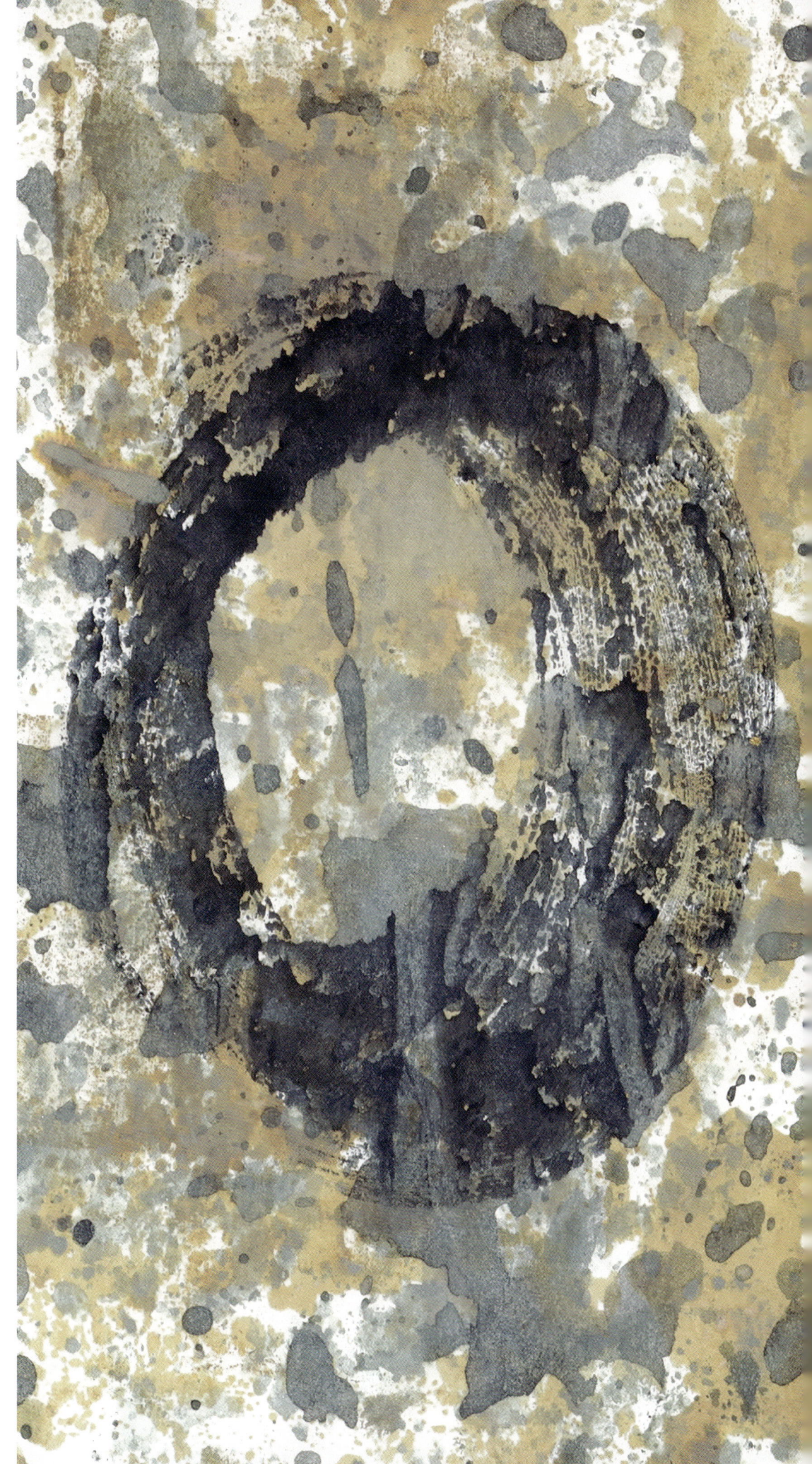

Stone pattern created from ink pad on the gel plate with alcohol with gel-printed circle

Paintbrush Strokes vs. Brayer on the Gel Plate

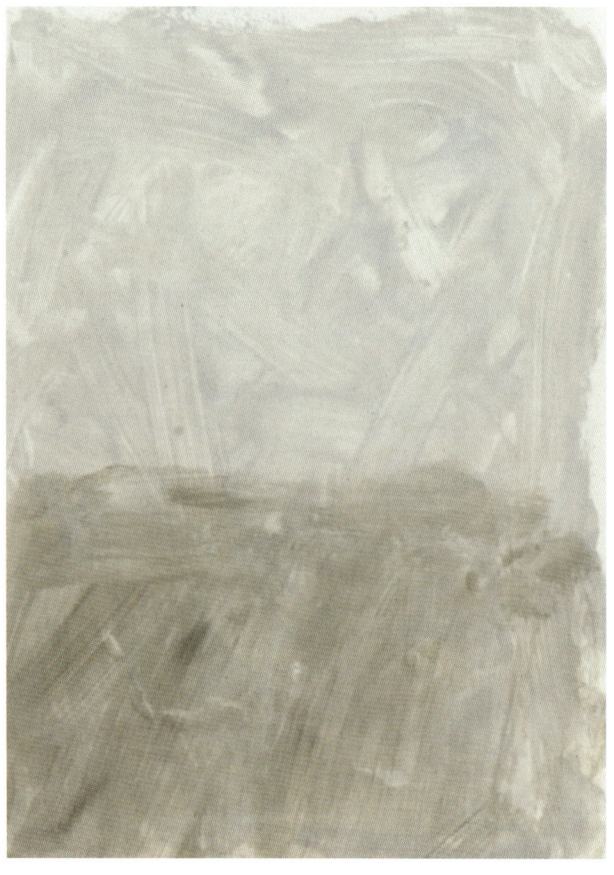

An example of brushstrokes on the gel plate

I, like so many, had been conditioned to use the brayer on the flat gelatin surface to create layers and transfer paint and image to paper. Using my paintbrush on the gel plate for the first time involved necessity being the mother of invention. I once moved across country and had carefully packed my gel plate and paints in the car for the cross-country journey. When I got to my home and set up my new art room and wanted to get right to gel printing, I realized I'd forgotten to pack the brayer. But I did have my paintbrushes.

To my absolute surprise and delight, the paint brushstrokes held up nice and firm on the gel plate, maintaining their texture and form in the pulled prints.

Use any acrylic paintbrush that you generally work with. I have a tendency to use a ¼″ flathead paintbrush, and it works best with acrylic or oil paints. Full-bodied or medium-bodied acrylic paint works better than fluid acrylics, though thinner-viscosity paints will work **1**–**2**. Once you have loaded your plate with paint and brushstrokes, lay your paper down and pull your print as usual **3**–**4**.

For a video of this technique, visit robynmcclendon.com.

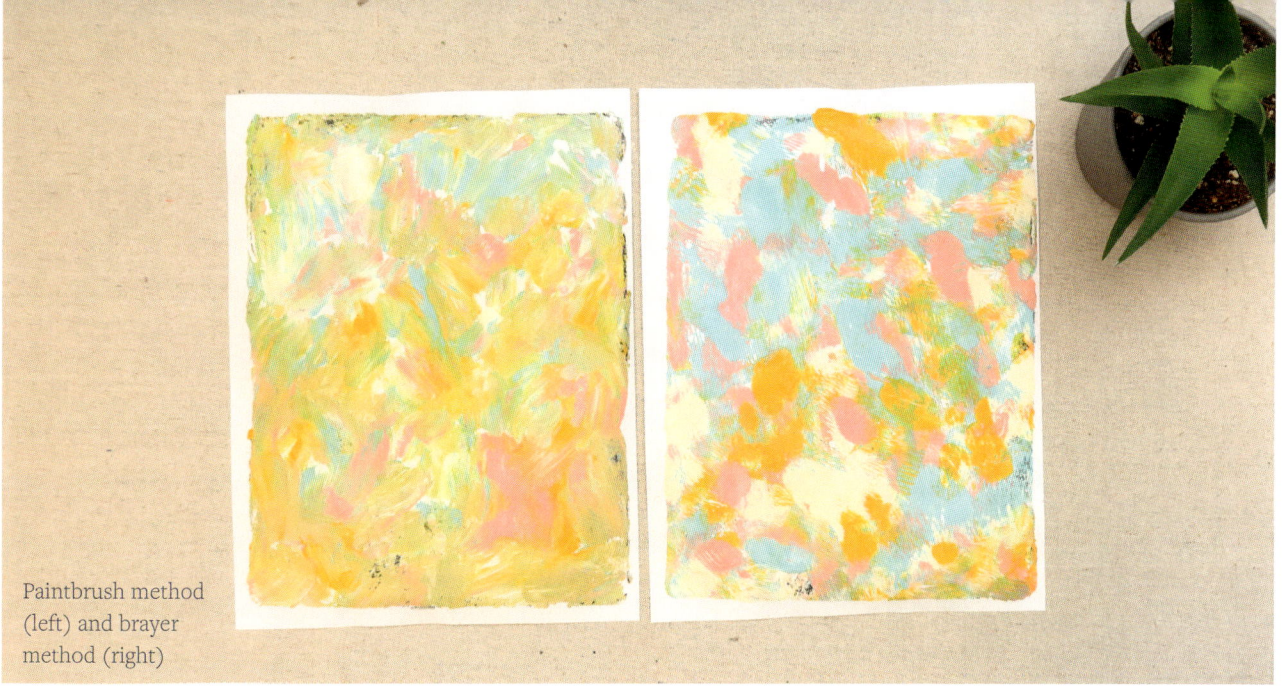

Paintbrush method (left) and brayer method (right)

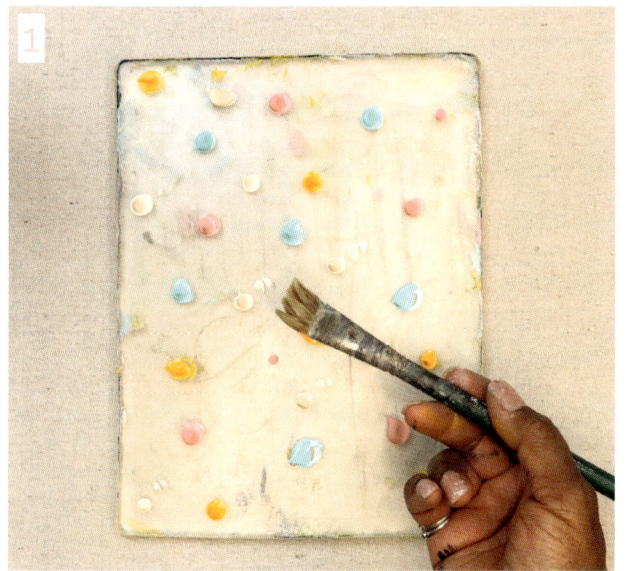

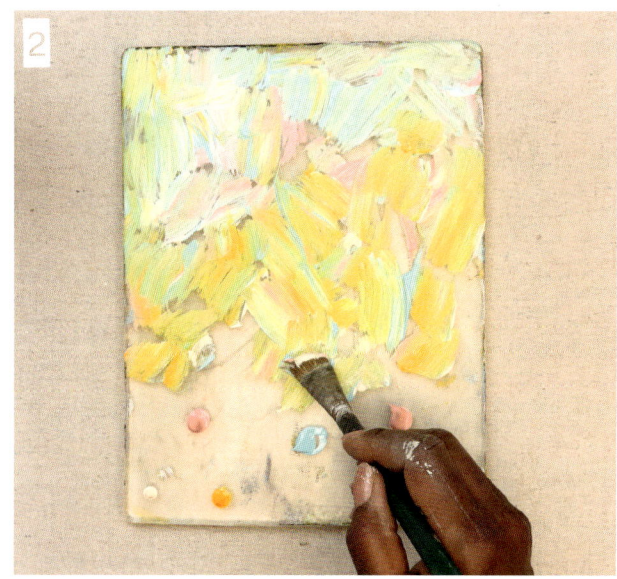

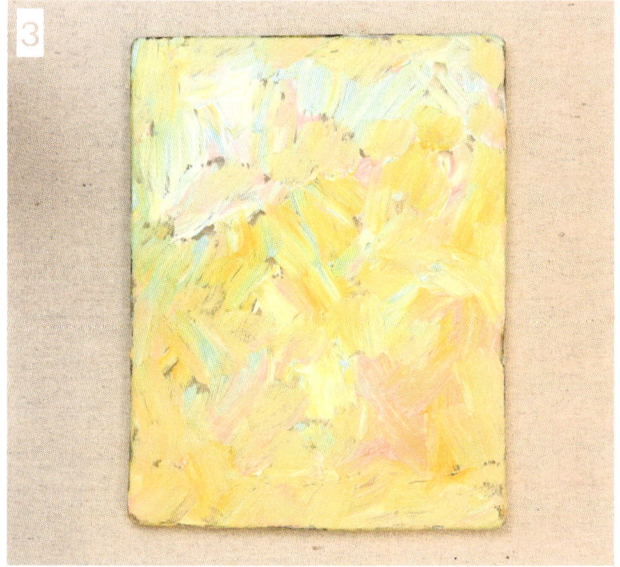

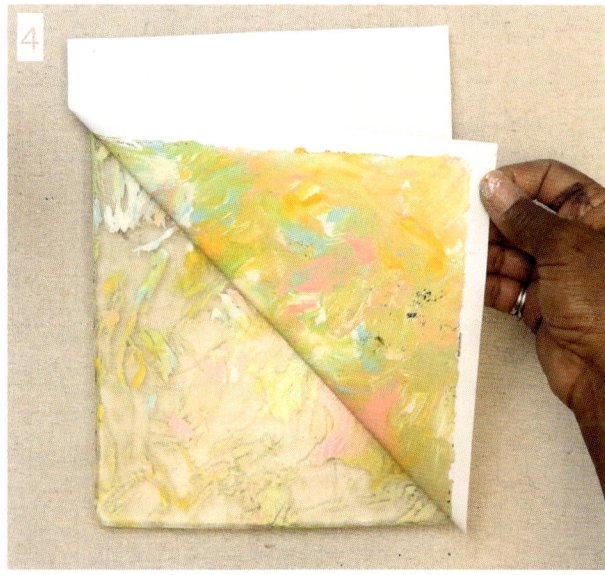

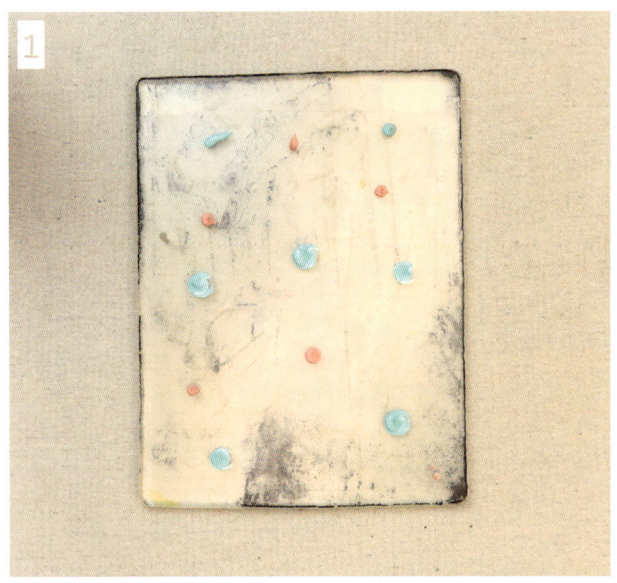

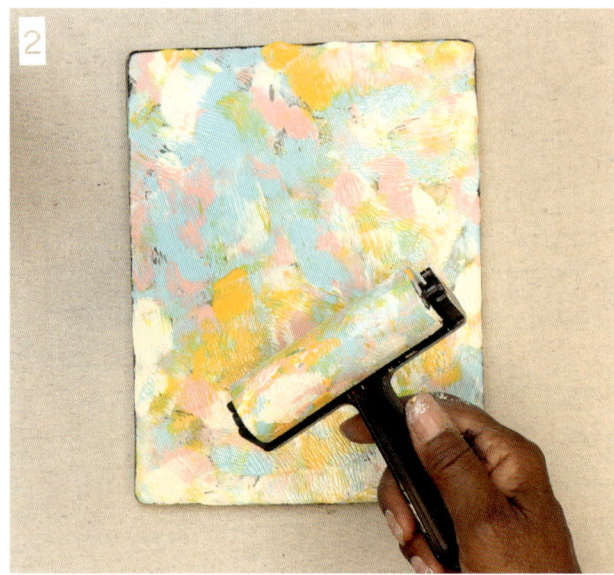

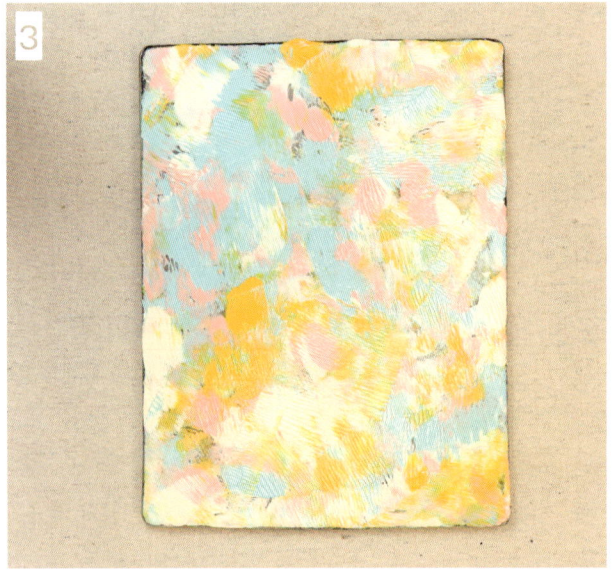

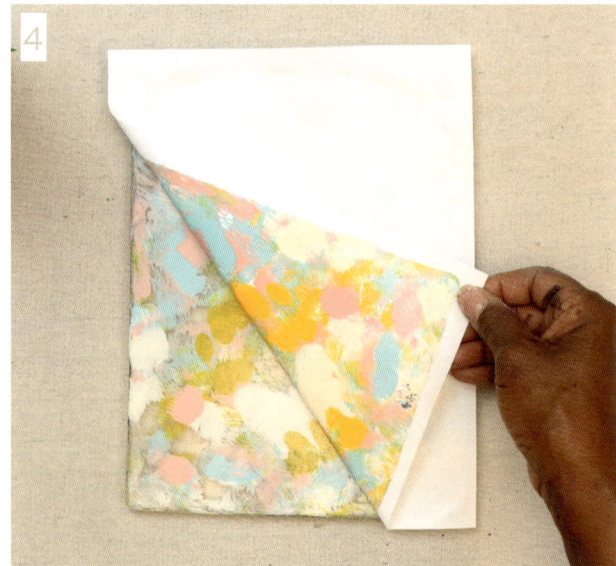

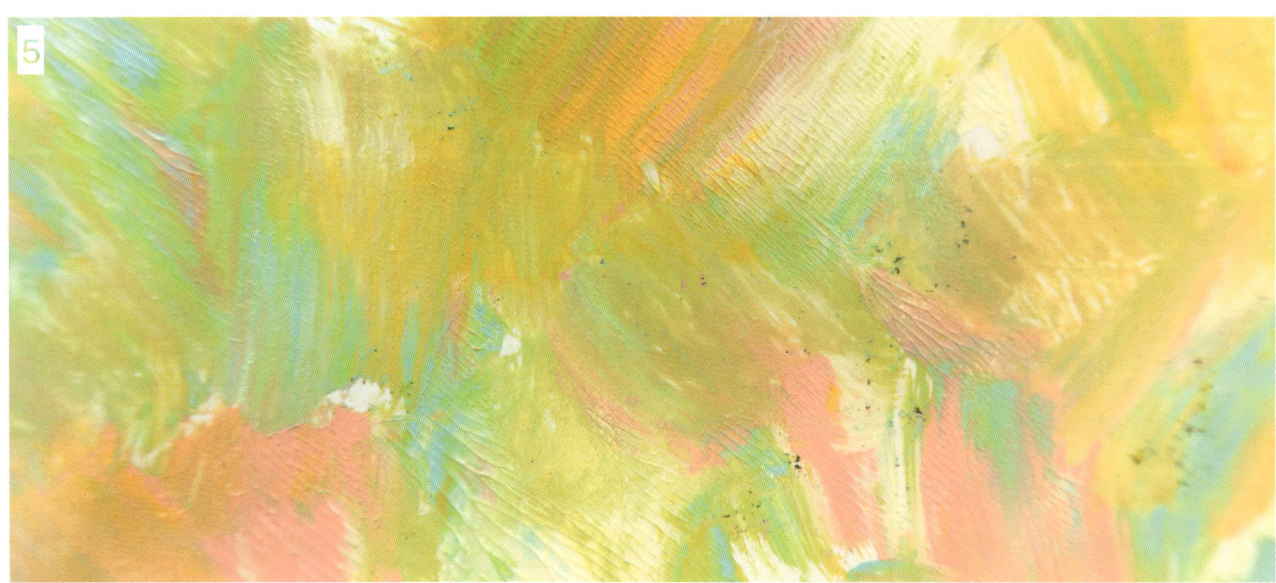

Detail, paintbrush method

Use your paintbrush the way you normally would paint—representative, figurative, abstract. Play with short and long strokes, cross-hatching patterns, and standard repeating patterns of circles, squares, and triangles. Portraiture and landscapes work well too; you get their benefits in monoprint form.

Fundamentally, when we use a brayer **1**–**4** we are rolling out and building up very thin layers of color. There is very little texture in the brayer. Conversely, a paintbrush results in texture, and the stroke of the brush creates emotion, mood, and movement. We are now able to bring all the things that happen in brush-work into the monoprinting process.

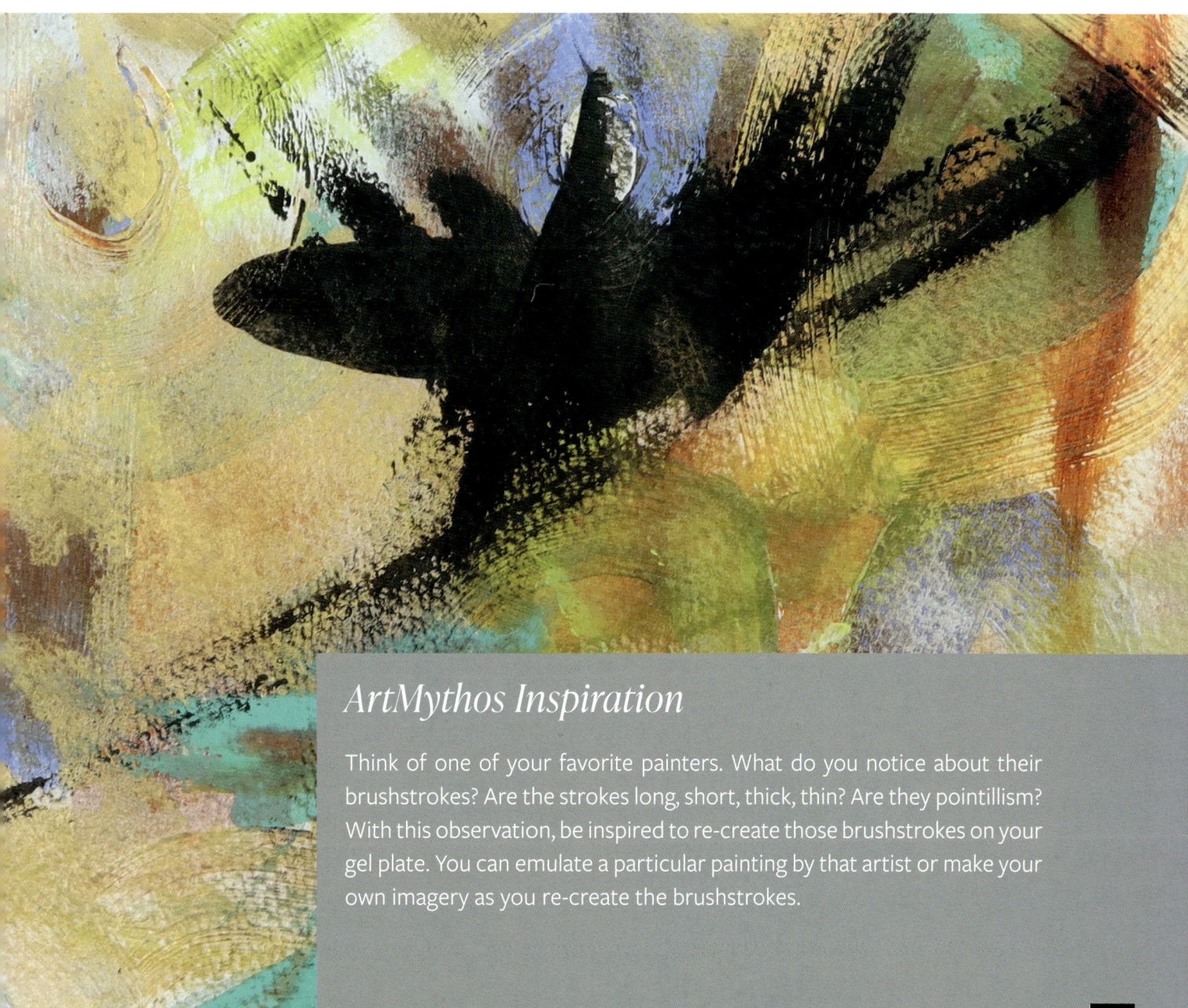

ArtMythos Inspiration

Think of one of your favorite painters. What do you notice about their brushstrokes? Are the strokes long, short, thick, thin? Are they pointillism? With this observation, be inspired to re-create those brushstrokes on your gel plate. You can emulate a particular painting by that artist or make your own imagery as you re-create the brushstrokes.

14

"Grunge" Photo Transfer

Photo transfer can be tricky no matter what the medium. For success, it always takes working with the medium for a period of time to really sort out the technique and other variables such as climate and viscosity.

This is particularly true for photo transfer with the gel plate. It's a matter of finding the paint that works best, while paying attention to your workspace's humidity (Is it dry? Is there more moisture in the air?). Both relate to the dry time on the plate, the papers you use to pull the print, and which transfer image papers are best. Certain clay-coat-based magazine images generally work best. You can use laser prints, but they require variations on the technique and so I don't recommend beginning with them. All in all, there are many variables to be considered when pulling a "perfect" print.

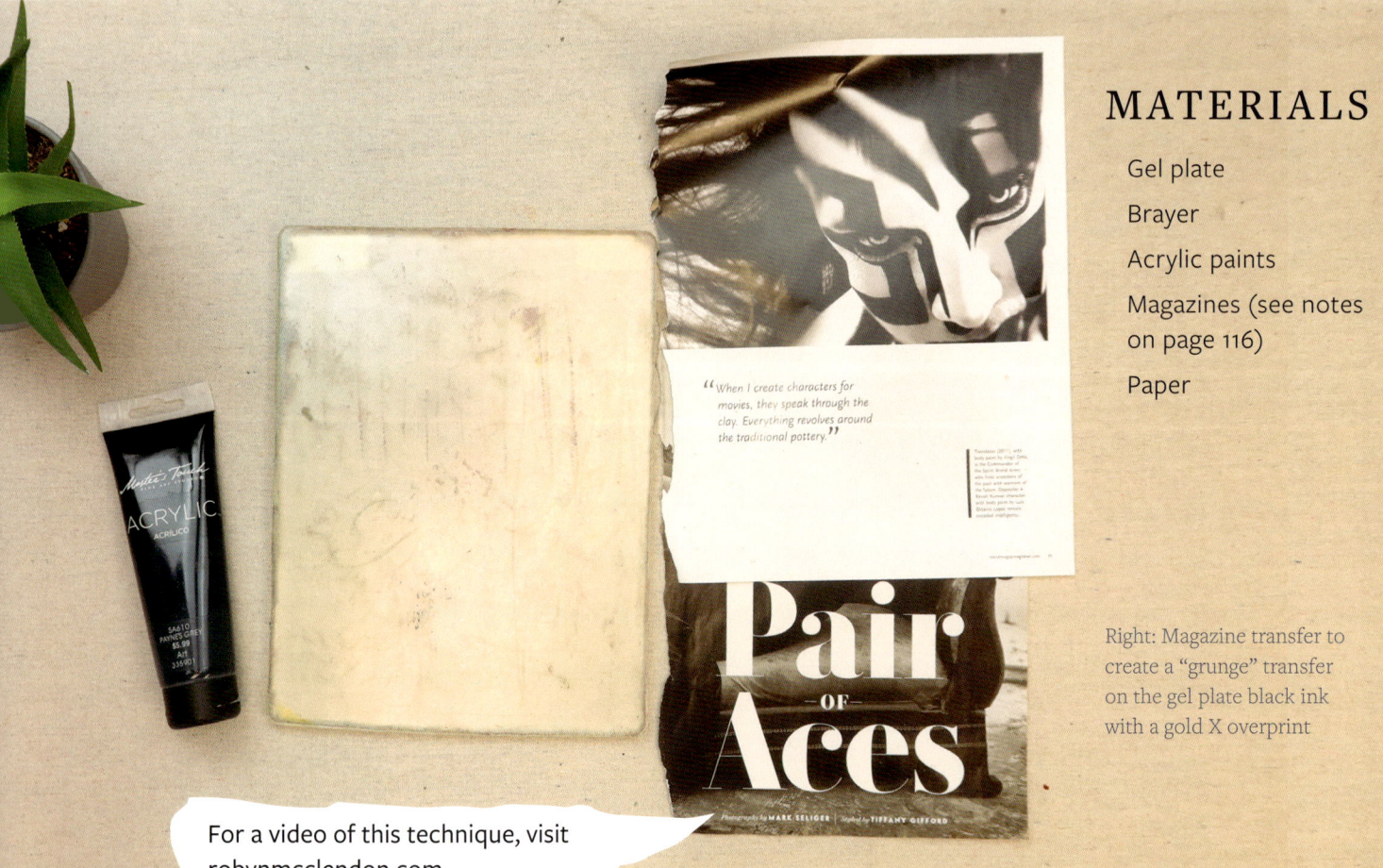

MATERIALS

Gel plate

Brayer

Acrylic paints

Magazines (see notes on page 116)

Paper

Right: Magazine transfer to create a "grunge" transfer on the gel plate black ink with a gold X overprint

For a video of this technique, visit robynmcclendon.com.

SEISMIC SHIFT

New York once did

...ers and artists pushes... ...the West Coast.

R...

...ring whether re... ...ominous mista... ...ase and disconnec... ...ertrude Stein... was no...

And then... ...ed to dinner. The eve... ...main with... Benedikt and Angelika Taschen at their landma... ...designed John La... ...seen it in films and iconic in... ...octagon... suspen... ...Hollywood Hills like a spaces... ...elebrating the Japa... ...tect Tadao Ando, and it turned ou... ...party at... a quin... ...vening. "First of all, to get to B... ...house you are alo... Mulhol... ...hrough what feels like deepest co... ...that you can se... the... ...low," Moby says. "And then I wa... ...ema... ...ver been in, where the guests inclu... ...only... livin... ...David Hockney and Jim Heimann, a loc... ...tr... ...stories about L.A.'s se... ...like the Black... ...tive of the uniqu... ...he city." ...bination of glamou... ...has always de... ...noir. But in the... ...70s the center... ...e ocean, and suddenly... ...all about good vibration... ...ast as people would go... ...Angeles Time... ...that time. "By the early '90s you... ...he'd vener... ...To the rest of the country, Angeles... living in car bubbles cruising from yoga to juice...

Around... ...that started to change... ...revi... ...eighborh... ...farther east: Hollywood, Silve... ...ticula... ...which has exploded in the past fe... ...ing center... ...art, and dining. "That geogr... ...M... says, "and... ...emphasis on darker urbanity ra... ...en aesthe... ...the city not only much-needed... ...imacy as... ...ural center."

...always feels like its own state... ...of nati... ...says art dealer Shaun Caley R... ...west in t... ...ame ...re's very little regard for hist... ...like it... ...Such... ...local designers say, ope... ...expansive creative environ... ...with fewer rules and preced... ...Wild West mentality... ...messy ...esh and risk-taking," says... ...with his twin bro... ...that... ...ly origi... ...rn... ...ings in their dow... ...studio. ...ture free than... ...rkolai. "There's... ...here, and no cul... ...living or express... ...other... ...en a... ...expected to behave to bec... ...ce... ...tes and Laura Mulleavy established their fashion label, Rodarte,... ...e... L.A.-base... fashion. And by never...

CONTINUED ON PAGE 189.

The MUSE... 900

Nathalie... Laura...

The sisters [sta]n... ...rea... Feliz and were tutored in fash... mother, *Vogue* editor Lisa L... style? Laura: "Comfort above a... Nathalie, but "I try not to wea... clothes to lunch. That's la... designer: Nathalie: "Rodarte... nothing like having a sister be... friend, like me and Laura. A... the way their clothes tell a sto... "Scott Sternberg, Jen Mey... J.C. Obando." **Classic film**: Laur... I watched it with my sister... times." **Classic song**: Nathal... by the Strokes, always re... driving around Hollywood... ...ood." **Favorite restaurant**... ...lat... for breakfast, Shibucho... ...cific Dining Car for old-scho...

...UT[E]R...[SON] ...ra and L... M... UNDER... RODARTE

...ura M... and Kate... Mulleavy, w... Nathal... Laura Love: On the Mus... ... blouses ($790 each)... Rodarte dresses and jew...

When I first attempted this technique on the gel plate, I experimented my way through all the above factors, and probably some others I've now forgotten, to pull a complete and clear print. Along the way, I noticed that I was getting great bits and pieces: some good text here, a part of a face there, a nice part of a background tree somewhere else. They were perfectly beautiful and usable pieces. I also knew that the way that I create art means I would never actually use an entire magazine image. So, there really wasn't a need for me to concern myself with trying to pull a perfect print all the time, when I was going to rip it up anyway.

It settled in my spirit that every print that I am pulling is usable at some level. Thus was born the idea of "grunge" photo transfer, a way I especially like to work in mixed media. This gives you permission to have funky prints! This changes the goals of what you are trying to accomplish. If you're thinking, "I'm pulling these great grunge prints," then just about every pull is perfect!

With the grunge photo transfer process, you want to select a medium-bodied paint because it will roll out thin enough yet have enough moisture and viscosity to act as a resist against the carbon on the image you want to transfer when you lay that image on the plate. However, that balance will vary from brand to brand and within a brand's colors. Certain colors won't work because of the chemistry in the pigments. It may be something that you have to be patient about as you experiment with the paints that you have. Pay attention both to the brand and the color, since if one color works, other colors from that brand may work too. When you find a paint that works, make sure to record that in your notes about this process. Keep adding to your go-to list as you try paints across different brands.

High-contrast images will work best. They need to have good black-to-white contrast. This doesn't mean that they have to be black-and-white images; other colors are fine as long as they have a high contrast.

For your transfer images, high-end fashion, home design, and decor magazines work best. The printing process that they use allows for the images to transfer well. This has to do with the clay surface of the papers.

Magazine transfers are a resist process. The inks that make up the image to be transferred resist the acrylic paint that's been rolled out onto the gel plate. The papers that are used in high-end magazines have a thin layer of a clay-based top coat. This coating is an ideal surface for the printing inks to lie on, creating a high-quality image with depth of image and clarity of color. These images are ideal for a monoprint transfer process, since the inks of the images resist the acrylic paint and absorb the paint in the low-ink/no-ink areas of the printed image, resulting in the acrylic paint being left on the plate in the areas of the image.

Most of the pages that have a glossy, slick feel to them are likely printed on this clay-coated paper and are of a heavier weight. Lower-end magazines have flat, dull pages and images, and generally the pages are thinner too. Experiment with magazines that seem to meet the above criteria and then make notes about each. With a little trial and error, you'll begin to learn which are best for your "grunge" transfer art.

After you settle on your photo images' paper and your paint, you need to select the kind of paper you will transfer to. Using a more premium photo paper with a nice smooth surface will allow you a successful print. The stronger the paper, the better the pull, in that you don't have to worry about the paper ripping. But you can get a great transfer with higher quality paper too.

Brayer out a thin layer of color **1**. Lay your magazine image or laser copy face down on the gel plate and smooth it out gently and evenly, making good contact with the plate **2**.

Lift your photo image from the surface of the gel plate, revealing the image transferred onto the plate **3**.

Immediately lay a fresh piece of paper on the plate, smoothing it out as before, ensuring that the paper makes good contact with the plate to transfer the

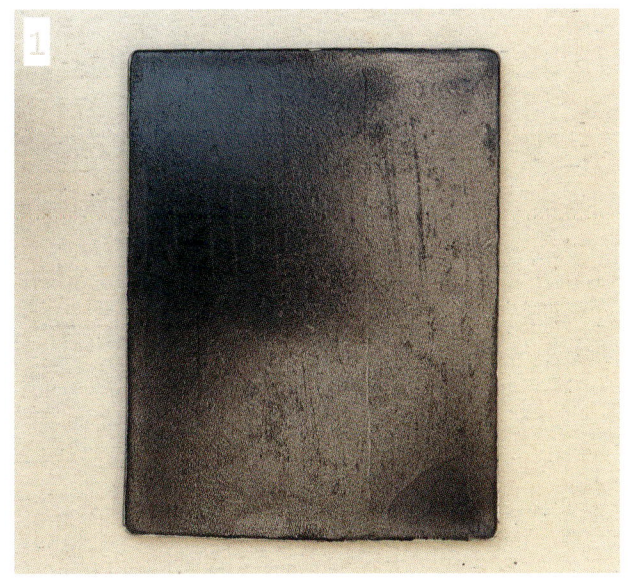

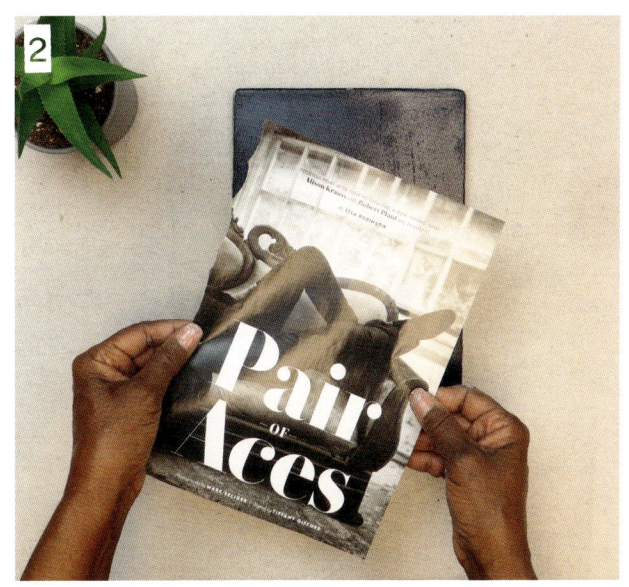

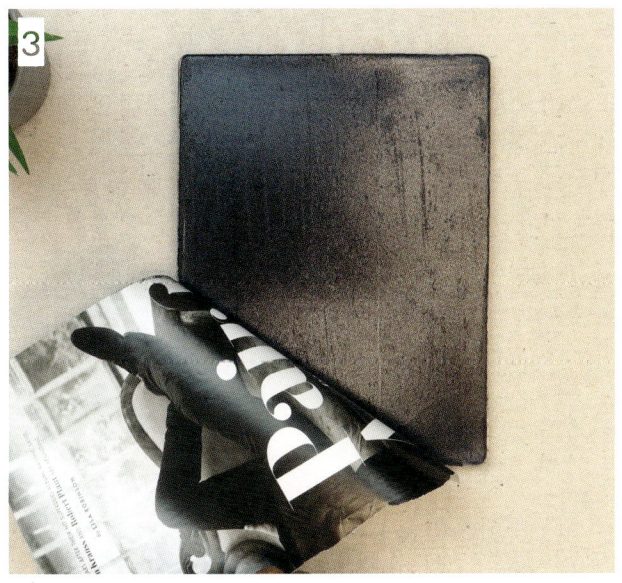

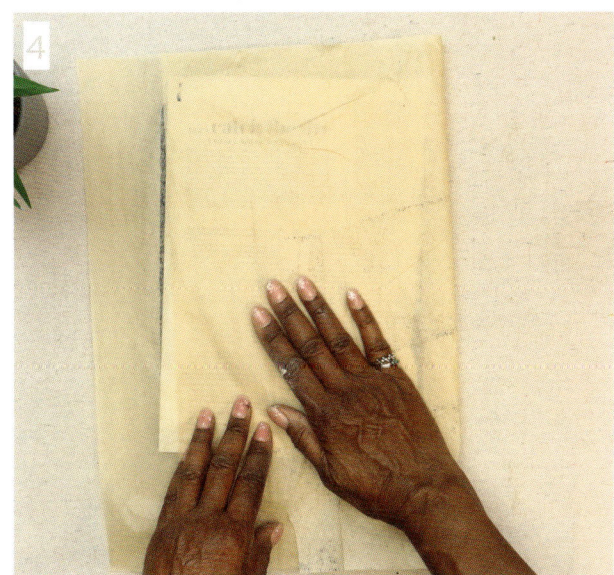

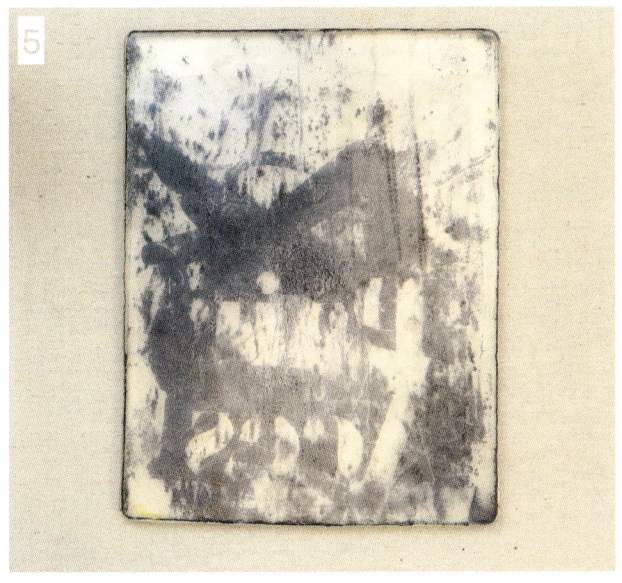

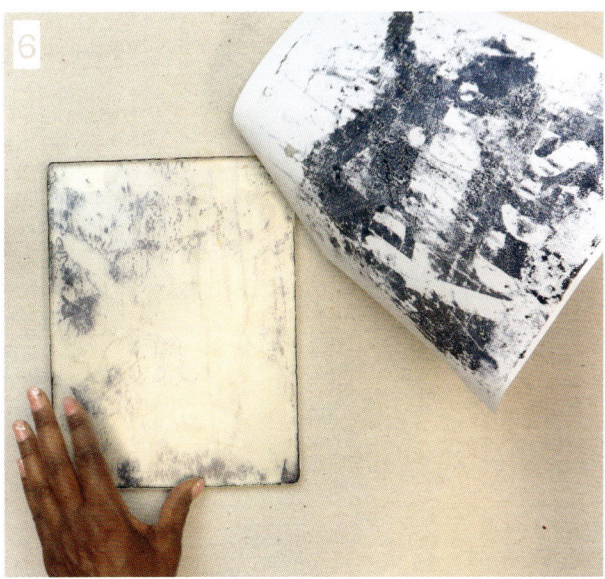

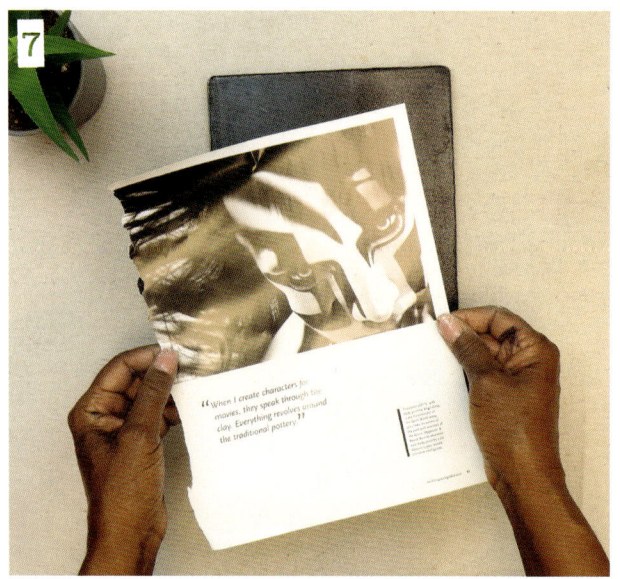

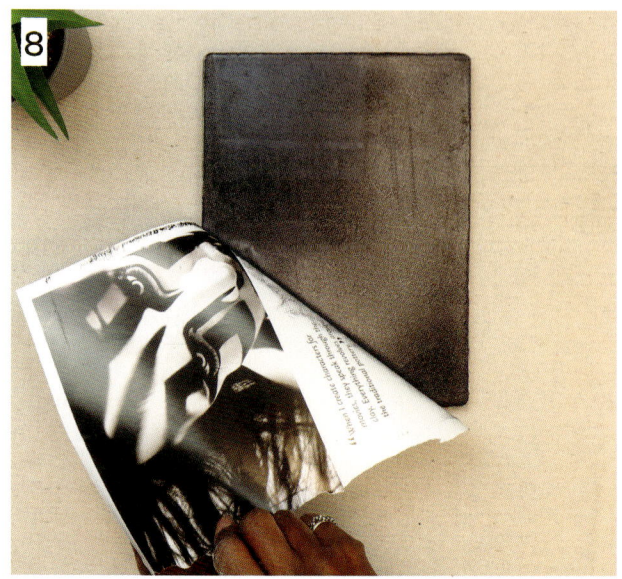

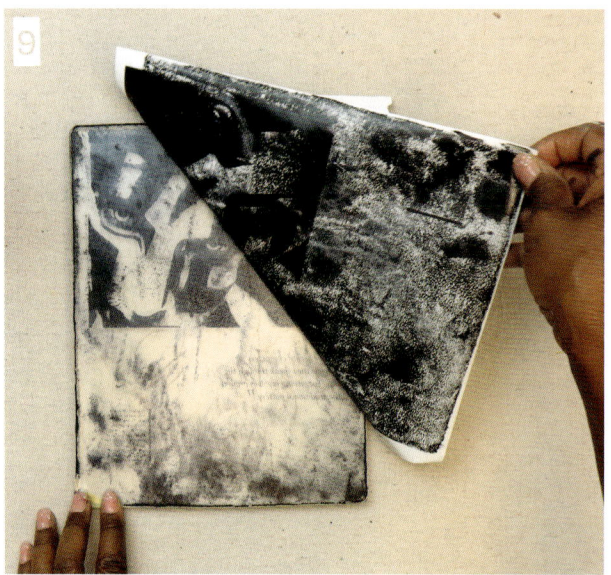

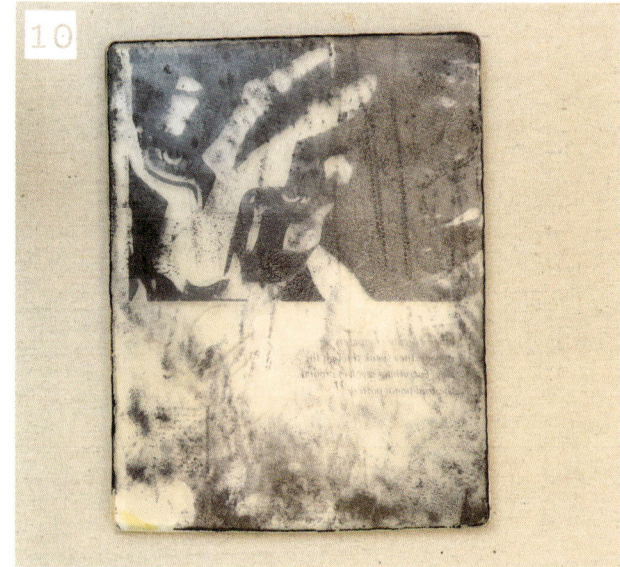

image from the plate to the paper **4**. Lift it off to capture the resist image **5**, **6**. We can see in this first example how incomplete the image pull is; oftentimes when you first come to the plate you will not get the best pull until the plate starts retaining moisture.

Or you can work differently by letting that image dry on the gel plate. When it is dry, you can brayer out another contrasting color in a nice smooth layer. Then lay paper down and pull; both layers of paint will come off the plate onto your paper **7**–**10**.

For example, let's say the first color you put down is Payne's grey. You wait for the Payne's grey to dry and then brayer out a layer of yellow. When you pull this, you will see the yellow layer and the gray image lying on top.

By following this process, you can have multiple colors layered on your prints. You could do this two or three more times, allowing dry time between each new layer. The final, wet layer will pull all the previous layers. It's up to you to decide how many layers you would like to work with. 🖌

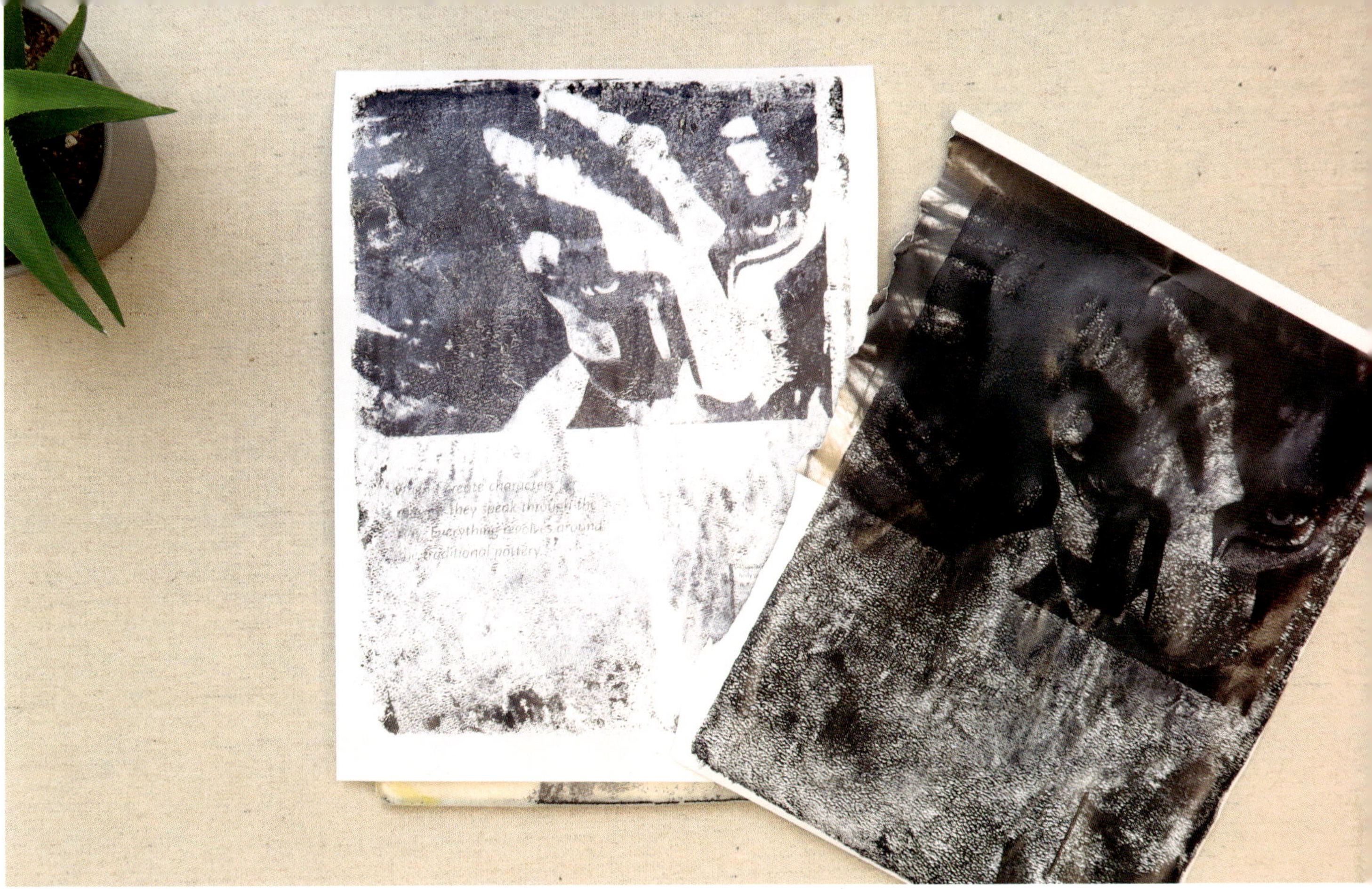

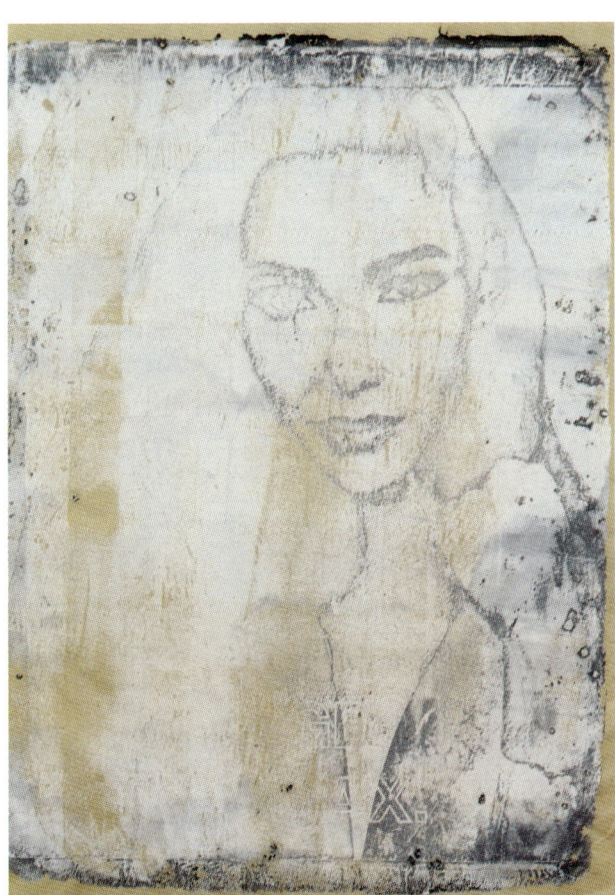

Magazine transfer to create a "grunge" transfer on the gel plate printed on kraft paper

ArtMythos Inspiration

Images in magazines usually have typography that goes with the picture. Whether you know it or not, when you choose an image to transfer, you may be drawn to the image *and* the typography. Challenge yourself to create a collage that balances images and typography in ways that you have never done before. This challenge is about seeing an enlarged letter, or a word, or a space, as art. You will notice that the letters become shapes that break up space in a collage, rather than just letters. Whether the letter is an *A* or *T* becomes inconsequential; what matters is that you are focusing on the relationship between the letter and balance in your collage. Size and scale will also come into play as you work with this. As you alter the size of the letters that you add to your imagery, you will feel how that changes your work.

Photocopied Gel Prints as an Activated Surface

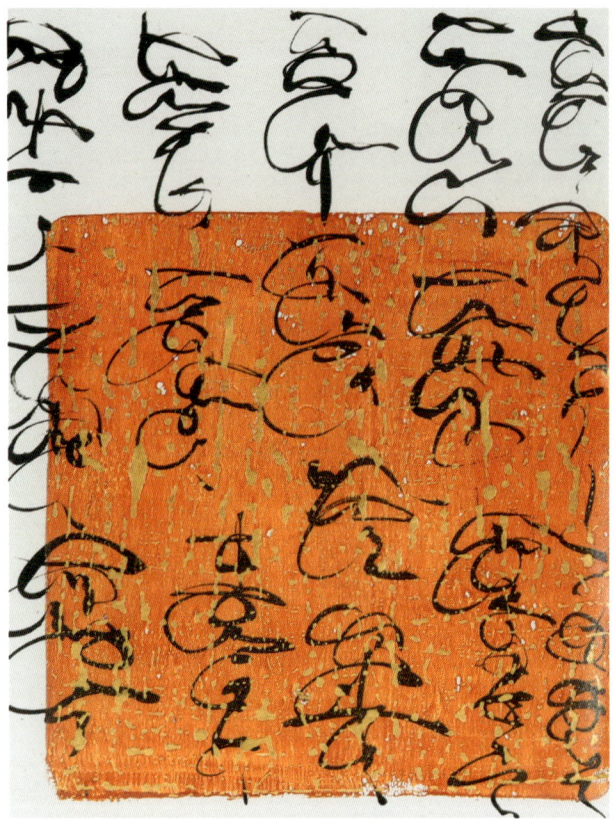

Gel printing on a laser print as activated surface

Eventually you may have a lot of your favorite gel prints that you don't want to alter. One of the methods I use is to photocopy the original, then work with the photocopy. This allows you to add to the image, perhaps stenciling or mark-making on top of it. A light glaze on top of it automatically will make the photocopy look like a monoprint **1**–**3**.

You can also make a photocopy of the paint left on your gel plate. When you pull a print you love, and what remains on the gel plate looks amazing but seems impossible to pull off the plate, this is where our camera phones come in handy **4**. You can take a picture of the image left on the plate and print it out to use as collage papers or as an activated surface to apply the glazing technique, or continue printing on top of it with stencils and masks.

For a video of this technique, visit robynmcclendon.com.

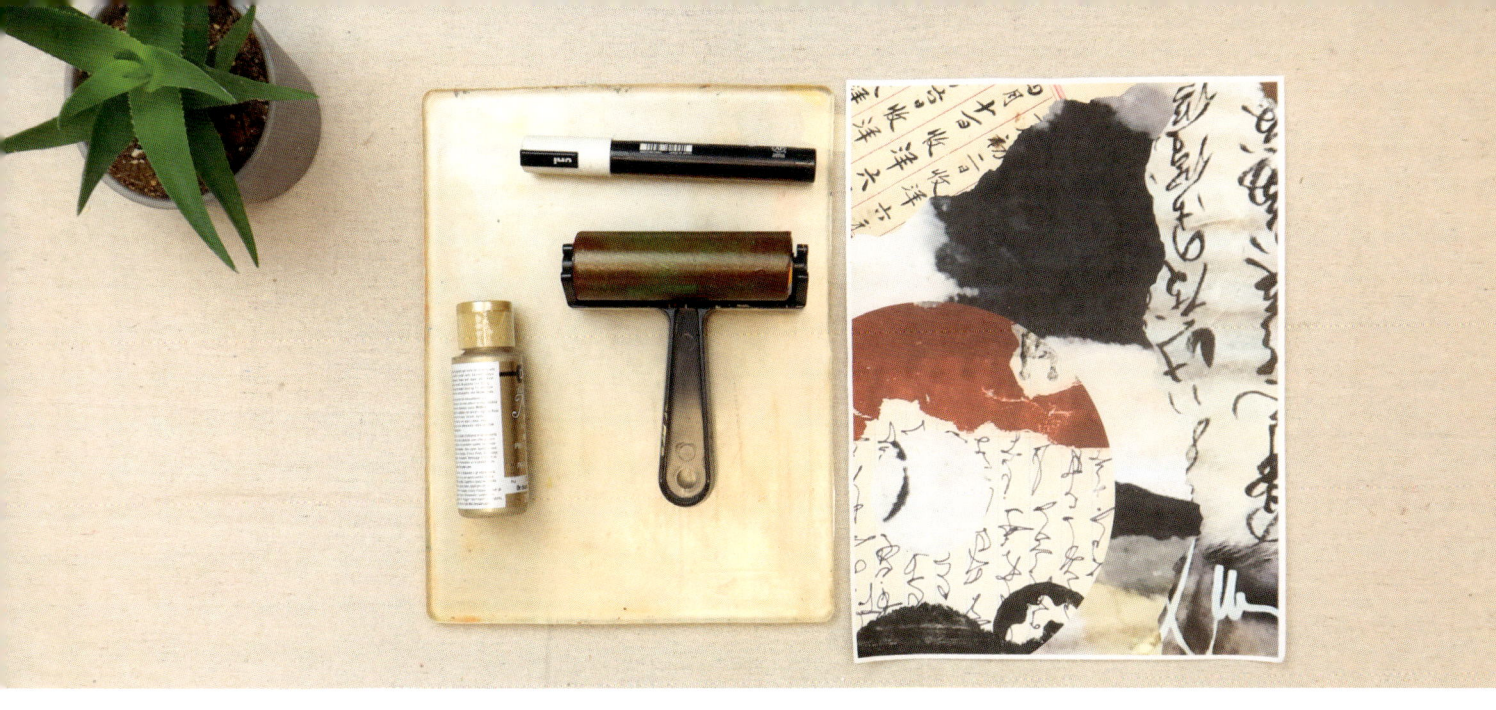

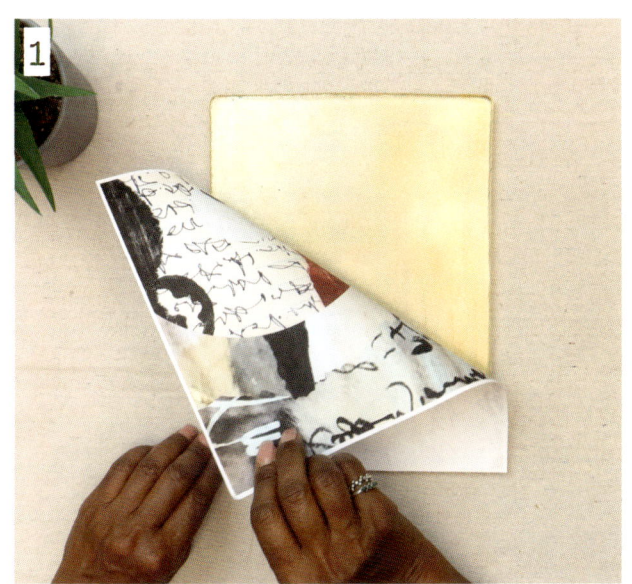

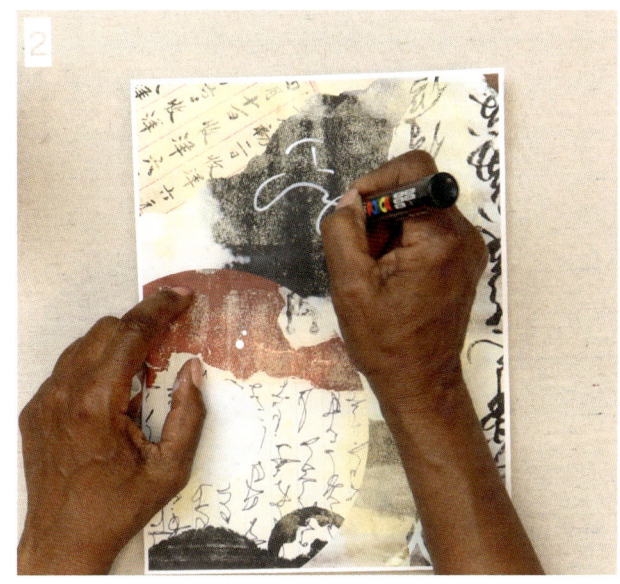

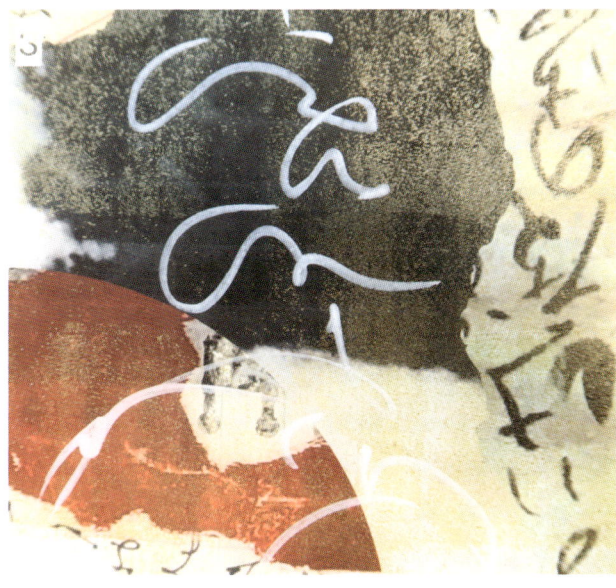

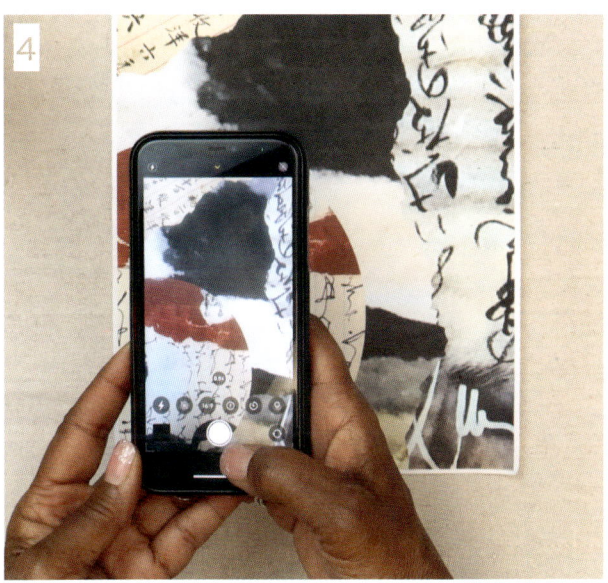

15

Fragments

As a mixed-media collage artist, I love taking bits and pieces of information and layering them into a more complex and harmonious image. The gel plate makes it so easy to create some of my favorite symbols that capture mood and emotion of line. I find myself painting circles, x's, lines, and dots on the gel plate and using very thin tissue paper to pull these prints for use as collage elements.

These bits and pieces or "fragments" are a part of my visual dialogue that can be separated from a completed gel-printed image. I apply them to collage compositions exactly where I want them. Fragments can be stored easily, so that when you're not gel printing yet want a monoprinted quality in your collage, they're ready to use.

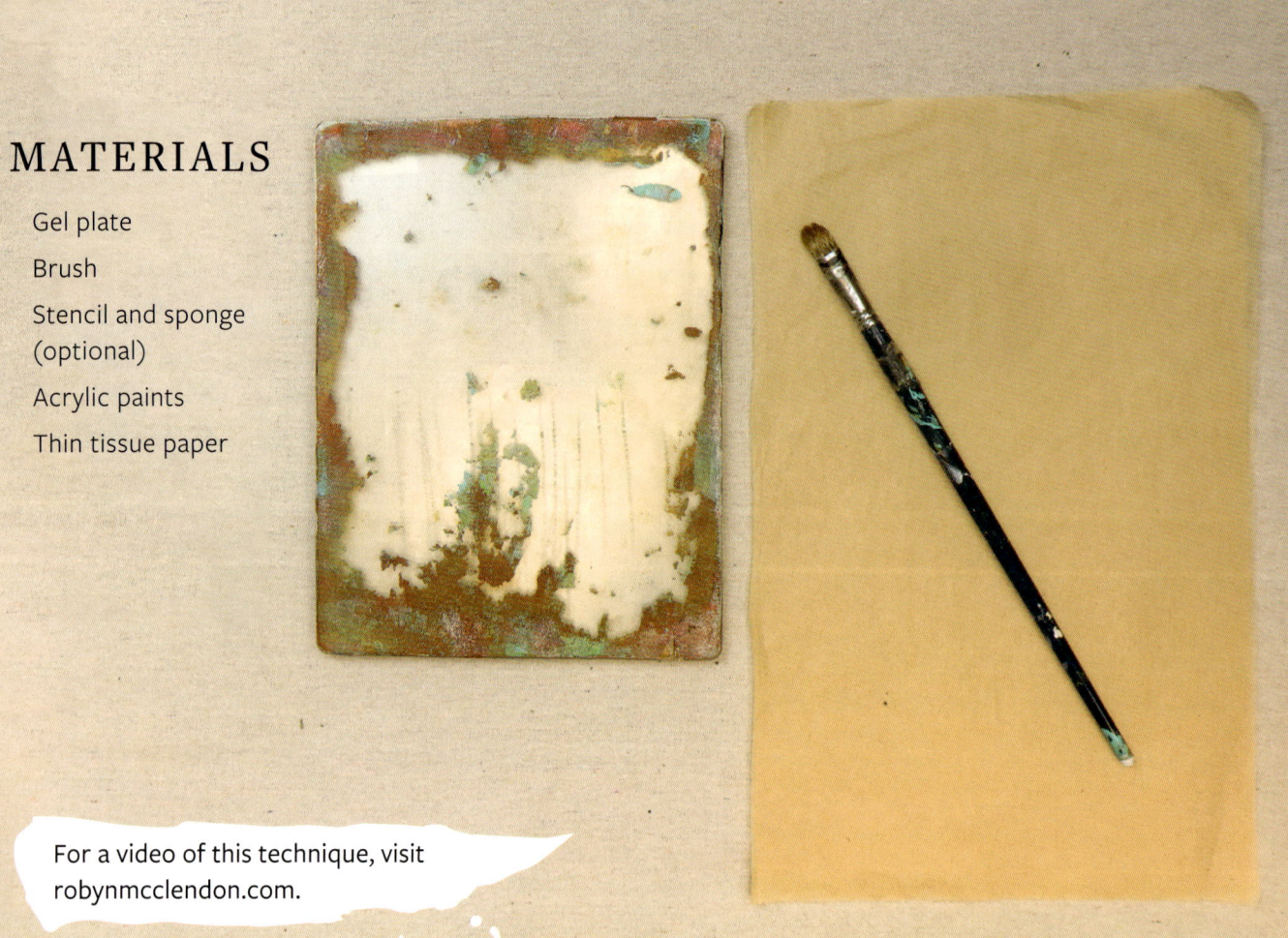

MATERIALS

Gel plate

Brush

Stencil and sponge (optional)

Acrylic paints

Thin tissue paper

For a video of this technique, visit robynmcclendon.com.

Right: Gold circle fragments on a gel-printed surface

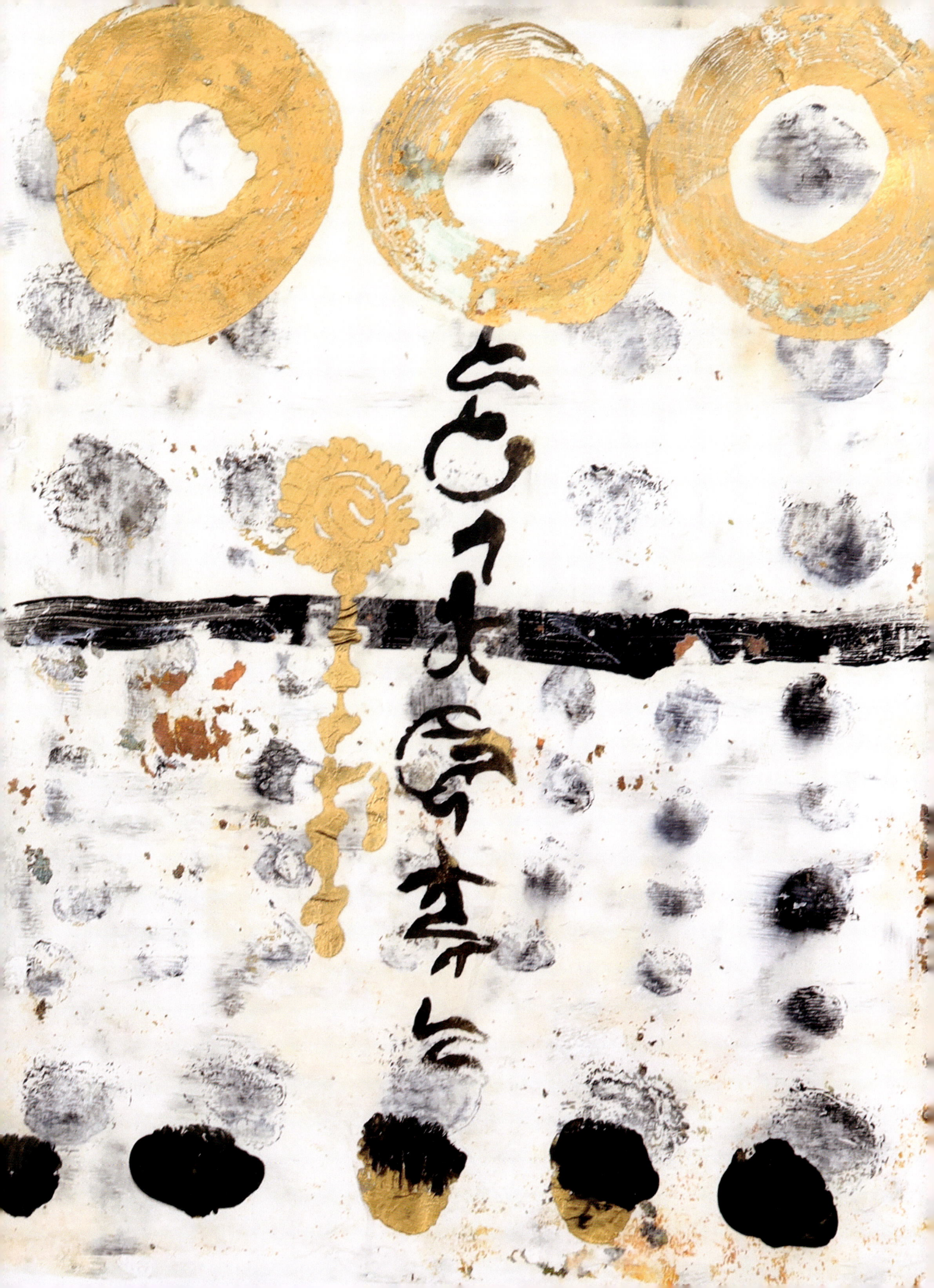

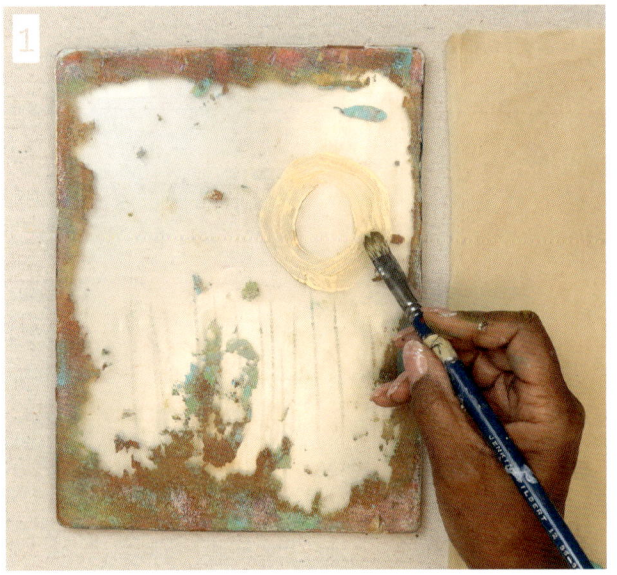

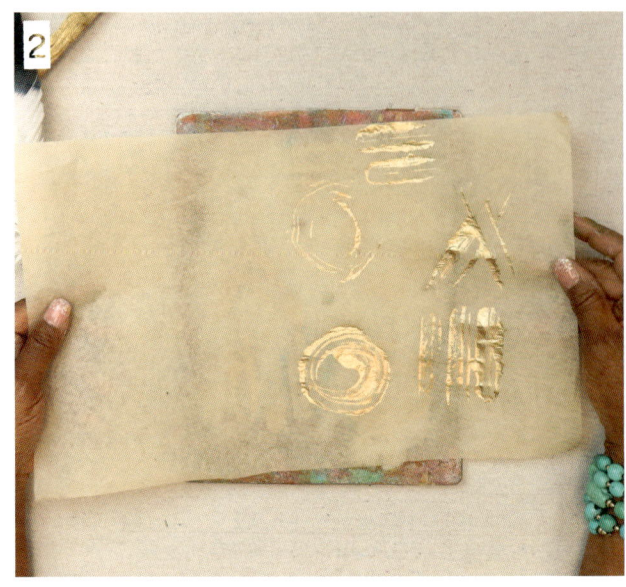

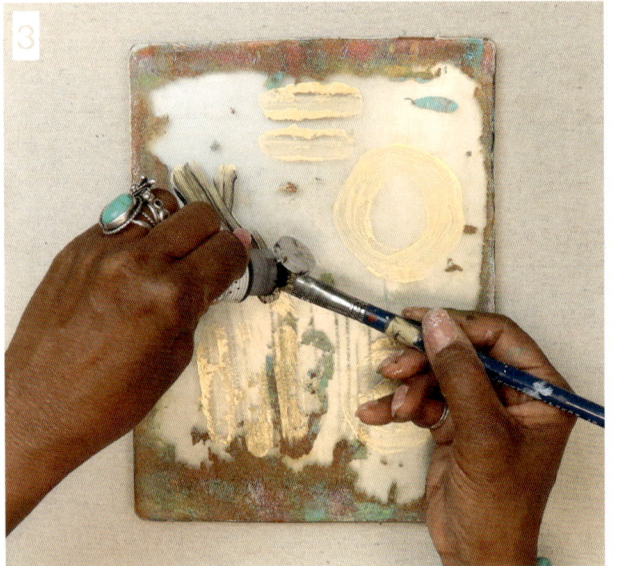

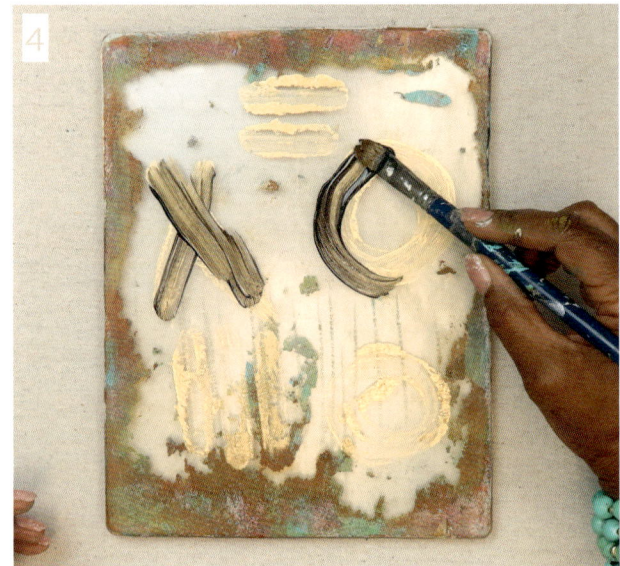

Fragments are easy and fun to make! I primarily use a paintbrush to paint the symbols, images, lines, and dots right onto my gel plate. I then use tissue paper to pull these images as a collection of individual elements that later will be torn off the tissue paper as needed **1**–**4**.

You can also use stencils. Lay a stencil on the gel plate and apply the paint through the stencil, using a small sponge, then remove the stencil and use tissue paper to pull the image.

When you're done, store the fragments among your collage fodder.

To work with gel plates, you don't always have to do a full session. You can create bits and pieces that you can store for later use in different ways.

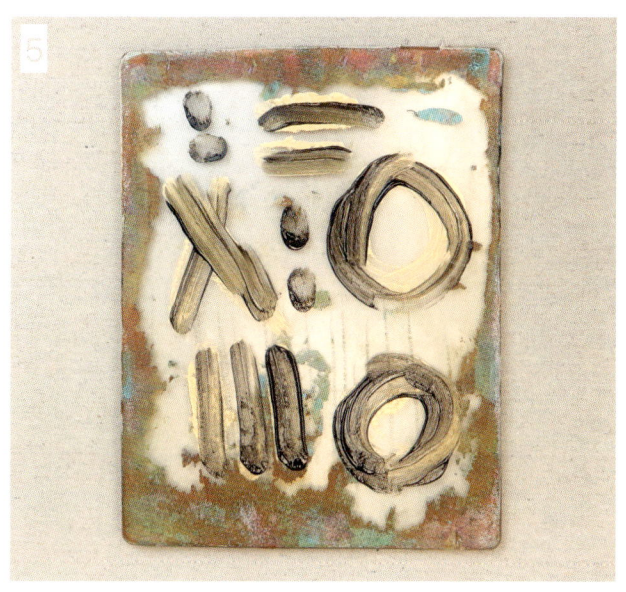

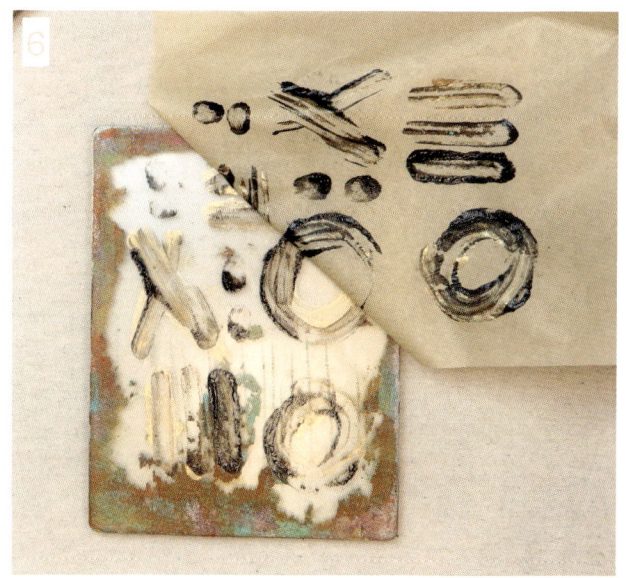

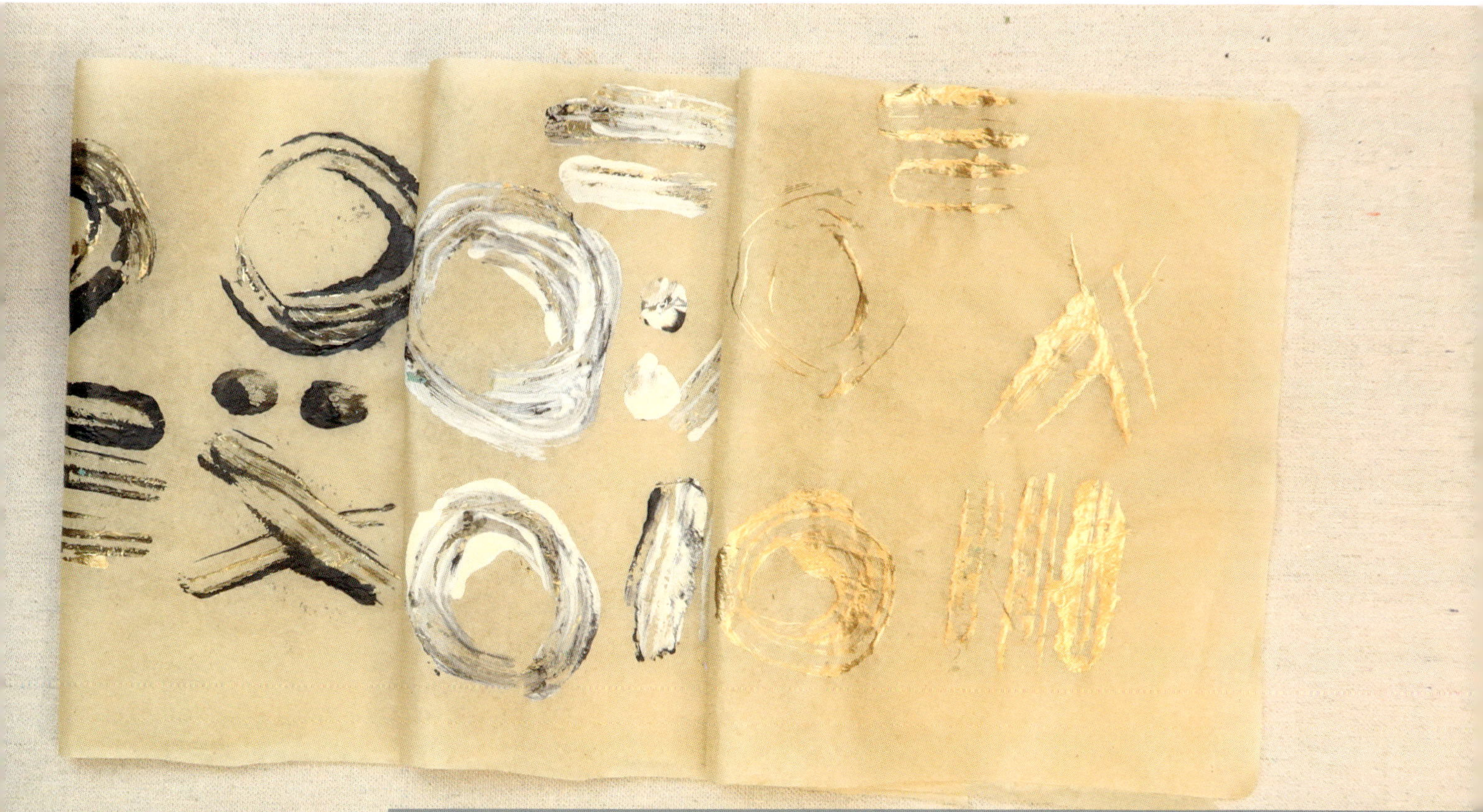

ArtMythos Inspiration

Using this fragments technique, put together a visual vocabulary that is unique to your aesthetic. Challenge yourself to gather your favorite symbols, shapes, and language. Letters, numbers, whatever you are inspired by. Look through your past work and see what shapes you use. You may be surprised to find that you have a symbol or shape that you use often. Use fragments to celebrate your relationship with this symbol or shape.

16

Oil Paints on the Gel Plate

When I am in my studio, it's often the case that I'm in a very experimental mood, and I found myself wondering how oil paints would interface with the gel plate. I thought that it would have to be similar to using traditional printer's inks on glass or acrylic surfaces in a monoprinting process on a flatbed press. So I pulled out my oils and began to experiment with oil paints on the gel plate, using both the brayer method and the paintbrush method. They both worked wonderfully.

The oil paints on the plate lie and stay in place similar to acrylic. There is a lot more open time because of the oil. You can really work your image. This is a great process for doing landscapes. It gives you the opportunity to work and play with the paints, and to get your subject matter fleshed out. The steps are similar to what you've already been doing many times by this point in the book.

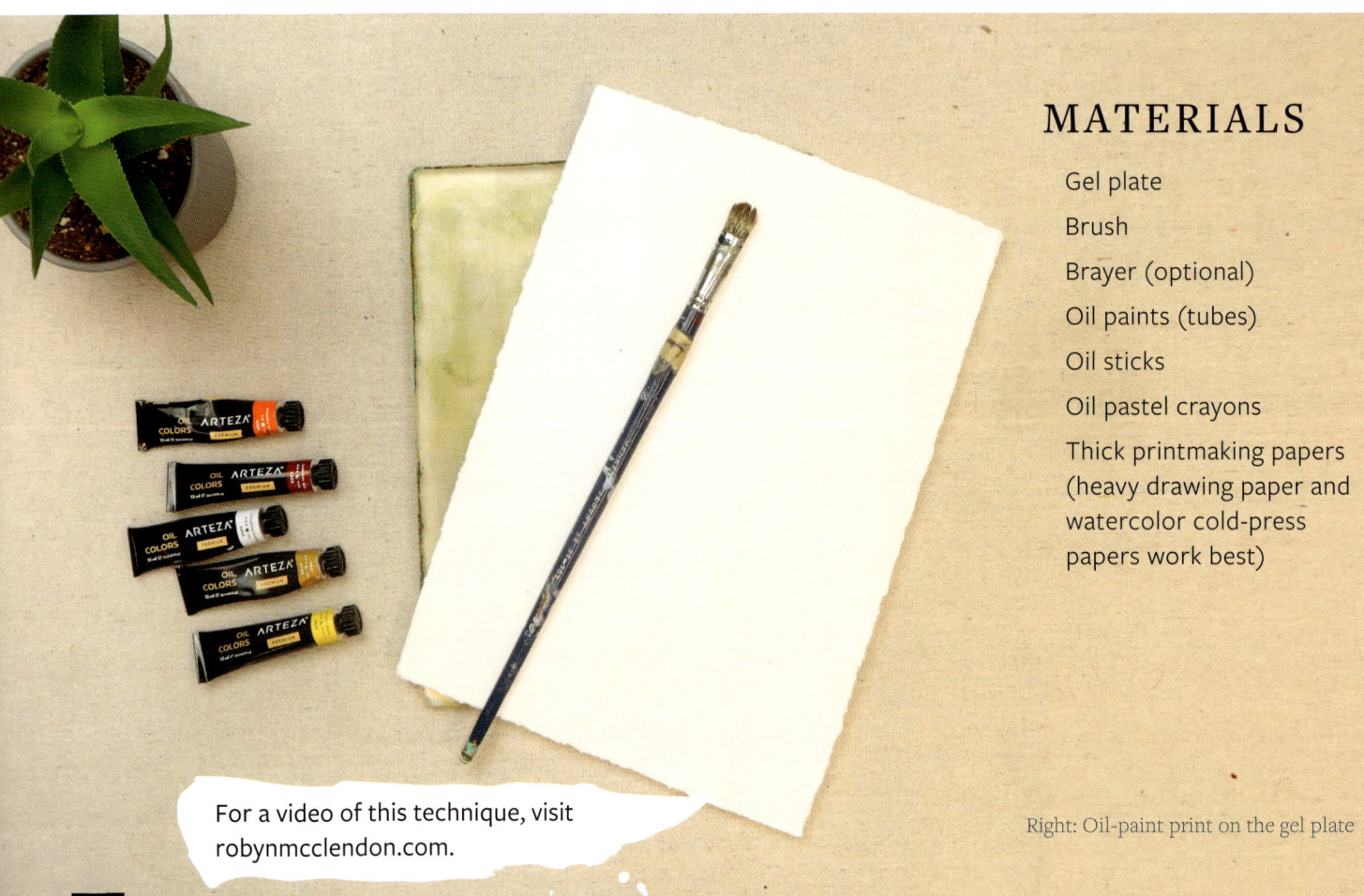

MATERIALS

Gel plate

Brush

Brayer (optional)

Oil paints (tubes)

Oil sticks

Oil pastel crayons

Thick printmaking papers (heavy drawing paper and watercolor cold-press papers work best)

For a video of this technique, visit robynmcclendon.com.

Right: Oil-paint print on the gel plate

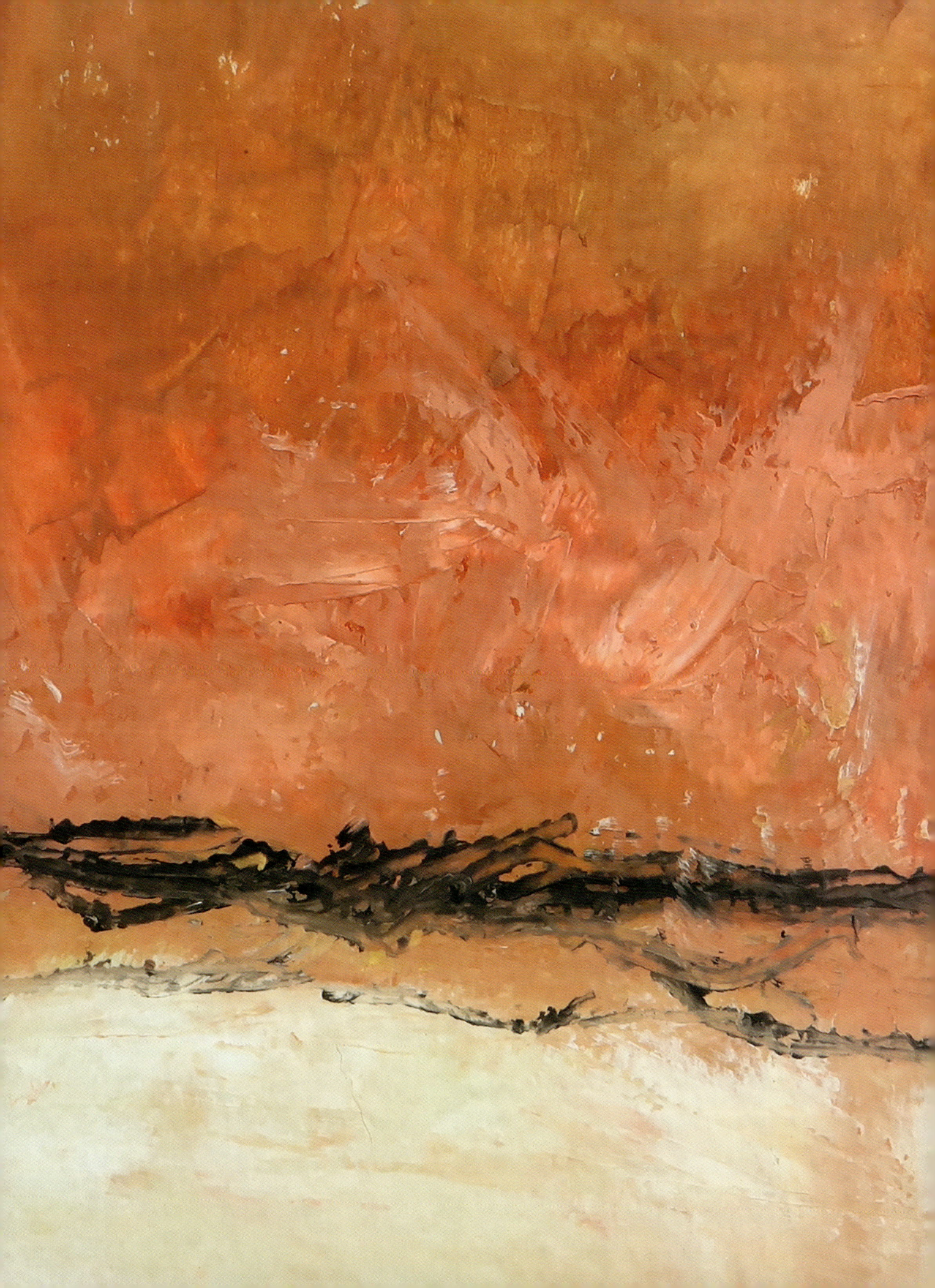

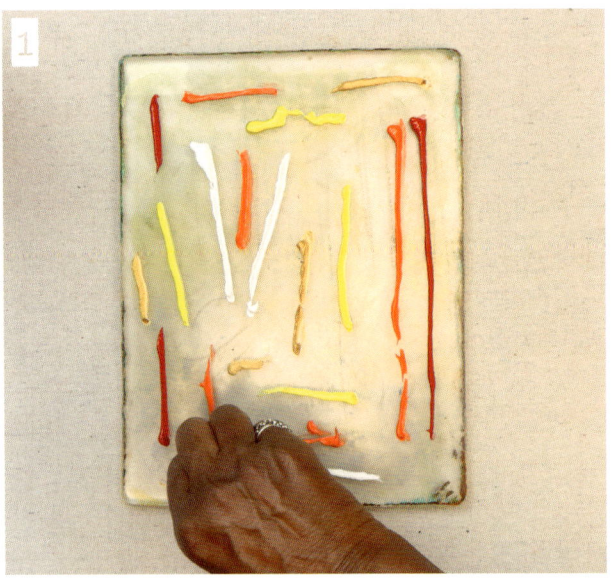

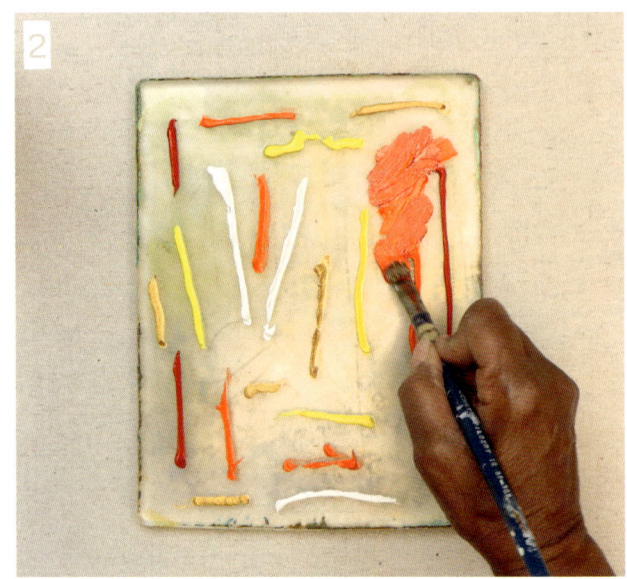

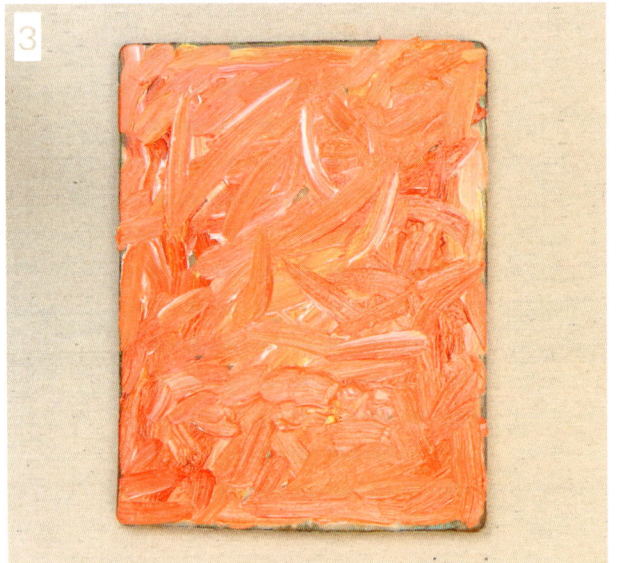

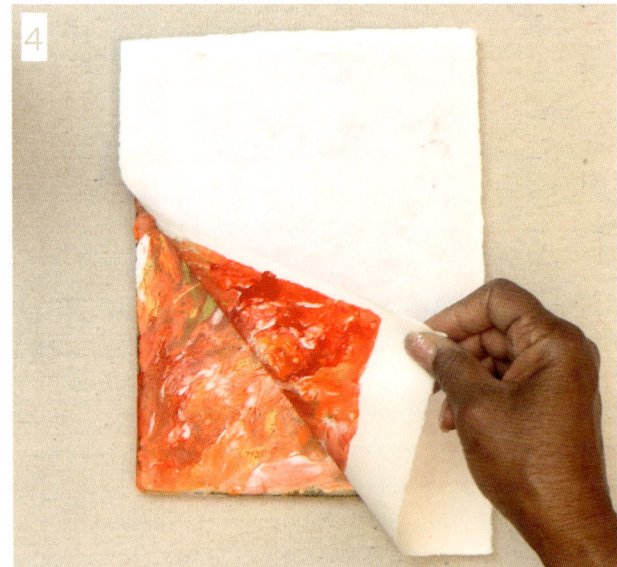

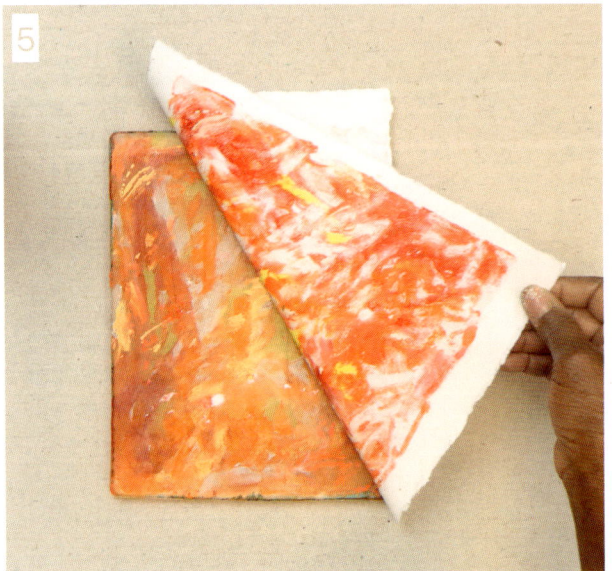

Put small stripes of paint on your plate **1**. Multiple coordinating colors work nicely.

Use your brayer or an oil-paint brush. Any size or shape will work. You'll discover the different patterns, textures, and shapes that the brushes will make **2**, **3**.

Lay paper down, gently make good contact, and remove **4**, **5**.

When you go to pull the print, there is some movement of the paint because laying the paper down and pressing it will cause flattening of the image. Yet, even so, it is amazing the amount of texture and volume that transfers off the plate onto the paper, leaving a really beautiful, rich oil-painted surface.

You can experiment with types of paper. I have used tissue paper, Japanese calligraphy paper, even copier paper. You can also use fabrics and a canvas cloth (see chapter 18) to transfer from the plate.

You can use oils in a tube, oil sticks, and oil pastels in combination. The tube oils will be creamier and buttery. They will have more impasto. The oil sticks offer more of a drawn line that brings a drawing element to your print. They are also great for creating definition. The sticks will also create a more identical image when you transfer, since they will not smush like the oil paints. This adds to the ability to control the line more.

When you are ready to change colors or clean the plate, you'll find it very easy. Put a quarter-sized amount of baby oil directly on the plate, and gently wipe it with a paper towel or baby wipe.

You can use large, open-pattern stencils such as large circles or squares. Open repeat pattern types of stencils are great for creating texture on the plate. Cloth is great too; you can use a heavy burlap. Working with oils allows you to pull some really neat textures, especially. Be experimental with creating your textures.

If you are looking for a quick and simple idea for creating during your first time using oils on the gel plate, a landscape is a great idea. An abstract expressionist landscape will have simple horizon lines and tree or mountain lines, and color backing those various elements. Pick a picture out of a magazine or a landscape that you admire. Try to copy the color field as you decide which paints to put on your plate.

These prints work best if you can hang them up to air-dry, since oil paints dry more slowly than other paints. You can use a clothesline or use shelves where you can lay them out individually. As with any oil painting, it will take a few weeks for the oil to dry.

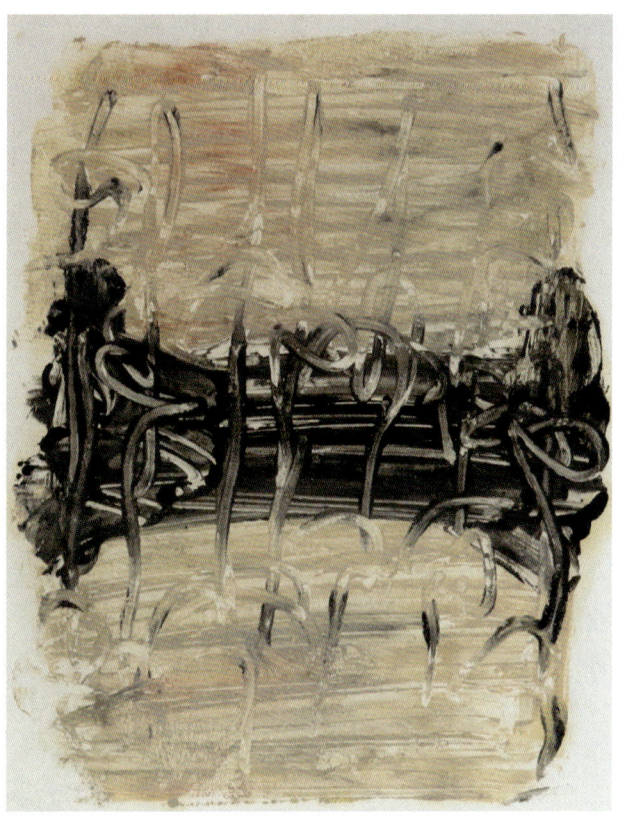

Oil-paint print on the gel plate

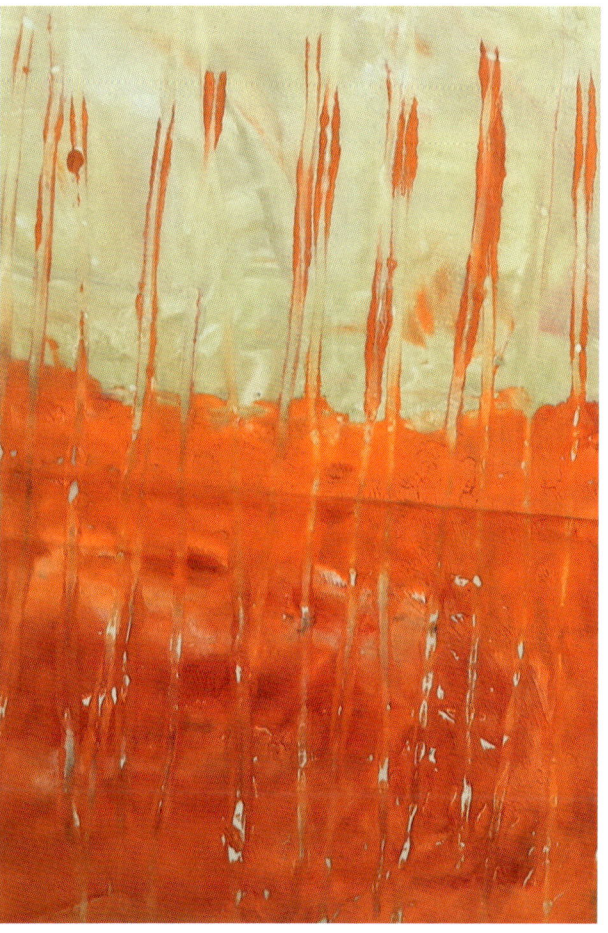

17

Block-Printing Inks and Intaglio Inks on the Gel Plate

Block printing and intaglio are traditional inks used in monoprinting processes. These inks work beautifully on the gel plate as well.

Block-printing inks are generally used on hard surfaces such as wood, and the surface can be worked without the inks drying out before the print can be transferred to paper. The cleanup is easy with these inks: soap and water will clean the brayer and plate, leaving no residue.

Intaglio inks are soy based, have a long open time, and are traditionally used on plexiglass and metal plates. However, I have had amazing success with them on the gel plate. These inks dry quickly when the images are transferred to high-quality papers, and otherwise they will stay open/wet indefinitely on the gel plate. They also offer an easy cleanup with soapy water.

MATERIALS

Gel plate

Brayer

Block-printing inks

Intaglio inks

Printing papers (cotton rag); Swarthmore and Rives are excellent brands. Cold-press watercolor or heavyweight drawing papers work well too.

For a video of this technique, visit robynmcclendon.com.

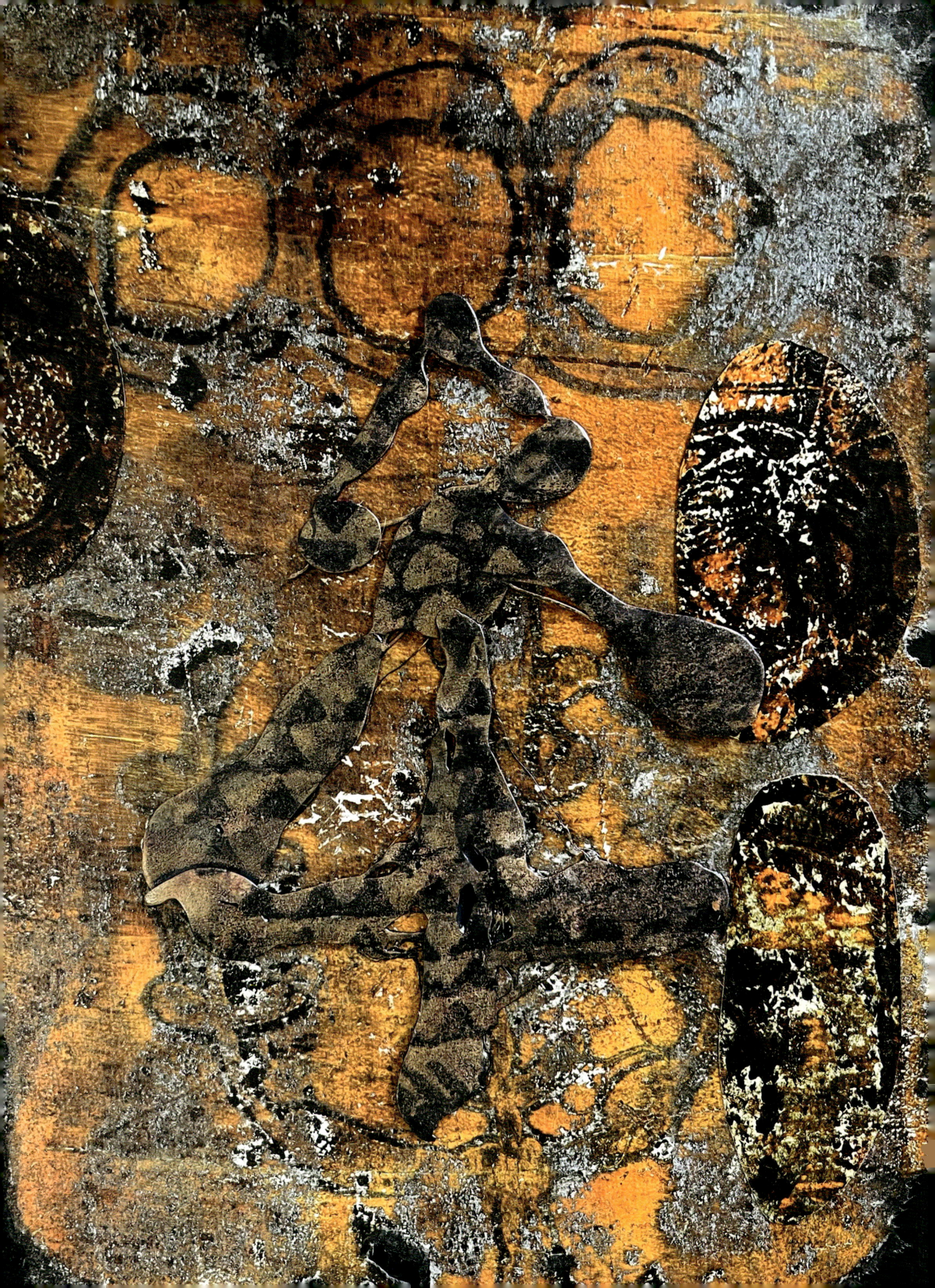

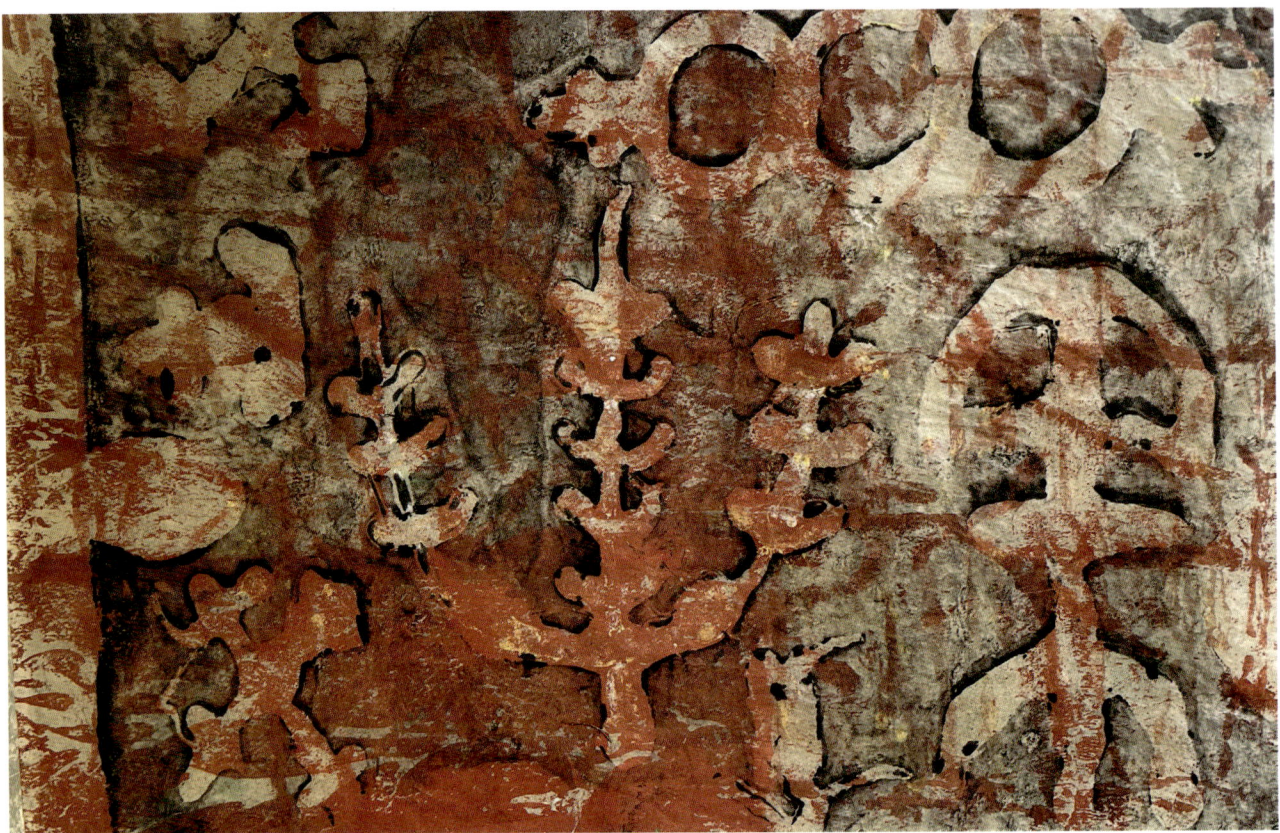

Apply a small amount of ink (pea size). It's important to start with small amounts and add to the plate, rather than having too much. With block printing inks, a little goes a long way. You will use far less than when working with acrylics. Brayer the ink out into a very thin layer.

You can draw into the surface by subtracting ink. Using masks and stencils will work beautifully in this process as well.

Lay the paper onto the surface, rubbing to smooth and form good contact with the plate. Remove the paper to view the transfer.

These steps can be repeated to build up images and color until you are satisfied with the results.

The images look very little like their cousins created with acrylic paints. The images are softer and more ethereal and have a level of sophistication reminiscent of traditional monoprinting methods.

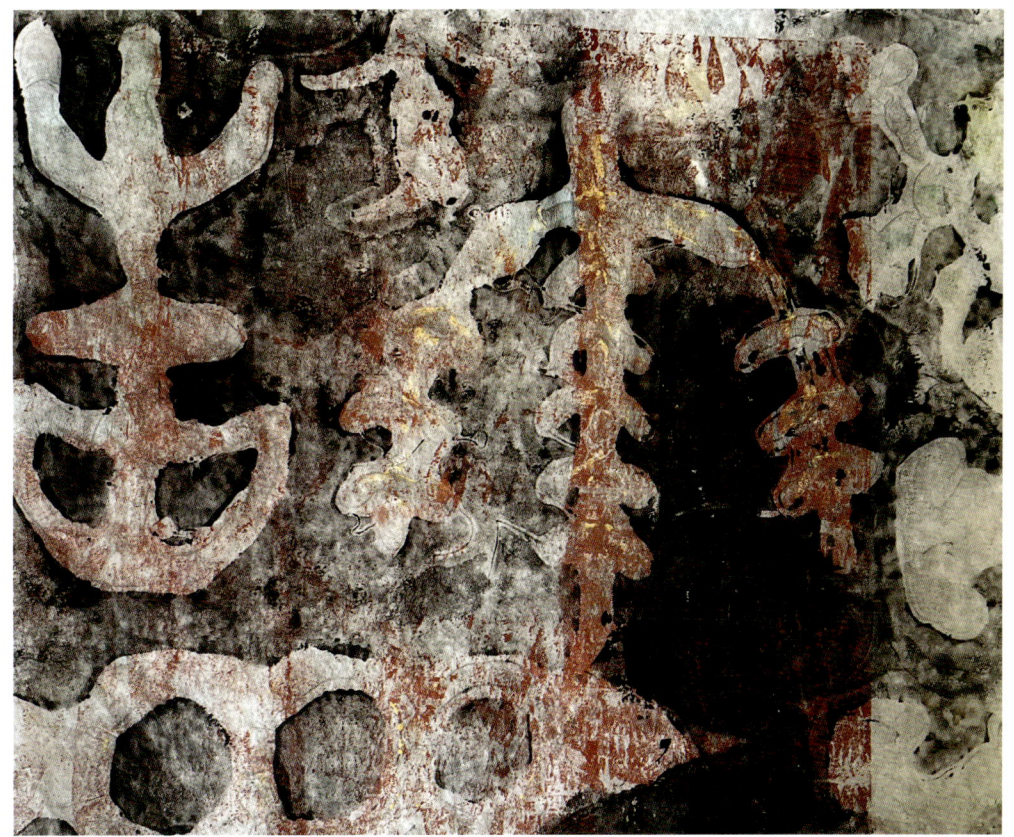

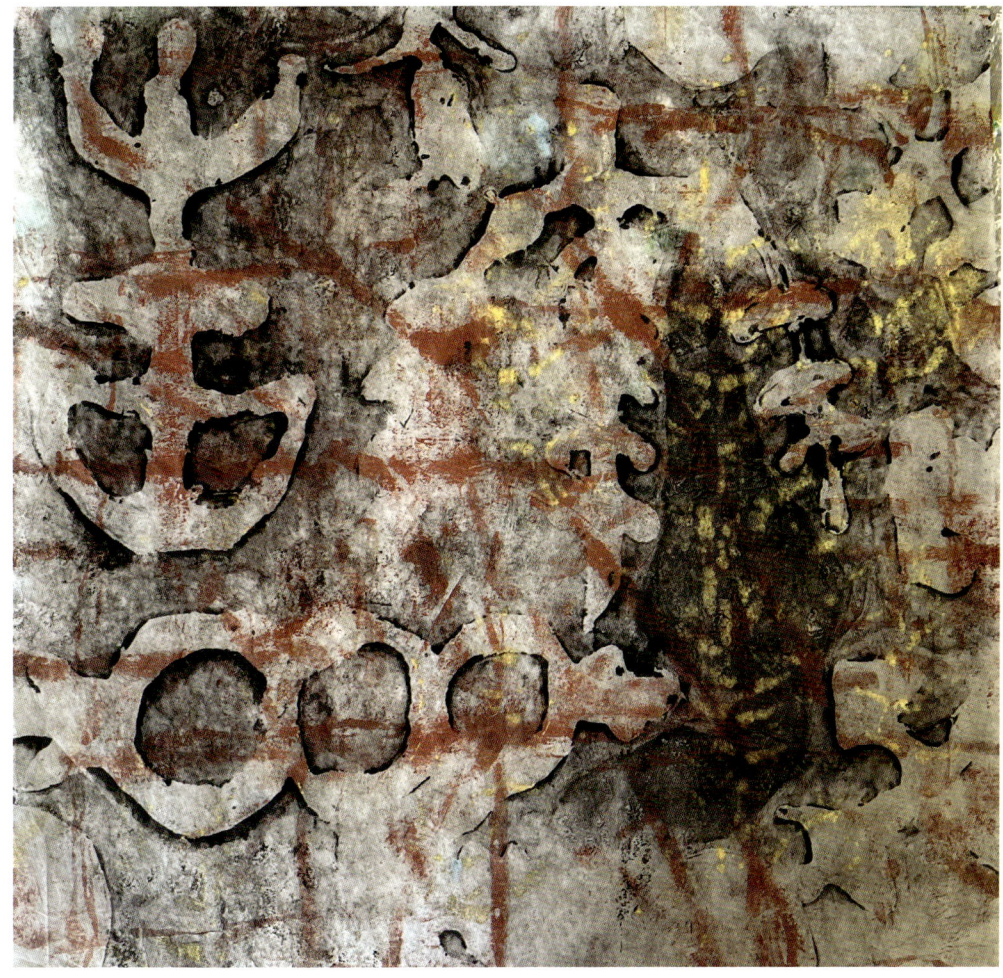

18

Gel Printing on Fabric

Historically, monoprinting has had so many applications in various genres, from wallpapers to fabric painting to fine-art printing. Because gel printing is a monoprinting process, it is inspiring to think of the ways you can push this technique. True to its historical foundations, we can use fabric on the plate!

There are many applications for using fabric in our artwork. You can use it as a collage element in art pieces, or as a foundation for covering your books and journals. It can also be used in quilt making, tapestries, and scrolls.

Thin fabrics and natural fibers such as cotton, linen, and silk work well. You can also use synthetics such as rayon or polyester. Any fabric that has a smooth surface will be good to print on. Sometimes synthetic fibers can resist paints or dyes; the organic fibers have a tendency to take paint and colors better. Jeans and canvas cloths work great, but it is important to gesso them due to their thick weave.

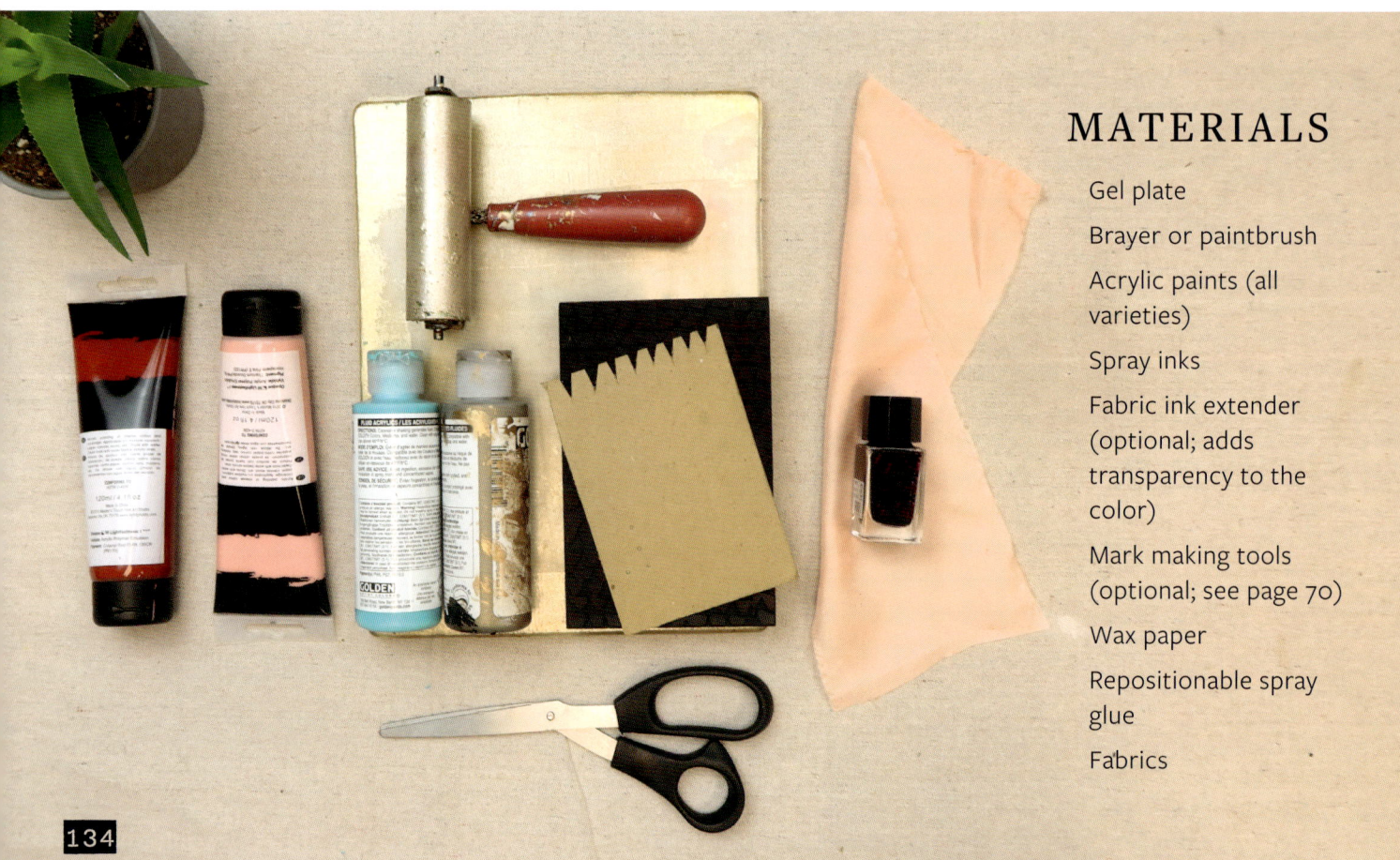

MATERIALS

Gel plate

Brayer or paintbrush

Acrylic paints (all varieties)

Spray inks

Fabric ink extender (optional; adds transparency to the color)

Mark making tools (optional; see page 70)

Wax paper

Repositionable spray glue

Fabrics

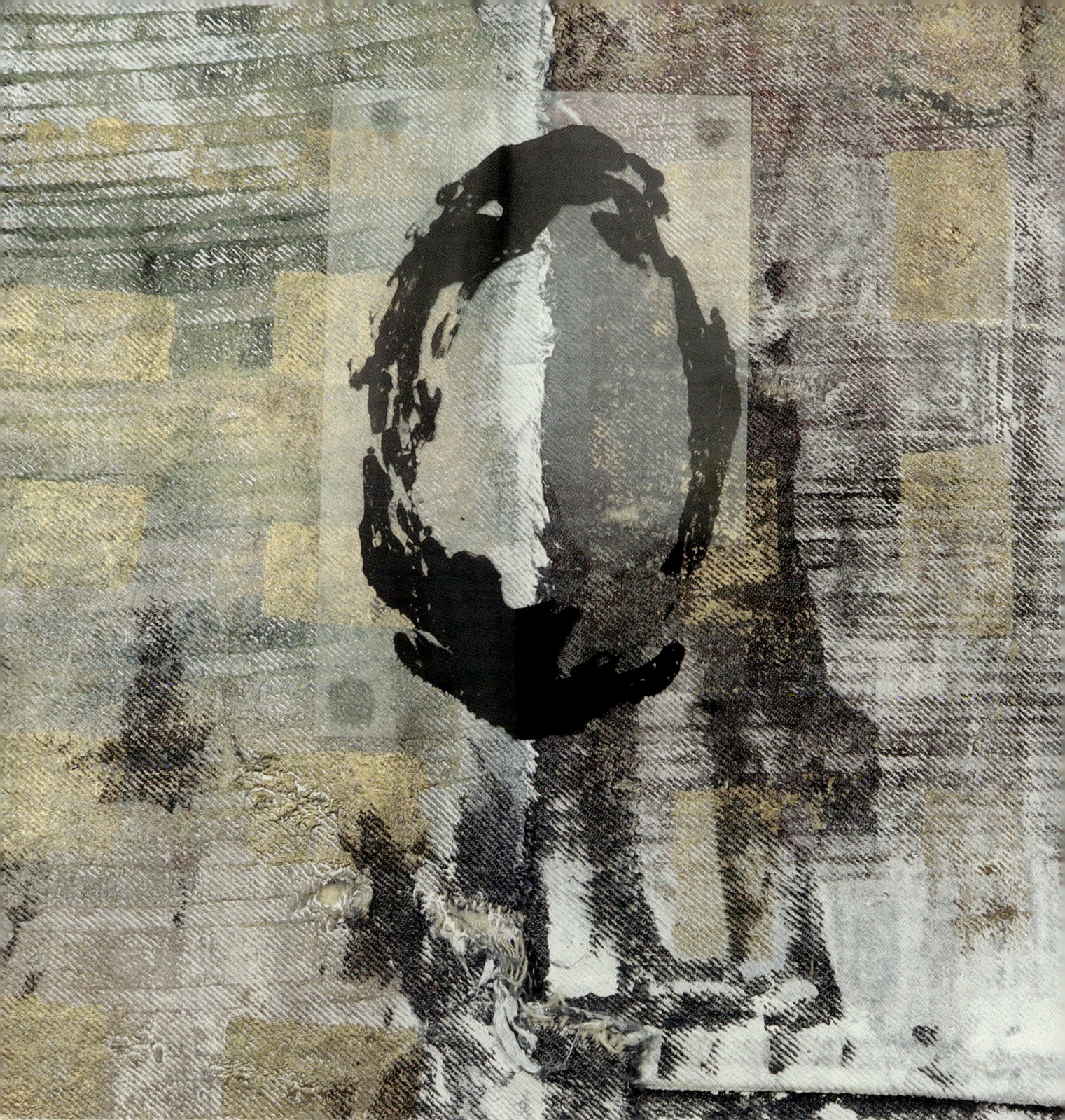

Gel print on fabric

For a video of this technique, visit
robynmcclendon.com.

Gessoing your piece of fabric is usually the first step. If you do not use gesso, the colors will bleed into the fabrics and give you a different finish. The color of the fabric will influence what the final print will look like. When you use gesso, the paint will lie right on the surface, and you won't have to worry about any of the resistance the fabric would give you. You will get crisper and more-definitive images with gesso.

It is a good idea to use a card over a paintbrush to get gesso onto your fabric. It will give you more-efficient use of the product. It will also give you more even coverage and a more even level of opacity.

Wait for the gesso to dry before doing any printing.

You always want to consider your substrate when picking out your color palette. This will often determine if you are going to use gesso or not. It is also a great idea to pick a color that harmonizes and integrates well with the fabric that you are using. For example, if you are using jeans, an indigo will be great to use in your printing.

When printing on fabric, the more stable you can keep your fabric, the better and easier your printing will be, especially if you will be doing several layers. What I like to do is back the fabric with paper. You especially want to create backing for thin fabrics such as silks, linens, and polyesters. Although backing is mainly for thinner fabrics, you can back your thicker fabrics such as denim too.

Use a good-quality waxed paper. When you iron the fabric onto the paper, you will get a temporary bond that holds while you print and reprint, until you are ready to separate it. You can also use paper and a repositionable spray glue, which makes a nonpermanent sticky surface. Spray your paper and smooth your fabric over it. Then when you are finished, just peel it off.

You can also use double-sided tape as a backing. This works especially well with thin fabrics.

I don't always back the fabric. It really depends on how specific I want an image transfer to be. If I'm okay with loose patterns, for example, I will omit backing. Experiment with both to see what you like and to observe the various applications' results.

Once you are ready to start printing, you can use any of the techniques you have learned in previous chapters, alone or in combinations.

Place small amounts of paint over your plate **1**. Multiple coordinating colors work nicely. Spritz on spray inks in complementary colors **2**. Doing this helps push the paints into the fabric and set the paints.

Use your brayer or a paintbrush of any size or shape to spread the paint **3**. You'll discover the different patterns, textures, and shapes that the brushstrokes will make.

Lay the fabric down, gently make good contact **4**, and remove **5**–**7**. 🖌

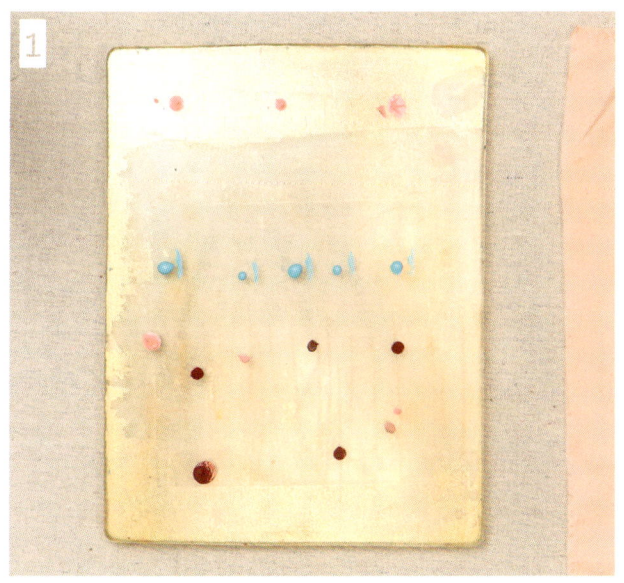

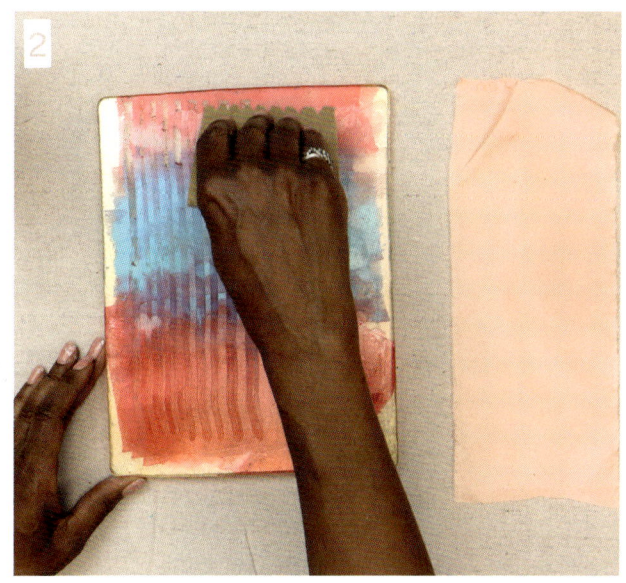

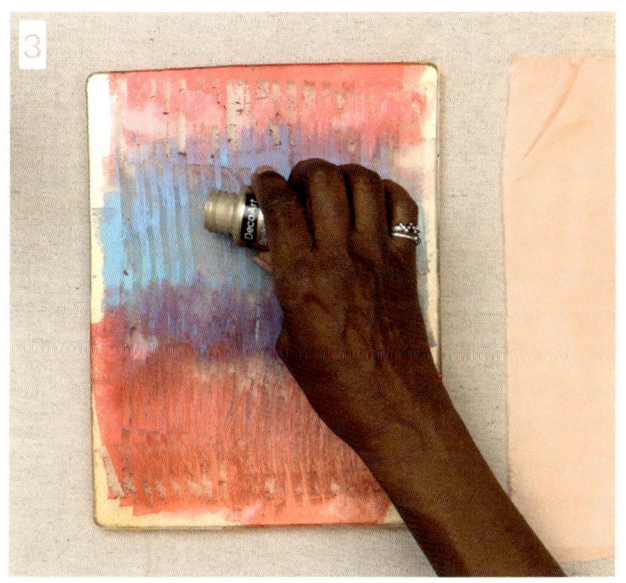

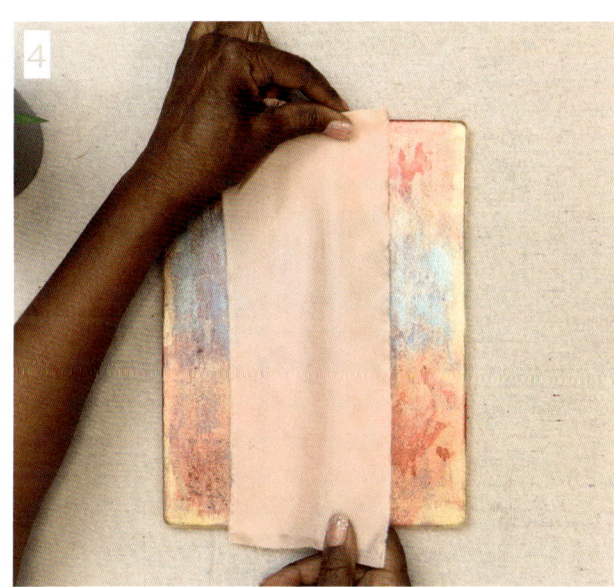

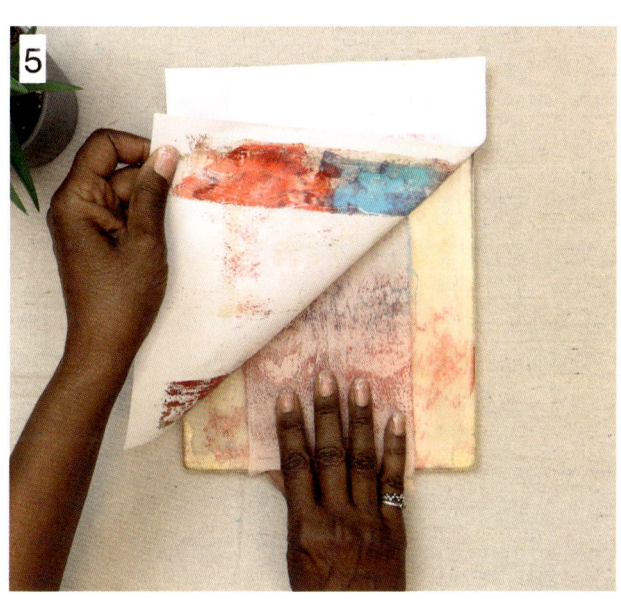

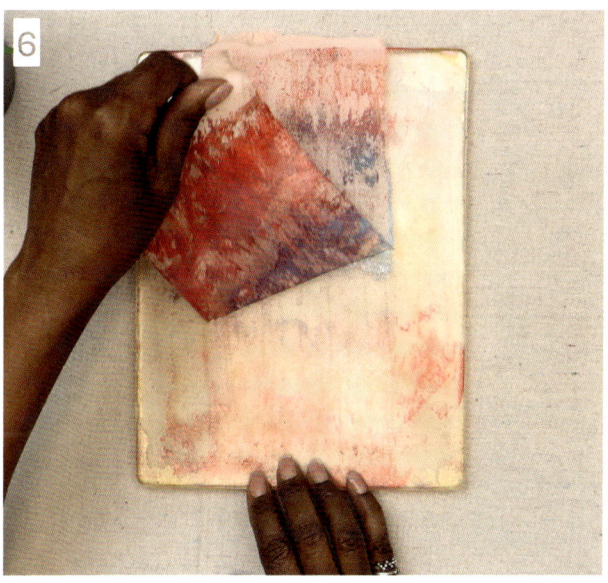

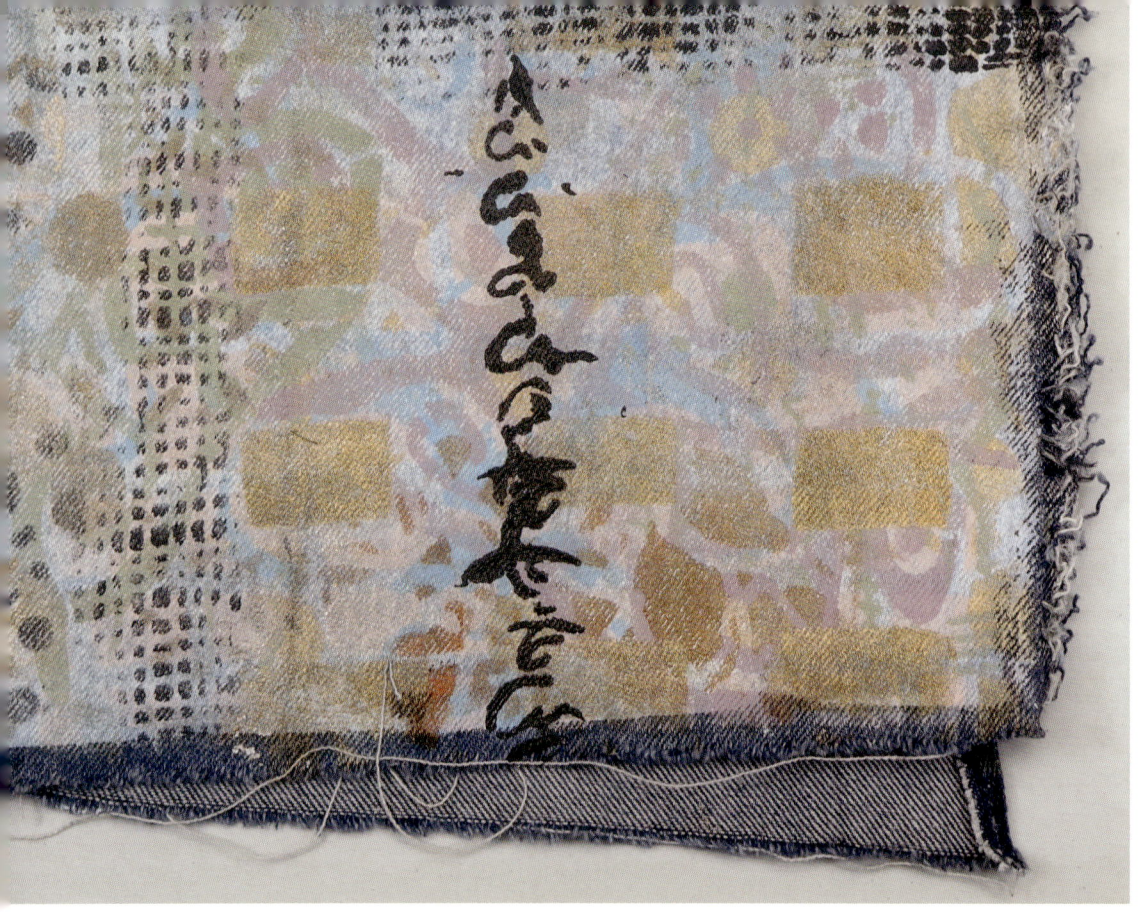

Gel print on denim

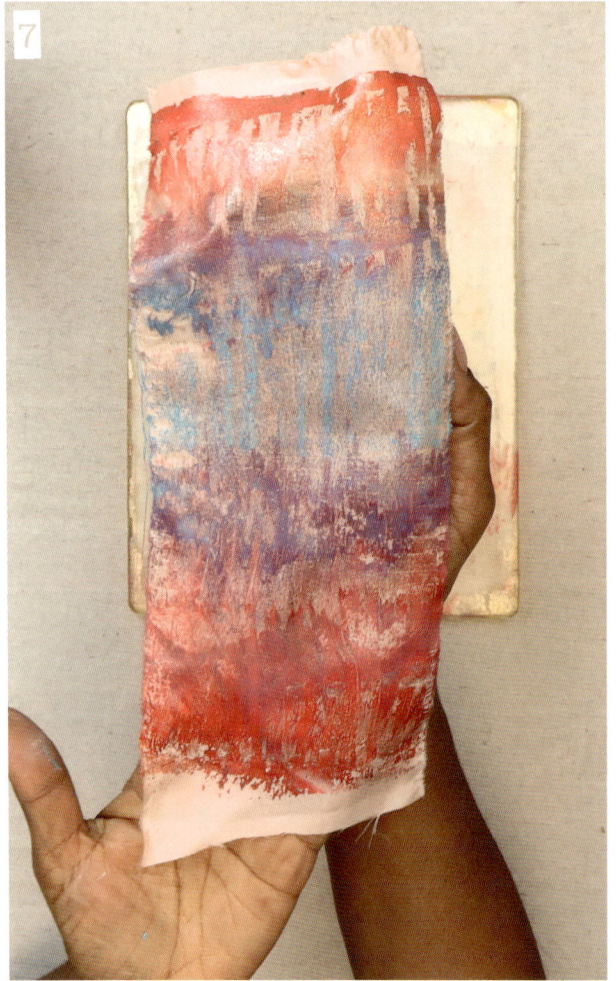

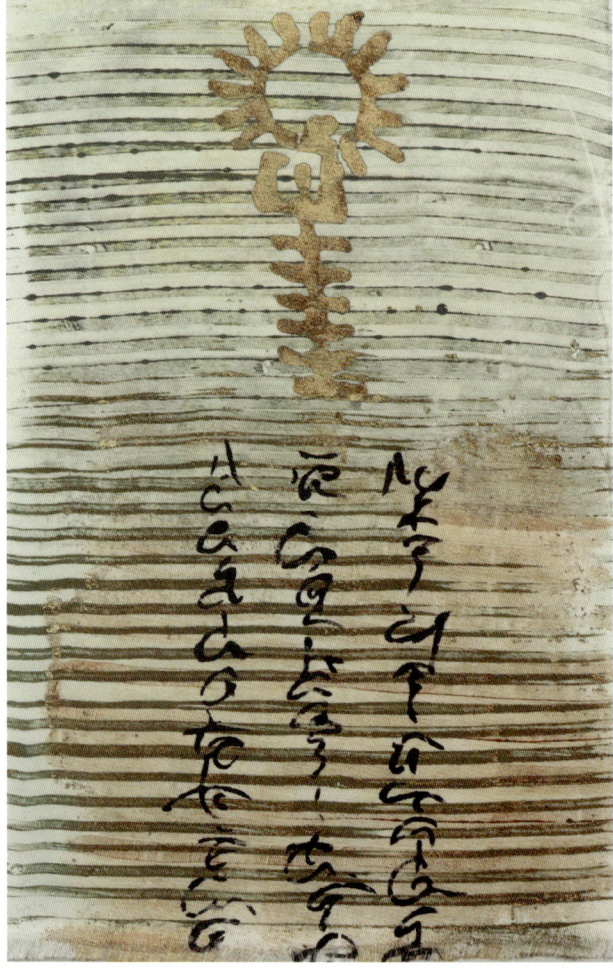

Gel print on sheer fabric

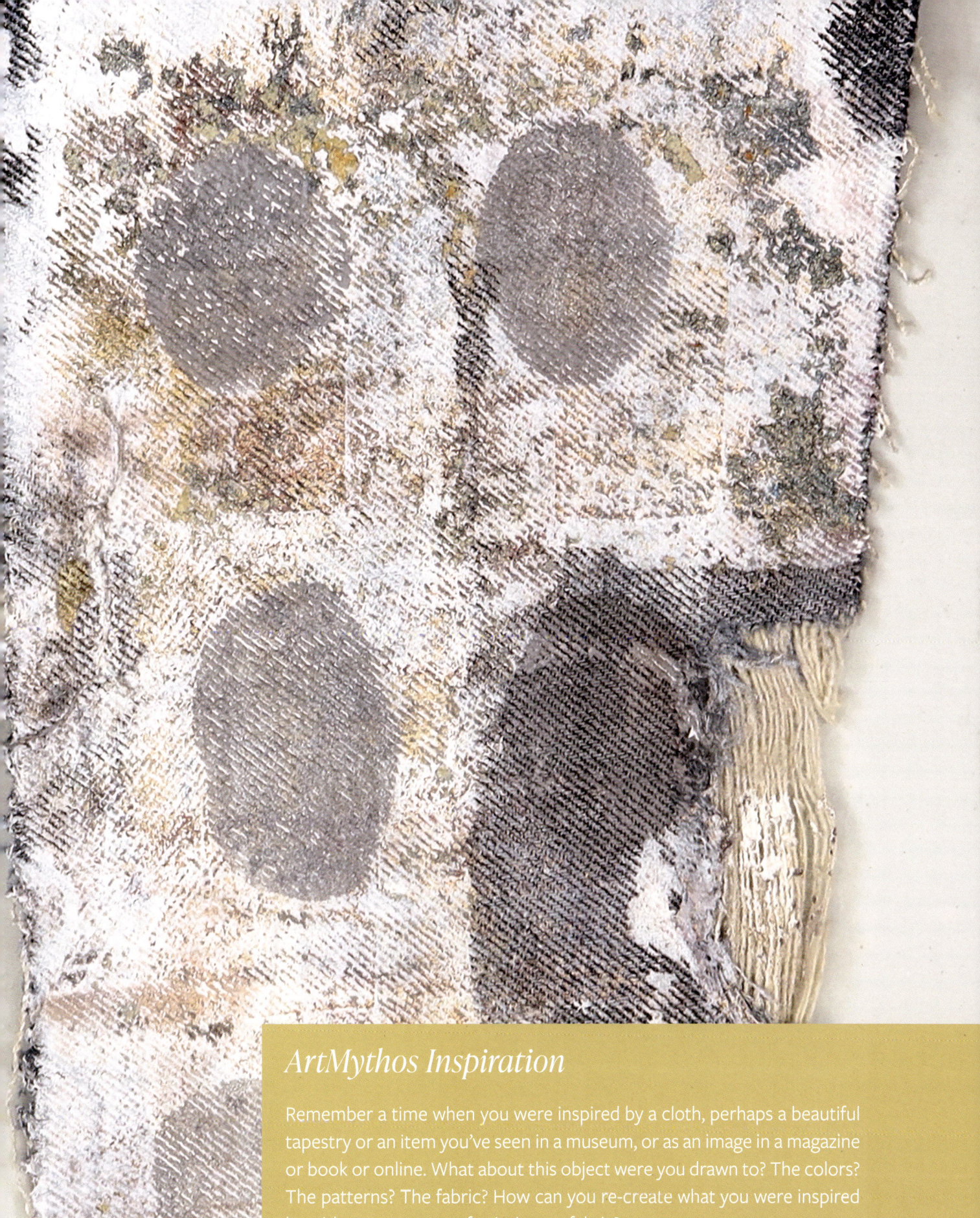

Gel print on denim

ArtMythos Inspiration

Remember a time when you were inspired by a cloth, perhaps a beautiful tapestry or an item you've seen in a museum, or as an image in a magazine or book or online. What about this object were you drawn to? The colors? The patterns? The fabric? How can you re-create what you were inspired by with your process of printing on fabric?

19

Large-Scale Gel Printing

Congratulations! You have reached the stage where you can combine everything you have learned into large-scale gel plate printing! Printing is a lot of fun, but as you can see, it is definitely a process that requires time for practicing the techniques and learning which ones work best for you, as well as for learning about your own color palette preferences.

All of this applies exponentially when you begin large-scale gel plate printing. When you start working with a surface that is larger than the largest gel plates available, you will have to change the nature of how you print.

The first thing to keep in mind is that you'll need to look at the work that you want to create in sections. Each section on very large sheets of paper can be equal to the size of the gel plate you are using. For example, if you have an 8″ by 10″ plate, you will need to view the entire work in 8″ by 10″ portions. The idea is that you will repeatedly use the plate as a giant stamp, filling up the sheet with the monoprinted images / painted sections until the entire page is filled with paint.

Phases and key ideas help with large-scale gel printin

1 Choosing a color palette

2 Finger painting

3 Stamping

4 First layer consists of vertical stamps

5 Second layer consists of horizontal stamps

6 6 Keeping the idea of weaving in mind

7 Using smaller plates to fill in the spaces

8 Using a smaller plate with white brayered out on it to create mark making

9 Deciding whether or not you want a border

10 Deciding which colors in your palette will work for the border

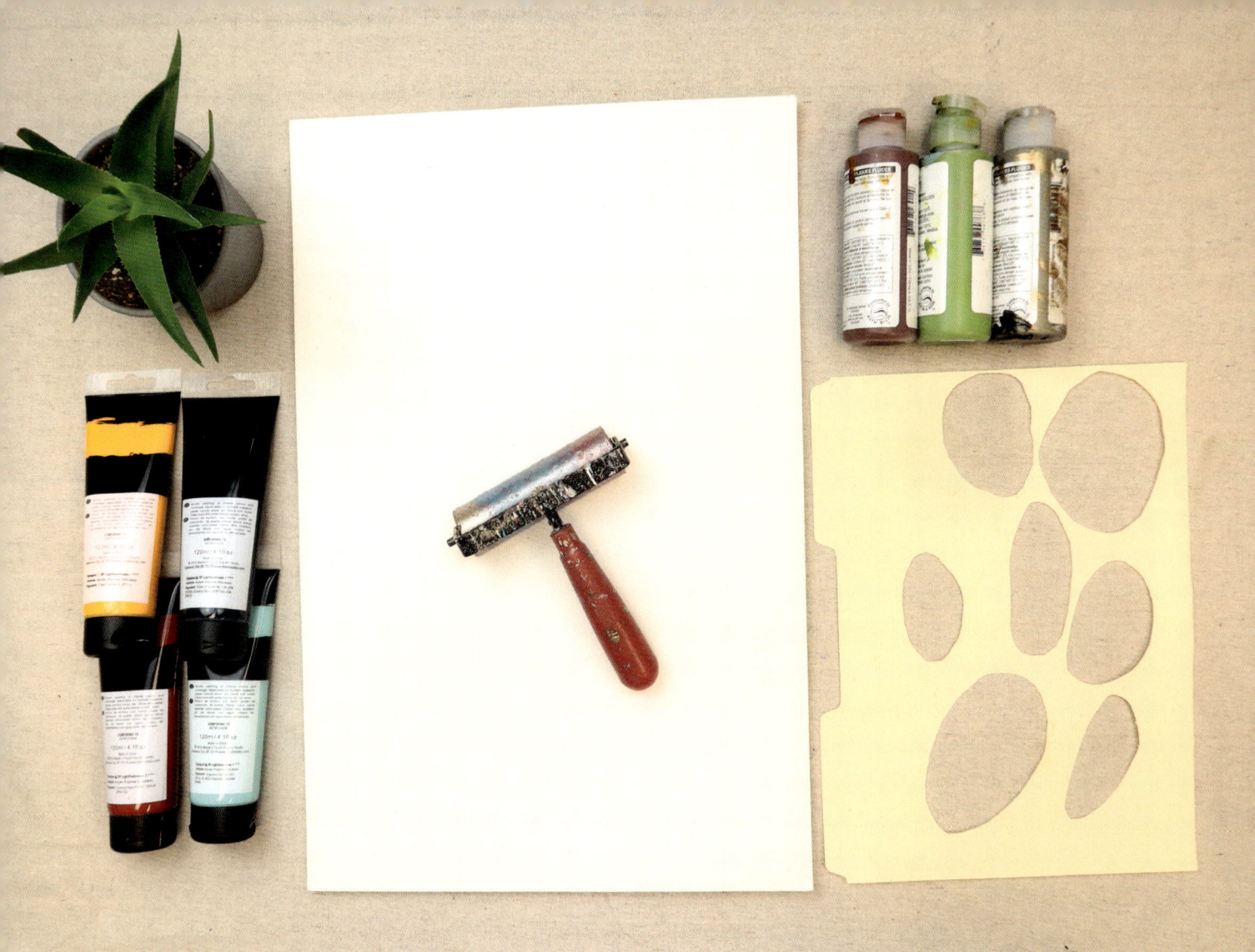

MATERIALS

Gel plate

Brayer

Acrylic paints, 4 to 5 colors

Spray inks

Paintbrush

Stencils and masks

Large papers: Printmaking paper or canvas paper works beautifully with this technique

For a video of this technique, visit robynmcclendon.com.

A Landscape

The easiest way to approach this technique initially is to create a landscape-style painting. This will really help with orientation on such a large piece of paper. Whether you choose to make it representational or abstract, thinking "landscape" will give your mind a reference point.

Start by deciding on a paper size. The standard US paper sizes of 12″ by 18″, 18″ by 24″, or 24″ by 36″ will work nicely for large-scale work.

Line up a paint palette. A minimum of four to five colors will give a nice variety.

We will begin with the one-color technique. Roll your first color out onto your gel plate **1**. Transfer this painted surface to a section of your paper **2**.

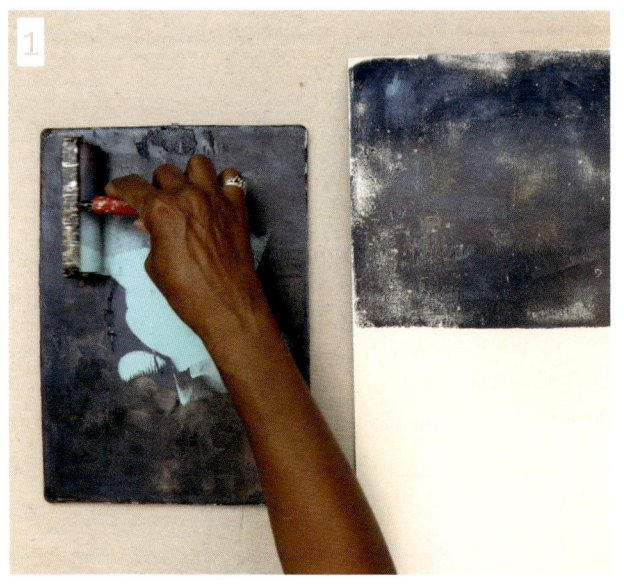

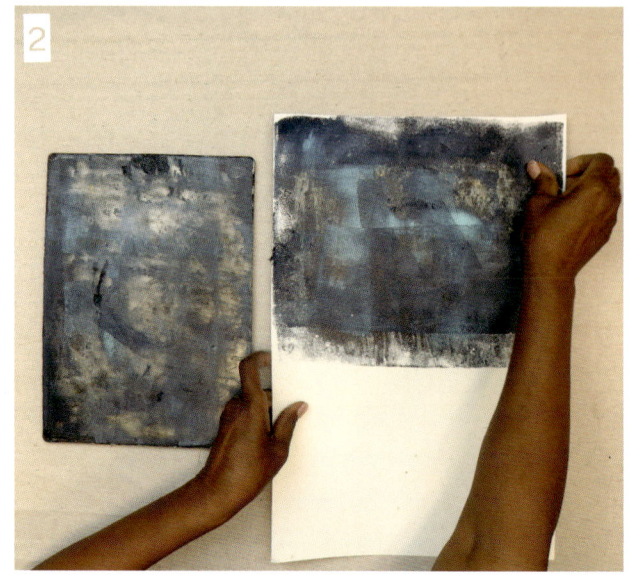

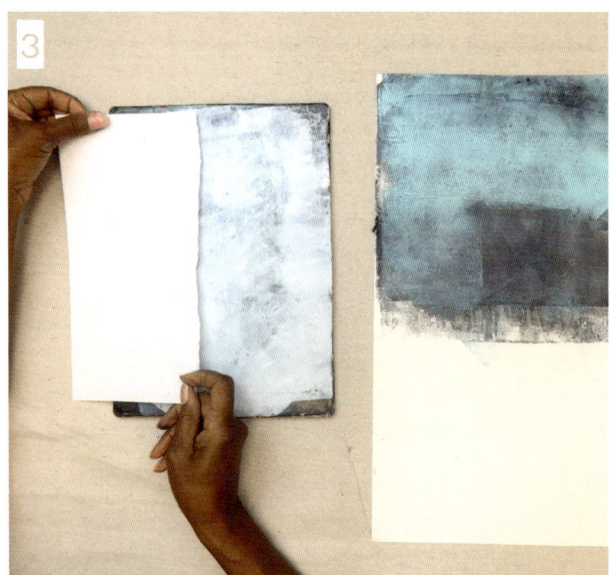

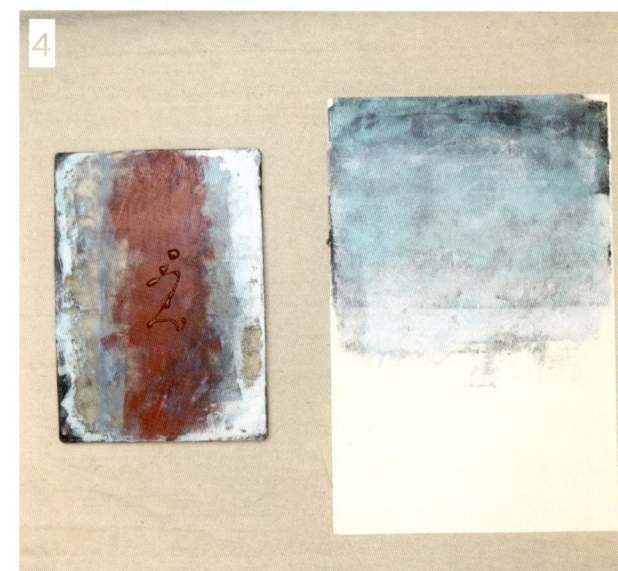

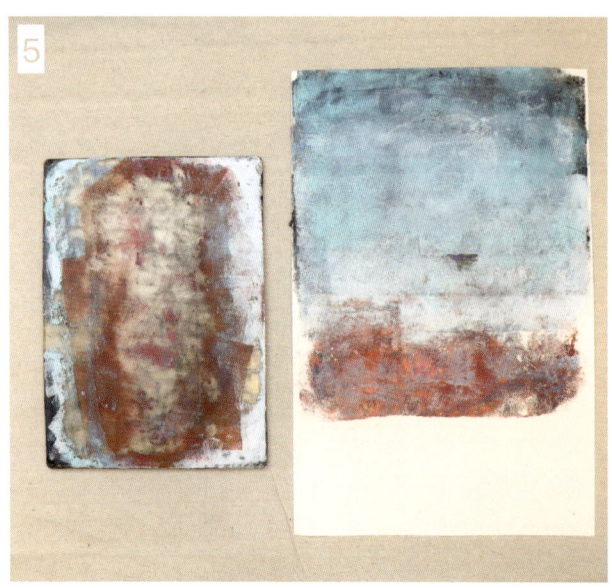

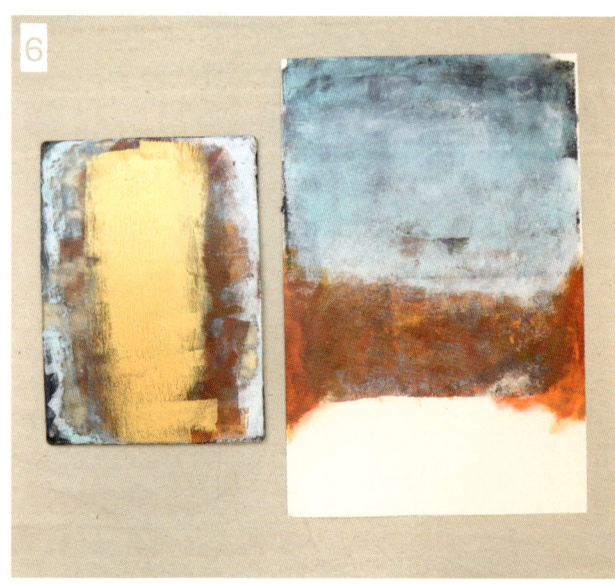

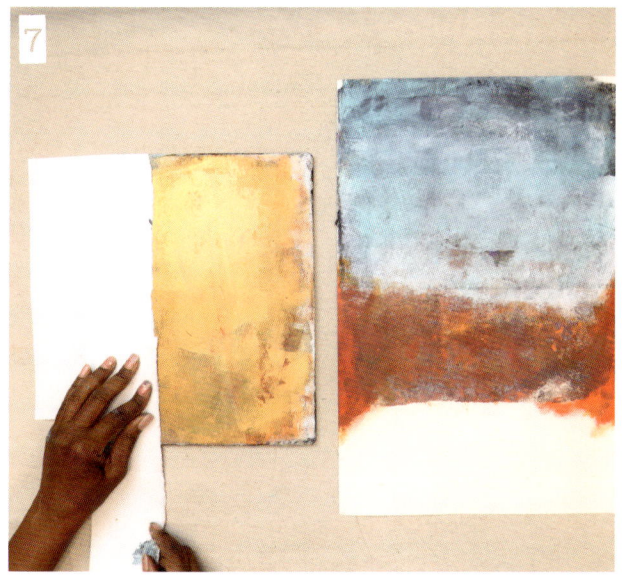

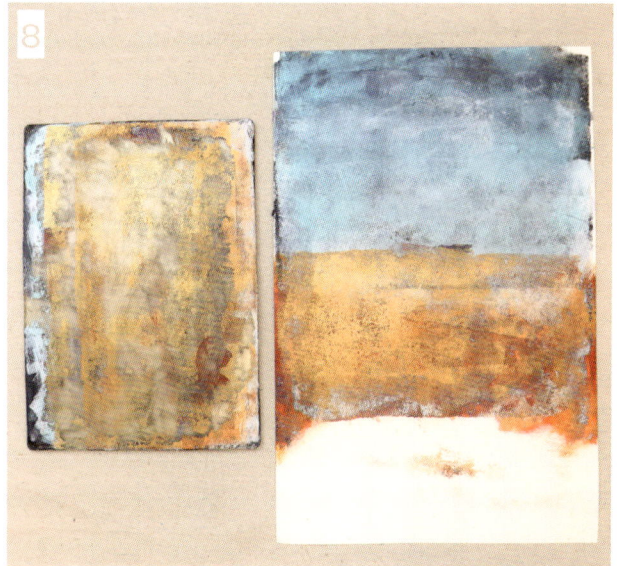

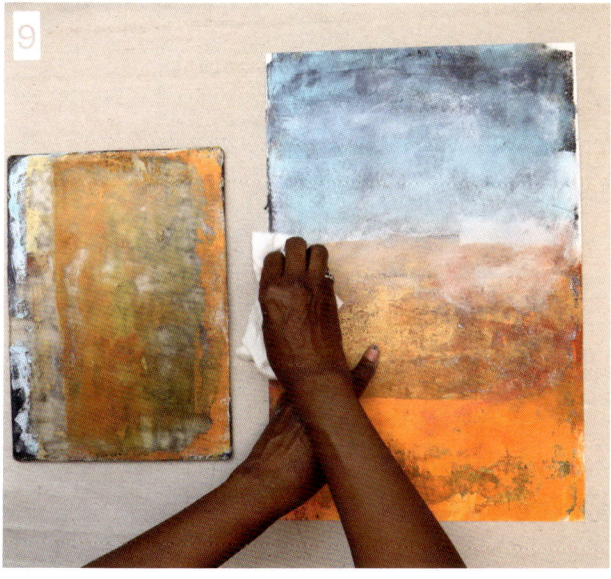

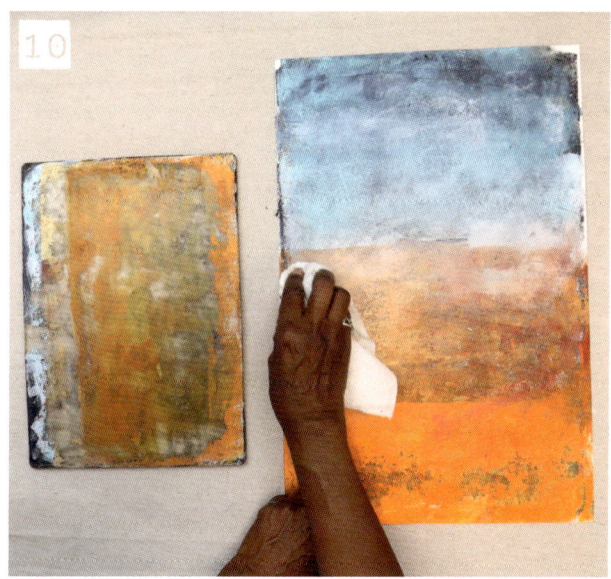

Continue to look at your paper as a landscape: divide it into thirds, with a top, middle, and bottom. Start with the top third of your paper and begin printing from left to right **3**. Fill the paper with the monoprint transfers until the top third is complete. Lay sections down one right next to the other, overlapping slightly, paying attention to covering the paper with paint.

Choose your next color, let's say a red, and repeat the same method across the middle third of the page **4**, **5**. We can think of this as our horizon line.

Choose a third color, perhaps a cream/gold, that can be mixed with both previous colors **6**. Add cream to the blue of the sky area **7**, **8** to blend it into the red. With a new color, in this case a yellow ochre, cover the bottom third in the same way as before, mixing in some cream to soften the edges between the two areas **9**, **10**. Our goal is to create an integrated color field. Take your time. It can be tricky at first, but have fun, play with it. There will be trial and error but eventually you'll develop a technique that you'll like.

With the color field now complete, we can add imagery. Select stencils or masks (or both) and begin adding these to the surface layer by layer, building up until you create a finished piece **1**–**6**.

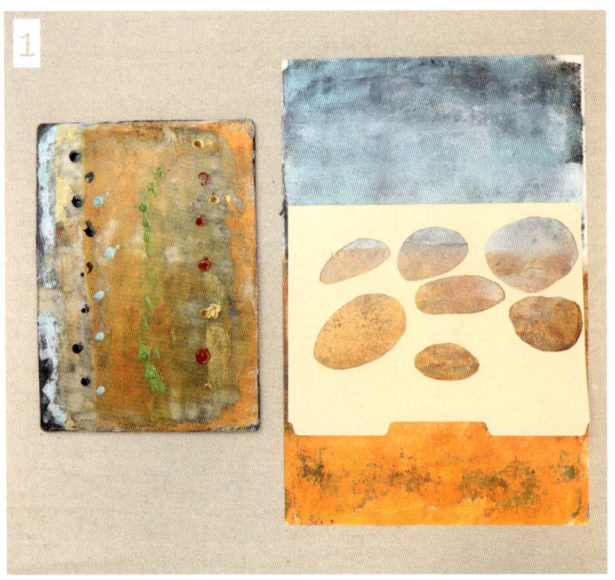

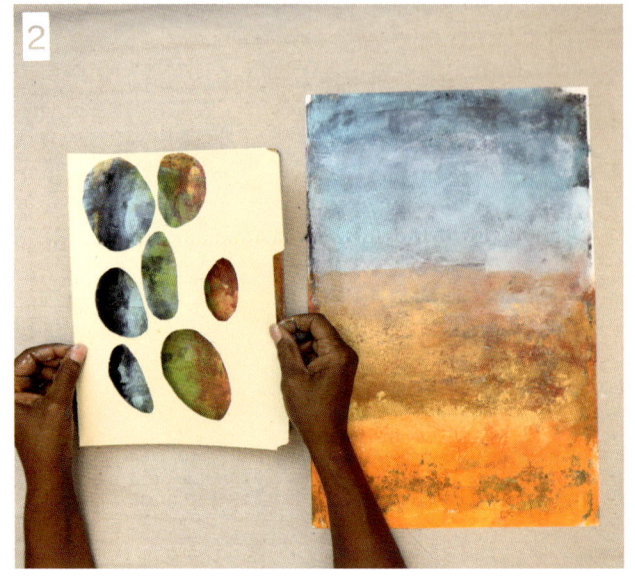

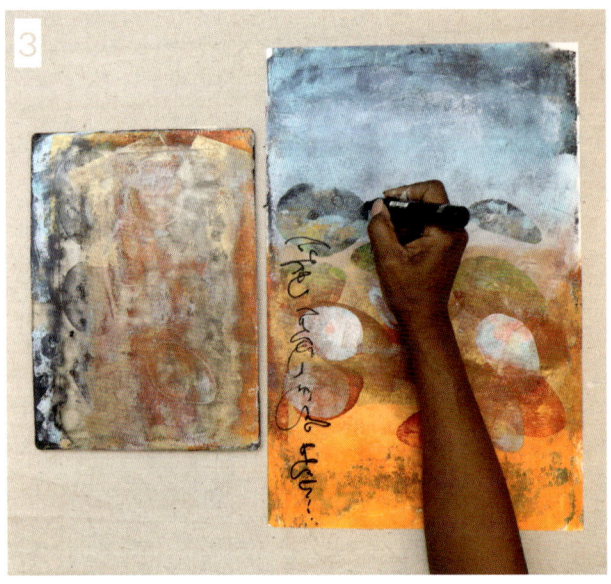

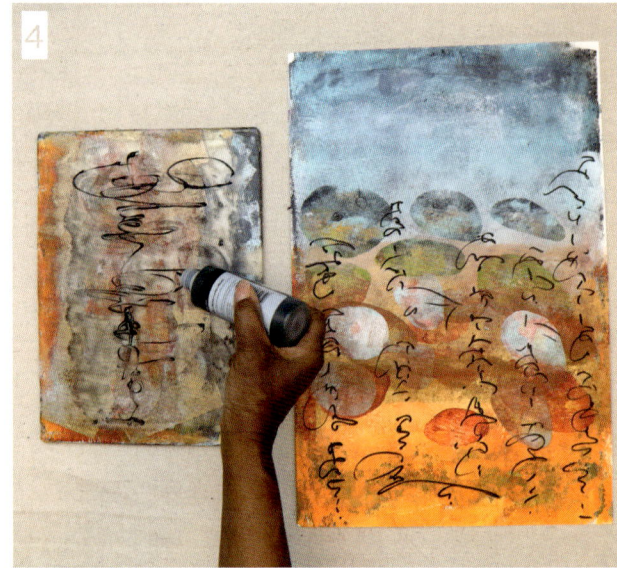

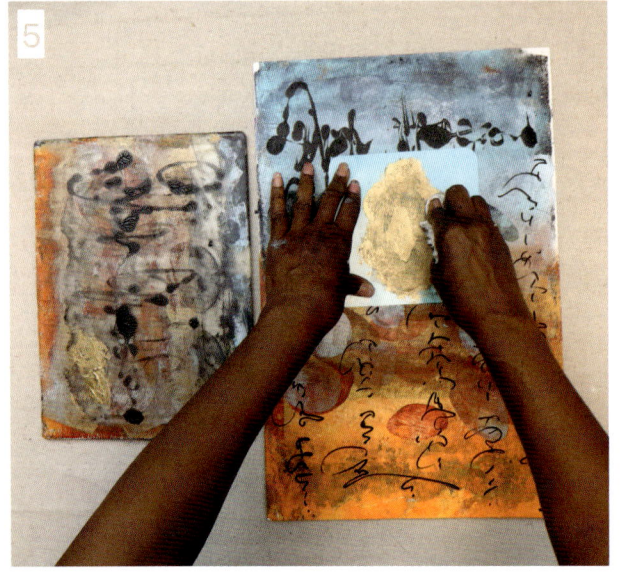

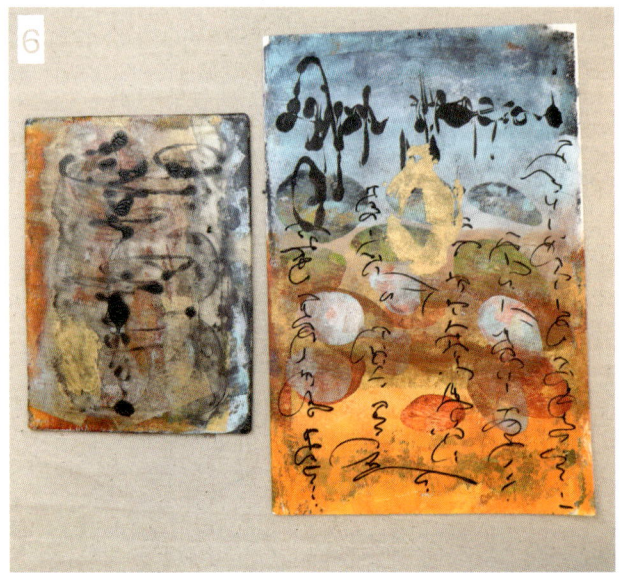

A Colorscape Using Hands-On Technique

Here's another way, a very tactile one, to use the plate as a stamp. We will be layering a variety of mixed-media techniques.

Work with 5″ by 5″ or 6″ by 6″ gel plates. Your finished piece will not look like a series of stamps when you use these sizes and get the overlapping correct.

Use a fun and bright color palette. Drop the colors in random places on the plate. Take your fingers and run them through the paint, just like finger painting. Begin stamping the gel plate, used vertically, onto the paper in the middle and then work around it, doing overprinting in a grid-like fashion. Your first series of stamping should create something that resembles the number "5" on a die. The "5 die" pattern will encourage you to distribute various colors all around the plate. When finished, your work will look more thought out, without areas of color clumping.

Create another finger-painted gel plate. Continue to stamp in a grid-like fashion with the same colors. Make sure to finger-paint in the same direction each time. For example, I did straight up-and-down lines.

Overlap your stamps in the grid as you wish, and try to change the strip of the print around.

Add other colors. Pull your fingers through the paint. Most of all, have fun. This is a new process that's very different from the others we have covered. As usual, the more you can create an atmosphere of fun, the more you will enjoy learning and playing.

Continue this process until you have your entire surface covered with your first layer.

The second layer is very much the same; however, you will be stamping your plate in the horizontal fashion instead of the vertical that you did for the first layer. The specific place where you will be stamping is on the white lines created from stamping your first layer. This is like creating a bridge between the previous stamps. A helpful idea to picture as you work is that you are weaving a pattern.

As you continue to work, pay attention to the color balance on your paper. For example, if I notice that the piece is beginning to have too much of one color, I will leave that color out when creating the next concoction on my plate.

To add interest to your borders, you can apply the technique of stamping: Once you have applied the design you want on your plate, stamp the plate along your border. This is a great place to use stencils in creating a border.

Next, add some touches to your piece that do not use the plate. Just as we practiced scripting and mark making on the plate, you can choose a few places to add your scripting directly onto your piece.

Think about what tools you would like to use at this stage to add even more interest and information to your piece.

At this point in the work, I usually do not use the plate anymore, unless I feel that the "Old Wall" technique would add to a certain section of the piece. 🖌

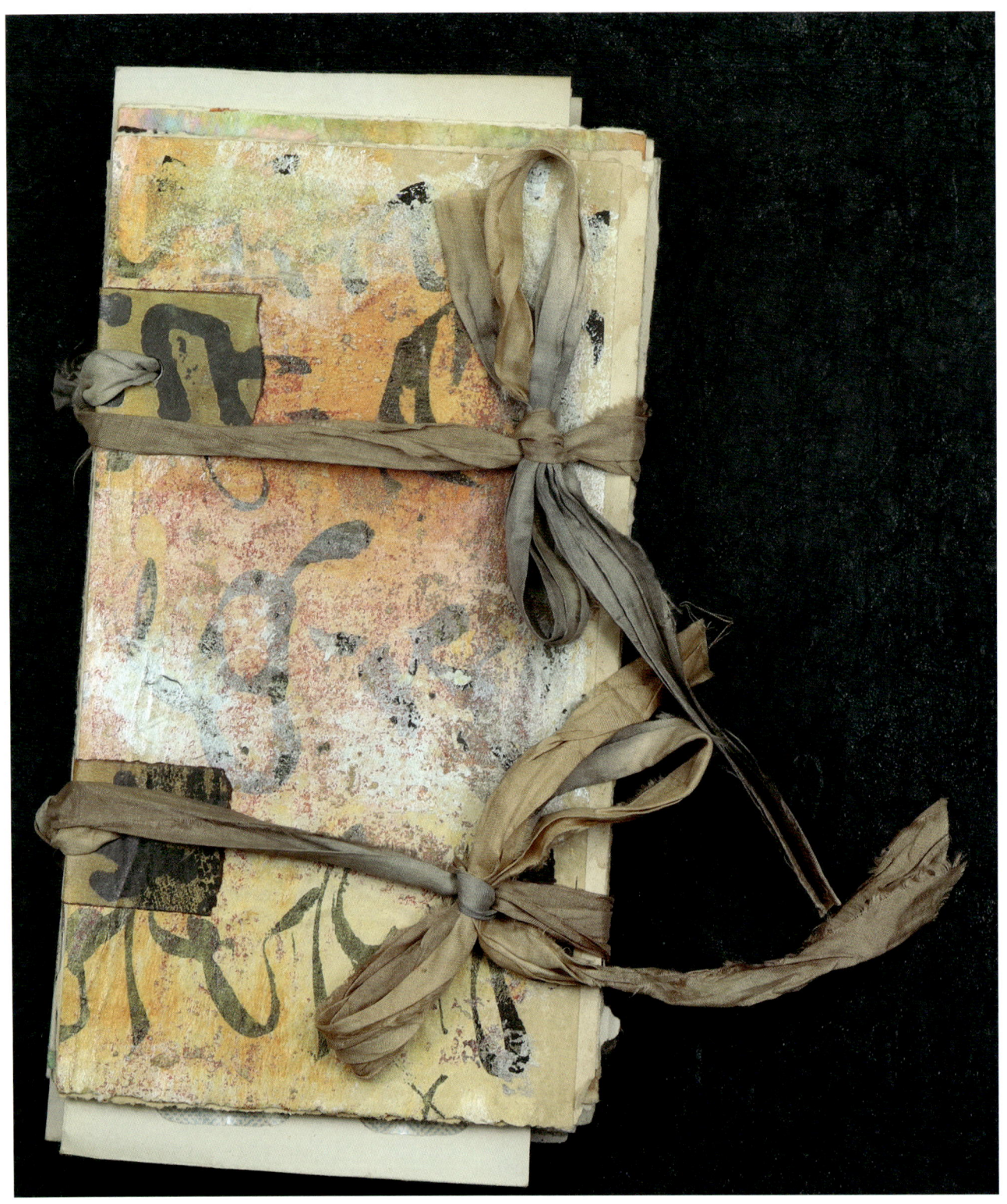

Custom binding on "Book As Art" project, with gel-printed papers of multiple layers of thin glazing on intuitive-scripted papers, using sumi ink

Books as an Art Genre

Books are natural projects in which to use gel prints. Some of the examples I show throughout these chapters are pages from my fine-art book projects.

I have enjoyed beautiful bound books since I was a little girl. I would go antiquing with my mother and while she was exploring her interests, I would find the nearest book shelf and look through the books. She'd buy me one during these outings, so I'd always come home with an old leather- or linen-bound book full of pages with deckle edges and gold leafing.

In the mid 1980s, as an artist learning hand papermaking, printmaking, and bookbinding techniques, I found myself among a community of artist who were exploring the book arts movement. I felt in perfect harmony.

The book arts movement is a term used to describe the resurgence of interest in the physicality of books during the late twentieth century. This movement was spearheaded by a group of artists comprising printmakers and papermakers, publishers, writers, and bookbinders who sought to bring the traditional craft of bookmaking into the world of art, while saving a dying art form.

It focused on the design, production, and display of handmade books, often incorporating elements of traditional bookbinding techniques such as decorative marbling and tooling. The book arts movement also sought to bring attention to the often overlooked aesthetics of the book form and its potential for creative expression. The book arts movement has had a lasting impact on the way books are produced, collected, and exhibited.

Creating books with our gel prints is a perfect union and expression of these two genres. Try this direction as a way to embrace the artistry of your prints.

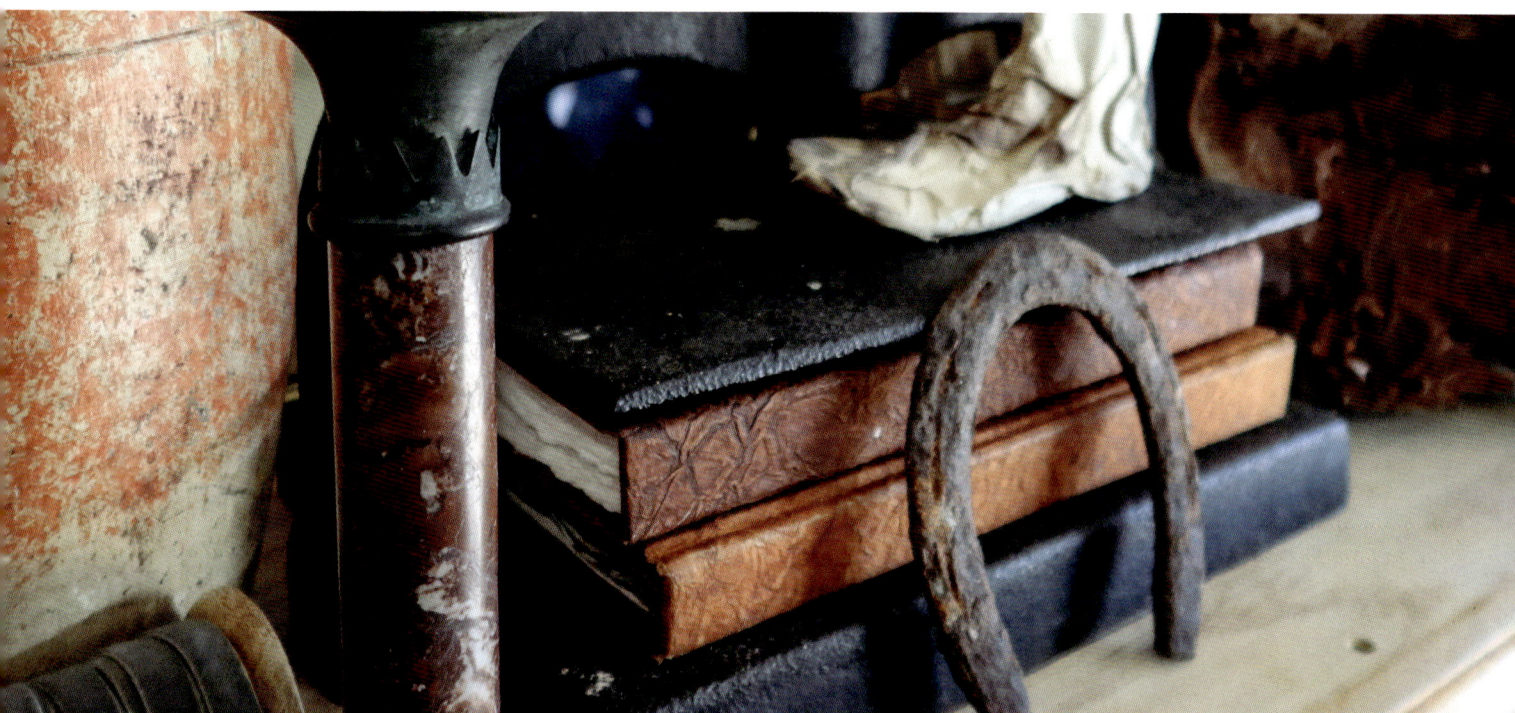

20

Eco-staining on "Throwaway" Gel Prints

Eco-staining is one of my favorite techniques to use on so many of my gel prints and papers that contain mark making. I really love an aged, textural sense in my work, and using natural pigments and spices is a wonderful way to "age" papers.

You can stain your papers first (white papers, for instance), allow them to dry, and then gel print on them. The other option—our focus in this chapter—is to take your finished gel prints, especially the so-so, "throwaway" prints, and stain them. This will go a long way to transform them.

In the process of gel printing you're going to make many prints that you don't like completely. There is no need to throw them in the trash, because eco-staining will fill in the white and open spots that don't look quite right, and will homogenize the color combinations you may not love. Eco-staining, including rust staining, gives these prints a beautiful Old World, found-element look.

MATERIALS

Gel plate

Paper ("throwaway" gel prints are ideal)

String or cloth for bundling papers

Coffee

Tea

Kitchen spices: turmeric, cinnamon, paprika

Onion skins, avocado pits

Water

For a video of this technique, visit robynmcclendon.com.

Right: Eco-staining on "throwaway" gel prints

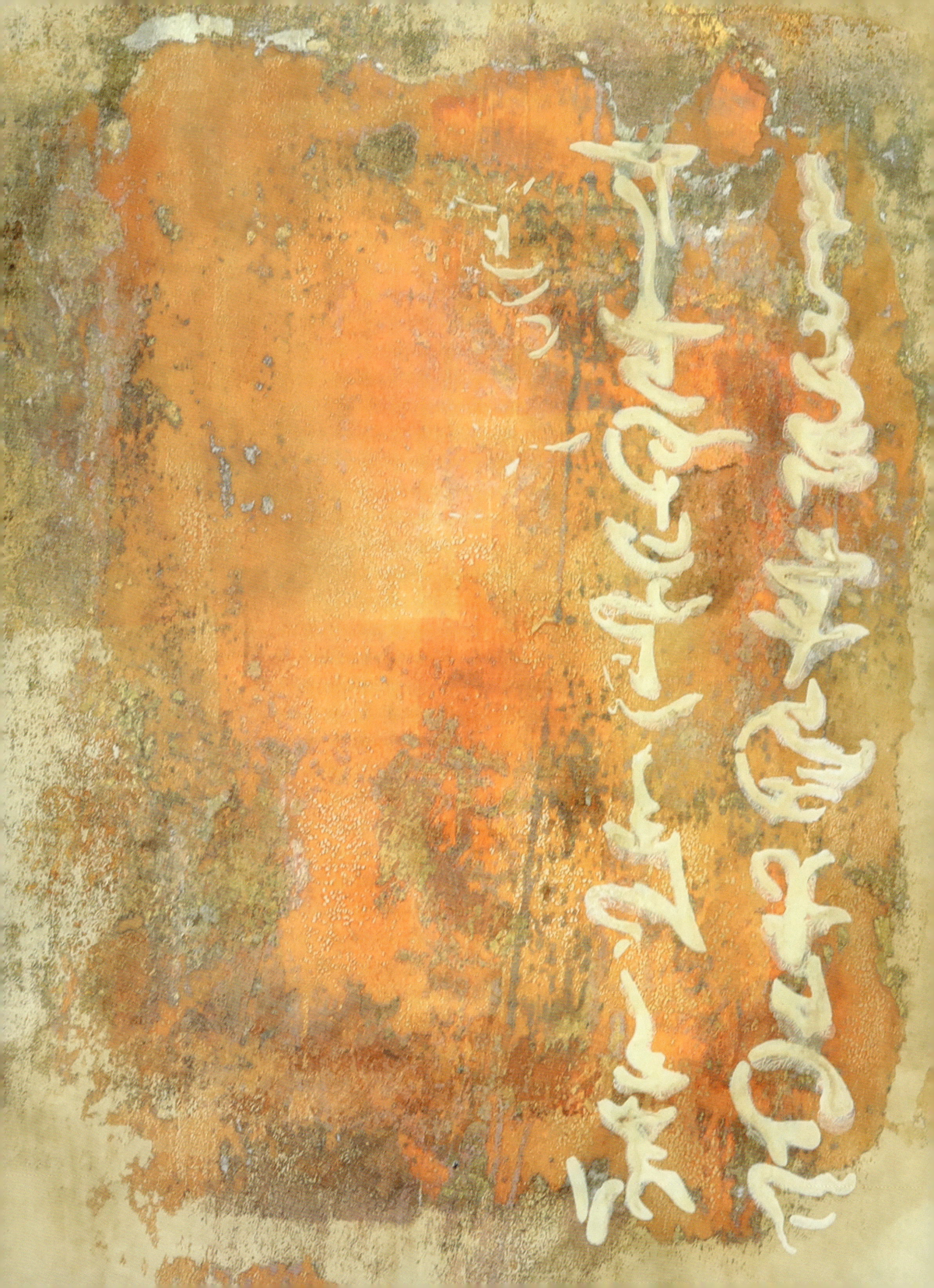

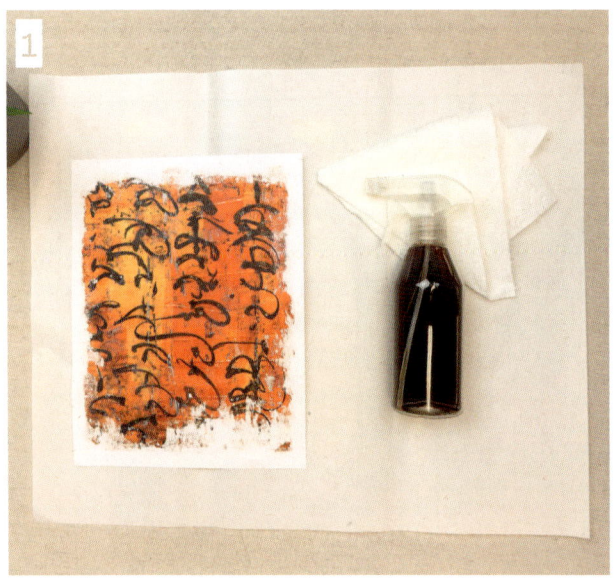

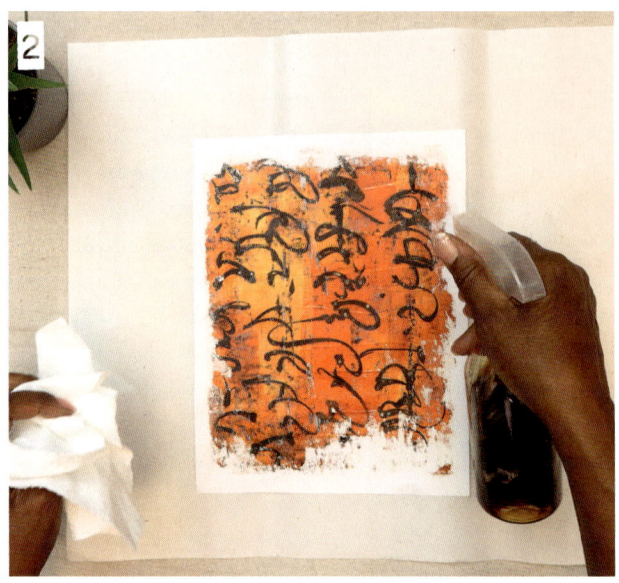

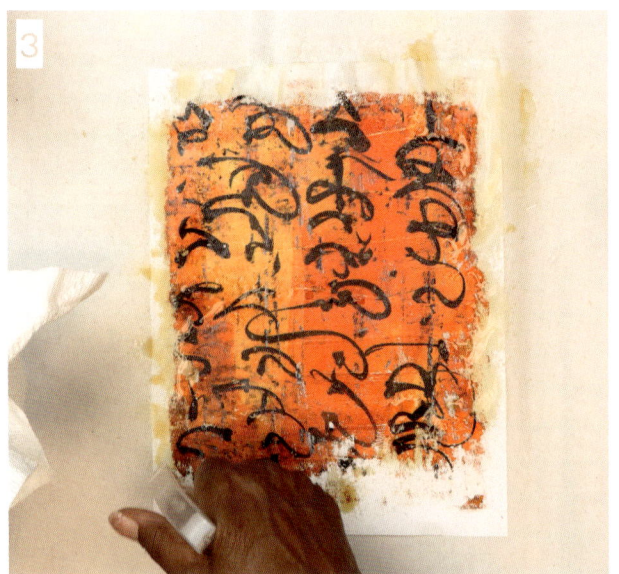

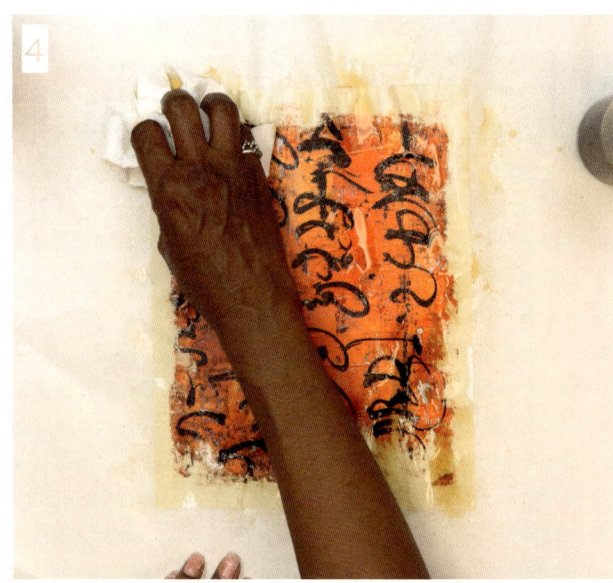

Coffee and Tea

Step 1. Make your eco-dyes. For coffee, 2 cups of boiling water to 1 cup of instant coffee mix is a good ratio to start with. For tea, six teabags in 2 cups of boiling water usually works great. You can experiment with different brands. Black tea will create different staining than herbal teas.

Step 2. You can either dip your papers (wrapped in bundles with string or cloth) into the mixture or put the mixture into a spray bottle and spray the papers.

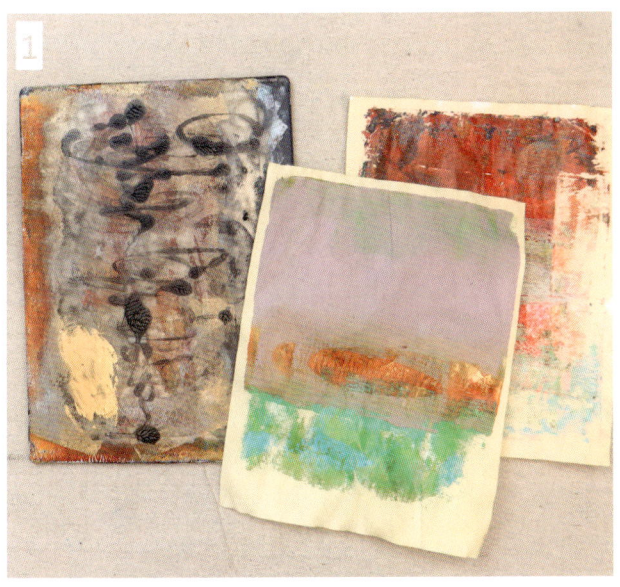

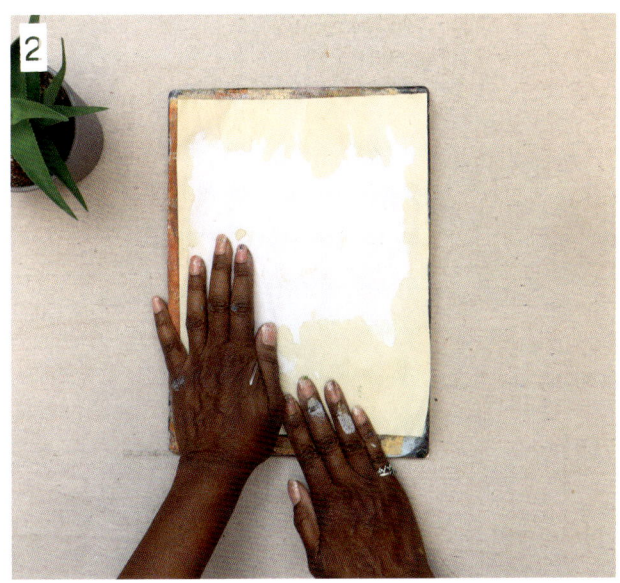

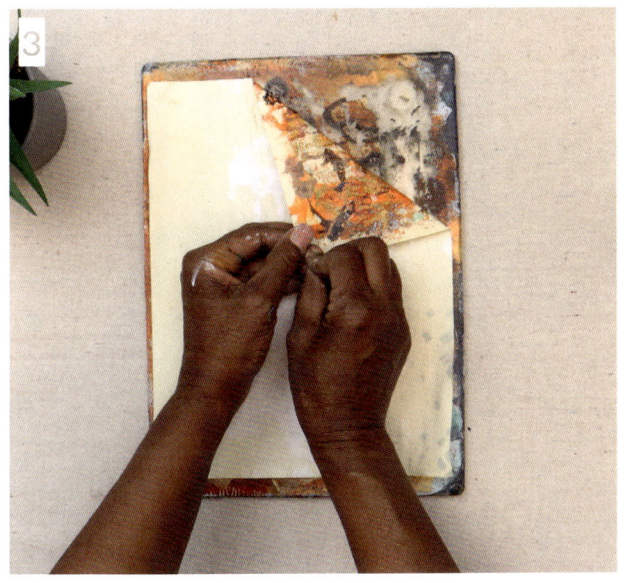

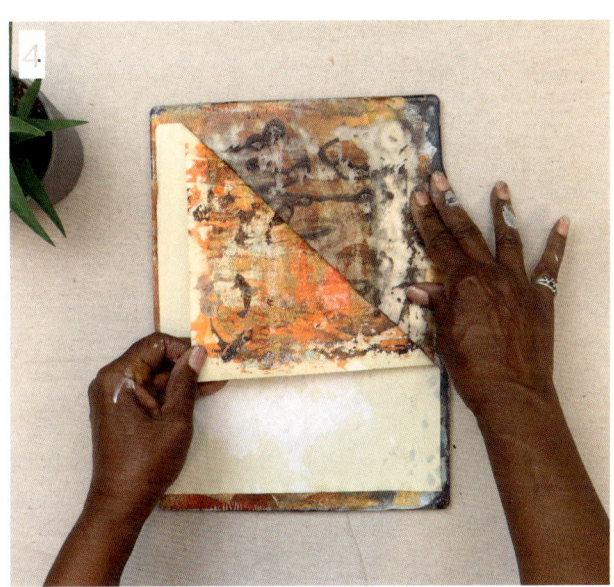

Turmeric, Onion Skins, Avocado Pits

Step 1. Make your eco-dyes.

Turmeric makes a pretty powerful yellow orange. Mix a cup of water with a couple of tablespoons of powdered turmeric.

Onion skins and avocado pits are boiled (separately) to create dye. Red and yellow onion skins create different colors. In a stockpot of water, place a cup of onion skins or three or four avocado pits. Let the skins or pits boil and simmer for thirty minutes to an hour. This will release a lot of the pigment.

Step 2. Take bundles of papers wrapped in string or cloth, and dip them into the hot water. You can also let the water cool and then put it in a spray bottle to spray the papers.

The less water you use, the more intense the color will be (and vice versa). So definitely play with the ratios. There really are no rules; these are general guidelines.

21

Techniques in Unison: Examples to Inspire You

I hope you have enjoyed learning the techniques in this book and that you feel great about creating art with your gel plate. On the following pages, I share works that demonstrate combinations of the techniques you've learned. May they inspire you to continue your discoveries.

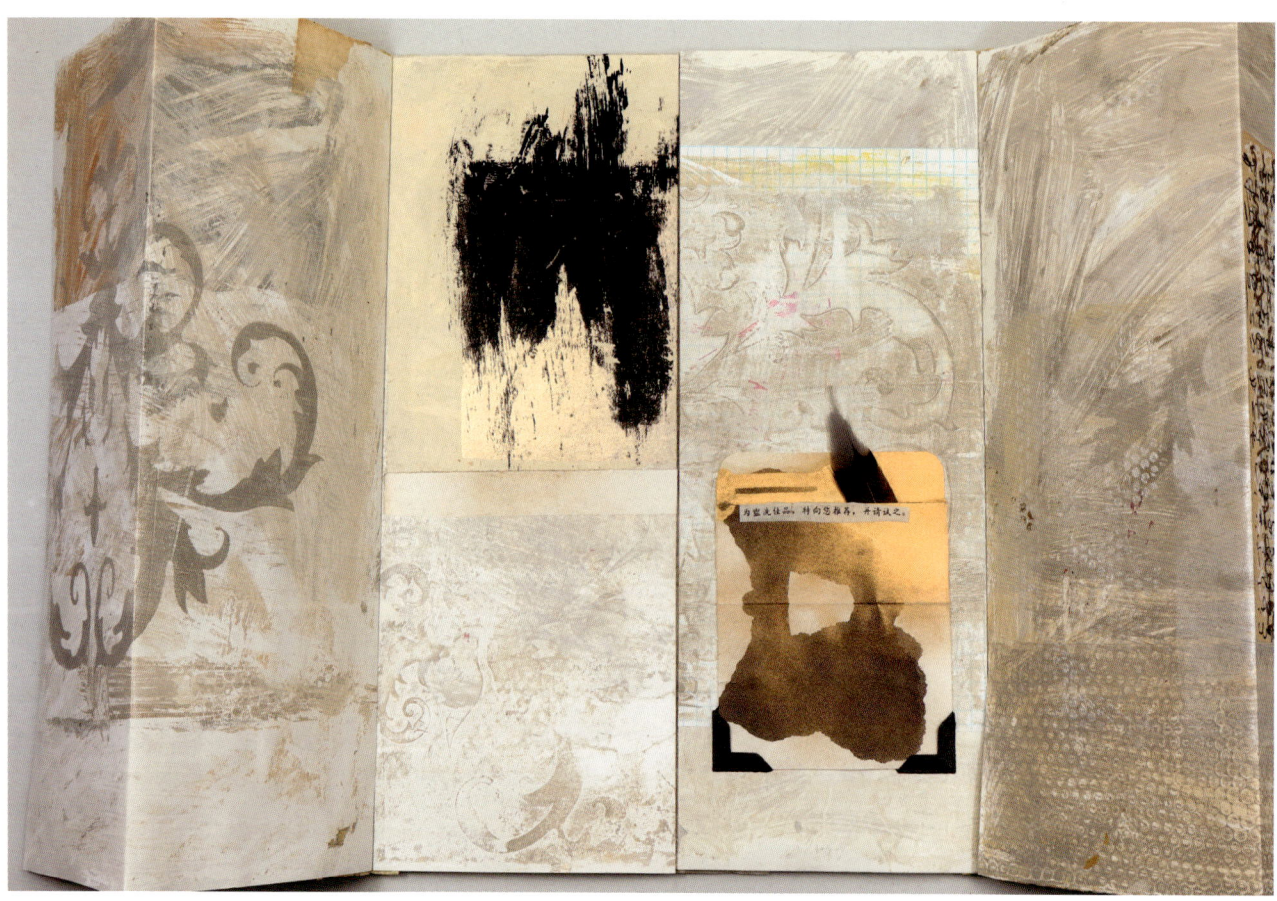

A page spread from a dual-accordion-fold book structure, using "Old Wall," stencil, paint applied to the gel plate with a brush, ink blot on the pocket with additional ink mark making and punchinello as a stencil, found elements collaged on the surface

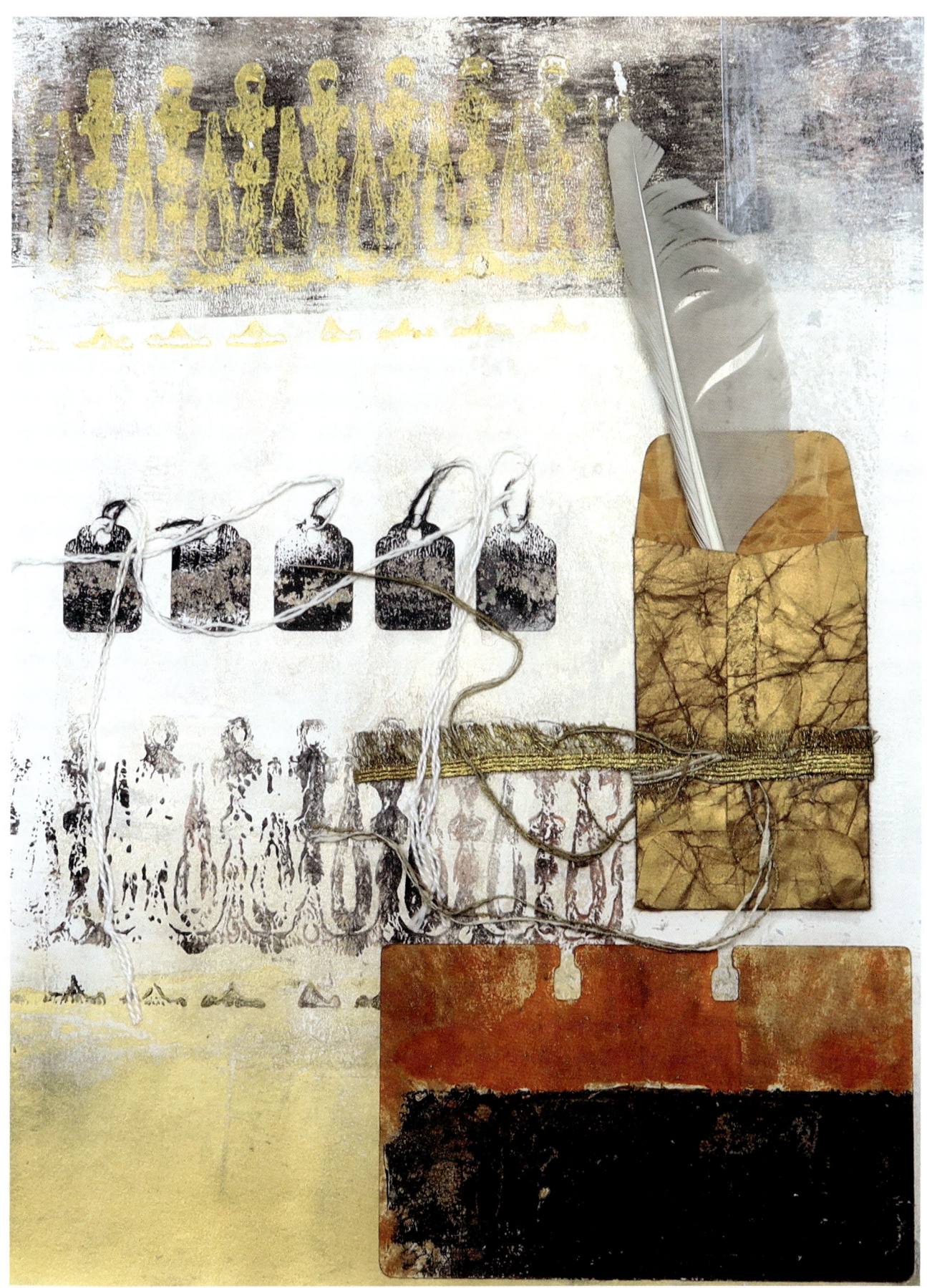

Collage using three-color background, stencils, two-color background on Rolodex card, patchwork
with found elements

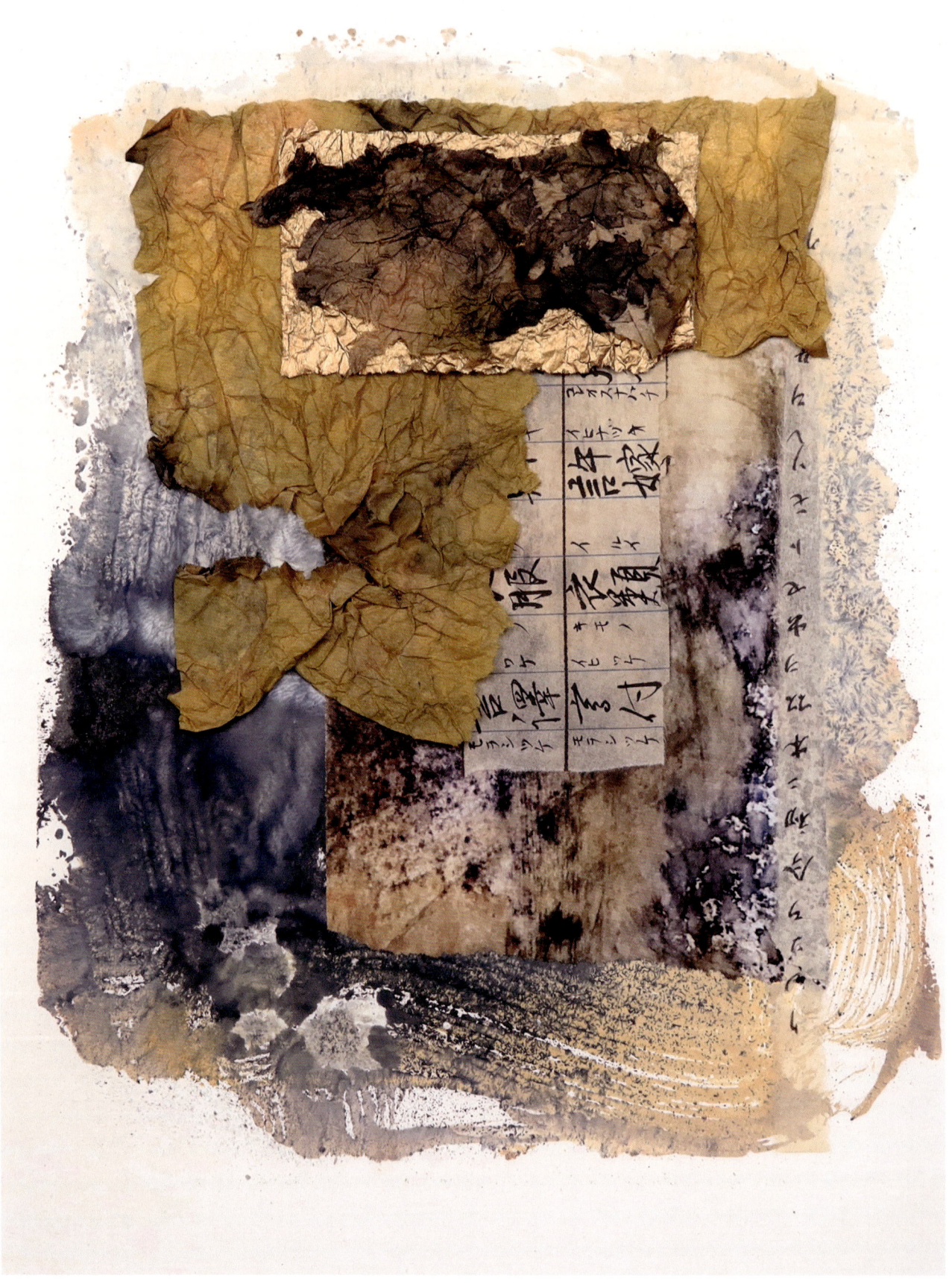

Watercolor acrylics with alcohol as background, turmeric eco-stained momigami paper, black sumi ink blot on archival tissue paper, black tea–stained calligraphy paper with sumi ink print on gel plate, with vintage Asian papers

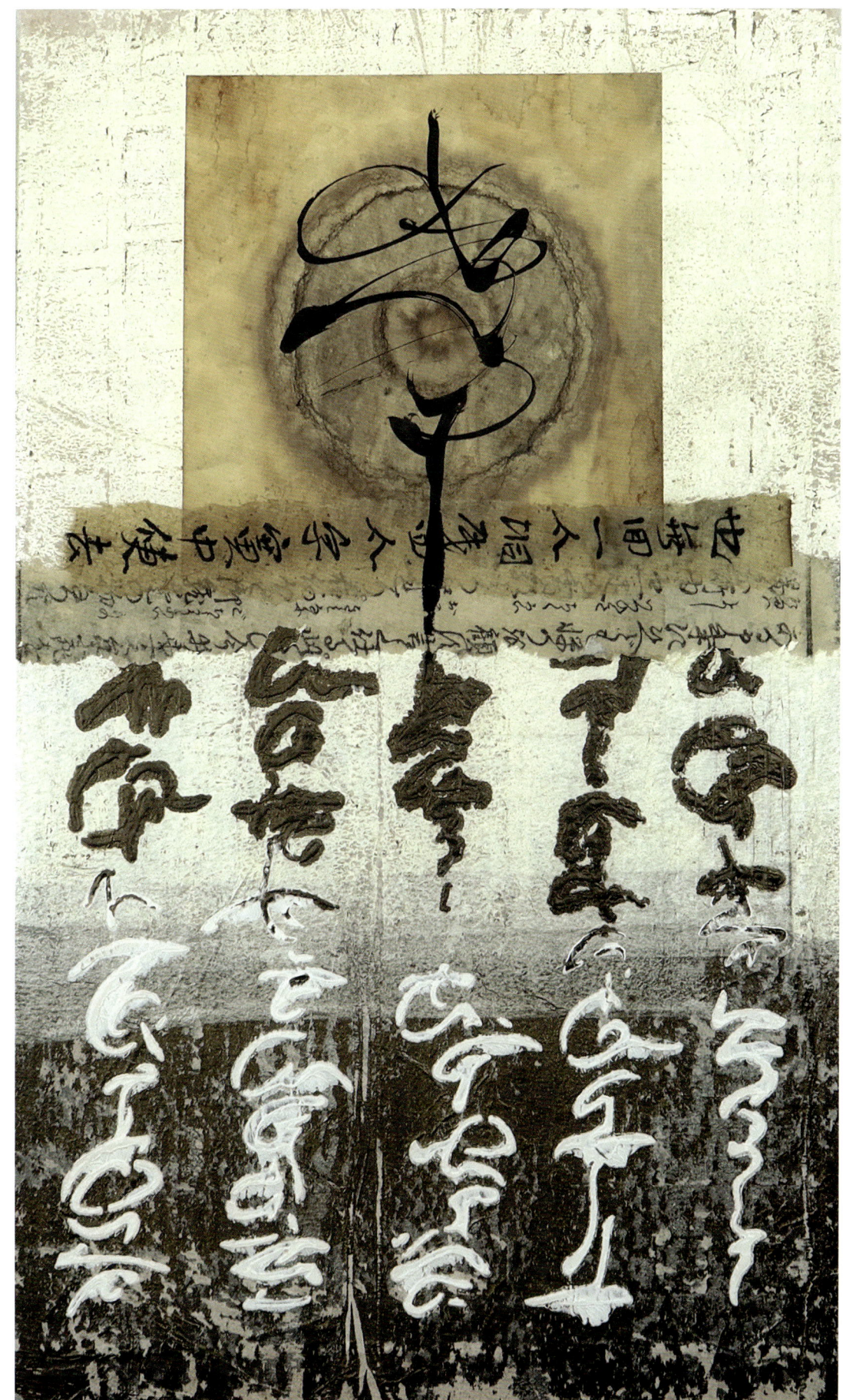

Collage using two-color backgrounds, metallic paints, my intuitive-scripting stencils, eco-stained image in the circle, intuitive scripting with sumi ink, and vintage Asian papers

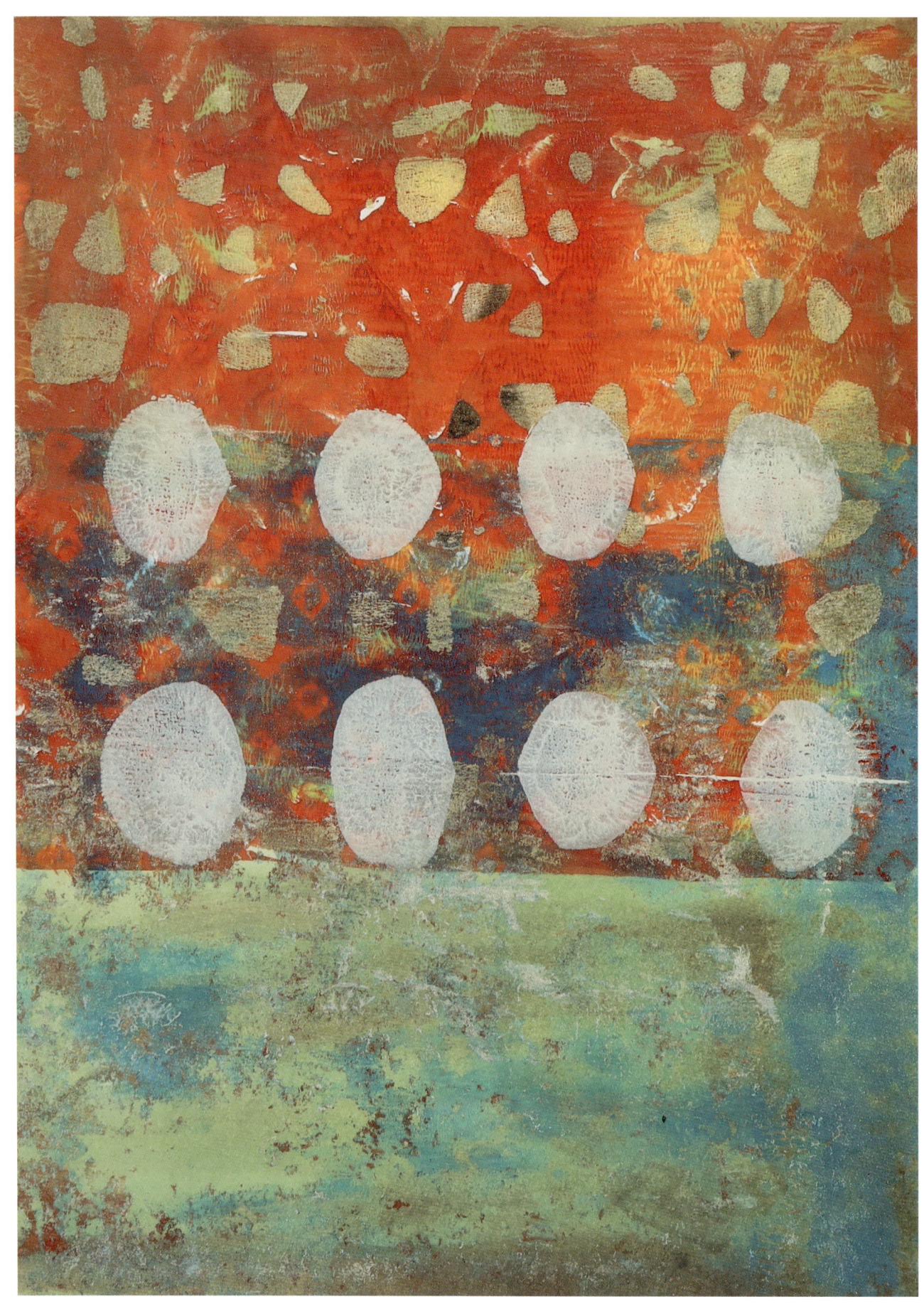

Gel print using "Old Wall," patchwork, page-protector stencil, organic paper stencil. This print has more than fifteen layers of thin color to create the complexity in the image.

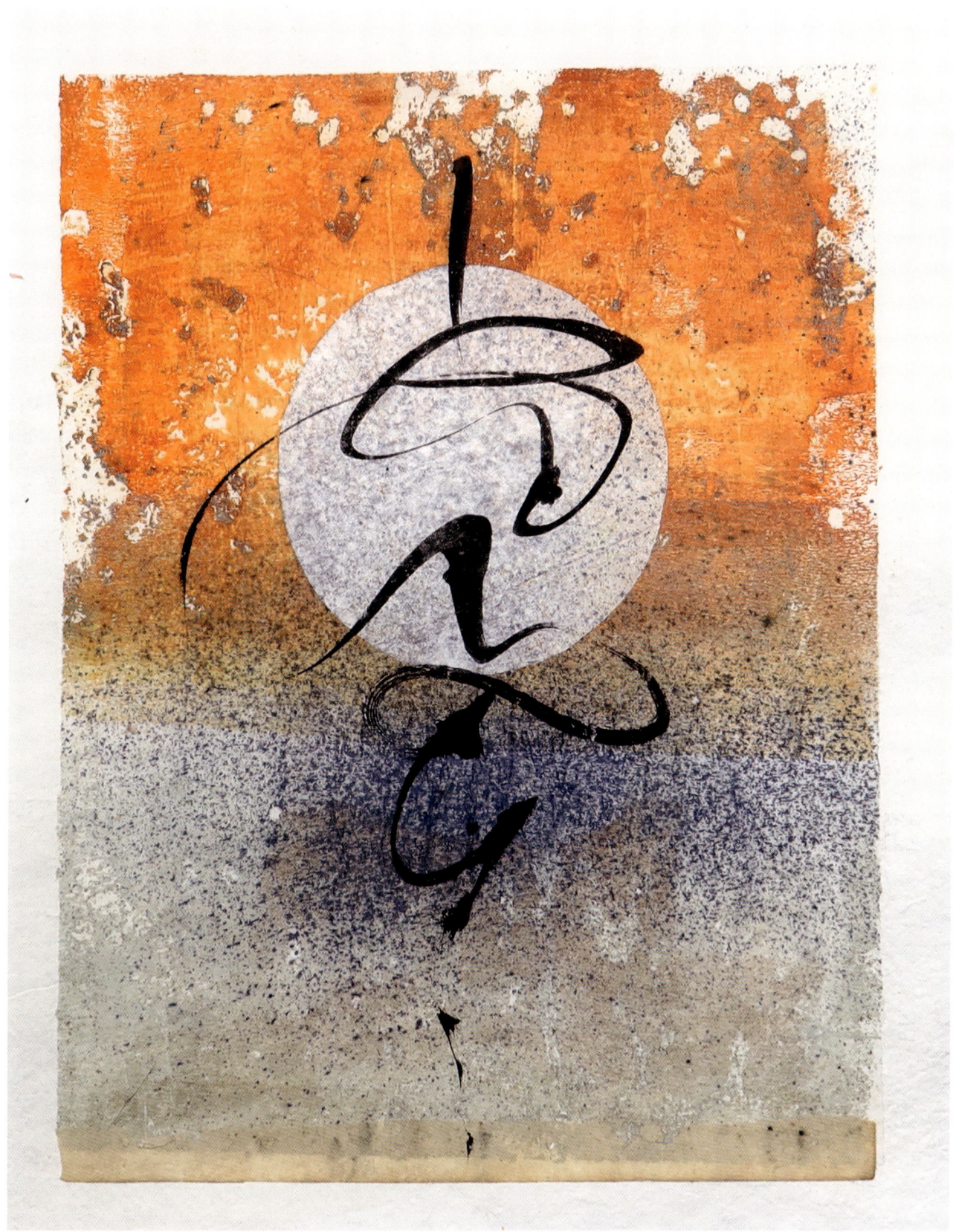

Collage: Two-color background, "Old Wall" buildup on plate, spray inks on plate as a layer, white gel-printed paper cut into a circle and collaged on to replicate chine colle, finished with intuitive scripting with sumi ink, vintage paper element on bottom

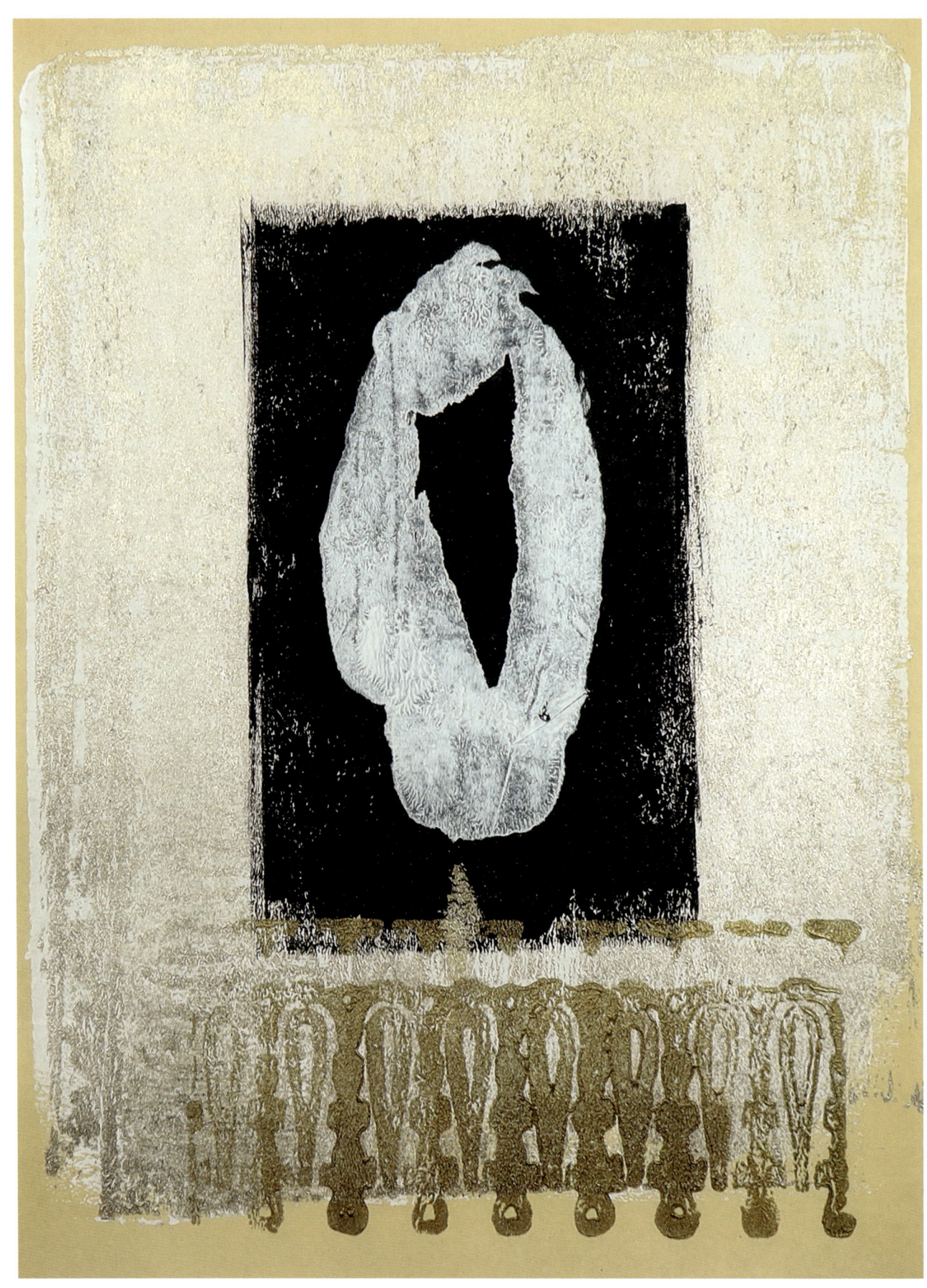

One-color background with black masked area, overprinted with white circle drawn on gel plate, and a wood stamp on top as final element

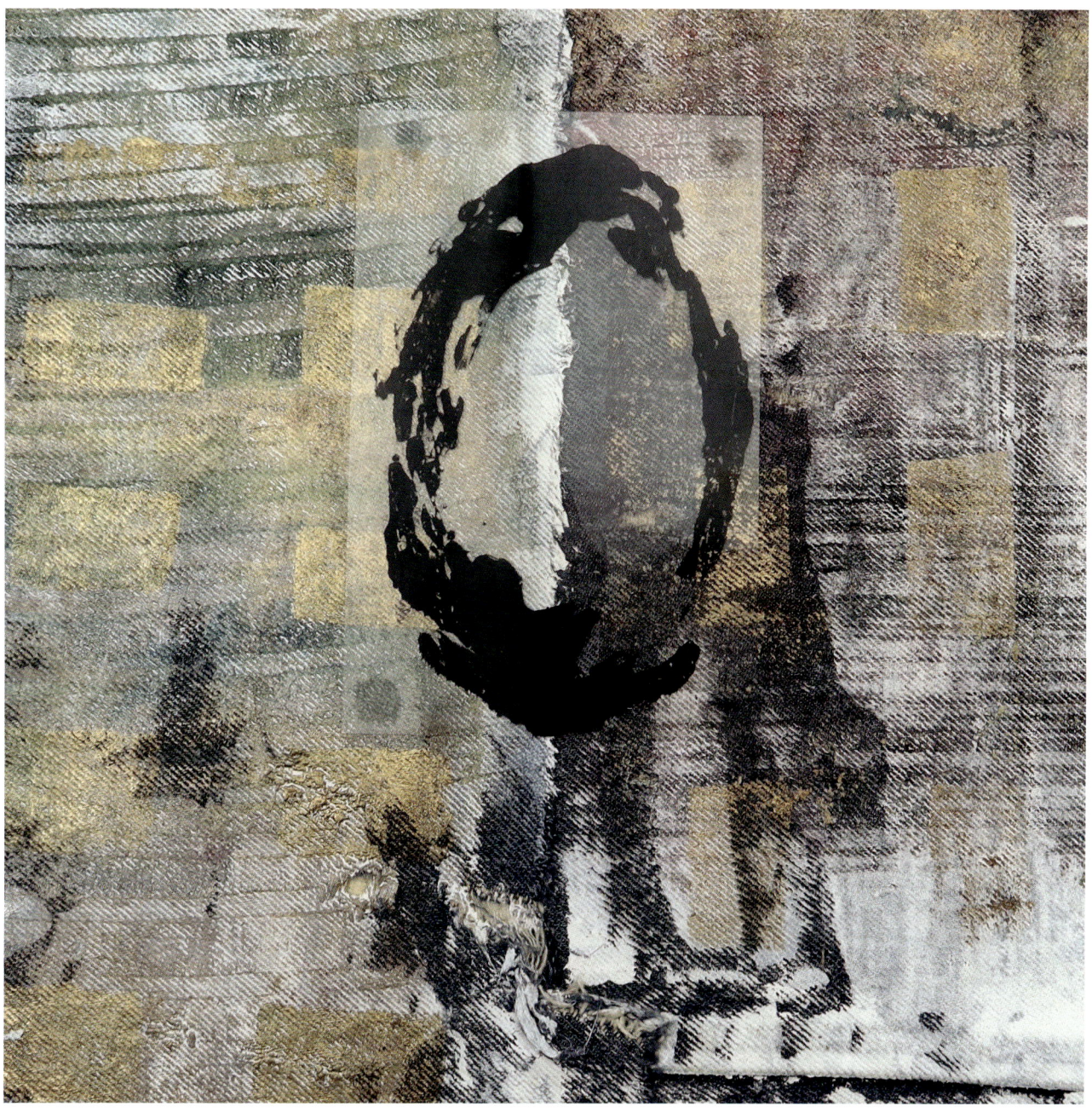

Fabric printing with patchwork technique, page-protector stencils, "Old Wall" buildup of paint, a gel-printed circle on transparency adhered to surface, jean surface collage

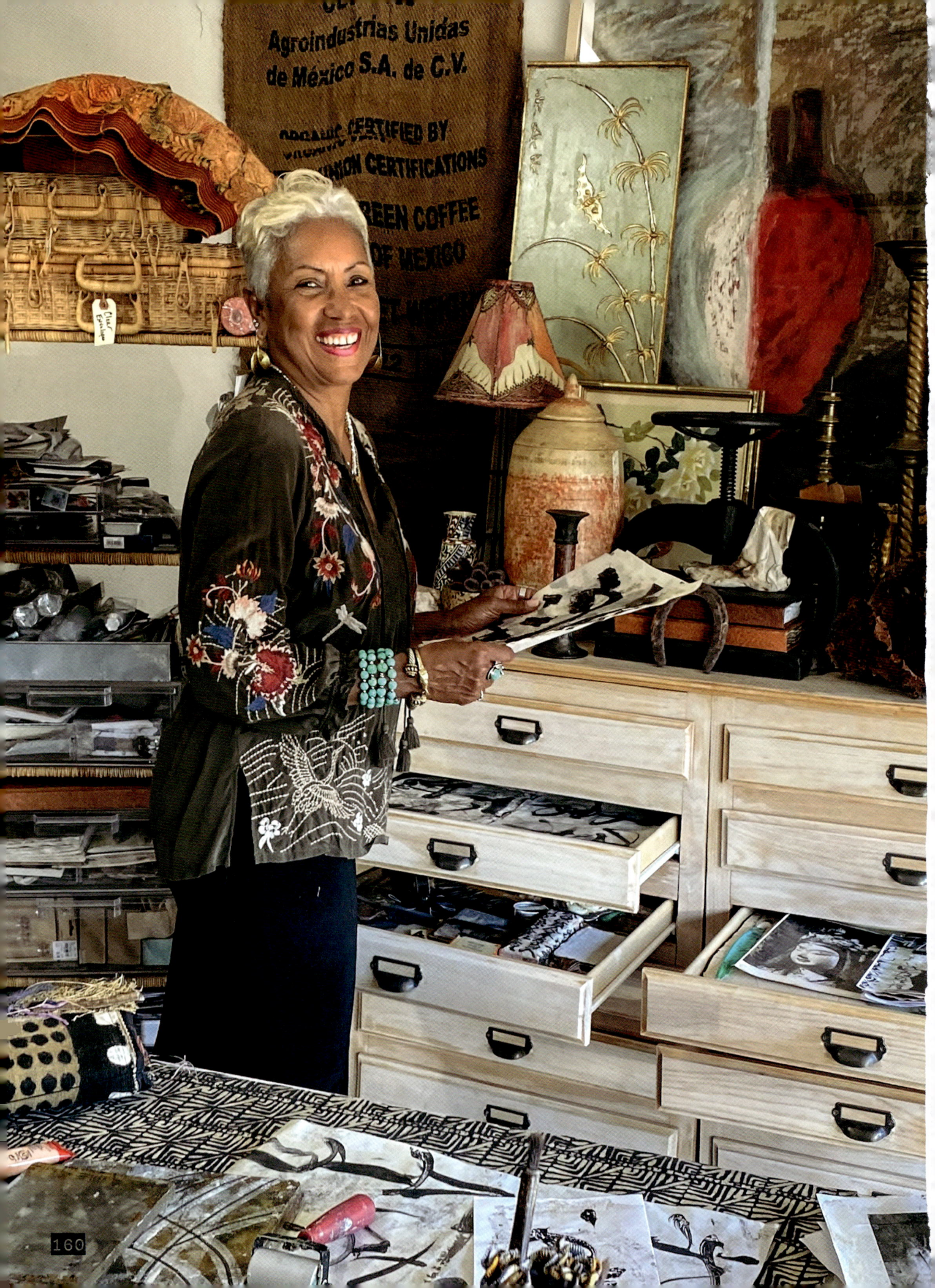

Resources

Workshops and Tutorials

On my website you will find a selection of video workshops and tutorials that are a companion to this book.

We learn in so many different ways, visual, audio, and/or kinesthetic, and because of that, I offer additional resources to help enhance every reader's experience in learning this amazing mixed-media art form. Many are free of charge.

Please visit my "Workshops" page at robynmcclendon.com to explore further.

Resources

There are many resources that I suggest to my community of products and brands that I have found that work best; this helps to take the guess work out. You'll find my resource section clearly marked with technique driven sections and links to easily find products.

Please visit my "Resources" page at robynmcclendon.com to explore further.

Artwork

I've been a working artist for more than thirty years, exhibiting nationally at museums and galleries. Creating my own artwork is at the core of my personal experience as an artist. The focus of this personal art exploration encourages me to push techniques further, innovate new approaches to traditional methods, and stay current with the changes and new technologies offered in the mixed-media genre.

If you are interested in seeing my body of work and learning about the motivations and philosophies that embody my approach, please visit my "Art Gallery" page at robynmcclendon.com.

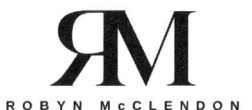

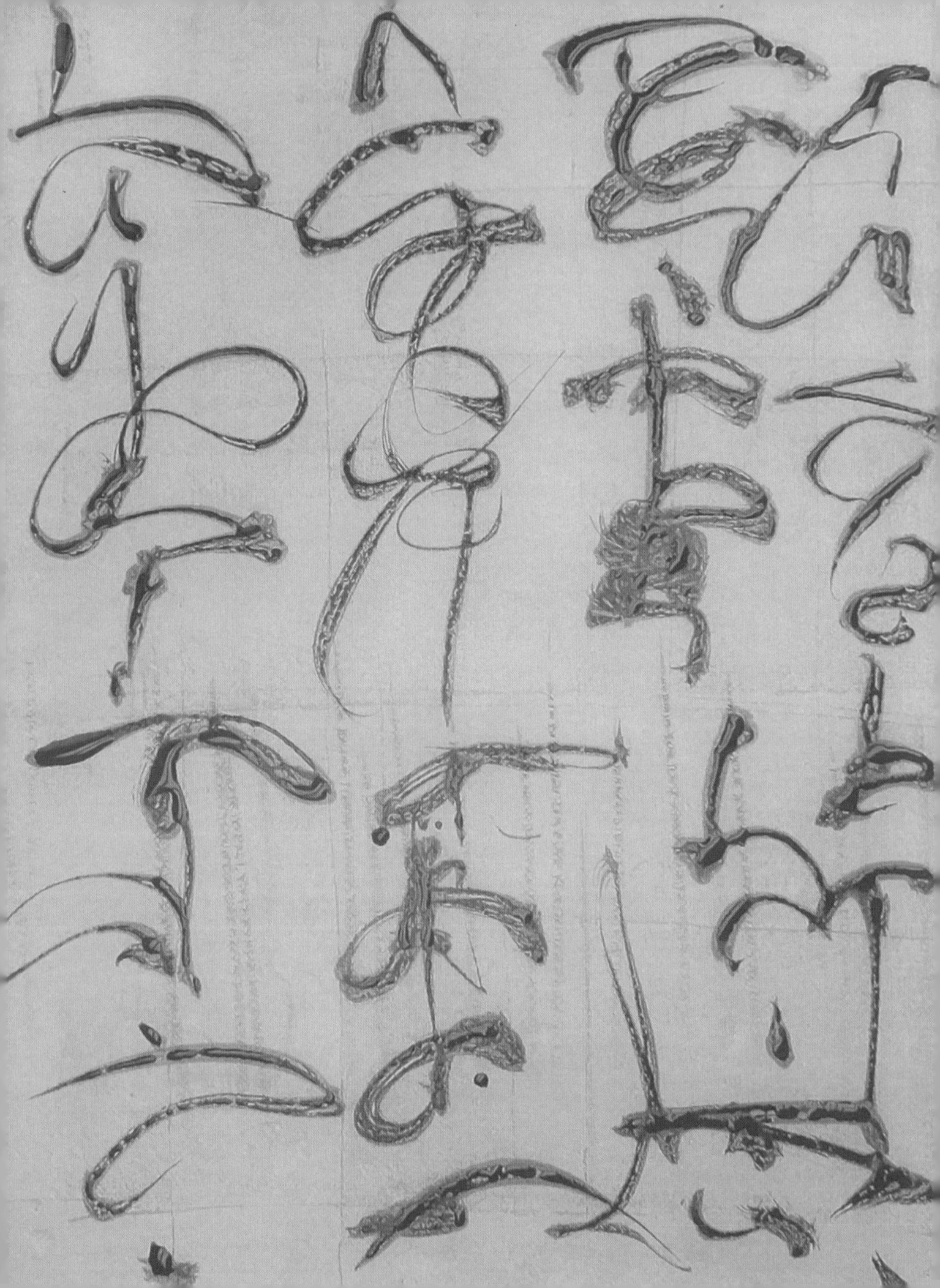